REALPOLITIK

A HISTORY

JOHN BEW

OXFORD
UNIVERSITY PRESS

OXFORD
UNIVERSITY PRESS

Oxford University Press is a department of the University of
Oxford. It furthers the University's objective of excellence in research,
scholarship, and education by publishing worldwide.

Oxford   New York
Auckland   Cape Town   Dar es Salaam   Hong Kong   Karachi
Kuala Lumpur   Madrid   Melbourne   Mexico City   Nairobi
New Delhi   Shanghai   Taipei   Toronto

With offices in
Argentina   Austria   Brazil   Chile   Czech Republic   France   Greece
Guatemala   Hungary   Italy   Japan   Poland   Portugal   Singapore
South Korea   Switzerland   Thailand   Turkey   Ukraine   Vietnam

Oxford is a registered trademark of Oxford University Press
in the UK and certain other countries.

Published in the United States of America by
Oxford University Press
198 Madison Avenue, New York, NY 10016

Library of Congress Cataloging-in-Publication Data
Bew, John.
Realpolitik : a history / John Bew.
pages cm
Includes bibliographical references and index.
ISBN 978-0-19-933193-2 (hardback)
1. Realism—Political aspects.   2. International relations—Philosophy.
3. World politics.   I. Title.
JZ1307.B48 2015
327.101—dc23
2015013935

3 5 7 9 8 6 4
Printed in the United States of America
on acid-free paper

Contents

IV REALPOLITIK AND THE TANGLED ROOTS OF AMERICAN REALISM

V PRACTICAL REALPOLITIK

REALPOLITIK

Introduction

The Return of *Realpolitik*

Realpolitik is back in fashion—again. The reasons for its most recent comeback are no mystery. The optimism and sense of triumph that crept into Anglo-American political thought following the end of the Cold War and peaked with the toppling of Saddam Hussein's statue in Baghdad's Firdos Square in April 2003 have been replaced by the "return of history," the "revenge of geography," and the "end of dreams."[1] In the 1990s, some regarded *Realpolitik* as a thing of the past—a relic of the Cold War era or a "necessary evil" that could be tossed finally into the dustbin of history. Yet a combination of ideological exhaustion, economic downturn, military overstretch, and a succession of crises in the Middle East, Eastern Europe, and the Pacific have ensured that *Realpolitik* has a receptive audience once more.[2]

This book offers the first comprehensive history of *Realpolitik* as a concept that moved from Germany into the mainstream of Anglo-American political discourse.[3] In times of strife, it is common to look again at history for guidance—or to seek to arm oneself with the intellectual armory of previous eras. Viewed over the longer term, this means that debates over politics, strategy, and foreign policy can appear somewhat cyclical. The waxing and waning of *Realpolitik* in Western political discourse is one example of this. Closely related is the periodic "rediscovery" of the writings of Niccolò Machiavelli, particularly his treatise *The Prince*, first published in 1532. As often happens when the world becomes a more challenging place, a flurry of new books on the Florentine statesman have appeared, including prominent offerings by Philip Bobbitt and Jonathan Powell, Tony Blair's former chief of staff.[4] As Michael Ignatieff has written, we are in the midst of another "Machiavellian moment," an instance "when public necessity requires actions that private ethics and religious values might condemn as unjust and immoral."[5] We have had many Machiavellian moments in the past.[6] The one that occurred in Germany in the mid-nineteenth century provided the context for the birth of *Realpolitik*, so it is not surprising that the two terms are often found side by side.

To many, Machiavelli remains the consensus father of *Realpolitik*—the individual with whom the term is most commonly associated. Yet other supposed heroes of *Realpolitik*, from later eras, have recently enjoyed a return to prestige. Among them are Viscount Castlereagh, Britain's foreign secretary from 1812 to 1822, and Count Klemens von Metternich, the Austrian Empire's foreign minister of the same era, and its chancellor from 1821 to 1848.[7] In *A World Restored*, published in 1957, Henry Kissinger described the achievements of Castlereagh and Metternich in stabilizing Europe after the defeat of Napoleon Bonaparte in 1815.[8] *Realpolitik* has also been closely associated with Otto von Bismarck, the Prussian chancellor who united Germany in 1871 after a successful war with France.[9] In a book about *Realpolitik*, Bismarck certainly deserves a prominent place, though—as we shall see—it is mistaken to see him as its theoretician-in-chief.

The canon of *Realpolitik*, as it is conventionally understood, links together these nineteenth-century statesmen with some of the most prominent figures of twentieth-century American foreign policy, particularly of the Cold War era. George Kennan, often taken as a paragon of American diplomatic realism, was a scholar of Bismarck's foreign policy.[10] Kissinger's doctoral thesis, which became *A World Restored*, was also originally intended to include a section on Bismarck, whom he wrote about at a later date and—as later chapters will discuss—of whom he had a different view than Kennan.[11] If Machiavelli is commonly understood to be the father of *Realpolitik*, Kissinger himself is assumed to be its most prominent torchbearer in the modern era. When the "return of *Realpolitik*" is discussed, it is no surprise to find his name often mentioned in the same breath. There was no greater indication of the influence that Kissinger's prognoses on foreign policy still have than the carefully crafted 2,000-word review of his 2014 book, *World Order*, written by former secretary of state Hillary Clinton.[12] Yet the assumption that Kissinger is the inheritor of a Bismarckian tradition of *Realpolitik* is, it will be argued, misleading.

As something born in the dark heart of Europe, imported from Germany—the great bogeyman of the two world wars—*Realpolitik* has always had an odd place in Anglo-American political discourse. Usages of it, both negative and positive, reveal much about British and American worldviews. The word began to seep into the English language in the era before the First World War. Even though it has been used frequently in foreign policy debates in Britain and America for more than a hundred years, it is still regarded as somewhat exotic. Consequently, even when *Realpolitik* has been used favourably in the United Kingdom or the United States, it has caused discomfort. In the 1930s in Britain and the 1970s in America, in very different contexts, the critics of foreign policy often cried foul about the ingestion of *Realpolitik* by their own statesmen and diplomats. A harsh Teutonic neologism, it has a tendency to get stuck in the craw. As Peter Viereck, a German American critic of *Realpolitik* wrote, in 1942, it was "pronounced with a long, throaty, truculent 'r', and connotes 'r-r-ruthless' (*r-r-rücksichtslos*, Hitler's favourite adjective) and 'r-r-realistic' (*r-r-realitsich*)."[13] One might well contrast it with the smoother inflexions of French—the traditional language of diplomacy—of which *détente* provides a notable example.

Over the last decade, *Realpolitik* has been shorn of some of these negative connotations for a number of reasons. The first is that the return of great power rivalries and the fraying of the international order has evoked comparisons with periods in our past when *Realpolitik* was seen to provide a useful tool of statecraft—chiefly, nineteenth-century Europe, when great powers buffeted each other. The second is that *Realpolitik* has been presented as a necessary antidote to the perceived excess of idealism in Anglo-American foreign policy of the post–Cold War era—a return to the "real" over the "utopian." In this incarnation, it is simply understood as a cool, circumspect approach to statecraft, deliberately contrasted to what is presented as the naïve idealism of others.

Today, this modernized version of *Realpolitik* has some new friends and unlikely advocates. Arguably the most liberal president to inhabit the White House in modern history has been as consciously "realist" as any of his predecessors in the field of foreign policy. For this reason, *Realpolitik* is no longer a dirty word in the Democratic Party as it was in the 1970s and 1990s. "Everybody always breaks it down between idealist and realist," remarked President Obama's former chief of staff, Rahm Emanuel, in an April 2010 article in the *New York Times*. "If you had to put him in a category, he's probably more realpolitik, like Bush 41 . . . you've got to be cold-blooded about the self-interests of your nation."[14] In May 2012, the German weekly *Der Spiegel* ran an article declaring that President Obama was the "unlikely heir to Kissinger's realpolitik" quoting the editor of the *National Interest* to the effect that he "may even start speaking about foreign affairs with a German accent."[15]

The reintroduction of this word as a term of praise can be dated from about 2005, when difficulties following the American-led invasion of Iraq were at their height, and the campaign in Afghanistan was also beginning to unravel. It was not so clear what it meant in practice, however. As a biographer of Lord Castlereagh, I had used it myself on a number of occasions to describe, in the broadest possible terms, aspects of Castlereagh's foreign policy, without much thought of its actual origin. Yet, when Castlereagh was put forward as an exemplar of *Realpolitik* and invoked in debates about contemporary foreign policy, I did not always recognize the individual who was portrayed. I also noted that in past periods such as the 1930s, historical analogies had been used to address contemporary foreign problems in ways that were not entirely accurate, or enlightening. Neville Chamberlain, British prime minister of the late 1930s, had been well versed in the foreign policies of Castlereagh, as well as George Canning, Castlereagh's successor. In rationalizing the policy of appeasement, Chamberlain had evoked these precedents as examples of *Realpolitik*. Yet, of course, this had not prevented the disastrous collapse of British foreign policy in 1938–9.[16] In other words, it seemed that the notion was a slippier signifier than I had once presumed. It was necessary to treat it with some care.

Realpolitik, it became clear on further investigation, was one of those words borrowed from another language that is much used but little understood. In modern usage, it has come to denote a posture, or a philosophical inclination, rather than anything more substantive (such as an approach to politics, or a theory of international relations). Of course, it is absurd to expect contemporary practitioners of foreign policy to know the provenance of every word they use, and it is perhaps all too typical of academics to retreat to the library with a roll of their eyes. In 1934, the English historian A. J. P. Taylor wrote that a nation's foreign policy was based on a series of assumptions, with which statesmen have lived since their earliest years, and which they regard as "so axiomatic as hardly to be worth stating." It was the duty of the historian, then, "to clarify these assumptions and to trace their influence upon the course of every-day policy."[17]

The true meaning of *Realpolitik* remains occluded by the partisan way the word has been used in Anglo-American political discourse. For one, as noted already, it has long had pejorative connotations. "The advocates of a

realist foreign policy are caricatured with the German term Realpolitik,"
Henry Kissinger has observed, "I suppose to facilitate the choosing of
sides."[18] It is significant, as later chapters will argue, that Kissinger has
generally eschewed the term himself. When he has used it, in fact, he has
sought to highlight its flaws.[19]

Others are more comfortable with the label than Kissinger. Yet some of
those who wear the badge with pride also tend to caricature the naïve idealists they set themselves up against. In the past, the critics of *Realpolitik* have
been denounced as "Wilsonians"; more recently they have been lumped
together as "neo-conservatives." Used in this way, *Realpolitik* has become
an accoutrement of sophistication, intended to signify one's worldliness
and historical depth and to distinguish oneself from dunderheaded ideo-
logues. "I will leave it to the self-described realists to explain in greater
detail the origins and meaning of 'realism' and 'realpolitik' to our confused
journalists and politicos," remarked the historian, Robert Kagan, in a 2010
discussion of President Obama's realist credentials. Kagan's point—the corollary of Kissinger's—was that those who claimed this mantle did so in a
self-satisfied manner, with the intention of dismissing their opponents as
unrealistic, unsophisticated, and ill informed.[20]

One can hardly blame politicians for using language in a way that suits
their agenda. In fact, if few satisfactory definitions of *Realpolitik* exist, the
fault lies elsewhere. It is more because scholars of international relations,
with a few notable exceptions, have remained largely uninterested in its
historical origins. For the most part, *Realpolitik* has been used interchangeably with "realism," "realist," or raison d'état—all of which, of course, are
sticky terms themselves.[21] As Lucian Ashworth has written, it remains the
case that scholars of international relations have sometimes been "lax in
the study of the ideas of their own discipline."[22] This book follows the
basic principles of the "Cambridge school" approach to intellectual history.
This holds that political ideas, and associated political discourse, should be
understood in the context of the historical era in which they were used.
They should be treated as products of time and place, rather than as vessels
of perennial "truths."[23]

This is not a merely an academic exercise. According to Quentin
Skinner, the most influential scholar of the Cambridge school, one useful
function that the historian can perform is "to uncover the often neglected
riches of our intellectual heritage and display them once more to view."
Yet, perhaps more important for our purposes, Skinner also warns that it is

"sometimes difficult to avoid falling under the spell of our own intellectual heritage"—that is, to become "bewitched" into believing that "the ways of thinking about certain ideas bequeathed to us by the mainstream of our intellectual traditions must be *the* ways of thinking about them."[24] As will be shown, the history of *Realpolitik* has been pockmarked by the existence of cultish devotees, overly impressed by the idea that they were the gate-keepers to reality.

A few common misconceptions can be lanced at the outset. *Realpolitik* is not, as is often assumed, as old as statecraft itself. Nor is it to be confused with "realism" writ large. As Jonathan Haslam makes clear in *No Virtue like Necessity: Realist Thought in International Relations since Machiavelli*, the best recent discussion of the concept, *Realpolitik* does have a place within the "realist" tradition.[25] Yet it is something distinct from raison d'état, pursuit of the "national interest," or Machiavellianism—concepts with which it has often been conflated.[26] *Realpolitik* is of more recent vintage. It has existed for just over a century and a half. It was created by the German journalist and liberal activist, August Ludwig von Rochau, in his 1853 treatise *Foundations of Realpolitik*. Rochau, who added a second volume in 1869, is almost entirely forgotten today. As will be seen, however, his creation has had a long and controversial afterlife.

The first goal of this book is best understood as an act of rediscovery. Part I begins by uncovering the origins of *Realpolitik* in mid-nineteenth-century Europe. It then goes on to outline and explicate the concept, as Ludwig von Rochau originally intended it to be understood, in his two-volume work. In contrast to modern incarnations, the original version of *Realpolitik* did not denote a philosophical *mood* so much as a *method* of analyzing complex political problems. According to Rochau, successful statecraft depended on an appreciation of the historical circumstances in which the statesman operated. Just as important, however, was the ability to anticipate, and adjust oneself to, the changing conditions of modernity. Ideas were important in politics—increasingly so, in the democratic age—but their importance was to be judged by their political force rather than their purity or elegance.

The second aim of the book (Parts II to V) is to examine how *Realpolitik* has been used in Anglo-American discourse about foreign affairs ever since its inception. This is dated from around 1890 when the word was first introduced into the English language. The history of *Realpolitik* in the English-speaking world should be distinguished from its earlier history in Germany.

Any sense of Rochau's original concept was almost lost entirely. The word was used in many different ways, to many different ends. This process of diffusion and proliferation tells a story in itself. It is the *usage* of the term that is explored in these chapters. Unlike liberalism or Marxism, there was no coherent or consistent view of what it meant. Parts II to IV should therefore be understood primarily as a study of discourse, rather than a study of the theory itself (provided in Part I). The reason for this is that the way *Realpolitik* has been used reveals much about the approaches to foreign affairs and the interpretations of international politics that have been prevalent in the two great superpowers of the nineteenth and twentieth centuries. In this way, *Realpolitik* is used as a window into the soul of what might be called the Anglo-American worldview.[27] Why did some individuals and groups so dislike and fear the notion? Why were others more comfortable with it and came to think of it more favourably? As will be demonstrated, what people thought about *Realpolitik* provided a clue for much else besides.

By beginning with Ludwig von Rochau, we can establish a true understanding of what *Realpolitik* was originally supposed to mean. Yet it is also important to understand that the notion Rochau created took on a life of its own. One of the main themes of the book is that *Realpolitik* has given birth to a number of bastardized and half-formed versions of itself, which have been the sources of misconception. The process began in Germany where Rochau's ideas were willfully twisted to serve other ends. By the time, *Realpolitik* arrived in the Anglo-American world it had become entangled with many other concepts such as *Machtpolitik* (the politics of force), *Weltpolitik* (taken to imply global power politics), and broader conceptions of "realism" in foreign affairs. In some cases, this distortion opened the door to great misunderstanding and, worse still, wrongdoing. So there is no desire to revive a cult of *Realpolitik* here. In fact, the book argues that much British and American foreign policy of the last century can be understood as deriving, in part, from a reaction against the more irredentist interpretations of *Realpolitik* that emerged in Germany after Rochau. In the English-speaking world, a form of "anti-*Realpolitik*" became a tangible phenomenon in its own right. In some respects, in fact, it provided a sort of glue between English and American foreign policy.

While the book often juxtaposes *Realpolitik* and its counterpart (anti-*Realpolitik*), some of the most fruitful insights into statecraft and foreign policy were to be found in the cracks between them, along with some of the best thinkers on foreign affairs. In outlining these debates, I do not attempt to offer a synthesis of the two traditions. The aim is not to present some sort of "middle-ground" ethics of statecraft. Those seeking to reconcile ideas and self-interest, in a coherent theory of international relations, will be better served by the work of the "English School" or Joseph Nye's more recent call for "liberal realism" in US foreign policy.[28] In any case, it might be said that that horse has long bolted. Reinhold Niebuhr outlined the founding precepts of "Christian realism," and all the dilemmas that came with it, more than half a century ago.[29] It is no surprise that President Obama has drawn on Niebuhr to help craft his own version of "liberal realism" and that Niebuhr's influence was evident in his Nobel Peace Prize acceptance speech of 2009.[30]

In one important respect, the original concept of *Realpolitik*—as its creator intended—can be understood as a form of liberal realism. Ludwig von Rochau was a committed liberal who wanted Germany to be united under the rule of law and constitutional and representative government. In calling for *Realpolitik*, he was appealing to his fellow liberals. In the simplest terms, they had to "get real" about the nature of politics if they were to achieve their aims. However, it is necessary to insert an important caveat here, that distinguishes his work from later attempts to articulate a coherent liberal realist theory of politics. Rochau was not concerned with the construction of worldviews but the business of politics, often at the most granular level. Theology and moral philosophy existed in another sphere to *Realpolitik*.

A book on *Realpolitik* cannot be separated from broader debates about "realism" in international affairs. However, those seeking a lengthy meditation on academic theories of realism—or International Relations theory—are best placed to look elsewhere. Nor is the book to be mistaken for an argument for a reinvigorated "classical realism." It does share some of the criticisms of the so-called neo-realist school, made by "classical" realists—particularly of the tendency to portray the international system in over-theorized and mechanized ways.[31] As the diplomatic historian Paul Schroeder has written, one flaw of neo-realism is precisely its use of terms such as *Realpolitik*, with little concern for the context in which they emerged.[32] At the broadest level, the book shares the view that many versions of realist thought—classical and otherwise—are dependent on subjective and time-bound vistas and axioms rather than fundamental "truths" about international affairs.[33]

While stressing the importance of historical methods, the conclusion of the book abandons something of the detachment to which historians hold themselves. I found myself in agreement with the historian Felix Gilbert who wrote, in 1970, that it would be a "declaration of bankruptcy on the part of historical scholarship if the work of the historian stopped short of the most burning issues of the day."[34] The book therefore begins and ends by arguing that the original concept of *Realpolitik*—as understood by Ludwig von Rochau—is ripe for rediscovery. To put it simply, Rochau's two-volume work, *Foundations of Realpolitik*, is an untapped and almost unknown source of wisdom about the nature of politics that still has uses in today's world.

Rediscovering real *Realpolitik* is, I believe, a more useful exercise than simply reverting to a rather jaded version of Machiavellianism, as we have done so many times in the past. That is not to say that Machiavelli's writing has suddenly lost its value after five hundred years. It is simply to make the point that the original concept of *Realpolitik* was born in an era that more closely resembles ours today than it does the world of Machiavelli. Ludwig von Rochau grappled with challenges that remain the quintessential problems of modernity. His version of *Realpolitik* provides a corrective to certain delusions that are still found in the Western liberal mind. But rather than rebelling against liberalism, Rochau's *Realpolitik* offered it a helping hand toward success.

A final word is necessary on the various usages of *Realpolitik* that appear in the five parts of the book, as this is important for the development of the argument. Thus far, the capitalized and italicized *Realpolitik* has been used. This practice is continued in Part I, which deals with the original concept of *Realpolitik*, as articulated by Ludwig von Rochau in his *Foundations of Realpolitik*. The capitalized and italicized version of *Realpolitik* is also used in the final chapter of Part I, which discusses the various uses of the word, in Germany, after Rochau's death. Even though Heinrich von Treitschke distorted Rochau's concept of *Realpolitik*—with lasting effects—he was building on the original. After Treitschke, Friedrich Meinecke's use of *Realpolitik* was closer to Rochau's original, which he had also read himself. Both Treitschke and Meinecke used *Realpolitik* to describe Bismarck's foreign policy. Even though Bismarck did not use the word himself, the italicized, capitalized form is maintained in discussions of Bismarckian *Realpolitik* (which appear in Part I and in later sections). The basic rule, continued in later chapters, is that German versions of *Realpolitik* are marked out in this way. It is important for the reader to understand that various German usages of the term were often vastly divergent from what Rochau intended. In the early twentieth century, General Bernhardi and other German nationalists often used it in very different ways, with no knowledge of who Rochau was. Rather than providing a detailed typology for each usage, the different delineations are explained in the course of the text. After Part I, in those instances where we return to Rochau's original concept, it is also referred to as "real *Realpolitik*," or "Rochau's *Realpolitik*," to mark it out from other German usages.

The rest of the book deals with the English-language history of *Realpolitik*. To distinguish it from the German original, the lower case, Roman version "realpolitik" is used. This is also the practice for the "anti-realpolitik" tradition that I begin to describe in Part II, which emerged in the period before the First World War. Initially, realpolitik was used in the English language in descriptions of German behavior on the international stage. But soon it began to take on a broader meaning. In Part II, for example, I note that early American discussants of realpolitik were always more comfortable with the term than their English counterparts. This is explained in a chapter on "American realpolitik." At the same time, a shared sense of anti-realpolitik did encourage the development of ideas of liberal internationalism in the 1910s. Thus anti-realpolitik shone most brightly when British and American interests seemed to converge.

As Part III shows, the meaning of realpolitik began to change in the interwar years. The word began to creep into diplomatic parlance in more generalized terms and became less associated with Germany. In Britain, in particular, this meant realpolitik lost some of its negative connotations. Instead, for the first time, it was used as an antidote to what were perceived to be the excesses of idealism of the period after the First World War (in which anti-realpolitik had been in the ascendancy). When British statesmen and scholars spoke of realpolitik in the interwar era, they did not mean German *Realpolitik* at all but a return to more traditional forms of nineteenth-century diplomacy. The ingestion of realpolitik reflected exasperation with the League of Nations and collective security. But the limits of this version of realpolitik were reflected in the failures of appeasement.

In the United States, increasingly, realpolitik assumed a variety of meanings. Part IV describes the further "Americanization of realpolitik." This had a number of strands. In the first instance, realpolitik was used interchangeably with geopolitics (derived from another German import,

Geopolitik), and the two were conflated. Whereas those in Britain who used realpolitik positively tended to support the policy of appeasement, the same was not the case in America. The American exponents of realpolitik of the 1930s and 1940s called for a front-footed stance on the global stage, and their main opponents were American isolationsists. In other words, they called for a greater emphasis on geopolitics.

After the Second World War, the meaning of realpolitik assumed different connotations in America again. The influx of a number of influential scholars from Germany (including those who understood the true origins of the term) meant that there was greater awareness of the German origins of *Realpolitik*. Most of the German-Americans who were engaged in the foreign policy debate avoided using the term and did not like to be associated with it. Part IV rejects the idea that there was a concerted attempt to insert German versions of *Realpolitik* into American strategic and political thought as simplistic. Nonetheless, it does argue that this tradition did have some influence on the shaping of American realism. An obvious example of its effects was the admiration often expressed for Bismarck's foreign policy, which played into debates about Cold War strategy. It was in this era that usage of the word became increasingly common, particularly in academia. Indeed, it became a discursive weapon in the so-called second Great Debate among theorists of international relations that occurred in the early years of the Cold War. The Roman form ("realpolitik") is maintained here. The one exception to this is in the last chapter of Part IV. This examines the debate between the Bismarckians and the anti-Bismarckians in which *Realpolitik* was understood to be something born in the particular context of nineteenth-century German history. It was in the historical profession that the faintest embers of Ludwig von Rochau's original concept were kept alive.

Part V, which examines "practical realpolitik," describes how the meaning of the word was cheapened from the late 1960s. During this era, it became caught up with a series of other controversies in the policymaking world. Some of this can be attributed to the number of those trained in the second Great Debate of the postwar era who assumed senior positions in office during this period. Realpolitik was one of the words they took with them from the universities into the foreign policy profession. The concept was to become associated with Henry Kissinger more than anyone else, of course. Yet there is a certain irony in this. Kissinger, distinguishing himself from Kennan, offered some of the most salient criticisms of Bismarckian *Realpolitik*. These nuances were largely lost in the highly charged debates of the 1970s between partisans and opponents of the administrations of Nixon and Ford, and then Carter. The presidency of Ronald Reagan, and the (ambiguous) notion of the "Reagan doctrine," demonstrated the inadequacy of the existing distinction between realpolitik and anti-realpolitik. By the 1990s, the term was so diluted as to become effectively meaningless—partly because it became entangled with the debates over intervention and non-intervention that characterized that decade. In the modern era, it is now the most vague of signifiers—a posture rather than a clear position on world affairs.

A Note on Methodology

My initial curiosity about the co-called "return of *Realpolitik*" in the modern era led to the discovery of Ludwig von Rochau's relativey obscure original work. This gave me a firm starting point for research. In tracing its evolution thereafter, I learned that the word had seeped into the English language from the early 1890s through to the outbreak of the First World War, and that it was treated with a certain degree of revulsion because of its harsh Germanic overtones. Nonetheless, its use fed into some of the most important debates of the era—from the causes of the First World War to the very creation of the field of international relations. It soon became clear that the English-language history of this idea and the genealogy of the word in Britain and the United States was a story in itself and was intimately related to the definitive foreign policy debates of the last century.

The "official" history of realpolitik, in national archives and legislative debates, provided a further dimension to the story. The index of the UK national archives (including Foreign Office, Cabinet, and Prime Ministerial files) and US State Department catalogues can now be searched for keywords, though only a portion of this can be viewed online. The initial searches provided a guide for archival research at the UK National Archives in London and the American National Archives at College Park, Maryland, where the CIA "CREST" archive is also available. This was supplemented by use of Hansard's Parliamentary Debates and the Congressional and Senatorial records. The Library of Congress housed a number of other useful digitized collections, such as the Frontline Diplomacy Archive and the ProQuest Historical Newspaper Database.

Searches of these files provided some basic intellectual scaffolding for the book, which was supplemented by broader exploration of a series of key themes, dealt with in the five parts of the book: the mid-nineteenth-century German liberal tradition, which gave birth to the *Realpolitik*; German debates about statecraft through the pre– and post–First World War period; English debates about imperialism and appeasement; American geopolitics and postwar American realism; through the controversies of the Nixon-Carter years and the foreign policy debates from Reagan to Obama. A fellowship at the Library of Congress offered access to the papers of Hans Morgenthau, Reinhold Niebuhr, and Daniel P. Moynihan—individuals who played an important part in these later debates.

Even ten years ago a book of this nature would have been more difficult to write. Digitized sources and databases (of newspapers and periodicals) allowed me to chart the changes in the meaning of the word over time. There are certain pitfalls in modern research methods that also should be acknowledged. The French historian Arlette Farge has observed that focusing on a particular theme (such as "drunkenness," "theft," or "adultery") "creates a specific viewpoint that requires explanation, because the space is necessarily reorganized by the research objective," along with an element of reconstruction.[35] My hope is that the precision afforded by the tools of modern research does not come at the expense of depth or breadth. I found the work of the cultural critic and literary historian, Franco Moretti, whose book on the "bourgeois" also used electronic databases, to be a useful model.[36] Other concept books that helped guide the research were Quentin Skinner's famous essay, *Liberty before Liberalism*, David Runciman's *Hypocrisy*, and Greta Jones's *Social Darwinism and English Thought*. Each discusses the use and misuse of a concept over time, attempts to rescue its original meaning, and cautions against false polarities.[37] In discussing a range of intellectual figureheads over time, there are similarities in my approach and that used by Perry Anderson in *American Foreign Policy and its Thinkers*.[38]

Finally, the work also takes inspiration from Raymond Williams's 1976 book *Keywords*, which examined the etymology and changing meaning of more than two hundred words commonly used in political discourse. Indeed, Williams's entry on "realism" is complementary to the argument made over the course of this book. In the eighteenth century, "realism" was taken to mean the general sense of an underlying truth or quality. From the mid-nineteenth century, it increasingly meant a facing up to things as they really are. In the second half of the twentieth century, the meaning morphed

again into implying one's acceptance of the limits of a situation. In the process, Williams argues, realism became increasingly self-limiting: it offered
a version of reality which stressed the limits of human wisdom and action,
rather than a true assessment of the whole picture.[39] It was in the earlier
sense of "realism" that Ludwig von Rochau's *Foundations of Realpolitik* was
conceived. A return to foundations, as the conclusion book argues, would
also be a return to a higher, truer form of realism.

PART
I

Real *Realpolitik*

The Realpolitik does not move in a foggy future, but in the present's field of vision, it does not consider its task to consist in the realization of ideals, but in the attainment of concrete ends, and it knows, with reservations, to content itself with partial results, if their complete attainment is not achievable for the time being. Ultimately, the Realpolitik is an enemy of all kinds of self-delusion.

(Ludwig von Rochau, *Foundations of Realpolitik*, vol. 2, 1868)[1]

I

Origins

*R*ealpolitik is not, as is often assumed, as old as statecraft itself. Nor is it part of a seamless creed stretching back to Thucydides and running through Niccolò Machiavelli, Cardinal Richelieu, Thomas Hobbes, and Lord Castlereagh, up to Hans Morgenthau, George Kennan, and Henry Kissinger. It is not to be discovered by dusting off the great tomes of statecraft from the Ancient or Renaissance worlds, or retelling the stories of sagacious statesmen of yesterday, in search of some form of timeless wisdom. To excavate its origins, one must return to the world in which it was conceived.

Real *Realpolitik*—as we might call it—was in fact born in an era that more closely resembles the one in which we find ourselves today, albeit with some obvious differences. It emerged in mid-nineteenth-century Europe from the collision of the Enlightenment with the bloody process of national state formation and great power politics. This was a world experiencing the quintessential problems of modernity: a combustion of new ideas about liberty and social order alongside rapid industrialization, class antagonism, sectarianism, the rise of nationalism (in both its civic and ethnic forms), and increasing international rivalry.

In the first instance, the creation of the concept of *Realpolitik* was an attempt to answer a domestic political conundrum: how to build a stable and liberal nation-state in an unsteady and rapidly changing environment, without recourse to violent convulsion or repression. *Realpolitik* held that it was the first act of statecraft to identify the contending social, economic, and ideological forces struggling for supremacy within the state. The second act of statecraft was to attempt to achieve some equilibrium and balance among these forces so that they would not hinder the development of the nation-state. To be successful, the statesman had to understand both the historical circumstances in which he operated and the conditions of modernity in an era of rapid economic, political, and intellectual development.

Lessons learned in domestic statecraft had relevance to the international theater too. The emergence of new nation-states—or aspiring nation-states—across Europe in the second half of the nineteenth century meant that the logic of *Realpolitik* was soon applied to the conduct of foreign affairs too. It was as an approach to foreign policy that *Realpolitik* spread to other nations, first in Europe, and eventually the United States. Underlying this was a deeper philosophical dilemma that remains central to today's debates about foreign policy: how to achieve liberal enlightened goals—which included balance and equilibrium—in a world that did not follow liberal enlightened rules.

The birth of *Realpolitik* was inextricably linked to the European revolutions of 1848. In some respects, the 1848 revolutions were nineteenth-century Europe's equivalent of the Arab spring.[1] A revolutionary wave began with uncoordinated revolts in Sicily and Paris in January and February 1848, respectively. By March the "contagion" had spread to Germany, Italy, Hungary, and Denmark, and the tremors were soon felt in Ireland, Belgium, Switzerland, Poland, and modern-day Romania.

Over the course of the next two years nearly all the 1848 revolutions (with the arguable exception of the Swiss) failed on their own terms. Uprisings that began in the name of political liberalism—ideas of the Enlightenment, along with constitutional rights and representative government—soon fell victim to other political phenomena. In some cases, revolutionary assemblies were shut down or neutered by coercive governments, which recovered from the initial shock and ruthlessly restored their authority. In others, movements for liberal reform were swallowed up by more powerful social and political forces—such as class, religion, ethnicity, and nationalism—or, in the case of Italy, Hungary, Poland, and the Romanian Principalities, snuffed out by foreign intervention.

While revolutionaries read about the deeds of their counterparts in other countries—and intellectual and ideological connections existed between them—the fate of each individual revolution was decided by circumstances unique to the context in which they occurred. This was to be a founding observation of *Realpolitik*. In France, for example, where most European liberals looked for inspiration, the so-called Second Republic got further than most in 1848, following the precedent of the First Republic, formed after the French Revolution of 1789. Ultimately, however, the

A caricature of the defeat of the 1848 revolutions across Europe, by Ferdinand Schröder, published in *Düsseldorfer Monatshefte*, in August 1849. Within eighteen months, nearly all of the revolutions had been defeated by the old regimes or foreign intervention. Courtesy of Wikimedia Creative Commons.

Second French Republic fell victim to the fate that befell the first. It was hijacked by Napoleon's nephew, Louis Napoleon, who dissolved the National Assembly and established a Second Empire instead. Following the Bonapartist method, he used the power of plebiscite to gird his regime with popular legitimacy, circumventing the representative process.

Realpolitik emerged against this broader European backdrop, but it was in the particular circumstances of Germany that the notion was formed. A month after the French Revolution began in Paris in February 1848, several states in the loosely federated German Confederation experienced uprisings. These included the two most powerful of the thirty-nine German states, Austria and Prussia. In Austria, the deeply conservative chancellor Prince Klemens von Metternich—in office for more than three decades and the nemesis of many European liberals—was forced to resign by angry protestors who flooded Vienna. In Prussia, King Frederick William IV was caught unawares by popular protests and forced to accede, in the short term, to liberal demands.

The liberals and radicals of the various German states shared many aims and sought to coordinate their efforts. Most of them believed that the liberal political cause was best served by a united Germany rather than a Germany divided into small states and principalities in which the old elites held political power. To that end, they formed a German National Assembly in Frankfurt, in the state of Hessen, including deputies elected from across the German Confederation, who met in order to debate a new draft constitution for Germany as a whole. Ideological and strategic divisions between them soon emerged. Should this united Germany contain Austria, for example, or was it preferable to have a smaller Germany (*Kleindeutsche*) led by Prussia? Should the constitution be based on universal suffrage or a limited franchise? Meanwhile, as the liberals argued among themselves in the cocoon of their parliament, the old regimes regained the upper hand.

In early 1849, a group of deputies chosen by the National Assembly offered Prussia's Frederick William IV the office of emperor in what they hoped would be a new German constitutional monarchy, excluding Austria in the south but unifying the north German states. When he declined the offer, the Frankfurt Assembly—with no king to lead it and no army to make good on its ideals—was left rudderless. If the existing regime had lost public authority momentarily, it still had most of the tools of state power in its control. The reason why power slipped through the fingers of the men of 1848 was that they had only ever really held it in their minds. Before long, many of the revolutionaries and reformers had been scattered into exile, arrested, or imprisoned. Some were simply scared off and others even embraced the governments that they had once opposed.

Liberals and radicals had been in the vanguard of German nationalism, but the revolution unleashed forces that were out of their control. Nationalism and liberalism were not, as some revolutionaries had believed, two sides of the same coin. Over the following two decades, Germany was indeed to be united but not by the means that the men of '48 had originally envisaged. Rather than constitutionalism and representative government, it was the "blood and iron" of the Prussian minister-president, Otto von Bismarck, that drove the creation of the German Empire in 1871.[2] The historian A. J. P. Taylor famously described the 1848 revolution in Germany as the moment when "history reached a turning point and failed to turn." By this he meant that Germany took a different path from that of most liberal and Western states—where economic modernization was matched by political liberalization.[3]

It is in the cracks of this fractured political landscape—of false hopes and frustrated ambitions—that one finds the notion of *Realpolitik*. For some, *Realpolitik* was welcomed as an important evolutionary development in political understanding; for others, *Realpolitik* resembled the spurts of an ugly, suffocating, and sinister weed. As the rest of this book will argue, both of these interpretations have some truth in them. But it is necessary to go back another fifteen years, before we can begin this story.

Ludwig von Rochau: A Liberal Mugged by Reality

On 3 April 1833, fifteen years before the revolutions of 1848, a group of around fifty German students, workers, and artisans—supported by a small number of Polish refugees and political activists—attempted to storm the main guard post of the military garrison at Frankfurt, a short walk from the seat of the parliament of the German Confederation. In what was to become known as the *Frankfurter Wachensturm* (the charge of the Frankfurt guard house), their ill-conceived plan was to gain control of the treasury of the confederation and spark a series of similar revolutions across the other German states. The army had received forewarning, however, and the attempt was a hopeless failure. Many of the ringleaders fled immediately and some ended up as far away as America. One became lieutenant governor of Illinois and another died serving Sam Houston in Texas.

Among those arrested trying to flee the scene was a twenty-three-year-old radical named August Ludwig von Rochau. This was the first stage in what was to be a rude awakening for Rochau about the unforgiving nature of politics and the limits of idealism. But his coming to political maturity did not occur overnight. Not until twenty years later, in 1853, did Rochau introduce the concept of *Realpolitik*.

Rochau was neither a great leader nor a great political theorist in a period replete with both. He is known to German historians of the period as one of a number of mid-century liberal activists rather than a particularly distinguished character in his own right. His political journey was, to some extent, typical of the general trajectory of German liberalism before and after 1848.[4] There are good reasons that Rochau's life and work have rarely been discussed in the English language outside the context of German liberal history in this period. With one notable exception, the man and his work have been almost entirely missed by historians of international relations.[5] Indeed, his two-volume treatise on *Realpolitik* has never been translated into English, despite his coining a word that is used so often today.

This neglect can partly be explained by the fact that Rochau's theory of politics—if it can even be called a theory—was messy. It contained an uneven mix of German, French, and English political philosophy and sociology and does not fit easily within the main intellectual traditions of the nineteenth century: liberalism, conservatism, socialism, or Marxism.[6] If anything, it borrowed elements from each. Also, *Realpolitik* became associated with other, more famous characters, which obscured its origins and its true meaning. Chief among them were Austria's Count Metternich and Prussia's Otto von Bismarck, the preeminent statesman of nineteenth-century Germany.

The association of *Realpolitik* with Metternich is misleading. It was against Metternich's illiberal regime that Rochau and his colleagues defined themselves before 1848, when Metternich fell from power. *Realpolitik* emerged only after Metternich was off the scene. The linkage of *Realpolitik* with Bismarck was more plausible but still misleading. After 1848, Rochau was an opponent of the Prussian monarchical regime of which Bismarck was the chief political representative, becoming minister-president in 1862. Yet, in 1867, a year after Prussia defeated Austria in a brief war for supremacy within Germany, Rochau was one of a number of liberals (the majority, in fact) who were willing to enter into a temporary alliance with Bismarck. The notion of *Realpolitik* was partly used to justify this accommodation. Soon after—in a twist of fate—it was also used to describe Bismarck's foreign policy. Significantly, however, Bismarck himself never used it.

So who was Ludwig August von Rochau? He was born on 20 August 1810 in the small town of Wolfenbüttel in Lower Saxony. This was the moment at which Napoleon Bonaparte's domination of Europe was at its height. Saxony had been the last German state to be allied with Napoleon before his defeat by the Sixth Coalition in 1814. Yet this was a choice forced upon it because of its vulnerability to the huge armies of the French, just a few days' march away. Saxony also had a tradition of anti-French resistance into which Rochau was born. He was the illegitimate son of an officer in the Braunschweig Hussars, a regiment raised in 1809 by the Duke of Brunswick-Wolfenbüttel to fight against Napoleonic occupation and which was to play a part in the battle of Waterloo in 1815, when Napoleon was defeated for the second and final time.[7]

The three decades after 1815—later referred to as the *Vormärz* (literally "before [the] March" revolutions of 1848)—were characterized by a flowering of intellectual and cultural activity in Germany, and the spread of liberalism and nationalism in particular. As a young man, Ludwig August von Rochau was very much a creature of the *Vormärz*. He began his adult life as a radical political activist, known to his friends to hold republican and anti-monarchical views. He studied law at the universities of Jena and Göttingen but never completed his studies and was expelled from the latter because of his political activities.

In his youth, Rochau spent most of his time trying to mobilize his peers in support of liberal causes, at home and abroad. He urged the formation of a German academic legion in support of the Polish uprising of 1831. Much of his optimism was dampened by the failed rebellion of 1833. When in custody, following the *Frankfurter Wachensturm*, he attempted suicide twice but was revived against his will. He was sentenced to life imprisonment and served three years before he escaped and fled, in disguise, to Paris in October 1836, where he would spend the next decade.

In Paris, like many exiles, Rochau made his career as a freelance journalist and writer. He sent articles on French politics back to the German liberal press for publication. His first book was an account of travels in southern France and Spain, which reaffirmed the anti-authoritarianism and anti-clericalism one would expect from a mid-nineteenth-century liberal. While he avoided any direct involvement with radical circles in Paris, he did write an essay in 1840 that expressed sympathy with the ideas of Charles Fourier, the French socialist thinker known for his utopianism and belief in the potential productive power of societies based on the cooperative principle. He also absorbed elements of the French positivist school of thought, associated with Henry de Saint-Simon and Auguste Comte—which held that society operated according to general laws. His theory of *Realpolitik* bears the marks of Comte's book, *Politique Positive*, which appeared around the same time. Comte argued that it was possible to have a science of social knowledge, based on empiricism.[8]

On the eve of the 1848 revolutions, with the authorities' attention elsewhere, Rochau returned to Germany to the liberal university town of Heidelberg and joined the staff of the liberal newspaper *Deutsche Zeitung*

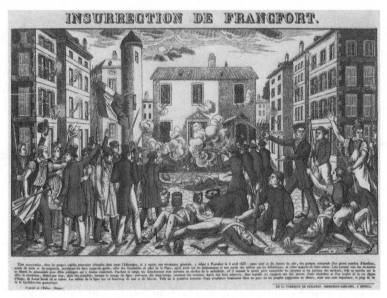

INSURRECTION DE FRANCFORT.

As a twenty-two-year-old, Ludwig von Rochau was part of a hopeless attempt to spark a liberal revolution in Germany in 1833, when students attempted to storm the police in Frankfurt and gain control of the German treasury. Rochau was arrested as he tried to flee the scene and was held in prison for three years, before he escaped to Paris. The *Frankfurter Wachensturm* uprising on 3 April 1833. Reproduction of a colored woodcarving by Francois Georgin (1801–1863). Courtesy of Wikimedia Creative Commons. PD-US.

(founded in July 1847). He played no significant part in the revolution which followed in March 1848, though he did support it. He failed in an effort to get elected to the Frankfurt Assembly created that year. As a newspaper correspondent, he sat in the chamber and reported on the debates over the constitution and future of Germany, which ultimately came to naught. After joining another newspaper, *Augsburger Allgemeine Zeitung*, his reports of the assembly debates mostly took the form of balanced reportage. He did, nonetheless, express sympathy with the more moderate delegates who believed that it was unrealistic to exclude the German princes from any reorganization of the German political system. By this stage, Rochau had softened his views and given up on republicanism. He supported those delegates who wanted to offer the throne of a North German Confederation to Frederick William IV. There would be an important role for the monarch to play if Germany was to be unified.

The Frankfurt Assembly was created following the German revolution of March 1848 and met inside St. Paul's Church in the city. While Ludwig von Rochau failed to get elected to it, he sat in on proceedings as a newspaper correspondent. He later accused the delegates of "building castles in the sky" and of being political juveniles, leading to the parliament's collapse a year later. Courtesy of Wikimedia Creative Commons. PD-US.

By 1850, however, the dream of German unity under Prussia was defeated by the Agreement of Olmütz. Under the terms of this arrangement, Prussia accepted, once again, the revival of the German Confederation under Austrian leadership. A disillusioned Rochau—who had seen both the nationalist and liberal causes suffer severe setbacks in the two years since the 1848 revolutions—was forced to flee Germany again, as the autocrats tightened the screw once more.[9] The liberals had been completely out-maneuvered.

Many European liberals had spent much of the period from 1815 to 1848 with faith that history was on their side, even if governments were not. What had gone wrong? Why had history, in A. J. P. Taylor's phrase, "failed to turn"? For Rochau, the men of 1848 had themselves to blame. They had been naïve and deluded, to the detriment of the liberal and national cause. They spoke in philosophical terms about their ideal political system while the tectonic plates of German politics rumbled and shifted beneath their feet. They dreamed up superstructures but they forgot the base. "A work that had been begun with aimless enthusiasm and carried out with an over-estimation of one's own capabilities ended in dishonour and injury," he was later to write.[10]

Across Europe, similar scenarios had played out. Europe's year of tumult in 1848 was to become known, disparagingly, as the "revolution of the intellectuals"—as described by the Polish-born British historian, Louis Namier. The revolutionaries failed to seize control of armies and treasuries and left their imprint "only in the realm of ideas." The liberal elites had failed to bring the masses with them. Outside the cities, the great bulk of the peasantry remained cautious, conservative, and loyal to church and Crown. The French Revolution of 1789 and the Russian Revolution of 1917 were sparked, and then sustained, by the convergence of great revolutionary forces. The "revolution of the intellectuals," by contrast, exhausted itself without achieving any of its aims and was defeated by, as Namier put it, "a perplexing mix of hubris and idealism."[11]

The events of 1848 prompted an intellectual revolution in another sense too. Across Europe, a new generation of thinkers began to reflect more deeply about the process of historical change. As Namier wrote, many of the participants in the failed revolutions came to understand their business better ("better, indeed, than many historians who have written about it since"). They learned that states were not created or destroyed by elegant speeches and majority votes. Instead, it dawned on them that "nations are freed, united, or broken by blood and iron, and not by generous application of liberty and tomato-sauce: violence is the instrument of national movements."[12] It is no surprise that 1848 was a spur to a new set of philosophies of radical change—revolutionary socialism, anarchism, and even the techniques of modern terrorism such as the cult of blood sacrifice to the "propaganda of the deed."[13]

In *The Communist Manifesto*, published in 1848, Karl Marx and Frederick Engels had argued that bourgeois revolution was the next step in historical development. So the failure of those revolutions required some explanation. Engels addressed these questions in a series of articles for the *New York Tribune* in 1851 while Marx wrote one of his most famous essays—a case study of the collapse of the Second Republic in France and the rise of Louis Napoleon as emperor, which was published in 1852. "Men make their own history," was how Marx famously began *The Eighteenth Brumaire of Louis Napoleon*, "but they do not make it as they please: they do not make it under self-selected circumstances, but under circumstances existing already, given and transmitted from the past." [14]

According to Marx, bourgeois revolutions such as those of 1848 had a pattern to them. At first, they "storm swiftly from success to success, their dramatic effects outdo each other, men and things seem set in sparkling diamonds, ecstasy is the order of the day." In the excitement, however, the revolutionaries failed to appreciate their weakness. They took "refuge in a belief in miracles, believed the enemy to be overcome when he was only conjured away in imagination." Their idealism was blinding. They "lost all understanding of the present in an inactive glorification of the future that was in store for it and the deeds it had in mind but did not want to carry out yet." Louis Napoleon's coup d'état of December 1851, when he simply dissolved the French National Assembly, "struck them like a thunderbolt from the sky." With liberal bourgeois revolutions, successes were inevitably short-lived. Soon "they have reached their zenith, and a long Katzenjammer [cat's cry, often used to express a sense of hangover] takes hold of society before it learns to assimilate the results of its storm and stress period soberly."

The Eighteenth Brumaire is now known as a foundational text in historical materialism but it did not dismiss the role of the individual or the role of ideas. In Marx's interpretation, they were all interlinked. Political ideas were a reflection of the socioeconomic foundations of society. "Upon the different forms of property, upon the social conditions of existence, rises an entire superstructure of distinct and peculiarly formed sentiments, illusions, modes of thought, and views of life," explained Marx. In rural areas in France, for example, there was little appetite for the civic republican view of freedom articulated by the liberal bourgeoisie. For that reason, it was important to treat political rhetoric with care—to distinguish "the phrases and fancies of parties from their real organism and their real interests, their conception of themselves from their reality." [15] Ludwig von Rochau never mentioned Marx directly, though he borrowed a number of phrases from him. A version of Marx's argument—that ideas separated from social forces are mere "illusions"—was to be another of the founding precepts of *Realpolitik*.

The debate over 1848 was to echo long into the future. The English historian E. H. Carr argued that what had emerged in Europe at this time, from the combination of the Renaissance and the Enlightenment, was a "marriage between Utopia and the Cult of Reason." Added to this was the impact of the Romantic movement of the early nineteenth century that "added its quota of encouragement and inspiration to utopian visions of the liberation of man from a constricting environment."

In the late eighteenth and early nineteenth century, the utopian tradition had gone into two streams. The first—encompassing Jean-Jacques Rousseau, the Jacobins, Charles Fourier, and Robert Owen—saw progress primarily in moral terms, as the triumph of virtue. The second—in which Carr included Anne-Robert-Jacques Turgot, Marquis de Condorcet, and Comte de Saint-Simon—saw progress primarily in economic and technical terms, in the rise of productivity and the diffusion of scientific knowledge. Carr argued that Marx synthesized these two tendencies in his *Communist Manifesto* of 1848. The failure of 1848, however, had "created a climate unpropitious to Utopias." Thus, without mentioning Rochau directly, Carr observed how, after 1848, the "age of *Realpolitik* . . . set in." Liberals, radicals, and even socialists "began to think in terms of what was practically possible rather than of what was ideally desirable."[16]

To achieve anything in the future, Rochau believed that Germany's liberals had to develop a true understanding of the material basis of politics in the country. Yet real *Realpolitik*, we shall see, was more than pure materialism—nor was it simply the art of the possible in politics, or the acceptance of existing political conditions as a fait accompli. The utopian element of Marxism and socialism was not entirely extinguished in 1848. It lived on, partly through the work of Engels, and partly in events such as the Paris Commune of 1871.[17] In the same way, real *Realpolitik* eschewed liberal utopianism but it did not jettison liberal idealism in itself. It held out a vision of the future and a guide for how to get there rather than a fatalistic acceptance of the world as it was.

At the dawn of the 1850s, the prospects for German liberalism looked bleak. According to Marx's confidante and co-author Engels, the liberal revolutionaries had been "more severely defeated in Germany than in any other country." They had been "worsted, broken, expelled from office in every individual State of Germany, and then put to rout, disgraced and hooted in the Central German Parliament." "Political Liberalism, the rule of the bourgeoisie, be it under a Monarchical or Republican form of government, is forever impossible in Germany," wrote Engels, in the *New York Tribune*.[18]

As Rochau soon learned, the picture elsewhere in Europe was not particularly encouraging either. After fleeing Germany again in 1850, he had returned to Paris just in time to witness the collapse of the French Revolution as well.[19] Hoping to make sense of what he had seen, he began work on a political history of France from 1814 to Louis Napoleon's coup d'état.[20] While the book was a basic narrative of events—unlike Marx's *Eighteenth Brumaire*—an English reviewer paid testament to the "vividness" of his descriptions. In a revealing phrase, Rochau's chapters had "none of the magic lantern style about them, no French polish or French exaggeration; but are marked by dignified, sober, earnestly truthful—in a word, *German*—fidelity to matter of fact, without German exuberance of reflection and theorizing."[21]

Rochau's experience of life outside his native Germany added another layer to his political understanding. It also heightened his sense of the way in which national circumstances conditioned political outcomes. He had already traveled in southern France and Spain. He now visited Italy, where the smoke was also clearing from a series of failed liberal nationalist revolutions. In 1851, he published an account of his travels, which was translated into English.

For the most part, *Wanderings in the Cities of Italy* contained observations on the weather, landscape, food, and art and amusing comments about his travel companions—an Englishman with two daughters, another German, a group of Swiss, and a flamboyant couple from Paris. In a preface for English readers, the translator observed that Rochau was "wedded to no theory of politics or art; enters into no profound disquisitions, classical or aesthetic," and was "amusingly anxious to disclaim the character of a learned traveller, having, perhaps, like most of his educated countrymen, suffered in his youth from overdoses of classical erudition." There were flashes of deeper political insight, however. When entering Austria-controlled Lombardy with the "dangerous Swiss Republicans," he made a self-effacing joke that as a "constitutional German citizen, the most harmless biped on the face of the earth," he was unlikely to cause any such concern for the authorities. He described a conversation with an old Sardinian colonel who could not quite grasp the idea of Italian unification that was increasingly popular among the young. "A war without a single General to conduct it—with officers acquainted neither with the theory nor the practice, who did not so much know the map of the country!" the exasperated colonel exclaimed, in a view which foreshadowed some of Rochau's own arguments. Italy's regionalism was an admirable trait in the Italian character—but, wrote Rochau, "unfortunately, as all history proves, and as it is to be feared it will be found in the future, an extremely active cause of division and political impotence."

A close reading of *Wanderings in the Cities of Italy* also reveals glimpses of Rochau's pessimism about the future of liberal nationalism in Germany. Unification, he wrote, was a prize that "might be won in Germany now—but it will not be won." His own view of the monarchy remained critical. Frederick William's continued popularity cast in "doubtful light the value of popularity and the judgement of the mass of mankind." But it could not be ignored. The aftermath of 1848 had proved that monarchism remained an extremely powerful force in Germany.[22]

The rest of Europe was waking up to the realities of the post-1848 era. It was time for Rochau's own countrymen to also get real. At the end of 1851, he returned to Heidelberg, and turned his hand, once again, to the German question. In 1852 he published an essay, "Geschichte des deutschen Landes und Volkes"—"A History of the German Lands and Peoples"—which analyzed the failure of the constitutional project to achieve a united Germany.[24] But this was just the prelude to his main work which appeared the following year.

2

Foundations

Sovereignty is a term of power and he who treats it as a legal term will
always arrive at unsustainable results.

(Ludwig von Rochau, *Foundations of Realpolitik*, vol. 1, 1853)[1]

In 1853, now forty-three years old, Ludwig von Rochau published
*Grundsätze der Realpolitik: Angewendet auf die staatlichen Zustände
Deutschlands* (which translates as *Foundations of Realpolitik, applied to the current state of Germany*). A second edition of the book was to follow in 1859,
in which Rochau added a new preface though the text remained otherwise unchanged.[2] In 1868, he produced a second, much longer volume, in
which he made more effort to define what he meant by his neologism and
addressed some of the criticisms—many of which have continued to this
day. This he presented as volume two of the *Foundations of Realpolitik*, making the 1853 book volume one by default.[3]

The first volume of *Foundations of Realpolitik* is just over two hundred
pages long. It is broken into twenty-one chapters and roughly divides into
two halves. The first half explores the structure of the state and the social
forces within it—what might be called the basis of the *Realpolitik* method.
The second half of the book applies those ideas to the immediate political
circumstances in Germany, as Rochau saw them. Rochau was a journalist
and an activist rather than a jurist, and he was not particularly interested in
philosophy or metaphysics for their own sake. Nonetheless, it would be to
undersell his achievement to say that what he produced has no value as a
work of political thought. As he was drawing on an eclectic range of thinkers and ideas, and attempting to synthesize them, his notion of *Realpolitik*
was certainly original, if not entirely flawless.

Foundations of Realpolitik is based on four interlinking assumptions.

- The law of the strong is the determining factor in politics. Thus sovereignty is not a natural right (for "the people" or the king) but a reflection of power. This is a message that Rochau directed primarily to his liberal colleagues, following their humiliation in 1848.

- The most effective form of government is one that incorporates the most powerful social forces within the state, harnesses their energies, and achieves a balance among them. The more harmonious a state is internally, the greater is its potential magnitude. This is a message Rochau directed at Germany's rulers, encouraging them to make an effort to incorporate the middle class into the polity by moving toward a more representative system of government.

- Ideas matter in politics but the role they play has been widely misunderstood. The purity or coherence of an idea—its "inherent truth"—barely matters in politics. In fact, immoral or uncultured ideas are often more powerful than noble ideas. What matters is how many people hold an idea and how strongly they hold it.

- Modernity has changed the nature of statecraft. Public opinion is ever more important and the *Zeitgeist* (the "spirit of the age") is the single most important factor in determining the trajectory of a nation's politics. In this rapidly transforming era, nationalism can provide a potential glue to reconcile those forces within the state that might otherwise go to war with each other.

The Law of the Strong

Rochau's first chapter begins with the assertion that the existence of the state is a "natural" phenomenon—by which he meant a given, or unavoidable, fact of life. Both Aristotle's statement that "Man is a political animal" and the Christian belief that the state originates from God were based on the same assumption—that the state was an inevitable part of human existence. This did not need lengthy explanation.

The next question, and the most important to politics, is who can claim sovereignty within the state. The Frankfurt Assembly had spent months arguing over the correct form of constitution for Germany in 1848–9. What the members had failed to realize was that sovereignty was not the natural property of the people any more than it was it the natural property of God, the king, or the aristocracy. Sovereignty was not a right but a reflection of power.

For Rochau, the law of the strong "dominates life inside the state in the same way as the force of gravity dominates the physical world." Debating the question of who or what *should* rule—law, wisdom, virtue, a single person, the few, or the many—was a matter that belonged to the field of philosophical speculation: "practical politics has to first of all contend with the fact that power alone is in a position to rule." At the simplest level ruling meant exerting power. "This immediate link between power [*Macht*] and rule/dominance/authority [*Herrschaft*] is the foundational truth underlying all politics and constitutes the key to all of history," he wrote. It was "misguided pride" that "refuses to recognise this relationship, or which regards it as an improper one, that can and must be corrected."

While the law of the strong had been recognized for centuries, a number of misconceptions had grown up around it. For example, theorists of state power (such as those who spoke of the "divine right of kings") had made the mistake of believing that, because the law of power dominates politics, the strongest therefore had *the right* to predominate. One of the great achievements of the Enlightenment had been to undermine the notion that "might makes right." In fact, Rochau believed this view was not only misguided but "immoral." Meanwhile, however, liberals had lost sight of the "foundational truth" of politics. In rejecting the alleged right of the strongest on moral grounds, they had misjudged the nature of power. This was the source of the "crudest mistakes," which the constitutionalists in the majority of the European states were all guilty of.

This realization had two important implications for liberal politics going forward. First, the notion that the state could be regulated or controlled by law was flawed. It was irrational to demand that power be subordinated to the law. Power obeyed only greater power. The second flawed notion at the heart of liberalism was the idea that political power could be contracted out (in the form of a constitution, for example). In the past, such contracts—between the governed and the government—had only been accepted by those who held power, so long as it suited their interests. The manner in which Prussia's King Frederick William had undercut the revolutionary Frankfurt Assembly so easily, after initially promising to accede to liberal demands in 1848, was fresh in Rochau's mind. Bitter experience now caused him to dismiss both Plato's *Republic* and Jean-Jacques Rousseau's *Social Contract* as "historically false," and "philosophically untenable." By paying blind homage to such "ghosts" of the past, the liberals had failed to see the changing structure of the society in which they operated. The "castles in the air [*Luftschlösser*] that have been built have dissolved into blue mist" and it was time to reject such "chimerical images [*Phantasiebilder*]."

What Rochau criticized his fellow liberals for was not their "conviction and conscience" but their assumption that these were political forces in their own right. "Conscientiousness is certainly a very desirable element in politics," he wrote, "but a policy which treats any given matter as a matter of conscience runs the greatest risk of ending in fruitless casuistry, and of splintering into insignificant atoms the very forces which can function effectively merely as part of a mass." Another lesson of 1848 was that political formulas could not be lifted from one state to another. Experience had shown that treating constitutional politics "along abstract-scientific lines or on the basis of principles" was rarely useful, due to "the variety of societal relationships" that existed in different states.[4]

There was, however, a sting in the tail of Rochau's argument. The question of which constitution was ideally *best* belonged to the realm of philosophical speculation. Liberals had failed to see this. But the question of which constitution was *most effective* was one that was crucial to every state. The job of a constitution was to reflect the interplay of social forces within the state, from classes and interest groups to ideas and opinions. The study of the forces that make up, support, and transform the state was, in fact, the starting point for achieving any political insight. Each societal force could legitimately claim recognition in the state—not by a claim to legal right, but by virtue of its power (its "breadth" or "reach"). The power of the state itself, meanwhile, was "merely the sum of the number of the different societal forces which the state has absorbed."

In effect, Rochau was conjuring up the image of a more robust, "full," and strong form of nation-state, superior to the small autocratic states that currently governed Germany. "The more profoundly the societal subject matter pervades and the more completely it fills out the state, the healthier is the body politic, even if its outer appearance shows irregularities," he argued.[5] As a member of the liberal bourgeoisie, Rochau still wanted to get access to that state. In fact, he believed that a healthy state would have to incorporate the middle classes. That said, he also realized that after the failures of 1848, he and his fellow bourgeois might have to take a circuitous route to gain entry. This would have to be a long march, rather than a quick seizure of power.

A Message to the Prince

What began with a critique of naïve liberalism now began to move in another direction. By arguing for a corporate, historicist understanding of the origins of the state over a legal-constitutional one, Rochau was departing from classical liberalism or natural law theories. Equally, however, he was preparing the ground for a critique of the autocratic regimes that had been restored across Germany after 1850. On a number of occasions in his book, he made sure to point out that theories of divine right were just as flawed and chimerical as those predicated on the idea of popular sovereignty. A political philosophy that attributed the "indelible character of sovereignty to monarchy," he wrote, "sins against reason and history as much as Rousseau's or any other doctrine which attributes sovereignty once and for all to the people."[6]

Autocratic or narrowly monarchical states had an inherent flaw in them that made them weak and restricted their growth. A weak constitution was one that denied participation in the state to powerful societal forces and therefore failed to harness their energy to make the state more powerful. Worse still was a constitution that artificially keeps alive the "passive and limbless elements" within the state. By the "passive and limbless" forces, Rochau meant the remnants of the ancien regime such as the aristocrats, princelings, and religious hierarchies whose societal power was in decline. Such trappings were a "dead burden."[7]

It was significant that Rochau used a quote from the English philosopher-statesman Sir Francis Bacon on the title page of *Foundations of Realpolitik*. What it reveals is that Rochau was not simply directing his book to his fellow liberals but also to Germany's existing rulers. In that quote, Bacon—himself a student of Machiavelli—criticizes the so-called wisdom of princes who relied on "fine deliveries and shifting of dangers and mischiefs when they are near" (short-term and reactive measures), rather "than solid and grounded courses to keep them aloof" (what might be called grand strategy). To those who confused tactical agility in the short term with a long-term strategy, he warned that they were relying on fortune, rather than long-term planning, "for no man can forbid the spark, nor tell whence it comes."[8]

In effect, Rochau was reminding those in power that they had already been caught unaware by the events of 1848. It was far wiser for them to anticipate future political demands than set themselves up as a bulwark against them. Arguably, it was a message that Otto von Bismarck took on board in his domestic statecraft as much as his foreign policy—by co-opting emerging social forces (bourgeois and proletarian) and by pre-empting the demands of liberals and then socialists, thus unifying the nation and building a welfare state.

When Rochau talked of new powerful societal forces emerging in Germany, he was of course referring to the increasingly powerful middle class to which he himself belonged. Viewed in another light, it could be said that the real purpose of his book was to make an assertive claim on behalf of the *Mittelstand* (middle class) to participation within the state, but on the basis of their power rather than natural right.[9] Their claim to representation came by virtue of their "education, wealth, entrepreneurial spirit, and appetite for work," which added up to a potent political force. The year 1848 had proved that the bourgeoisie did not necessarily see themselves as a homogenous interest group, of course. But just because they did not act with a unified "class consciousness" (a phrase Rochau lifted from Marx), it was a mistake to underestimate their true force. Even those with "under-developed abilities and 'sleeping' dispositions also counted as societal forces."[10]

In this way, Rochau was throwing down the gauntlet to Germany's existing rulers on terms they would understand, rather than claims to abstract rights they did not recognize. "Politics cannot without impunity disdain the middle class as if it were an appendage to a doctrine," he warned; statesmen had to come to terms with it.[11] Was the old regime capable of absorbing the bourgeoisie, as he put it, "in order to exploit them for the benefit of the state" (through taxation revenues, for example)?[12] Perhaps they were not up to the task, he hinted. "The ruling societal forces, thanks to the natural selfishness that is inherent in all living beings, fear every new competitor wishing to increase his importance in the state."

What Rochau was saying about the power of an emerging societal force and its challenge to the state (particularly as it came to consciousness) contained echoes of Marx, but he was equally at pains to stress that there was no predetermined outcome. Rather than presenting a linear theory of historical development, his argument was that a smart politician could construct a strategy that recognized such changes and adapt to them intelligently.

To that end, Rochau went on to argue that the first job of the statesman was to assess the various social forces presenting a challenge to the existing order. Once he had done this, he had "from a purely political point of view no choice but to either incorporate these forces or to suppress them." The "middle way" was "apolitical and the state risks conflict and danger if it goes down this path." This was "because the force which the state does not incorporate, will necessarily become its opponent." Many states had been defeated by "opponents of this kind which it had previously either despised or tried to eliminate." The violent elimination of any societal force, which had not yet acted out its full potential, was one of the most difficult tasks in politics. The stiffer a constitution was, the more brittle the state; the stiffer the constitution, the greater the effort of the new force to gain entry, and "the more violent the impact of an eventual breakthrough."[13]

While history provided instructive lessons, it was not the source of immutable rules. Here Rochau made the first of a number of points about how the conditions of modernity had changed the nature of statecraft—how the tactics on offer in the age of Machiavelli were no longer so easy to apply. In previous historical eras, the state had often been able to flatten and subdue challenges to its authority through the use of violence, as Machiavelli had described in *The Prince*.[14] In the modern era, however, such examples had "become ever more rare, be it that the state does not have the same choice of arms with which such a struggle can be fought in the same way as before, be it that the increased mobility of the more recent centuries has made impossible the necessary stamina."[15]

In some ways it was easier to tackle a foreign invader than a serious internal challenger. A state dependent on violent methods to maintain its authority would inevitably weaken its organic bond with society. By taking this road, it "becomes ever more certain that the state will succumb to degeneration and decrepitude." Such a state—an illiberal state—poisoned its own body politic. By contrast, a healthy state was one that was inevitably more powerful when compared to its rivals. "The political magnitude of the state depends crucially on a certain extent of stability, not regarding the state's institutions but regarding the actual societal conditions and their development," he explained. Only by virtue of this stability was it possible to incorporate "a significant sum of societal forces in a unified and unchanging direction towards a particular state aim," and "only in virtue of this stability may time be won which is in all circumstances necessary in order to achieve great and lasting political success."[16] In essence, Rochau was evoking the image of a strong unified German nation-state of the future.

There is almost a conservative, organicist feel to this version of state development. Just as slow growth ensures a long life in the world of nature, "in politics painstaking acquisition ensures lasting possession." A state with greater "elasticity" was a state that was likely to be healthier and more effective in the long run.[17] In this respect and others, Rochau—combining broadly liberal political principles with a conservative understanding of historical development—resembled a German version of the Anglo-Irish writer Edmund Burke. Burke's work was well known in Germany, his *Reflections on the Revolution in France* having been translated by Metternich's advisor, the counter-revolutionary publicist Friedrich von Gentz.[18]

Following Burke, Rochau expressed a preference for representative government. But as Burke had also argued, viable political institutions must reflect the specific national circumstances in which they existed. In this spirit, Rochau suggested that the Senate in America and the House of Lords in Britain—based on franchise and property, respectively—were equally viable, as they reflected the balance of social forces in each. It was "the most hopeless of all endeavours" to try and force ideas onto people that were "allegedly in their interests and yet that are incongruent with their natural and historical disposition."

Thus, Rochau wrote, in a memorable phrase, that it was "absurd to attempt to transfer the European idea of civic liberty onto a Turkish or Hindu state." Even if some elites in those states were amenable to these ideas of governance, it was highly unlikely that the mass of people were. As 1848 had proved, advanced philosophies of government rarely extended beyond the senate or the city. The "form and fate of states is by and large determined by the forces that constitute the masses, and wherever forces join together to form a mass they will achieve influence and standing within the state."[19]

The Power of Ideas

Rochau was a child of the Enlightenment. He had a classic bourgeois understanding of progress that held that liberal ideas had brought more sophistication, intelligence, and morality into public life. Thus, the gradual dissemination of education and wealth was the driving force of historical

change. As Rochau described, this was the reason that power was "transferred from the hand of a single individual into the hands of the few and
finally into the hands of the many." Education and wealth were "the bridge
that leads to political power for one popular class after another." Rulers
could do little to prevent this. The only way to do so was "the perpetua-
tion of ignorance and poverty," but a statesman who tried to perpetuate the
ignorance of his people was a statesman not worthy of the name.[20]

Yet modernity was not a one-way street to liberal political outcomes or
moral improvement. Statesmen must also take into account "those latent
forces of habit, tradition and sluggishness" which still existed throughout
society. Alongside the wealth and intelligence he associated with the middle classes, there was still a high degree of "poverty, lack of knowledge,
prejudice, and . . . stupidity." Society could bemoan and object to immoral
practice, of course, but it would also have to confront such behavior as a fact
of life: "Lies and all other kinds of immoral behaviour, even crime, can not
only demand but even exact a certain political recognition regardless of the
fact that their nature is hostile to society and the state."[21]

It is worth pausing here to consider what Rochau says about the role of
morality in statecraft. It was not to be jettisoned and had a rightful place
in political calculations. At the same time, moral principles were always
subject to compromise. This was not to say that "there is no moral obligation in politics, but rather that there is a limit where the actual possibility
to fulfil this obligation ends," he wrote. To elucidate his point, Rochau
offered a list of examples in which moral considerations might have to be
downgraded to second-order concerns. First, if the state made a "usurious
deal with finance in a situation in which it is pressed for money, it thereby
makes a concession to immorality, but not because it wants to but because
it must." Second, in the face of "an insurgency or a soldiers' mutiny," politicians "may have to make a deal with crime itself" by negotiating with
the insurgents or rebels. It may even be that the government of a great
state "cannot avoid having to come to tolerate the presence of a robber."
Rochau gave the example of José María Morelos, the priest and revolutionary rebel leader who led the Mexican War of Independence movement in
the 1810s before being captured and killed by Spanish authorities in 1815.
If the government of Ferdinand the VII had not been able to catch José
María, he argued, it would have been the right political choice to negotiate with him and make peace. Rochau anticipated the criticism that he
was advocating immorality in statecraft, and he already had an answer.

"Such a course could only be considered 'right' or 'good' policy for a paltry government and a decrepit state," he made clear. Nonetheless, he did note that the church had made many such compromises on moral issues such as slavery and that it was unfair to hold governments to higher standards. Morality "may not be harder on politics than on religion," he observed.[22]

Like Marx, Rochau believed that the dominant ideological currents in a society were shaped by changes in the underlying socioeconomic structure. Inevitably, with the emergence of new societal forces came the growth of new ideas about how to organize the state. The example Rochau gave was the decreasing wealth of landed property in proportion to the mobile wealth associated with the bourgeoisie. The consequence of this was the decline in the political leverage of the landed aristocracy. The idea that this upper strata of society should be granted unconditional authority "to which in the past even the most savage forces submitted themselves has been criticised to an extent that today only some puny ruins survive." "Things like bourgeois class consciousness, the idea of freedom, nationalism, the idea of human equality are completely new factors of social life for many of today's states," Rochau was prepared to concede. They had already exhibited their power, however, in the events of 1848, when public opinion had shown its force. The modern statesman should not deny them recognition.[23]

How could the power of public opinion be assessed in *Realpolitik* terms, then? To answer this question, Rochau drew a distinction between different gradations of it in ascending order of importance. In the first instance, he believed that the "feeble self-conscious opinion of the day" is not entitled to claim political consideration, as it is merely fleeting and unfocused. From this starting point, however, the more consolidated public opinion becomes, and the more it transforms itself into a firm conviction, the more important it becomes for the state. It was when a mood or a prejudice became transformed into a "belief" that a government could no longer afford to ignore it. The most important expression of public opinion is *Volksglaube* (popular belief), which should always be treated with "care and protection, not blandishment."[24]

Notably, Rochau also made clear that the "accuracy and rationality" of an idea was of secondary concern. Sometimes governments had to bow to popular opinion even if it made unreasonable or irrational demands; or, at least, the government had to pretend to accede to public opinion so as not to make enemies. "Even if stupid prejudice or blindfold error weigh heavier than truth in the stable of public opinion," he wrote, the government "may, if it is reasonable, not exactly follow prejudice and error blindfold, but give in at least a little and as much as possible so as to not make enemies of these forces." Equally, in recognizing the importance of "popular belief," governments should also aim to preserve a plurality of opinion (through free speech). Thus, popular belief must not be treated preferentially at the cost of other intellectual forces that helped encourage the intellectual development of the people.[25]

While the popular belief was the highest peak of popular opinion, the *Zeitgeist* was its broadest foundation. The *Zeitgeist* was the "consolidated opinion of the century as expressed in certain principles, opinions and habits of reason." An opinion transformed itself into the *Zeitgeist* to the extent that it stood the test of time. The *Zeitgeist* represented in all circumstances the most important influence on the overall direction of politics. For a state to act in defiance of the *Zeitgeist* was completely self-defeating. A policy that attempts to "emancipate itself" from the people's convictions would have "very limited space of manoeuvre."[26] To put it simply, liberalism and nationalism could not be put back in the box. With the help of a strong police force, it may be "possible to manipulate citizenry like puppets," but the ideals they held on to could not be smothered forever.[27]

There was a temptation for states to play a subtler game of divide and rule—to sow dissension between different strands within the *Zeitgeist*. In the long run, however, a strong state depended on "the support of a potent public spirit." A healthy state needed some degree of internal struggle for its overall development. But some struggles risked damaging the state when they were not mediated. Instead, the modern state could take advantage of two modern political phenomena of the Enlightenment era—"patriotism" and "rationalism." Both rationalism and patriotism were "the natural conciliatory forces in conflicts between different political parties."

> When all political bonds and public societal bonds are slacking, ambitions and wishes push in different directions, when passionate conflict between different political parties are menacing to tear apart the polity, the last resort to achieve reconciliation is to be conscious of one's obligation to save the nation. This is why human judgement has been very firm regarding the view that it is the utmost sacrilege to question the national spirit, the last and most valuable guarantee of the natural order of society. And policies designed to humiliate and break this spirit thereby descend to the lowest rank of despicability.[28]

While he did not cite Machiavelli here—or at any point—Rochau's discussion of these phenomena was reminiscent of Machiavelli's belief that a
government had an interest in encouraging a civil religion for the purpose
of maintaining and promoting the state's authority.[29] In lieu of the civic
republicanism of the Renaissance era, nationalism could provide the necessary glue in modern society. A state that aimed to suppress the national
spirit would be setting itself against one of "the most noble and strongest
mainsprings of public life."[30]

On the one hand, Rochau's definition of the core ingredients for nationality demonstrated a classic liberal form of nationalism. This was a compos-
ite of Romantic and civic ideas of nationhood that stressed the importance
of shared ancestry, shared language, and a similarity of "civic views, attitudes and habits." He was quite aware that nationality rarely existed in
"entire pureness and perfection" because historical conditions were always
more complicated. So common language was desirable and common values were to be encouraged but the state was best advised to promote these
gradually, "by proceeding slowly and by indirect means." [31]

On the other hand, *Realpolitik* also implied that there were certain limitations on just who was welcome within the national fold. Along with a majority of 1848 liberals, as we have seen, Rochau inclined toward a *Kleindeutsch*
(smaller Germany) solution on the national question. This held that the
Austrian monarchy was too wide and sprawling (and composed of too many
competing nationalities) to become an effective part of a unified German
state. A state that united many different nationalities within its borders was,
Rochau made clear, in danger of disintegration over the longer term. Even
dormant nationalisms, such as existed in the farther regions of the Austro-
Hungarian Empire, among the Slavic peoples, were likely to awaken at some
point. Attempting to incorporate a number of competing nationalities at
once would be a recipe for disaster.[32] This reflected the fact that German
nationalism—even of the civic brand favored by Rochau—was created in
the pressure cooker of multi-ethnic central Europe. It also revealed that
Realpolitik had a markedly illiberal edge when it came to the national cause.

Realpolitik and Foreign Policy

The first volume of *Foundations of Realpolitik* was a discourse on domestic
state-building rather than a treatise on foreign affairs. Yet the question of

the future of the German nation was not, of course, merely a domestic political question. It entailed the reconfiguration of the state system in central Europe and therefore had huge foreign policy implications for all the major European states—not just Prussia, Austria, and the German states but also France, Poland, Russia, the Italian states, and even Great Britain. It was no coincidence that Germany's immediate neighbors were opposed to unity as they recognized that this would make it the strongest state in Europe.

As a liberal nationalist, Rochau's understanding of national freedom depended, first and foremost, on protection of the country from foreign molestation. He lamented the disunity of the German states because it had long made them weaker in the face of external threats. The sectionalism (*Partikularismus*) of some south German states—which manifested itself in strange customs and pride in things like traditional dress—was particularly irritating as it confused local independence with political freedom. An even greater obstacle to national unity was the rivalry between Catholic Austria in the south and Protestant Prussia in the north.[33] Rochau had no time for sectarianism but he understood its political force.

It was in the final chapter of the first volume of *The Foundations of Realpolitik* that Rochau began to turn his attention to foreign affairs. The rise to power of Louis Napoleon (now Emperor Napoleon III) in France was viewed with great alarm in Germany because it raised the prospect—once more—of French armies marching through German land under the banner of another Napoleon. The conclusion that Rochau drew from this, therefore, was that the unification of Germany was too urgent a matter to be left to history to take care of. Only "a superior force which swallows the others, not a principle, an idea nor a contract" would be capable of ensuring this. By a superior force, of course, Rochau meant Prussia, Germany's strongest state.[34]

By the time the second edition of *Realpolitik* was produced in 1859, six years after the first, a growing international crisis had given the question of German unification much greater urgency. In a new preface, Rochau turned his attention directly to foreign affairs and national security. There was a growing conviction that France was likely to launch an assault on Austria on some concocted premise—such as "faked jealousy" of Austria's influence in northern Italy, where France also had designs. Nothing in the preceding six years had convinced Rochau of anything other than Napoleon III's "lust for war"; when Napoleon "shivers, Europe must shake." But

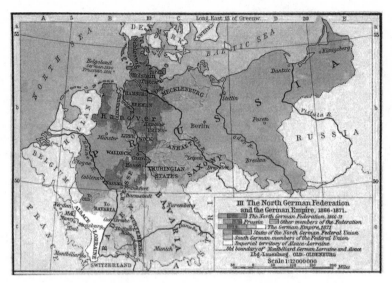

The German Confederation was a loose association of thirty-nine German states created in 1815, at the end of the Napoleonic Wars. Many nationalists felt that federalism left the country vulnerable to external threats from France and Russia and urged the unification of the country. From *The Historical Atlas* by William R. Shepherd, 1926.

Germany's weakness had also fed his hubris. Austria, in particular, had adopted a doomed attempt to placate the French by appeasing them. Every concession it had granted amounted to nothing more than an avowal of weakness.

Rochau had very little sympathy for Austria, which he still saw as an enemy to both German unity and liberalism. Despite this, however, he argued that it was necessary for Prussia to establish a defensive alliance with Austria as soon as possible. The collapse of Austria in the face of French aggression would put Prussia's status as a great power at risk. Austria was not a dependable ally and could not be trusted in the long term. Nevertheless, a defensive alliance was the only option in the short term.

Here Rochau rejected both *Gefühlspolitik* (sentimental politics) and *Prinzipienpolitik* (principled politics) as the basis for a nation's foreign policy. A Prussian alliance with Austria was a matter of pure self-interest. Moreover, the future of Prussia as the leading state in Germany depended on a "long overdue reconciliation" with the German public. Allowing Austria to be flattened by France would be treated as an unspeakable infamy in the other states—a humiliating return to when Germany was the "match-ball of its enemies" and the "mockery of history."[35] A force of a different kind could also be mobilized against France. This was the German *Volksgeist* that was already rallying itself and had no sense of state boundaries. The *Volksgeist*, which Rochau personified, was "no admirer of Austria, whether today's or that of Metternich's era." Nationalist liberals disapproved of Austrian domination over northern Italy, for example, but they did understand the need to resist France at all costs.[36]

The general population was far ahead of the traditional elites in their willingness to stand firm against external enemies. Indeed, Rochau criticized the Prussian *Landtag* (the upper chamber of parliament, dominated by aristocrats and the landed gentry) for its over-cautious approach to France. "Diplomacy is not the realm of parliament," he argued. The "moderation and the self-control for which the Landtag is lauded are easily mistaken for impotence." In demanding "wholehearted preparations for the potential war," Rochau called on the *Landtag* to take the practical step of banning the sale of horses to France in case they were used against German states in battle. Put simply, unification was a matter of national security. The inevitable sluggishness of a military campaign that relied on a federal army constituted by more than thirty different contingents gave France the advantage—always able to pre-empt and surprise its enemy. Germany would never match its powerful neighbor completely until it decided to implement a "federal reform" centralizing the conduct of its foreign policy and its military power in one single hand.[37]

Rochau was not alone in making this point. Johann Gustav Droysen, the Prussian historian and prominent member of the Frankfurt Assembly, wrote that the "Lilliputianism" of the small German states was suicidal in the modern era. The era of small states was over. "In political life, as in manufacturing, only large mass structures will come to anything. . . . Alongside the world powers of England, Russia, North America and China (which is reforming itself), the southern European and the Germanic races must either crumble or join together as a mass."[38]

For the first time, *Realpolitik* was turned to the conduct of warfare itself. Germany would also have to learn to turn the table on its traditional enemies—to take the fight to them first and to develop the capacity for pre-emptive war. "Military authorities have claimed in cold blood that Germany was due to its political and military situation not in a condition of being able to initiate a war of attack [*Angriffskrieg*], but could only fight

a defensive war," Rochau wrote. By such a view, however, Rochau complained, Germany was destined to serve as the theater of all wars it fights.
If Germany seized the initiative now, it would do so in circumstances that
were more favorable to it and less favorable to France than they had been in
the last thirty years.[39] Rather than waiting for the rest of Europe to act on it
again, and accepting its station, Rochau demanded that Germany change
the rules of the game itself.

3

Liberalism and Bismarck:
A Fatal Compromise?

Across Europe, liberalism and nationalism were to have an increasingly strained relationship. Nowhere was this more the case than in Germany. Even at the height of German liberal optimism in 1848, there had been recognition that questions of freedom were only one component of a deeper desire for national glory. "The path of power," claimed the liberal delegate Friedrich Christoph Dahlmann in the Frankfurt parliament on 22 January 1849, "is the only one that will satisfy and appease the fermenting impulse to freedom—for it is not solely freedom that the German is thinking of, it is rather power, which has hitherto been refused to him, and after which he hankers."[1]

By becoming the champions of German unification, Germany's liberals had created a political force that conservatives could not ignore. Yet nationalism was not a phenomenon that was bound by liberal principles or any single ideology. Others proved adept at harnessing nationalism to their own agendas—no one more so than Otto von Bismarck, the man who was to unite the country by force of arms. In his first speech as Prussian minister-president in September 1862, Bismarck famously asserted that the "great questions of our time will not be decided by speeches and majority decisions—that was the mistake of 1848–9—but by Blood and Iron." Germany did not look to Prussia for her liberalism but because of her military power.[2]

It was because of such unsentimental logic that Bismarck was to become forever associated with the concept of *Realpolitik* (and *Realpolitik* became associated with blood and iron). There was a certain irony in this, however. First, Bismarck never used the word himself, and there is no evidence that he ever read Rochau's work.[3] Second, Rochau remained a fierce critic of

Bismarck for much of the 1850s and 1860s. In 1859, just after the second edition of his book was published, he was appointed secretary of the National Union (an umbrella group for German liberals).[4] In that position he published *Wochenschrift des Nationalvereins*, a weekly newspaper that was strongly critical of Bismarck and was banned by the government.[5] In 1861, Rochau was also involved in the formation of the Progressive Party, created as an umbrella group for liberal and radical opponents of the government. The Progressive Party was the largest grouping in Prussia's lower chamber but it was the upper chamber, the *Landtag*, which still held ultimate authority. During the Prussian constitutional crisis of the early 1860s, in an attempt to bring the government to a standstill, the Progressives refused to vote for the army reforms put forth by General Albert von Roon, the minister of war. When appointed minister-president midway through the crisis in 1862, however, Bismarck called their bluff by using a flimsy constitutional pretext to govern without the support of parliament.

The Progressives remained in opposition to Bismarck for the next five years. On one crucial issue, however, they were willing to allow him considerable freedom to maneuver. So long as he continued to make progress on German unification—under Prussian leadership—many in the center and center right of the Progressive Party were prepared to hold their fire on his government.

In 1866, then, Bismarck used his victory over Austria in the Seven Weeks' War to re-set his relationship with the liberals in the Prussian parliament, attempting to bring an end to years of constitutional conflict. He hoped to provide a new basis for cooperation between the lower chamber and the *Landtag* through an Indemnity Bill that retroactively legalized the state budgets from 1862 to 1866. He spoke in conciliatory terms to his liberal opponents. The liberals were split on how to respond, but a large majority agreed to support the new dispensation on the condition that Bismarck push ahead with unification of the north German states.[6] In 1868, the Progressive Party split on the issue of cooperation with Bismarck, and the National Liberal Party was formed out of its remnants. The National Liberals continued their uneasy accommodation with Bismarck—agreeing to support him in his efforts to unify Germany—for the next decade.

Rochau—who stood on the center-right of the Progressive Party—was a founding member of the National Liberal Party and supported the parliamentary accommodation with Bismarck. There was no simple capitulation to Prussian authoritarianism or a casual jettisoning of

Otto von Bismarck, appointed minister-president of Prussia in 1862, led
Germany to unification in 1871, and became chancellor of the German Empire
until 1890. The majority of National Liberals came to an uneasy accommodation
with his government on the grounds that he seemed to offer the best hope for
unification, while others believed this was a fatal compromise. Courtesy of
Wikimedia Creative Commons.

liberal values. Rochau and his liberal colleagues continued to hold their liberal goals dear, and they pushed for reform within the state.[7] Nonetheless, it
was in the seeds of this accommodation that some saw a fatal compromise.
Rochau had not envisaged this scenario when he wrote the first volume of
Foundations of Realpolitik in 1853. But he reached again for the concept he

had created in order to defend the arrangement with Bismarck fifteen years later. Thus, *Realpolitik* was reinvigorated for the 1860s. Crucially, however, for its critics the word came to imply a slippage of German liberalism—a willingness to trade liberal beliefs as the price of national glory—that was to have lasting consequences in Germany history.[8]

Debating *Realpolitik*

The fact that *Realpolitik* was used to justify the accommodation with Bismarck means that it has been chiefly associated with those on the center right of the Progressive Party, where Rochau himself stood. In fact, *Realpolitik* was also used favorably by a number of individuals to the left of Rochau. In 1863, for example, the socialist politician Karl Rodbertus argued that *Realpolitik* could provide the most effective formula for alleviating and improving the social and economic conditions of the working classes. Rodbertus was much more radical than Rochau and was a supporter of universal suffrage, but he also believed that social questions should precede those of political liberty. The moderate socialist version of *Realpolitik* held that Social Democrats should harness themselves to the monarchy and achieve their goals by making the state dependent on their support. Thus, he tried to convince the Progressive Party to form itself into a "monarchical democratic party which can later be used to bring the 'state-idea' again to account while it acts for the strength of the governmental power, absolutely necessary under the present circumstances, as for the social demands of the working classes, and which pursues . . . Realpolitik."[9] Also to the left of Rochau was liberal radical Hermann Schulze-Delitzsch, a supporter of universal suffrage. Yet he, too, believed that the wisest policy was for liberal radicals to prioritize the national question first and fight for political liberty later: "We Germans have not pursued *Realpolitik* enough," he wrote, proving that use of the word was beginning to spread. They must accept Prussian hegemony and focus on "the attainable."[10]

The most salient criticism of Rochau's *Realpolitik*—which looked more convincing with the passing of time—was that it was not as realistic as he claimed. In its emphasis on "the facts"—the obstacles to political change—it was in danger of meekly succumbing to them. In 1864, the democratic activist, Jakob Venedey, produced a pamphlet called *The Cardinal Sin of the National Union* (referring to the liberal organisation of which Rochau was then secretary). Venedey—who had traveled extensively in Europe—offered the most articulate criticism of *Realpolitik* to date by comparing the behavior of German liberals and radicals to those who had forced change in other countries.[11]

In Venedey's view, *Realpolitik* did not reflect hard-headedness but timidity. It claimed to have history on its side, but it failed to understand the way in which reformers, liberals, and radicals had changed the course of history in the past, through the force of their idealism. For Venedey, what sounded like great wisdom was in fact a sign of the immaturity of his countrymen. *Realpolitik* was "nothing but German political twaddle." If the leaders of the National Union wanted to transform the political system, their task should be to pursue something completely opposite: "*Idealpolitik.*" The founders of German Protestantism, the heroes of English and American Revolutions, Irish nationalists, and the champions of free trade in England did not meekly acquiesce to existing conditions. Martin Luther, John Hampden, Oliver Cromwell, Benjamin Franklin, George Washington, Daniel O'Connell, and Richard Cobden had all been *Idealpolitikers,* who maintained their principles "until they finally achieved the power to be *Realpolitiker.*"[12] Here Venedey added two new innovations in the discourse surrounding Rochau's word. The first was the use of *Realpolitiker* as an adjective, or a label, for those acting in this way. The second, of greater importance, was the idea of *Idealpolitik* as an opposing force, which also had great political successes to its name. In the English-speaking world, this was to live on in the form of the anti-realpolitik tradition described in subsequent chapters of this book.

Attacks on *Realpolitik* did not necessarily come from the left of the political spectrum. One of the most influential critics of *Realpolitik* was the former Prussian diplomat and philosopher, Constantin Frantz, born in Halberstadt in 1817. The son of an evangelical pastor, Frantz had worked for a decade and half in the Prussian civil service and then in the Prussian consulate in Barcelona. Disillusioned with the direction of German politics, he had left government in 1862 in order to concentrate on political writing. He was a critic of both Bismarck and the Progressives, whom he believed were assuming warlike tendencies.

Frantz believed that a modified version of the Holy Roman Empire—a loose federal arrangement, in other words—was the best hope for Germany. Federalism was Germany's gift to civilization and it was her "historical vocation" to lead Europe back to equilibrium and peace. He wanted

Austria and Prussia to abandon their self-defeating efforts to be independent great powers and act through and within the German confederation.
Indeed, Frantz believed that a German confederation cooperating on these
terms could be a model for European international relations as a whole.
The tumults of the 1850s and 1860s—from the Crimean War, through
Italian unification and Bismarck's war against Austria—underlined to him
the dangers of national vanity.

In Frantz's view, the erosion of Christian values in the name of rationality and materialism risked setting Europe on a path to perpetual conflict.
"Christianity imposes on us duties paramount to those we owe our country, by declaring that our true home is, indeed, not at all on this earth. . . .
First come our duties to God, then those towards our neighbour, no matter
whether he be German or French, and only then our duty to our country," he wrote. Where, he asked, would *Realpolitik* lead in the long run? If
politics drifted away from the gospel, and Europeans confined their minds
"within the narrow sphere of supposed national interests," they were creating a recipe for perpetual war. Christianity knew nothing of *Realpolitik* and
those who taught it disowned the Bible, "in order to place the worship of
nationality in its stead."[13]

Frantz also rejected Rochau's argument that nationalism soothed internal divisions within the state. Rather than healing internal tension between
different societal forces, Frantz believed that Bismarck's foreign policy successes had actually allowed him to skirt around growing tensions within
German society. Germany had "won external peace, but no inward satisfaction," he wrote, pointing to a surge in support for socialism. Religious
tension between Catholics and Protestants was also likely to increase. This
had been made worse by the failure to include Catholic Austria in the new
Germany, to act as a natural balancer against Protestant Prussia. In the past,
Frantz argued, Germany's acceptance of plurality had been a great influence in preventing the inflaming of sectarianism across Europe as a whole.
This had been jettisoned.[14]

Frantz was later celebrated as an opponent of German imperialism during
the First World War. He held up as a hero of *Freie Zeitung*, a German radical
opposition newspaper run out of Vienna during 1914–8, for his opposition
to *Realpolitik*.[15] Under the surface of Frantz's Christian federalism, however,
lurked a more mendacious interpretation of national liberalism. Frantz's
worldview was informed by an odd mix of Christian faith, romanticism,
and the most flagrant anti-Semitism. He saw the national movement as

a Jewish conspiracy, characterized by the spread of materialism and the erosion of Christian values in favor of commercial ones. In this delusional view, Bismarck's German Empire was dismissed as an "Empire of Jewish Nationality."[16] It was an idea that was to reappear in later years, in different forms. While Frantz accused Jews of being behind the nationalist movement, later anti-Semites attacked them for betraying it. The issue loomed ominously in the background.

Defending *Realpolitik*

By the time Rochau produced the second volume of *The Foundations of Realpolitik*, in 1868, a decade and a half had passed since publication of the first volume. In the preceding years, Bismarck had been able to take control of the national agenda on his own terms. After the Seven Weeks' War with Austria in 1866, Bismarck created the North German Confederation in 1867 (which was to be the basis for the German Empire he completed in 1871, following war with France).[17]

It was in the wake of the creation of the North German Confederation— and the glow of Bismarck's success—that Rochau produced the second volume of *Foundations of Realpolitik*. His motivation for writing was to address the criticism that had been made of *Realpolitik* since the publication of the first volume, fifteen years earlier. Simply by means of its title, the first volume of *Foundations of Realpolitik* had "placed itself straight away not only in opposition to the political idealism but also against the policies of phantasy and sentimentality whose opaque impulses" had fooled the German people for too long. "Formless ideas, impulses, emotional surges, melodic slogans, naively accepted catchwords"—these had been the targets of his first book. "A number of general liberal misunderstandings and the opposition's habitual self-delusions were made the victim of political truth," he sniffed, so criticism was inevitable.[18]

In the preface to volume two, dated October 1868, Rochau insisted that there was not one sentence that he wanted to take back, or that he considered outdated. Yet he was aware that, as others began to use the word, *Realpolitik* was already beginning to take on a life of its own. He rejected the criticism that had been leveled at the title of the book, if not so much against the content itself. Previously he had regarded any definition of *Realpolitik* as gratuitous, as the notion seemed self-evident. But now he felt he must define it, because, he complained, his fellow Germans were very slow on the uptake.

First, Rochau turned his sights on Constantin Frantz, who had criticized the notion of *Realpolitik* as consisting "only in disdain or despair regarding all ideals, whereby any kind of violent act and meanness is sanctioned in advance." For Rochau, the idea that he was an anti-idealist was a gross mis-representation of his position. In attacking *Realpolitik*, Frantz had created a false dichotomy between a politics of idealism and a politics of compromise. On the contrary, Rochau argued that the "the pursuit of the highest aims" was quite compatible with making temporary deals in order to achieve short-term goals. Second, he believed that there was a fundamental difference between a "recognition of success" and the "sanctioning" of success (its justification), of which he had been accused by Frantz. German liberals had come to terms with the fact that Bismarck had seized the initiative on the German national question. For now they were prepared to deal with him on these grounds. But this did "not entail the renunciation of individual judgement and it requires least of all an uncritical kind of submission" to the powers that be.[19] To advocate a momentary compromise with the status quo was not the same as converting to the belief system that underlay it.

Realpolitik was not some sort of revolutionary science of politics that rejected all that had gone before. It was more appropriate to think of it as a mere "measuring and weighing and calculating of facts that need to be processed politically." Yet one could not pick and choose the facts that one must process. It did not matter whether these facts "are the result of violent acts and meanness or of justice and nobleness." It was the essence of *Realpolitik* to deal with the "historical product," accepting it as it is, with an open eye for its strengths and its weaknesses. *Realpolitik* would not be "bribed by the noble origin of a fleeting momentary appearance"; nor would it ignore political facts in "virtuous indignation," simply because these may be of immoral or criminal origin. "In the scales of *Realpolitik*," for example, Louis Napoleon's coup d'état of 1852 outweighed the French Revolution of 1848 by a factor of ten.[20]

Yet Rochau was not a fatalist. To recognize the facts of political life was not to succumb to them. To recognize Bismarck's strength was not to bow down to him uncritically. The practitioner of *Realpolitik*, "far from avoiding opposition or struggle," believed that he was the one most seriously engaged in trying to effect political change. *Realpolitik* did not "move in a foggy future, but in the present's field of vision, it does not consider its task to consist in the realization of ideals, but in the attainment of concrete ends." The practitioner of *Realpolitik* knew to content himself with partial results, if complete victory was not yet attainable. Above all, *Realpolitik* was "an enemy of all kinds of self-delusion." To seek to change what one could, and to accept that change was not always possible, was in fact a moral choice. It was a "matter of conscience" to see men and things for what they really are.[21] In this, Rochau anticipated the so-called ethical realism of twentieth-century realists (often traced back to Max Weber and his "ethics of responsibility").[22] It is worth noting, in fact, that Weber's father was a contemporary of Rochau, closely involved in the National Liberal movement.[23]

What irritated Rochau most about the critics of *Realpolitik*, such as Frantz, was their suggestion that his was a theory of "political materialism." This could not be further from the truth. As German nationalism had proved, ideas remained a central component of political life. Even Bismarck, for example, had been forced to adjust his policies to reflect German national sentiment. For this reason, *Realpolitik* would contradict itself if it were to "deny the rights of the intellect, of ideas, of religion or any other of the moral forces to which the human soul renders homage."[24]

As in 1853, Rochau was eager to distinguish between the philosophical sophistication and moral purity of an idea and its actual political force. These were not one and the same. The intellect and everything that is related to it was factored into *Realpolitik* "only to the extent that there inheres in it a force that can be turned to account in public life," he explained. Equally, even the "craziest chimera" may become a serious matter. This was how Rochau viewed the increasing influence of socialism in German politics. However one might regard it as being based on absurd notions, its strength could not be denied because of its appeal to "thousands of weak minds, desirous hearts and spry arms." Conversely, it was common that "the most beautiful ideal that enthuses noble souls is a political nullity." The examples he gave were ideas such as eternal peace, democratic fraternity, gender equality, and equality of the races. Phantasms like this, which were based on "no real belief, no will and no force . . . *Realpolitik* passes by shrugging its shoulders."[25]

While Rochau retained his faith in the power of ideas, however, one can discern a greater appreciation of military power in his writing by 1868. Volume one of *Realpolitik* had argued that the *Zeitgeist* was the single most important factor in shaping the direction of political life. Fifteen years later, in the wake of the Austro-Prussian War, there was a subtle but significant change of emphasis: "when it is a matter of trying to bring down the walls of Jericho, the Realpolitik thinks that lacking better tools, the most simple pickaxe is more effective than the sound of the most powerful trumpets."[26]

Political Idealism and Reality

In the preface to the second volume of *Foundations of Realpolitik*, Rochau had directed his remarks chiefly at Constantin Frantz. In the fifth chapter of volume two, "Political Idealism and Reality," he turned his sights on the left-wing liberals and socialists, such as Venedey, who had split from the Progressive Party over the decision to enter a coalition with Bismarck in 1868. Politics should be understood as an "empirical science" rather than a field of "speculation" or "random abstraction." For Rochau, the state was a natural *Realpolitiker.* The state had long had to put up with being portrayed as "a poor sinner" by political idealists. It was only on rare occasions that the state "pursues a chimera, indulges in a silly idea, [and] involves itself in undertakings that go beyond its strength." In most cases, however, one could assume that the state "understands its position, its advantage and its tasks by and large better than all its critics."[27]

Statecraft, as its name suggested, was "nothing more than the art of success, applied to the specific ends of the state." Every reasonable human activity was geared toward success. For Rochau, those idealists who regarded political success as a "marginal matter" were pursuing a "vain game under a pretentious name, however solemn the ideas and principles serving as catchwords may sound." He gave the example of the Prussian democrats whose dogged abstention from voting in the 1850s meant that "much was missed and nothing was achieved" other than humiliation. In fact, he noted, a growing number of them had now confessed to their mistake in taking such a line of "irresponsible stubbornness."

Again this was not to reject political idealism out of hand. It still had a role in shaping the future trajectory of politics in state and society. Political idealism may "build its systems, pursue its bold sprints and attempt its upswing to sky-high aims," he wrote. Such "gymnastic exercises of the intellect," although they often became absurd and farcical, were by no means useless. On the contrary, idealism often played an important role as "a harbinger and trailblazer of events," setting the trajectory for a country's political development. However, where radicals tended to assess political ideas by virtue of their "metaphysical or religious or ethical worth," the *Realpolitiker* knew that their "market value" was the real test. Mad fanaticism was potentially just as powerful a force as the most noble enthusiasm. There were many "dirty superstitions" in European culture that were embarrassing and out-dated—anti-Semitism, for example—but so long as they persisted one should not deny them recognition.

The more one understood reality, the better one could serve higher ideals. Too often, groups of like-minded people who believed themselves to possess the "true doctrine of the good" adopted a purist and utopian approach to political change. Giving another example, Rochau criticized a faction of democrats in Berlin who had just issued a manifesto proposing a radical republican government. Their plan had no foundation in German history. Were they expecting "the millennial empire which supposedly falls from the sky overnight or which is achieved in the twinkling of an eye by means of a street battle"? Such philosophical absolutism, in Rochau's view, was actually illiberal. It arose from a despotic spirit that considered nothing valid but itself. Tyranny, as the history of religious persecution had shown, was not less tyrannical if it arose from idealism.

Politics consisted of "unending series of fights and compromises." But the so-called idealists would hear nothing about sober calculation and the apprehension of the moment. By splitting themselves into factions, the opposition only strengthened the government's hand. Worse still, Rochau believed that the behavior of extreme radicals—in refusing to respect the rule of law—gave Bismarck the pretext to practice repression against the moderate opposition. Radicalism discouraged people from "political work in the real world." It intimidated "weak minds and hearts" and provided reactionaries with welcome excuses.[28]

In Search of Equilibrium

Rochau's book was not simply an attack on the naïve versions of liberalism that he saw around him. Others were equally guilty of self-delusion. In the second volume of *The Foundations of Realpolitik* he also criticized Bismarck's Conservative Party as an "anachronism." He denounced the tools of reactionary conservatism—emergency powers or curtailed press freedom—as dictatorial and therefore unsustainable.[29] Autocratic government went against the things that comprised the greatness of the nation—patriotism, nationalism, lawful ambition, manly and civic pride, the spirit of enterprise, self-confidence, strength of character, and prosperity.[30]

The basic postulates of *Vormärz* liberalism—political freedom, self-government, equality before the law, and freedom of expression—were still peppered throughout his work. His preferred strategy for achieving these goals was through constitutional political pressure and influencing public opinion. This had been the task that the National Union, which Rochau had co-founded in 1859, had set itself. Faced with the triumph of reactionary forces, Rochau believed that the liberal bourgeoisie had two choices. The first was to hold on to the ideals of the 1848 revolution regardless of the fact that these were now unattainable. The second was to adapt to the new situation. Rather than stressing the power of ideas, principles, and abstract constitutional idealism, the *Realpolitik* course was to highlight and harness the actual societal power of the bourgeoisie and to bring it to bear on the new Germany at the moment of its creation.[31] He remained convinced that the existing regime was inherently unsustainable in its present form.

It was at this point that Rochau developed an idea of equilibrium as a desirable social and political outcome within the state. By this, he meant a balance between the various social forces in Germany. This required mutual recognition and a general compromise between these different societal forces. Germany's rulers had to respect the rising power, wealth, and education of the middle classes. Liberals and radicals had to accept that monarchy, and the popular attachment to the royal family, could not simply be wished away. Monarchism was woven into the cultural fabric of Germany and people disposed to monarchical government had "never been turned into a people of Spartans over night." In another passage which was reminiscent of Edmund Burke's critique of the French Revolution, Rochau argued that one could behead the king and all his relatives, but a people used to a monarchy would most likely elevate an Oliver Cromwell or a Napoleon Bonaparte to the empty throne.[32] After the regicide, Burke had famously predicted that disorder would reign until some popular general, "who possesses the true spirit of command, shall draw the eyes of all men upon himself."[33]

As with volume one of *Foundations of Realpolitik*, then, Rochau placed much emphasis on the changing conditions of modernity in an industrializing society. By virtue of their education, their wealth, their entrepreneurial spirit, and their appetite for work, the middle classes had become the driving force of modern Germany. But German society was also changing in other ways that also needed to be taken into consideration. It was not just the middle classes who had been created by modernization and industrialization but a new proletarian class, which had also grown in political importance. The "poor and uneducated sections of the population for their part are politically significant by virtue of their number," and their recognition in the political system could no longer be ignored. "The great masses which formerly appeared only in exceptional situations in the political arena, are nowadays appointed to regular participation in the running of the state," he wrote. Although Rochau opposed universal suffrage, he believed that the participation and co-option of the working class was "undoubtedly desirable." "Even diehard reactionaries nowadays do not even consider denying the masses at least a certain degree of participation in the running of the state," he observed.[34]

In fact, Rochau exhibited a striking degree of optimism about the prospect of all classes working in harmony. Another positive aspect of modernity was the greater levels of toleration it had created in society. The mutual relationship between different political forces within the state was to be understood similarly to the relationship between different religious groups in Germany. One could not expect them be united in "heart and in soul," of course, but it was "completely legitimate to demand of both in the name of the spirit of the nineteenth century a mutual and external tolerance which excludes any crude forms of hostility and all assaults upon the continued existence of one or the other." The "renunciation of any plans or attempts to achieve mass conquest" by one societal force over another, such as had occurred in past centuries, was "dictated by public reason and self-interest."[35]

Running alongside this notion of equilibrium—bolstered by tolerance and reason—was a further elaboration of the Burkean idea of the organic development of society and state, which Rochau had introduced in volume one of *Foundations of Realpolitik*. Again, Rochau did not cite Burke directly. However, he did use precisely the same analogy that Burke had used to describe the English constitution—that of a great oak tree growingly slowly and unevenly over time.[36] When taking a knife to this "societal organism," one should only remove the dead branches, or those that were showing signs of disease. Some branches were abnormal and ugly but they had to be accepted as part of the tree. If one attempted to remove every disfigured branch, because it was offensive to the eye, the whole operation would end in failure.[37]

This was followed by the use of another Burkean precept—that historical and national circumstances determined the characteristics of every political situation. "The circumstances are what render every civil and political scheme beneficial or noxious to mankind," Burke had written.[38] Here Rochau appealed directly to the more "advanced minds" among the liberal opposition, whom he distinguished from the radicals. Specifically he addressed the "reasonably sensible" reformers who did not hope to create a state in the image of Plato's *Republic* or Thomas More's *Utopia* but instead looked to the federal republics of Switzerland and the United States as possible models for Germany. While he agreed that one people could learn from another, he was dubious about imitating the constitutions of other nations. To replace one system of governance with one lifted from another country would effectively be an "imposition." In Germany the most obvious obstacle to republicanism was the strength of the Prussian monarchy. However much liberals and radicals hated the fact, there was no evidence that it was in decline.

Rochau believed that Prussia's success in the Seven Weeks' War, which Bismarck and the monarchists could claim credit for, had made the potential for revolution almost disappear. On the other hand, the creation of the North German Confederation had created the "broadest leeway" for political reform. Small state particularities and national barriers had been swept aside, as manifested in the eradication of tariff barriers. Turning his attention back to the anti-Bismarck opposition, Rochau was eager to impress upon them that this was the critical moment to make their voices heard, by cooperating in the formation of the new German nation-state—abandoning their scruples and leveraging their influence on the state through political participation. He denounced "all kinds of pessimism which rejects the good in order to avoid being distracted in its pursuit of the better."[39] In fact, when the National Union dissolved itself in 1867, believing its task complete, Rochau protested vehemently, believing that it was more important than ever for it to influence the future of Germany. If anything, he feared Bismarck and Prussia would be too timid in completing the work that had begun.[40]

War or Peace?

While the second volume of *The Foundations of Realpolitik* was written before the Franco-Prussian War of 1870, the prospect of that war loomed large over its pages. In the final chapters of volume two, Rochau turned his attention to the "unsettling tension" that had arisen in European affairs. The first basic observation that Rochau made about international relations was that the internal political structures of states had a significant influence on the course of their foreign policy. France was a prime example. The Bonapartist Empire of Napoleon III, for example, was so entwined with one man's personality that it depended on the perception of his virility—something tested in the international arena. This was reflected in the erratic behavior of the government-controlled French press, which frequently raised the prospect of an attack on Germany, only to go silent on the issue a few weeks later. Rochau warned that such a "swing system" was a dangerous one and "brings us closer and closer to the brink of war."

Europe sat on a "powder keg." Germany was particularly vulnerable because it was sandwiched between the two most powerful armies in the world—those of France and Russia—both of which had designs on expanding their influence in German territory. This circumstance required a tough choice. Given that French hostility was the number one threat at this time, however, Rochau believed that the smartest policy was to seek a temporary alliance with Russia. This might not be easy, as Russia was still exerting its influence on several German states. Such interference was "very distressing to the German ego." Nonetheless, it was shortsighted, for the moment, to let one's ego dictate policy.[41]

Like the liberals in the Prussian parliament, German nationalists would have to reconcile themselves to this reality in the short term. While Rochau was not the only one to have argued this, it is worth noting that Bismarck came to the same conclusion: that a war on two fronts, with France and Russia at the same time, was a suicidal course for Germany. Indeed, it was this notion that was said to constitute one of the foundation stones of what became known as Bismarckian foreign policy: something that Kaiser II and post-Bismarckian German Imperialists jettisoned after 1890.

Of the other major powers, England was Germany's most natural ally. As the offshore balancer in European affairs, English statesmen had long believed in preserving a central European bulwark to maintain the balance

of power in Europe (and to prevent France or Russia from gaining hegemony). Since 1815, England had been torn between supporting Prussia or
Austria but had largely sided with the latter. Prussia's victory in 1866, however, had made that choice easier in London, as it was now the preeminent
German state. In the event of a war, the North German Confederation
could at least count on England to secure its coastlines and free navigation of
northern European rivers, if only to protect its own trade. Rochau was far
from sentimental about such an alliance, and he understood international
politics—like domestic politics—as a great game in which interests were
paramount. It remained to be seen whether this momentary community of
interests would stand the test of time.[42] It is no coincidence that *Realpolitik*,
as applied to the international system, came to be taken to imply a break
with the "concert diplomacy" associated with the policies of Klemens von
Metternich from 1815 to 1848. The previous conservative consensus—and
preference for stability and harmony—had been weakened by the rise of
new nation states.[43] Ultimately, Germany would have to carve out an independent course for itself in which it did not depend on obtaining guarantees for its security from other states.

In the long term, Rochau felt that the combined threat from France and
Russia was nothing short of "existential." The most important step in dealing with it, therefore, was to achieve internal unity within Germany. On
these grounds, Rochau turned his ire on both radicals in northern Germany
and Ultramontane Catholics in the southern states, such as Bavaria. He
denounced the radicals for blaming Prussian militarism for the deterioration in European relations—thereby ignoring the mendacious behavior of
other nations. He accused the Catholics of being more loyal to the Catholic
Church than to their fellow Germans, thereby opening the door to the
French to sow dissension by acting as the protector of the papacy. "In order
to survive this coming confrontation with two military powers, Germany
must "finally prove its legitimate right to national existence" and be "united
in its civil and military might." In a hardening of tone, something that was
to become a feature of German nationalism, Rochau claimed that "anyone
who presents an obstacle to this unity will be rightly accused of complicity
in the murder of their homeland."[44]

If Rochau's view of future political and economic development within
Germany was optimistic, the same could not be said for his assessment of the
international arena. While the threat from Russia was currently dormant, it
would soon come to a head. Diplomacy would only work for so long. Russia

and Germany were set on a collision course. The gradual Russification of Poland was, in particular, a strategic threat to Prussia—doubly so, as Russia resented having its access to German rivers blocked by the tolls of the North German Confederation. Likewise, enclaves of German-speaking peoples dotted outside the German states were particularly vulnerable to unrest in the event of increased national rivalries. In a prophetic remark, Rochau also warned that "the great and constantly growing number of German colonies on Polish–Russian soil contain much flammable matter."[45]

A related concern was the growth of Pan-Slavism. To the east and south of the North German Confederation, the Slavic peoples of Europe (Czechs, Croats, and Serbs) increasingly emphasized their distinctiveness and made their own national demands. Austria, because of its multi-national empire, had the most to lose from such developments. There was also a fear that the Russians would champion the Pan-Slavic cause to weaken Germany for their own interests. The Czechs and other Slav nationalists had already demonstrated that they were "prepared to tackle the transition from theory to practice, in the face of which Germany cannot remain indifferent and inactive."[46]

Before 1848, as noted earlier, there was some support for Polish independence among German liberals. Indeed, Rochau had campaigned alongside Polish nationalists in the 1830s. German liberal nationalists were attracted to the idea of a viable buffer state to the east built on similar principles. After all, it would have a common interest in opposing reactionary cabinets in Prussia, Austria, and, above all, Russia. Thus Germany could be afforded protection, space and time in which to make its transformation to a liberal state. This began to change once the Polish question began to impinge on German interests. This problem presented itself in the form of the Polish majority in Posen, a small state which German nationalists envisaged as part of a unified German state. The Poles of Posen had different ideas, of course. Here was the rub: the rise of new nationalist agendas across Europe would lead, inevitably, to competing national aims.

In this, there was no small degree of hypocrisy and chauvinism. Attitudes to "new" nationalisms among the Slavic peoples (Czechs, Croats, and Serbs) were even less sympathetic than they were to the Poles. One justification offered for this sense of superiority was that such nationalisms were recent constructs and merely mimicked German nationalism. More important was the fear that Slavic nationalisms were potentially anti-German and pro-Russian. In 1848, then, no bond was formed between those Czechs or

Germans who were actually fighting for the same thing. When the Czech rebellion was put down in 1848, many in the Frankfurt Assembly regarded it as a good thing for Germany. Overriding any sense of international fraternity was a geopolitical concern about the viability of a German state that was so vulnerable on both its flanks. As the historian Brendan Simms has explained, each new threat to the Rhine frontier to the west, and each new threat to German interests in the east, "combined to hasten the formation of a hard-headed liberal nationalist *Realpolitik*."[47] Thus Rochau's word became ever more associated with debates about foreign policy. As an interesting subplot, German-speaking Czechs began to evoke their own version of *Realpolitik*, in the name of their own nationalist goals. In 1876, for example, the Czech politician Johann Kaspar Bluntschli introduced a distinction between *Realpolitik* (entailing the "real" needs of the Czech people) and *Idealpolitik* (their abstract demands). In turn, Bluntschli's writings guided Thomas Masaryk, the great hero of Czech independence, who was later credited with the practice of a specifically Czech form of *Realpolitik*.[48]

In his hostility to Slavic nationalism, Rochau failed one of the litmus tests set by A. J. P. Taylor in his discussion of the limits of German liberalism.[49] Nevertheless, Rochau did avoid some of the other traps of chauvinistic nationalism into which many of his counterparts fell. While it is possible to accuse him of opening the door to Bismarck, he was certainly innocent of the racialism that characterized later manifestations of German nationalism. In fact, Rochau tackled one of the most poisonous issues in German society head-on: anti-Semitism. In the second volume of *The Foundations of Realpolitik* he denounced it as both morally wrong and illogical. Rochau, as we have seen, was prepared to denounce such "superstitions"—sectarianism and ethnic hatred—on ethical grounds. More to the point, the integration of Jews into the national cause was an example of the sort of modernization that Rochau believed was so important to the future of Germany. Due to their social force, wealth, and intelligence, he believed German Jews were not only entitled to political representation; they were an indispensable asset to the German nation-state of the future. Anti-Semitism was neither rational nor pragmatic; it had no place in Rochau's understanding of *Realpolitik*.[50] By forgetting this lesson, and succumbing to the irrationality of hatred, many those who boasted of their *Realpolitik* after Rochau fell at the very first hurdle.

4

Realpolitik after Rochau

Having failed to attain a seat in the Frankfurt parliament of 1848, Ludwig von Rochau finally won a seat in the Reichstag in 1871. He had lived to see the formation of the German Empire, following Bismarck's emphatic defeat of France in 1870 in the Franco-Prussian War. In 1870–2, he produced a small two-volume history of Germany, but he was approaching the end of his life.[1] Rochau died of a stroke in Heidelberg in 1873 while working on a biography of Count Camillo Cavour, founder of the Liberal Party in Piedmont and a leading figure in the unification of Italy.

From 1871 to 1879 the National Liberals were the chief allies of Bismarck in the Reichstag and could make a good case that they were able to exert influence on his government by agreeing to cooperate with it. On the one hand, they could point to the reduction of tariffs on trade; relaxation on questions of religious liberties (including for Jews); and a new criminal code and other judicial reforms. On the other hand, the National Liberals had blind spots in their worldview. These arose in part from their tendency to see modernization and secularization as a litmus test for liberal advancement. Thus they happily cooperated with Bismarck's *Kulturkampf* legislation, which was an assault on the political structures of German Catholicism—signaling a willingness to side with the bureaucracy over the rights of self-identifying communities within the state. To say that they "capitulated" to Bismarck does not quite tell the full story. Nevertheless, the weakness of the National Liberals was to be exposed when Bismarck unceremoniously dropped them as allies in 1879. He formed an alliance with the Centre Party instead, casting the liberals into the wilderness.[2] The thing about *Realpolitik* was that others could play the game, too.

The emergence of *Realpolitik* had also coincided with broader developments in European politics and culture. Writing in the 1930s, the historian Robert Binkley argued that many of Europe's ills could be traced back to the undermining of the "federative policy" of the Holy Roman Empire, by new trends of rationalism and realism. "Inductive science, literary and artistic realism, commodity economics and *Realpolitik* betray a certain harmony of design," he wrote. It was the combined presence of these forces that led the "federative polity [to yield] to centralization and violence in the basic group relations of Europe—political, clerical and social." The rot had begun to set in with political tracts such as Rochau's *Realpolitik* and Auguste Comte's *Cours de Politique Positive*. Then followed Darwin's *Origin of Species* in 1859, which, in turn, popularized the notion that human development could be understood in scientific terms. According to Binkley, this broad and ill-defined realism ran counter to internationalism and cosmopolitanism in its repudiation of myths, sentiments, and metaphysical idealism. Finally, the same logic began to infect the conduct of foreign policy. To materialism in natural science and economic thought and to realism in the world of ascetics, there corresponded *Realpolitik* in the sphere of foreign affairs.[3]

The cultural historian Franco Moretti has placed *Realpolitik* within a broader literary milieu. This era saw the increasing number of "realist" literary novels such as those by Walter Scott, Maria Edgeworth, Honore de Balzac, William Makepeace Thackeray, Jean de La Fontaine, Henry James, Gustave Flaubert, and Thomas Mann. Nineteenth-century descriptions of social and political conditions became analytical and impersonal, Moretti argues: a change of mood encapsulated by the creation of *Realpolitik*.[4]

To some this was a worrying trend, criticized by one contemporary liberal observer as *Realismus der Stabilität*—a realism of stability and fait accompli. Against this idea, another literary scholar has argued that hidden within this literary turn was actually a political trick—an effort by liberals and radicals to keep alive the possibility of change in a period of conservative reaction. It has been argued that there was a *Realpoetik* tradition in French, Italian, and German Romanticism in the post-Napoleonic period. Continental romantics used literature and poetry to prevent the post-1815 restoration from embedding itself too deeply.[5] This interpretation is perhaps closer to Rochau's real intentions: to keep liberalism alive in a world that looked unfavorable to it.

The Role of *Realpolitik* in Germany's "Special Path"

The history of Germany in the century after 1848 gave credence to the argument that something had gone seriously wrong in its national development.

After the Second World War, when the full scale of Nazi evil became clear, historians began to talk about the *Sonderweg* (special path) that the country had taken from the middle of the nineteenth century. It was in the context of these debates that increased scrutiny was turned on the notion of *Realpolitik*. *Realpolitik* was to become associated with two things in particular. The first was the flimsiness of German liberalism in the face of rapidly changing circumstances, creating a void into which illiberal forces flowered.[6] The second was Bismarck's foreign policy—characterized, above all, by the break from the congress diplomacy of the Metternich era.[7]

This fed into a broader narrative. After the Second World War, an influential school of thought emerged in Germany which held that Germany's development had been corrupted by having undergone economic modernization without the type of political liberalization experienced in the other leading industrial nations in the West.[8] It is significant, then, that Hans-Ulrich Wehler, one of the historians most closely associated with the *Sonderweg* thesis, produced the only edition of Rochau's *Realpolitik* in the twentieth century.[9]

The *Sonderweg* thesis was highly controversial—not least because it assumed that there was only one version of political development in industrializing societies.[10] Why should Germany be expected to develop along similar lines to Britain and France? The Marxist historians Geoff Eley and David Blackbourn also made the countervailing point that the German bourgeoisie had actually been more powerful than the theory *Sonderweg* suggested. If anything, the British political system remained more dominated by the old landed elite, and one could make the case that Germany was more democratic and free than Britain before the First World War. There had indeed been a bourgeois revolution—just not one reflected at the level of parliamentary democracy. The *Realpolitik* of the German bourgeoisie, as Eley and Blackbourn labeled it, had seen them form a partnership with the pre-industrial power elite, represented by the Junker classes from which Bismarck came. Again, there were echoes of Rochau in this argument (though they used the word *Realpolitik* without attributing it to him).[11]

While some pointed the finger at the fatal compromise that German liberals made with Bismarck, others argued that the opportunity to set Germany on a different path had been missed before 1848—the point at which A. J. P. Taylor had said history had failed to turn. The German American historian Peter Viereck, writing in the 1940s and 1950s, argued that much of the blame lay with Metternich. Instead of co-opting liberals, Metternich's policies of repression had forced them to gamble that the new phenomenon of

nationalism was going to be a liberalizing force. Liberals and conservatives should have combined their "respective half-truths against the whole-
lies of their real enemies: the self-styled realists ... racists, the militarists,
the war-planning Irredentists." But in 1848 "middle-class internationalism" and "monarchico-aristocratic internationalism" wounded each other
fatally, creating a vacuum into which extremist nationalism flowed.[12] This,
in turn, had a profound impact on international relations in Europe.

For all its flaws, Viereck argued, Metternich's Europe had seen a lengthy
period of peace. He understood European politics as a league of nations
in which states respected general laws of conduct—an idea that was to be
thrown aside under Bismarck. In Viereck's view, *Realpolitik* in the international arena entailed a despair of anything better and a lack of faith in any
universal code of good or bad.[13] While all nations practiced an element of
Realpolitik, it was to be Germany that "went further in rationalizing this
deplorable practice into a glorification of theory."[14] This was to have disastrous consequences.

Heinrich von Treitschke and the Distortion of *Realpolitik*

Even before Rochau's death, *Realpolitik* was being deployed in ways its creator would not have recognized. Writing a century later, the Harvard-based
historian of Germany, Hajo Holborn, insists that the term should not be used
except for statesmen who entered the scene in the decade after 1848, and even
then it needed exact definition. As use of the word proliferated after 1853,
however, its original meaning became blurred. It either came to denote a policy contemptuous of all ideas and ideologies, or a policy exclusively employ-
ing power for the achievement of its ends.[15] Gradually, too, an understanding
of the liberal context in which Rochau had written was extinguished.[16] It was
after this period that *Realpolitik*, born on the left of the political spectrum, was
to become chiefly associated with those on the right.

One figure was more important than any other in keeping alive the
notion of *Realpolitik,* and equally responsible for distorting its meaning. This was Rochau's fellow National Liberal politician and historian,
Heinrich von Treitschke. It was largely due to Treitschke's efforts that the
word became associated ever more closely with Bismarck. It was through
Treitschke, also, that *Realpolitik* became associated with a cultish devotion

to the importance of power in the German national ideal. Above all, it was through Treitschke that the Anglo-Saxon world was first confronted with the discomfiting concept of *Realpolitik*—one that recycled some key observations by Rochau but added much of its own. By the onset of the Second World War, some would even call Treitschke the "prophet" of National Socialism.[17]

Treitschke was born on 15 December 1834 in Dresden, the son of a distinguished Saxon army officer of Czech descent, who had (like Rochau's father) first experienced military action against Napoleon's armies. Treitschke's maternal grandfather had actually fought under George Washington in the American War of Independence. As a young man, Treitschke had suffered from poor hearing, which deteriorated over the years. He was also a poet and his writing had much greater appeal to readers than Rochau's rather workmanlike prose. Though only fourteen, he was excited by the 1848 revolutions and his sympathies lay with republicanism. By the early 1850s, however, as he came into adulthood, he became increasingly fascinated by the question of what had gone wrong in 1848.

Treitschke discovered the first volume of Rochau's *Foundations of Realpolitik* in the university library in Heidelberg in 1853. He believed that it contained "more that was useful for scholarship than a thick textbook on politics" and claimed to know "of no book that destroyed preconceived illusions with a more cutting logic."[18] What particularly impressed Treitschke was the final sentence in the first volume of *Foundations of Realpolitik*, which asserted that the only thing that could unite Germany was "some superior force which swallows up the others." This impressed upon him the importance of Prussia in the German national cause.[19] Significantly, though, he took Rochau's logic further in the extent to which he prioritized the national question over the liberal program in Germany. The path that led most quickly to national unification was the one he cherished most, even if it led to despotism, Treitschke confessed in 1854.[20]

One can see the influence of Rochau in Treitschke's intellectual development in the 1850s. He borrowed some of the metaphors Rochau used, such as the notion that the men of 1848 had built "castles in the sky." Treitschke wrote that "it can never be the task of political science to build up for itself a phantastic structure in the air; for only that is truly human which has its roots in the historical facts of actual life."[21] In 1857, he presented an essay at the University of Leipzig in which he argued that there was no such thing as an ideal state. In 1859, he expressed admiration for Rochau's history of

Heinrich Gotthard von Treitschke (1834–1896), the nationalist German historian, was an admirer of Ludwig von Rochau and set out to show the world "how brilliant *Realpolitik* is." However, Treitschke was later accused of being the "prophet of National Socialism" and encouraging extreme militarism and anti-Semitism. Courtesy of Wikimedia Creative Commons. PD-US; PD-old.

France, published that year. Indeed, he hoped to write a history of Germany in the same style, "but better than that work, wherever possible."[22]

Treitschke even read Rochau's more obscure work, such as his account of his travels in Italy (the only one of his books translated into English). He commented, admiringly, on the disproportionate time that Rochau devoted to discussing the economic and social customs and institutions of the country (rather than an average traveler's account of art galleries or sights of interest).[23] He read Rochau's short history of Germany (published in two volumes in 1870 and 1872), although he was not so impressed, and his work on Italy's Count Cavour, produced in the final years of his life.[24] When composing his own book on Italy in 1870, Treitschke expressed his desire to show Germans "how brilliant *Realpolitik* is."[25]

Like Rochau, Treitschke remained a liberal in his political instincts. "Everything new which the nineteenth century has created is the work of Liberalism," he wrote. But it was nationalism rather than liberalism that represented the ultimate, final, and crowning stage of political evolution.[26]

It was on these grounds that Treitschke began to pick at the foundations of Anglo-Saxon conceptions of liberalism in an 1861 essay on John Stuart Mill. In the essay, he articulated a concept of freedom and liberty *within* the state rather than freedom *from* the state, as Mill had done. In an 1864 essay titled "The Federal State and the Unitary State," Treitschke linked the "freedom of people" in Germany to the "state power of Prussia."[27] What Germany lacked was the self-confidence and sense of destiny that existed in many other nations. To serve this end, Treitschke began a history of Germany in the nineteenth century. Politics was applied history. The state, building on a now familiar idea, was a living organism. The grandeur of history lay in the perpetual conflict between nations. Cosmopolitanism and provincialism were both enemies to this.[28]

In Treitschke's hands, *Realpolitik* became interwoven with other currents of thought. In addition to Rochau and Mill, Treitschke immersed himself in Aristotle's *Politics* and Machiavelli's *The Prince*. He cited Aristotle (as Rochau had done) in support of his argument that the state was the supreme moralizing and humanizing agency in human life. Thus the state must live by its own imperative of preserving its existence and developing its full potential. Of Machiavelli he wrote, he was "more fitted than any other to destroy the illusion that one can reform the world with cannon loaded only with ideas of Right and Truth." Treitschke was not simply attracted to Machiavelli's realism. He also saw him as a patriot, who was willing to set aside his republicanism if it meant the strengthening of the Florentine state. Machiavelli sacrificed "Right and Virtue to a great idea, the might and unity of his people."[29] In *The Prince* he saw "fiery patriotism and the conviction that even the most oppressive despotism must be welcomed if it warrants the might and unity of the fatherland—these are the ideas which reconcile me with the many objectionable and terrible opinions of the great Florentine."[30] Other neo-Machiavellians in Germany at the time included Karl Bollman, who wrote *Defence of Machiavellianism* in 1858, with the motto "The Fatherland before everything else."[31]

Treitschke's strong Protestant faith also gave his writing a tincture of providentialism. His belief in the destiny of German nationhood gave his writings an almost evangelical tone. He shared Hegel's faith in history and the state as vehicles for the Divine. The destinies of nations followed courses that were veiled from mortal eyes. Men must not seek to dominate history. The noblest quality of the practical statesman was "his ability to point to the signs of the times, and to realize in some measure how universal history may develop at a given moment." The statesman must resign himself "to desiring only the really attainable" and to keeping this aim perpetually and steadfastly in view.[32]

Before the Austro-Prussian War, Treitschke's attitude toward Bismarck was one of qualified respect. He was still, as his first English biographer later put it, "half a Liberal," still wedded to the liberal constitutional doctrines he had learned as a student.[33] In 1866, Bismarck tried to recruit him to write his War Manifesto during the Austro-Prussian War. Treitschke replied that while he would support Bismarck's external foreign policy, he refused to become a functionary of the state until the constitution was re-established.[34]

Like Rochau, however, Treitschke believed that Prussia's victory over Austria in the Seven Week War in 1867 was a transformative moment in the German question. Despite the fact that he was from Saxony, he went so far as to call for Bismarck to invade his home state—something that made him rather unpopular among the natives. As a committed Protestant, suspicious of the supranational loyalties of the Catholic hierarchy, he was also support-ive of Bismarck's *Kulturkampf* legislation.[35] After the war, Bismarck granted him unrestricted use of the state archives, and Treitschke's wounded brother—who had fought in the war—was put under Bismarck's care.[36]

While Treitschke remained nominally independent of Bismarck, he soon became, in effect, the propagandist-in-chief of the Prussian court. By 1870, Treitschke urged that "We must become more radical in questions of unity and more conservative in questions of liberty."[37] When Bismarck achieved unifi-cation in 1871, Treitschke's nationalism had completely taken over his lib-eralism. He went so far as to claim that the foundation of the Reich in 1871 had "fulfilled the liberal programme."[38] In a study of Treitschke written in 1945, the Czech Jewish émigré Hans Kohn argued that German liberalism lost its soul in the nationalist excitement of these years. While Rochau had maintained a distance from the regime, Treitschke had embraced it. Thus, Kohn argued, "Bismarck's *Realpolitik* had conquered not only in the field of diplomacy and battle, but even more disastrously in the field of the German mind."[39]

Realpolitik and International Relations

By the early 1870s, Treitschke was one of the most influential historians in Germany. Through his lectures and speeches, he had amassed a huge following. In 1874, he took a prestigious position at the University of Berlin (which he held until his death in 1896), where he became a colleague of Leopold von Ranke, arguably the most influential figure in the professionalization of the historical profession in the nineteenth century.[40] Ranke had sent Treitschke his essay titled "Genius of the Prussian State," which was a matter of great pride to the younger Treitschke.[41] Behind the scenes, however, Ranke opposed Treitschke's appointment on the grounds that he was too vehement a partisan of Bismarck and lacked sufficient scholarly detachment.[42]

Ranke's contribution to the historical profession is famous, in his emphasis on empirical treatment of primary sources and the role of narrative. It can also be argued that he had a small but significant part in the story of *Realpolitik*. Ranke's historicism defended the peculiarity of the Prussian state from the so-called norms of liberalism. He spoke of how the German understanding of the state had been "emancipated" from the French Revolutionary example. German nationalism was a response to the existential threat from France. "As we are now attacked by a spiritual power, so must we oppose it with spiritual force," Ranke wrote. Germans needed to develop their own sense of nationality, as expressed through the state. To this he added another argument—that foreign affairs were the supreme factor in political life, and the ultimate test of a nation.[43]

In the hands of others, Ranke's notion of the "primacy of foreign policy" could take a more militant form, in which a nation's health was measured in terms of military power. "Behind the radiant Ranke there looms in the background the sinister Bismarck, not to speak of other even more sinister personages, the man of blood and iron, who forged his empire in the furnace of war," wrote the Czech-born sociologist Werner Stark a century later.[44] In the hands of Treitschke, elements of Ranke and Rochau were fused to project forward a path to further glory for the new German state. "The possession of a powerful and well-disciplined Army is a sign of great excellence in a nation," Treitschke wrote. As Carl von Clausewitz had argued, war was simply a continuation of politics. When it came to war, there was no limit on a nation's conduct. The sharpest weapons could be used and the first aim must be to "pierce the enemy to the heart."[45]

Treitschke's view of international relations was perhaps more complex and subtle than might seem at first glance. He argued that there were two dominant conceptions of international relations, both of which were untenable. One, "the so-called naturalistic theory," dated back to Machiavelli and was based on the notion that a state is "merely might personified" and "has the right to do anything that it is profitable to it." In Treitschke's view, this was an absurdity. It was to go against *Realpolitik* to behave in such a way (a test the Nazis would fail). If a state aspired to military might alone and paid no heed to reason or conscience, its successes would be short-lived. By exhibiting contempt for good faith or treaty agreements it would soon raise a crowd of enemies. Even Cesare Borgia, whom Machiavelli had admired, "ultimately fell into the pit which he had dug for others." Thus the doctrine of "pure might" was actually immoral because it could not justify its own existence.[46]

Treitschke believed that there was a naturally regulating element in inter-state behavior. This was humanity itself, which was an irreducible factor in international affairs. In making this case, in fact, he offered an elegant warning about the dangers of falling too hard for the temptations of *Realpolitik*. The man who declared that might and the mailed fist alone decided the fate of nations was "often a soured fanatic who in his youth smoked away at the pipe of peace, discovered that that was too good for this poor world, rushed off to the other extreme, and now declares that the basis of all things is brutality and cynicism." All great political thinkers showed a "touch of cynical contempt for mankind." But the most effective statesmen were those who could awaken "the finer energies which, despite all frailties and brutish instincts, lie dormant in man."[47]

On the other hand, Treitschke rejected the "moral" conception of the state that he believed was predominant in German liberal theories of politics. "The State is here regarded as a good little boy, to be washed, brushed, and sent to school; he must have his ears pulled to keep him good, and in return he is to be thankful, just-minded, and Heaven knows what else," he wrote. This had fed into a misunderstanding of the international system as an arena regulated by rules and self-limiting good behavior. The doctrinaire exponent of international law "fondly imagines that he need only emit a few aphorisms and that other nations of the world will forthwith, as reasonable men, accept them." Such a view ignored the fact that "stupidity and passion matter, and have always mattered, in history."[48]

Most striking about Treitschke's surveying of the international scene was that he had a new target in mind. For him, the state that did most to manipulate the international system to its own ends was not France or Russia—Rochau's chief concerns—but England, which was the "home of barbarism in all matters of international law." England had risen to predominance by its ruthless domination of the seas and its bullying and bombardment of other nations. Thanks to England, maritime international law was "nothing better than a system of privileged piracy." Yet it was England that still somehow saw fit to lecture the world on liberalism, with its "empty commonplaces about humanity."[49]

In England, Treitschke saw not only hypocrisy but weakness. He admired the old English soldiers and diplomats of the Napoleonic era and its immediate aftermath—such as Wellington, Castlereagh, Canning, and Palmerston—who spoke honestly about their pursuit of self-interest. In recent decades, however, England had become beholden to "self-satisfied" and insipid commercialism. Citing the influence of men such as Richard Cobden, the English radical who had led the free trade movement, he argued that the commercial spirit poisoned the English character: "the duel went out of fashion . . . the riding-whip supplanted the sword and the pistol" and, referring to the professionalization of cricket and football, the youth of the nation even turned their sport into a business.

England was also more secure than other European nations—something that had fed into a general rot in the English mind. "The fallacious security of insular life has bred in the English State and people an arrogant disregard for the feelings of foreign nations, such as no continental nation would dare to indulge." There were many examples of English hypocrisy, such as the bombardment of Copenhagen in 1807, when English troops had firebombed the city, killing three thousand citizens. The English annexation of the Transvaal Republic in 1877 was yet another case in point. The English strategy was to bully the weak and act morally superior when confronted with the strong.[50]

As Treitschke considered the potential of German power, his eyes began to turn beyond Europe and to the dream of a German Empire that would rival that of the British and the French. In this we can see the seeds of what was to be called *Weltpolitik* (world politics). Paving the way for German colonialism, Treitschke argued that international law is "mere clap-trap when these principles are applied to barbarian nations." It was a "scandalous weakness" for German statesmen not to seek a great role in the battle for new colonies in which other nations were engaged. The expansionist tone in German nationalism also had an unashamedly racist dimension to it too. "A negro tribe must be punished by having its villages burnt," wrote Treitschke, in an infamous passage, discussing how the German Empire could be built.[51]

As the man who wanted to show the world "how brilliant *Realpolitik* is," Treitschke had moved away from the original ideas of Rochau. Rochau had been highly conscious of German weakness in Europe. Thus Rochau's vision for the German Empire was restrained by comparison. He had argued, in the second volume of *Foundations of Realpolitik*, that the condition of lasting German greatness would be the continual exercise of moderation, and he had never talked about colonies or *Weltpolitik*.[52]

For Rochau, instead, *Realpolitik* was a weighing of facts, and, above all "an enemy of self-delusion." In Treitschke's hands, the emotional detachment that this demanded was diluted by militarism and chauvinism. Tellingly, the clearest break with Rochau was on the Jewish question. Rochau had seen German Jews as an integral part of the future German nation-state. He regarded anti-Semitism as irrational and therefore incompatible with *Realpolitik*. Sounding more like Constantin Frantz, one of Rochau's greatest critics, Treitschke believed that Jews encouraged anti-German tendencies in their commercialism and control of the press.[53] He expressed regret that the Pharaoh's policy toward the Jews had not been pursued with more vigor in ancient Egypt. In an ominous statement, he suggested that this had left Germany with a Jewish problem that would need to be solved.[54]

Friedrich Meinecke and *Staatsräson*

Treitschke died in 1896 but he had a successor—albeit a critical one—in the form of Friedrich Meinecke, who was to take *Realpolitik* into the twentieth century but attempt to cleanse it of some of the notions that it had become associated with. There was a connection between the two in that Meinecke succeeded Treitschke as the editor of *Historische Zeitschrift*, the most important historical journal of the period.[55] For Meinecke, Treitschke had become the foremost German thinker on questions of raison d'état (*Staatsräson* in German). In Meinecke's hands, *Staatsräson* was used interchangeably with *Realpolitik*—a practice that many twentieth century "realist" scholars would follow. It was Meinecke who did more than any other to fuse the two concepts together, to the extent that they are often presumed to mean the same thing by theorists of international relations to this day.[56]

Meinecke was born in Salzwedel in Saxony-Anhalt, in October 1862, which meant that he belonged to the next generation to Rochau and

Treitscke. He was educated at the University of Bonn and the University of Berlin. From 1887 to 1901 he worked as an archivist at the German State Archives. After assuming editorship of the *Historische Zeitschrift* from Treitschke, he held that position until 1935, when he was finally pushed aside by the Nazis. While not a Nazi supporter, he was a lifelong anti-Semite and believer in the German *Lebensraum* (living space) at the expense of the Slavic peoples in Eastern Europe.

Meinecke lived for ninety-two years, which means that his career went through a number of phases that can loosely be categorized as before and including the First World War; interwar Germany; and post-Nazi Germany. His thought was molded by the context in which he operated, prompting E. H. Carr to describe him as the archetypal *Zeitgeist* historian.[57] Before the First World War, he became one of the scholars associated with the drumbeat of German nationalism. Inevitably, his scholarship was shaped by the rise of Bismarckism and German imperialism, but he was not uncritical of either.[58]

It was through his reading of Treitschke that Meinecke discovered Rochau.[59] He too placed great emphasis on the role of 1848 in shaping the German political psyche. Indeed, Meinecke made the argument that Treitschke discerned in Rochau an "idealist who was doing no more than predicting the victory of that power which was supported by the idea." Rather than rejecting idealism, Treitschke, following Rochau, was trying to do something the German idealists had failed to do before. "To unite the world of power and the world of ideas under the leadership of ideas, this was and remained the higher intent of Treitscke's patriotism," argued Meinecke.[60]

At the core of all of Meinecke's writing was the dialectic between reality and morality. In 1907–8 he published his first magnum opus, *Weltbürgertum und Nationalstaat* (*Cosmopolitanism and the Nation-State*). This dealt with the development of German thinking on the subject of the state in the century before the foundation of the Reich in 1871. He approved of the increasing realism and departure from utopianism and idealism in German thought. Three "liberators"—Hegel, Ranke, and Bismarck—had led the charge. Meinecke was not unsympathetic to German idealism and romanticism associated with Immanuel Kant and Johann Wolfgang von Goethe. Yet he called humanitarianism "a poison which the body had to evacuate if it was to function naturally," and described Bismarck as the "doctor" who had seen to this.[61]

Meinecke came closer to the essence of real *Realpolitik* than Treitschke did and his work has strong echoes of Rochau.[62] He described how Germans of the mid-nineteenth century felt themselves internally divided and oppressed, but also weak and despised in the council of nations—"like Hamlet, a prey to the disproportion between intellectual overproduction and an inert will, uncertain whether the latter was due to the fault of others or of themselves." Even the great intellectual achievements of German idealism seemed in the middle of the century to be overtaken by decay. Produced in an era of purely intellectual effort, they had no answer for "the problems of modern existence, the constitutional struggles and the imminent economic rivalry of the classes."[63]

Meinecke also made extensive use of Edmund Burke. In Burke he saw the best defense of an organic conception of state development. In his opposition to the French Revolution in the 1790s, Burke struck the most effective blow against prevalent notions of natural law. He taught his readers a deeper respect and understanding for the irrational components of political life, for the power of tradition, customs, instinct, and impulsive feelings. Burke had not discovered these things himself but he had been the first thinker to truly understand their importance. In contrast to the rationalizing theoreticians of the French Revolution, they had been seen as a mere "pudendum."[64]

This idea—that the irrational components of politics were more than a pudendum (superfluous external genitalia)—was highly evocative. Like Rochau, Meinecke also used Burke's more elegant metaphor of the state as a great oak tree. According to Meinecke, Burke taught respect and even love for this "entire interwoven mass of natural and half-wild growth" that wound its way through the society and state, providing both a "snug cocoon" and a "hidden support." For Meinecke, too, as a religious man, there was something comforting in the idea that there was a hidden wisdom in the chaos of historical development.[65]

In making this case, Meinecke was providing a historical justification—or rationale—for the creation of the German Empire under Bismarck. It was his belief that the state which had been created was not artificial or imposed but was a product of the national will and had its roots in the past. Those who had excluded themselves from that process had therefore acted against the logic of *Realpolitik*. "They moralized from the outside instead of trying to understand the nature of the state from the inside," he argued, in a criticism that fitted perfectly with that offered by Rochau in both volumes of *Foundations of Realpolitik*.[66]

Meinecke's influence as a theorist of *Realpolitik* was to outlast the influence of Rochau and Treitschke too (despite the latter's anti-Semitism and adoption by Nazi propagandists). His later works are discussed in subsequent chapters. He had many students who went on to become world-renowned historians and international relations experts. These included Hajo Holborn and Felix Gilbert, who also taught some of the next generation of scholars and foreign policy practitioners in the United States.[67] It has been argued that many of the leading "realist" thinkers of the twentieth century—such as E. H. Carr, Hans Morgenthau, and Kenneth Waltz—"consciously or not built their structures on foundations he laid."[68] It is partly through the work of these thinkers that the changing meaning of *Realpolitik* is examined in subsequent chapters.

The Emergence of *Weltpolitik*

In the short term, use of the word *Realpolitik* became eclipsed by another word from the 1890s: *Weltpolitik*. Rather than the triumph of Bismarck, it was his fall from power in 1890, at the behest of Kaiser Wilhelm II, that marked a watershed in this regard. *Weltpolitik* was an aggregate ideology based on the vision of German imperial expansion beyond Europe—to give Germans a "place in the sun" by the acquisition of colonies. In essence, it was the expression of Germany's desire to be a world power, like Britain, and it was to drive it headlong into a clash of interests with the Anglo-Saxon nations and the French.

Like *Realpolitik, Weltpolitik* was, as one scholar later wrote, "one of those well-known but ill-defined catchwords with which the vocabulary of politics abounds." In the 1890s, in the post-Bismarck era, it began to proliferate among an influential group of journalists and advocates of economic imperialism. Within government, it was those officials who had helped engineer Bismarck's fall who put forward the most detailed expositions of *Weltpolitik*. By the First World War, it had become regularly used in the German Foreign Office, Colonial Office, and *Deutsche Bank*—and existed in the links between business interests and various strands of the bureaucracy. *Weltpolitik* was most obviously associated with the policies of Bernhard

The historian Friedrich Meinecke (1862–1954) offered an interpretation of
Realpolitik that was closer to Ludwig von Rochau's original than many others, but
he also succumbed to the anti-Semitism and chauvinism that Rochau rejected.
Federal Archives, Bild 183-H27525, o.Ang.

von Bülow, German foreign secretary from 1897 to 1900, and chancellor
from 1900 to 1909. Other prominent *Weltpolitikers* included Friedrich von
Holstein, the most influential figure at the Foreign Office in this period;
Paul Kayser, head of the new Colonial Department; and both Baron Adolf
von Marschall von Bieberstein and Alfred von Kiderlen-Wächter, who also
followed Bülow to the Foreign Office. [69]

One can overstate the significance of the emergence of *Weltpolitik*, just
as one can overstate the importance of *Realpolitik* after 1848. Those who
subscribed to it did not abandon all of the tenets of Bismarck's foreign policy, such as the balance of power and the approach to alliance making. Of
greater importance was the personal influence of the Kaiser. It was due

to this factor, above all, that *Weltpolitik* became an inconsistent guide to German behavior in foreign affairs. There were also other new ingredients in German foreign policy which were distinct from *Weltpolitik*—such as Social Darwinism and a growing emphasis on the importance of securing German *Lebensraum* ("living space") within Europe.[70] Yet those watching Germany from the outside did not necessarily see these tensions and complexities.

In making its entry on the world stage, Germany imposed itself on the consciousness of other nations, particularly those whom it identified as rivals. In trying to make sense of German foreign policy, observers of Germany looked to terms such as *Weltpolitik* as a possible explanation for, and predictor of, German behavior in the future. In discovering *Weltpolitik* in the 1890s—along with *Machtpolitik* (the politics of force)—they also encountered *Realpolitik* for the first time, even though a generation had passed since its creation. In the process of discovery, *Realpolitik* not only became conflated with *Weltpolitik*, but it also became associated with a list of other ills that were to play a role in the outbreak of European war in 1914. By that time, Ludwig von Rochau was long forgotten and *Realpolitik* had taken on a life of its own.

PART II

Anti-Realpolitik and the Anglo-American Worldview

"We Germans," a Berlin professor recently assured me, "write fat volumes about *Realpolitik* but understand it no better than babies in a nursery." "You Americans," he added, I thought enviously, "understand it far too well to talk about it."

(Walter Weyl, "American Policy and European Opinion," July 1916)[1]

5

The English Discovery
of *Realpolitik*

For the English, and to a lesser extent the Americans, *Realpolitik* was a disconcerting discovery. It was the distinguishing mark of a dangerous new rival but also, more broadly, it implied a menacing and uncivilized worldview—a new way of looking at politics and international affairs—which set itself against those prevalent among the English-speaking peoples. The early English-language history of *Realpolitik* coincided with the Anglo-German rivalry that began in earnest in the last decade of the nineteenth century and culminated in the First World War. As a consequence of this rivalry, the word began to seep into the English press from the mid-1890s, in discussions of German domestic and foreign policy. By the 1900s, it was peppered across a range of British newspapers, journals, and periodicals. In the early 1910s, as Germany began to challenge America in its own sphere of influence, discussions of German *Realpolitik* also began to find their way into the American press and academia. By 1914, it had even crept into the official parlance and diplomatic correspondence of a number of the leading states that went to war that year. Thus, it soon became a tangible phenomenon in international affairs—something recognized by practitioners and not merely theorists.

For many in the English-speaking world, *Realpolitik* was to be seen in an almost entirely negative light. It was usually interpreted as an outgrowth of Prussian militarism and German imperialism. By the time the notion arrived in Britain and America it had gone through many iterations in Germany already. As we have seen, the voice of Ludwig von Rochau had faded and it was Treitschke—the self-appointed inheritor of the term—who was known as its preeminent disciple. That the word had originally been used in discussions of domestic politics was soon forgotten. It was taken to imply dastardly conduct on the international stage, in diplomacy and war. In this interpretation, *Weltpolitik* and *Realpolitik* were two sides of the same coin and little was done to distinguish between them. Into the mix was thrown *Machtpolitik*, the politics of force, which denoted Germany's lurch to militarism. The capitalized and italicized forms of these words were used to underline the point that these were notions alien to Anglo-Saxon culture. Put simply, these were things that the Germans did.

At the same time, however, some influential voices cautioned their countrymen in England and America against adopting a simplistic view of *Realpolitik* as a uniquely German sin. Liberals, radicals, and socialists— such as the economist J. A. Hobson and Irish playwright George Bernard Shaw—rejected the idea that Germany was somehow more self-interested or dishonest in its foreign policy than the rest. Every leading power pursued its self-interest relentlessly, they pointed out. Indeed, this argument became central to the debate about who was to blame for the war—which was not just a matter for historians but also important in determining the terms of the peace that was to follow. Defenders of Germany, such as Friedrich Meinecke, decried the rank hypocrisy of its Anglo-Saxon and French opponents. In fact, there was an odd interchange between the ideas of Shaw and Meinecke (and, later, E. H. Carr) and, when it came to criticism of Anglo-Saxon imperialism, Hobson and Vladimir Lenin.

A search for the word in newspapers, periodicals, pamphlets, and official documents from the period provides a window onto a whole series of debates about the premise of the international system and the foundations of Western political thought before the First World War. The eclecticism and diversity of the views expressed warn against simplistic categorization of intellectual trends such as "realism" or "idealism."[1] Nonetheless it is possible to discern some broad themes in the early Anglo-American history of *Realpolitik*. First, before 1914, it was mostly seen as a symptom of "the German problem" in international affairs. Second, as the Allies approached victory, it was agreed that Germany's version of *Realpolitik* had failed on its own terms—that what it stood for was anything but realistic. Third, while it retained pejorative connotations in England, it did prompt a significant degree of soul-searching about Britain's approach to the world (and the question of empire). This was reflected in a desire to set international affairs on a more equitable footing after 1918. Tied to liberal internationalism in Britain and America, this fed into an emerging tradition described here as "anti-realpolitik." It is not italicized or capitalized because it is the author's own construct. What I take to be anti-realpolitik was a loose notion that was not simply directed against German foreign policy but designed as an antidote to the ills that existed in the international system as a whole.

Fourth, while many Americans objected to German *Realpolitik* on similar terms to those of the English, the word was also used in a positive sense in the United States. As Chapter 6 explains, America crafted its own version of "realpolitik" (first articulated by Walter Lippmann but derived from ideas put forward by Captain Alfred Thayer Mahan and Theodore Roosevelt). This manifestation of the word is also presented in its lower case and Roman form, because it was consciously distinct from the *Realpolitik* practiced by German and other "old world" diplomats. In fact, the American version had almost nothing to do with the original term and was based on what might be called an early version of "geopolitics," set in opposition to isolationism in the United States.

Bringing this all together, the liberal internationalist movement of the period, embodied in support for the League of Nations, grew out of a fusion of two trends. The first was the emerging tradition of anti-realpolitik in the English-speaking world. This held that international affairs could be placed on a surer footing, with multilateralism trumping the pursuit of narrow national interests. The second was America's alternative version of realpolitik, which was distinct from the German. This essentially indicated a willingness to play a leading role on the global stage. Hopes for a League of Nations depended on both operating at the same time but they were not as compatible as some had hoped. This is explained in Chapter 7 (the final one in Part II). The Anglo-American moment shone brightly for a moment but soon faded, as the coalition on which it was based fragmented after 1918—within both countries, and in the growing gap between them.

The Anglo-German Antagonism

The first time *Realpolitik* was used in an English-language publication was in the *London Illustrated Review* in 1872. It appeared in a review of Constantin Frantz's critique of Ludwig von Rochau and the National Liberals in Germany (discussed in Chapter 3). The reviewer noted, with regret, that Immanuel Kant, Germany's most respected international philosopher—who had spoken of perpetual peace among nations—had increasingly come under attack in his native country by the theoreticians of

Realpolitik. There was widespread admiration for German culture, philoso-phy, and Protestantism in England. It was the fact that unified Germany seemed to be drifting away from these cultural traditions—which stressed morality and aesthetism—that was the source of regret.[2] That the German professoriate and religious leaders seemed to be willing participants in this transformation was something that their counterparts in England could not quite comprehend.[3]

The marginalization of Kant, alongside the rejection of other romantic writers such as Johann Wolfgang von Goethe, was to become a recurrent motif in English discussions of German politics at the end of the nine-teenth century. Likewise, the renewed interest in the ideas of Machiavelli across Europe—the latest "Machiavellian moment"—was another cause for concern. England, supreme and self-confident, saw itself as a place apart—something reflected in its distaste for the neo-Machiavellianism in Germany and Italy.[4] In 1897, the English liberal politician and scholar Viscount John Morley warned that Machiavelli was "haunting men's minds; exciting, frightening, provoking, perplexing, like some unholy necromancer bewildering reason and conscience by paradox and riddle."[5]

There was no natural enmity for Germany in England. On the contrary, England had good relations with both Prussia and Austria that stretched back to the Napoleonic wars. There was nothing inevitable about the Anglo-German rivalry or the path toward war.[6] There were strong dynastic ties: Kaiser Wilhelm II was Queen Victoria's grandson. Still, as chancellor between 1871 and 1890, Otto von Bismarck had shown flashes of irritation at England, and particularly at his Liberal counterpart for much of this period, William Gladstone, who served as prime minister four times between 1868 and 1894. Hypocrisy was usually the allegation that Germans lobbed at Britain. After being condemned in the English press for his attack on Paris dur-ing the Franco-Prussian War, Bismarck complained about the humanitarian "*cant* of English public opinion." This was "a feeling which England expects other Powers to respect, though she does not always allow her opponents to have the benefit of it." Another source of grievance, which was to intensify in future years, was the perception that Britain deemed her naval suprem-acy to be almost a moral right, which others were not allowed to challenge.[7] Nevertheless, Bismarck had held back from confrontation with London. He had enough on his plate on the Continent. When it came to Germany's future strategy, Bismarck believed in a "natural alliance" with England.[8]

It was the fall of Bismarck that signaled the start of the slide into antagonism. Germany's conscious move toward *Weltpolitik* in foreign affairs increased the likelihood of a struggle between two European powers—one with a pre-existing empire and the other with global ambitions to have one of its own. It was not so much that German and British interests clashed, but the perception that they clashed that had a deleterious effect on relations. The fact that the social and political systems in both countries were constructed so differently added to the growing sense of distance. As Rochau had observed in the second volume of *Foundations of Realpolitik*, internal dynamics within states could have a radicalizing effect on a nation's foreign policy. As an example of this, Admiral von Tirpitz—the secretary of the German Imperial Navy—hyped up the Anglo-German rivalry in order to raise more money for his fleet. Treitschke died in 1896, but the extent of his popularity in Germany, along with his bitter denunciations of the British, only became well known in Britain after diplomatic relations worsened between the two countries.[9]

While the first English-language mention of *Realpolitik* had been in 1872, the second did not come until 1895, long after Bismarck's demise. The fact that the German government seemed to be taking an authoritarian turn underscored the growing distance between the two countries. In December 1895, the *Times* described a crackdown by the German police on the activities of the Social Democrat opposition, bemoaning the fact there were few survivors of a period when the old-fashioned idealism of the German character had not been superseded by what was now called *Realpolitik*. The "matter-of-fact realism" of the modern German Empire was having a corrosive effect on what was once "a nation of thinkers."[10]

The following month, January 1896, saw the first serious diplomatic incident between the two countries: the so-called Kruger telegram episode. This referred to a message sent by Germany's Kaiser Wilhelm II to Stephanus Johannes Paulus Kruger, president of the Transvaal Republic, which congratulated him on repelling a raid by a few hundred British irregulars from the Cape Colony in South Africa. Treitschke, of course, had specifically condemned British behavior in Transvaal as the epitome of British hypocrisy. Many in England took the Kruger telegram as deliberate interference in the British sphere of influence. There was an anti-German backlash in England, with the windows of German shops smashed in London.[11]

Despite the efforts of diplomats in both countries, tensions increased throughout the second half the 1890s. In January 1898, the British military attaché in Germany described having been subject to one of the Kaiser's tirades, "with which he has frequently favoured me, against British foreign policy". He claimed that for the previous eight years he had striven to be friendly with Great Britain to gain her alliance, "and to work hand in hand with her, but had failed." Britain, he suggested, would never have such an opportunity again because never would a grandson of the queen be heir to the German throne.[12] The Kaiser also claimed that during his last visit to England he had been attacked by the press so much that it was impossible for him to return there. Indeed, he believed that English newspaper reports on Germany "were far worse than anything even in the Chauvinist French press."[13]

Britain did explore the offer of a defensive alliance with Germany. Yet, its own growing suspicion of Germany led officials at the Foreign Office to conclude that it was not the best option. Not only was Germany hard to trust in the long run, but it was also increasingly unpopular among the other nations of Europe. Francis Bertie, assistant under-secretary at the Foreign Office, warned his colleagues to "remember the history of Prussia as regards alliances and the conduct of the Bismarck Government in making a treaty with Russia concerning and behind the back of Austria the ally of Germany." What was more, Germany was "in a dangerous situation in Europe . . . surrounded by Governments who distrust her and peoples who dislike or at all events do not like her." It was better for Britain to remain aloof rather than cast her lot in with an unreliable and unpredictable friend who seemed to bear her ill will.[14]

The Anglo-Boer War, which lasted from 1899 to 1902, was a source of further antagonism between the two nations. For Germans, British behavior in that war—which had seen them introduce mass concentration camps for the first time in history—was yet another example of Anglo-Saxon hypocrisy. In early 1902, the British Liberal Unionist politician Austin Chamberlain—who had heard Treitschke's lectures at the University of Berlin firsthand in the 1880s, with great alarm—caused a diplomatic storm with a speech in Edinburgh in which he replied to these criticisms by stating that the measures were less severe than those used by the Germans against the French in 1870. This speech provoked outrage in Germany and was condemned by Count von Bülow, German chancellor from 1900 to 1909, in a speech to the Reichstag.[15]

In 1902, it was feared that the death of Count Hatzfeldt, the level-headed German ambassador in London, would bring about a further alienation. The *Times* wondered whether Britain might have seen the last German ambassador who would lay stress on "considerations which do not specifically belong to the realm of diplomatic business, or, as the Germans say, *realpolitik*, in dealing with the political relations of the two countries."[16] Another visit to England by the kaiser in late 1902 was intended to soothe some of these tensions, but the verdict of *Die Zeit*, Germany's equivalent of the *Times*, suggested that the opportunity for rapprochement had passed. "*Realpolitik* and a policy of sentiment follow quite different ways," noted *Die Zeit*. In the long run, the former was the only policy that could be pursued by a great nation.[17] Anglo-German affinity had run its course.

Earth Hunger and Imperialism

Not everyone accepted the implication that *Realpolitik* was a uniquely German condition. In 1902, J. A. Hobson, who had reported on the Boer War for the *Manchester Guardian*, published *Imperialism: A Study* in which he argued that Germany's *Realpolitik* was just one symptom of a general gangrene in international relations. The scramble for Africa and Asia was a battle in which all the major powers were engaged. This had created "alliances which cut across all natural lines of sympathy and historical association," had led to unprecedented spending on military and naval armaments, and had even drawn the United States into the great game. Imperial ambitions fed into "a calculated, greedy type of Machiavellianism, entitled 'real-politik' in Germany, where it was made, which has remodelled the whole art of diplomacy and has erected national aggrandisement without pity or scruple as the conscious motive force of foreign policy."[18]

What Hobson called "earth hunger"—the scramble for markets and resources—had led to the repudiation of treaty obligations and a narrow focus on self-interest. The result was a gradual deterioration of behavior by all states in the international system. This was reflected in the "sliding scale of diplomatic language" and the prevalence of notions such as "hinterland, sphere of interest, sphere of influence, paramountcy, suzerainty, [and] protectorate." These were used to veil imperial ambitions and to rationalize the forcible seizure or annexation of land and the garrisoning of foreign ports.

While Germany and Russia were bolder in their "professed adoption of the material gain of their country as the sole criterion of public conduct," other nations had "not been slow to accept the standard." Hobson warned that there were perils in such behavior. Although the conduct of states in dealing with one another had always been determined by selfish and short-sighted considerations, things were getting worse. The conscious and deliberate adoption of these standards by all the major powers was "a retrograde step fraught with grave perils to the cause of civilisation."[19]

The challenge for Britain was not to build an empire but to preserve one. In getting to a position of such global power, so-called liberal imperialists such as Sidney Low—supporters of the Liberal Party who approved the maintenance of the British Empire but in a looser, more federal form, with greater self-government in the colonies—could make the case that Britain's methods arose out of self-interest, but that her liberal self-image acted as a check on imperialist excess. Low sought a middle ground between the arguments of historian Sir John Seeley—who famously claimed that the British Empire had been founded in "a fit of absence of mind"—and George Peel, who claimed that Britain had consciously, systematically, and forcefully defended its trade and liberties against aggressive rivals. In Low's measured view, Britain was "neither so good nor so bad" as it had been painted. British statesmen, as a general rule, first wanted to make England safe, and second, to make her prosperous and wealthy. This brought Britain into antagonism with any nation that seemed likely to threaten its maritime position or colonial possessions. But the primacy of self-interest had never been pursued in a particularly cultish way. "There was no such resolute concentration on *Realpolitik* as we should perhaps like to imagine," he wrote, beyond the vague idea "that we ought, somehow or other, to prevent anybody else from becoming very strong or very big." Added to this was the belief that if it was unable to play an effective role on the international stage, Britain would have abdicated its position as "a leading member of the international family," losing some of the prestige that a self-respecting nation ought to possess.[20]

The effects of modernization and industrialization raised the stakes of the game considerably. The dynastic period in international history was passing. Entire nations now mobilized themselves for international competition. The challenge from Germany and other nations contributed to a new debate about the British world role and how it was to be maintained, or systematized, to gird it for coming struggles. Late Victorian Britain had seen the emergence of a new idea of imperial governance—a "global state," loosely federated dominions in the image of Great Britain.[21]

The so-called "new" imperialism that emerged at the dawn of the Edwardian era (1901–10) reflected a further expansion of these ideas. One of the earliest books on British "Grand Strategy" described Edwardian imperialism as both a response to German *Realpolitik* and, following this, also a development of a new, anglicized realpolitik of its own. Led by Cecil Rhodes and Austin Chamberlain—whose memory of Treitschke's lectures never left him—calls for tariff reform and imperial federation were intended to toughen up the British imperial system. But the break away from free trade and the notion of an informal empire—one that was not systematized—was an explicit break with British strategy to that point and proved too much to stomach. Like German imperialists, the new British imperialists attempted to raise this cause to a higher ethical plain—by talking of the White Man's Burden, for example. But to many these efforts seemed rather contrived and too overtly self-interested. Ultimately, the new imperialists were to fail in their efforts to revolutionize the British system in anticipation of the coming threat from Germany.[22] Liberals and radicals feared that the new emphasis on robustness in the international arena would damage the domestic polity—that to follow the logic of *Realpolitik* was to open the door to the "Prussianisation" of the British state through centralization. In another pamphlet, *The German Panic*, published in 1913, Hobson accused the government of playing up the Anglo-German trade rivalry as part of a cynical attempt to divert money away from social reform projects in Britain.[23]

It was one thing to criticize British imperialism but another to fail to understand the nature and seriousness of the German challenge to Britain. In 1904, two years after Hobson published *Imperialism*, J. L. Garvin, the influential English journalist who went on to take over editorship of the *Observer*, produced a "psychological analysis" of the German official mind in the *Fortnightly Review*. Garvin was an admirer of German culture but he set out to "reveal a mechanism of wheels within wheels" in which the national interest was followed with an almost cultish devotion. Germany worked "exclusively upon a science of self-interest, more definitely methodized than in any other Foreign Office, and applied with more tenacious consistency." British cultural affinity for Germany had obscured the nature of the threat it posed. Radicals like Hobson had a tendency "to magnify the mote in our own eye, and to accept the assurances of our brother that there is none in his own." Impartiality was normally an asset, but the effort to be impartial became a snare when it led "to special pleading for an enemy or a competitor."[24]

Aptly, Garvin wrote under the pseudonym "Calchus," the Greek prophet of the Trojan War. Britain not only needed to wake up to German intentions, it had to counter them with a new realism of its own. It was a disaster to pursue a foreign policy "merely in the spirit of nebulous benevolence towards mankind." The Germans had bemused elements of British opinion by a "full-dress parade of a whole regiment of venerable platitudes" about their long-term intentions for peaceful coexistence, "all true in the abstract, all irrelevant to the concrete issue." Such language appealed "to the incorrigible idealism of man," and satisfied "his sense of symmetry," by suggesting that every nation was similar in its pursuit of interests. Yet, it was naïve to fall into this trap. The German scheme for a railway to connect Berlin and Baghdad, begun in 1903, provided irrefutable evidence of German pretensions to *Weltpolitik*.[25] Influential elements of the British Foreign Office also saw the move in this way. Indeed, it was in response to this threat that Britain and France signed the Entente Cordiale in April 1904. This saw Britain make a decisive break from its traditional position of non-alignment in European affairs, with long-term consequences.

Confronting Germany's *Realpolitik*

There were serious divisions within the British Foreign Office about how to deal with the German challenge in this period.[26] The most important document in outlining the parameters of the challenge was the "Memorandum on the Present State of British Relations with France and Germany," produced by Eyre Crowe, a senior official at the British Foreign Office, on 1 January 1907, for the foreign secretary Sir Edward Grey. Crowe offered the clearest exposition of the argument that the British world system—and worldview—was predicated on a fundamentally different premise than that of its German rival. This was not to say that Britain was necessarily more noble or benign in her pursuit of self-interest. Crucially, however, the nature of British power gave it a built-in advantage in that its interests were more inherently compatible with the interests of others.

This did not mean that Britain was without enemies, of course. The nature of British power—"with vast overseas colonies and dependencies" and as "the neighbour of every country accessible by sea"—would inevitably cause jealousy and resistance. For that very reason, however, it was in the self-interest of such a nation—one dependent on free commerce and global access—to "harmonize with the general desires and ideals common to all mankind" and to ensure that it was "closely identified with the primary and vital interests of a majority, or as many as possible, of the other nations." It followed, therefore, that Britain had a selfish interest in the maintenance of the independence of other nations—outside its own empire—and therefore must be the natural enemy of any country threatening the independence of others, and the "natural protector of the weaker communities." Belgium, invaded by Germany in 1914, was to fall into this category.

Second only to the ideal of independence was free trade. Most nations had "always cherished the right of free intercourse and trade in the world's markets." In proportion to the extent that England remained the champion of free trade, "she undoubtedly strengthens her hold on the interested friendship of other nations, at least to the extent of making them feel less apprehensive of naval supremacy in the hands of a free trade England than they would in the face of a predominant protectionist Power." Every nation, of course, would prefer to hold supremacy at sea. But, "this choice being excluded, it would rather see England hold that power than any other State." If this view of British policy was correct, Crowe argued, it followed that England must inevitably be driven to oppose any country threatening this equilibrium, aspiring to dictatorship over other nations, or disrupting free trade.

Like Garvin and many others in the English elite, Crowe had no instinctive enmity or dislike of Germany. Both his wife and his mother were German and he had spent many years in Germany as a diplomat. Nonetheless, he saw something in the recent history of the country that he believed was of great concern. With the events of 1871 the spirit of Prussia passed into the new Germany, and it was with "blood and iron" that Germany forged her position on the international stage. German aspirations to empire meant that it was inevitable that Germany would become a challenger to the status quo that had benefited Britain heretofore. No one who had knowledge of German political thought could deny that these were ideas "proclaimed on the housetops, and that inability to sympathise with them is regarded in Germany as the mark of the prejudiced foreigner." No modern German would plead guilty to a mere "lust of conquest." But "vague and undefined schemes of Teutonic expansion" were the expression of a deeply rooted feeling that Germany had "established for herself the right to assert the primacy of German national ideals."[27]

Other influential officials, such as Thomas Sanderson, argued for a more conciliatory approach to Germany. But it was Eyre Crowe's advice that ultimately held more sway.[28] Its impact was undoubtedly increased by the events of the second Hague Convention, which met shortly afterward, from June to October 1907. At the Convention, called by President Roosevelt, Germany rejected British suggestions for a limitation on armaments and compulsory arbitration in international disputes, eluding any attempt to box Germany into the status quo. In Britain, the outcome of the discussions confirmed the impression that Germany was the main obstacle to world peace. The *Times* alleged that the Germans had lulled Britain into a false sense of complacency as part of a deliberate strategy of dishonest diplomacy. "To close the eyes of those whom she had marked out for attack," it was claimed, had been the constant maxim of the *Realpolitik* that the rulers of Germany professed.[29]

Offering a unique perspective from within Germany, Count Osten-Sacken, Russian ambassador in Berlin, reported to his superiors that German behavior over the Hague Convention was part of a broader strategy to challenge British predominance from a position of heightened naval strength. "The theory of an armed peace is the basis of a German *Realpolitik*," he wrote in a secret memorandum, "and this principle Germany employs chiefly as regards to England."[30] The strategy was put to the test in June 1911 when Germany responded to French assertion of its claims on Morocco by deploying its gunboat, *Panther*, in the port of Agadir. Here was the theory put in practice. Tellingly, British Liberal Prime Minister Herbert Asquith described the incident as "an interesting illustration of *Realpolitik*" designed to test Britain's nerve and the strength of its commitment to its entente with France.[31]

Nothing spoke more to the extremes of Prussian militarism than the publication of *Germany and the Next War* by the veteran Prussian General Friedrich von Bernhardi in 1911. Bernhardi's bellicose book rejected international law and treaties as fallacious nonsense and described war as a "biological necessity." Attempts to abolish it through international arbitration were "poisonous" and "immoral." He announced that England was the greatest enemy of Germany, which could only be dealt with by force.[32]

Here one can see how the meaning of *Realpolitik* was to become increasingly confused with other dastardly practices that seemed to emanate from Prussia. Above all, English-language commentators took it to mean much the same as the old tradition of *Machtpolitik* (an approach to politics that emphasized the primacy of force and power). When Bernhardi's book was translated into English in 1912, it was no surprise that the English press protested against it as the epitome of the "full-blooded school of *Realpolitik*."[33] The translation also made a considerable impression in the United States. In 1912, the (Baltimore) *Sun* ran an article explaining the "Prussian Jingo" to its readers as an accompaniment to the book. This was an example of the "famous *Realpolitik* of the Prussian school," which asserted that Germany must win her "place in the sun" by defeating Britain.[34] In response to Bernhardi, the *Times* still expressed confidence that such extreme views could only gain a "passing influence over the German mind." Against Bernhardi, typically, the newspaper invoked Immanuel Kant's categorical imperative—that one should seek to act on the basis that your own behavior might be adopted as a canon by all good men. Such an approach, a "general conscience" in international relations, might allow nations to pursue their self-interest without recourse to war.[35] This was wishful thinking.

Realpolitik minus Bismarck

Even as Anglo-German antagonism became increasingly febrile, English opinion-formers retained some hope that this nobler tradition of German thinking would reassert itself. J. L. Garvin, now editor of the *Observer*, told a German magazine in 1912 that his bookshelves were full of the work of Goethe, Kant, Ranke, Sybel, and Mommsen but that they sat beside a growing number of reports about German naval armament and the work of Bernhardi and Treitschke. In early 1914, the year that war broke out, George Saunders, the Berlin correspondent of the *Times* who played a significant role in raising awareness of the German threat, wrote that it was "true that the Germans have been absurdly overbearing about their 'Kultur.'" But the attempt to make out that they were uncultured and uncivilized was "equally monstrous."[36]

When Treitschke's *Politics* was translated into English for the first time, in early 1914, Sir Edward Grey—the British foreign secretary—was horrified at its contents. It was a book in which "every ideal except that of force is abolished." But Grey also refused to believe that such beliefs were widespread among Treitschke's countrymen. The Germans were "more akin to ourselves than any other race," he said.[37] In fact, Treitschke was given a relatively sympathetic treatment by the Oxford University historian, H. W. C. Davis, in a study of his political thought that also appeared in 1914, before the outbreak of war in late July. Outside his own country, Davis noted, Treitschke was known "either as the most brilliant historian of the Prussian School, or a German Machiavelli, the most outspoken advocate of *Realpolitik* in the Bismarckian period." In Germany, he had a broader popularity as one of the "professor-prophets" who gave his countrymen the confidence necessary for the realization of national unity.

So did Treitschke really hate England, Davis asked? On the one hand, he wrote critically of utilitarianism and John Stewart Mill's *Essay on Liberty*. On the other hand, Treitschke showed a certain admiration for the representatives of the British national interest earlier in the nineteenth century—before Gladstone at least—for their forthright pursuit of the national interest. Wellington, Castlereagh, Canning, and Palmerston all had traits that were admirable—not least their willingness to see honor and value in the pursuit of national self-interest, rather than seeing these things as incompatible. It was the cant of late nineteenth-century "liberal imperialism"—the idea that the empire was a benevolent project based on a broad consensus—that had so enraged Treitschke. This was not too different from the British radical critique of empire. On closer inspection, then, Davis concluded that it was "surprising how much of humanism and of Liberalism" Treitschke had retained in his work.[38]

All was not lost in translation. Some English commentators were able to distinguish between extreme nationalism and genuine *Realpolitik*. Thus, according to the *Spectator*, the English conservative magazine, the problem with Germany was not the existence of *Realpolitik* but the fact that it was in increasingly short supply. It was the other tendencies in German political culture—militarism and aggression—that were the true danger. As an example, the *Spectator* cited the death of the most recent German ambassador to London, Baron Marschall von Bieberstein—sent to Britain just a few months before to turn around rapidly deteriorating Anglo-German relations—as another blow to diplomatic efforts to re-establish harmony. Bieberstein was described, not unfavorably, as "the most commanding representative of German *Realpolitik* since Bismarck" and a "most sagacious diplomatist."[39] Bismarck and his followers, the implication was, had not been that bad after all.

The *Spectator* was more concerned about what it called a "Byzantine Machiavellianism" emanating from Germany. Even as late as 1913, it was still hoped that those who subscribed to this school were numerically in the minority. But such sentiments became much more dangerous when they were not controlled by "such masters of political statecraft" as Bismarck. The risk was that the German nation, "imagining that there is some Bismarck behind the scenes," would "allow the men who usurp the forms without the substance of Bismarck's *Realpolitik* to have their way."[40] Bismarck, in other words, would have known when to end the game of brinkmanship. Germany's new generation were playing a high stakes game with no end in sight. In a similar vein, in August 1914, the month that England declared war, the *Saturday Review* described German policy as "blundering Machiavellianism." It was "the tyranny of Bismarckism, minus Bismarck's genius." This was an argument that Rochau himself may have recognized. With its "unbounded faith in *Realpolitik*, Germany had forgot the one thing that makes politics real"; it had forgotten the existence of patriotism in other nations, and the likely response that its behavior would engender in those nations that were on the receiving end. So confident in its own strength, it "trampled ruthlessly on this nation and that, scattering ultimatums like visiting cards, respecting no right or sentiment." In England, it was pointed out, there had been no inherent dislike of Germany—"only a curious lack of belief that Germany's intentions could be quite as bad as her manners." Indeed, the Germans had banked on the fact that so many Englishmen had claimed that Germany was misunderstood. But the threats against England and the ultimatum to Belgium proved too much. In the end, "no sane man could harbour illusions as to what the *Realpolitik* meant" in practice. Thus evaporated the "vague cosmopolitanism" associated with men such as Hobson, which had held that most of the major powers were as bad as each other.[41]

Rather than seeing him as the source of evil, then, some in Britain longed for Bismarck's return as the First World War began. In September, a month into the fighting, the editor of the *English Review* dated the war's origins back to the day when the Kaiser dismissed Bismarck in 1890 and proclaimed "full steam ahead." Within two decades, *Machtpolitik* (the politics of force), had become the state religion of the empire. Again, this was seen as "materialism, based on force, as opposed to the old Germanic ideal of Goethe."

German diplomats had played on English sentimentality about the "Old Fatherland of Kant and Goethe, of music and the professors, of Michael with his beer and sausage sandwiches." But the Kaiser's militarization of German society had had the effect of the "brutalisation of the finer feelings of humanity." The perversion of German politics and philosophy had not ended there. Not only Bismarck but even Treitschke had fallen into the Kaiser's disfavor at one point. Friedrich Nietzsche and his notions of "will to power" and life-affirming struggle had been popularized in German nationalist discourse. But even much of this, it was argued, was based on a misreading of Nietzsche's philosophy and a tendency to see only "ego-centric theories of life" in his writing. In reality, "the general attitude of the Germans has been moulded on the copybook of the drill sergeant." And the condition was not simply a Prussian one. Ultimately, even the Bavarians of southern Germany—despite their Catholicism and "aesthetic tastes"—had succumbed to the Prussian way of doing things.[42]

The implication of this argument was that German strategy was ultimately deluded and self-defeating. It spoke in cultish terms about the national interest, yet had become entangled with the highly idealized belief that Germany was destined to be a great imperial power. For some, Germany's greatest strategic flaw was its misunderstanding of the nature of empire. On these lines, a different critique of German statecraft was produced by the American scholar of ancient Rome, Tenney Frank. Frank was known for his theory that Rome's imperialism in the Middle East stemmed, above all, from a desire to keep peace by preventing the rise of a rival (*pax Romana*). The expansion of ancient Rome, Frank argued, had been justified both in terms of self-interest and ideology (undertaken in the name of the gods, in other words). The instinct for acquisition had disguised itself in religious language. Germany's nationalistic ambitions too, he suggested, juggled both this ideological and materialist justification. The difference was that German statesmen had failed to recognize the duality. Their behavior was often contradictory, therefore. "While the Kaiser spoke of 'manifest destiny', his chancellor was calling for *Realpolitik*, and both, working in perfect unison, were ready to assert that sentiment and individual ethics had no place in questions of national expansion," argued Frank. By contrast, the Roman senate matured enough to discuss each individual case on its own merits, and it could resist the temptation to devour the conquered "under the pretext of pleasing heaven." Unlike Germany, then, the Roman senate had avoided becoming "lost in the slough of *Realpolitik*." As Polybius had described, the Roman senate was sensitive "to the good opinion of the civilised world," a lesson that Germany had forgotten.[43] In other words, Germany's strategy was not Roman; it was inherently self-defeating.

Writing in 1914, Ramsay Muir, an academic at Manchester University and future Liberal member of Parliament (MP), also claimed to have identified a strategic blind spot in German *Realpolitik*. "The masters of *Realpolitik* pride themselves upon shutting out sentimentalism and looking only at brutal facts," he wrote in *Britain's Case against Germany*. In doing so, however, they had missed some less obvious but hugely important forces in political life. Honor was a political fact too. The "unconquerable soul of man" was a fact, though it could not be measured in centimeters like the barrel of a gun built by Krupp, the great German arms manufacturer. It was also a fact, missed by the Germans, that the passion and patriotism of a small and ruined country may burn even stronger than that in a powerful or superior state such as Germany. All these were things "which the Treitschkean realist forgets," causing him to make strange miscalculations. Above all, German strategists had failed to understand that the strength of the British Empire came from its ad hoc and informal nature. The hidden secret of the British global position escaped the German, for that secret was to be found in something "alien to German civilization. . . . The believers in *Realpolitik* concluded that the British Empire was an unreal thing because it lacked System." It was to be more resilient in the face of aggression, therefore, than the Germans had calculated.[44]

For Muir, Germany's behavior on the international stage could be explained by "a theory of international politics which has taken possession of the minds of the German people since the middle of the nineteenth century," in which brute force was the driving element. Set against this, however, was "a far nobler and saner view of the way in which international relations should be conducted." This alternative version of international politics had expressed itself in the development of the Concert of Europe, in the establishment of treaties for the protection of small states, in the growth of international arbitration, and "in the whole remarkable movement which culminated in the Hague conferences of 1899 and 1907." In Muir's reductionist view, therefore, the war was not simply a battle between nations but a conflict between "two conflicting views in regard to international relations." The German vision was based on the triumph of pure strength. Against this was "a rival doctrine, not quite so ancient, since it is only as old as civilization." It was the notion "that war is in itself a bad thing, which though it calls forth many great qualities, also destroys many fine and noble things; that it ought to be avoided as far as possible; that though it may be Utopian to hope to banish it wholly from the world, societies of rational men ought to be able to make it more and more rare."

This was both self-justificatory and one-sided, of course. Yet that should not disguise its importance. At the outset of the war, the Allies were laying claim to be fighting for a nobler vision of international relations. Aware of the German critique of English cant, Muir countered that the English vision, "which the adherents of its rival stigmatise as sentimentalism or hypocrisy, has made far more progress than most people realise." Muir went so far as to outline five steps for its fruition; the idea of a Concert of Powers striving for compromise; the establishment of a group of small states under the general protection of Europe; the spread of the practice of international arbitration; the restriction of armaments among the leading states; and the development of an agreed code on the conduct of warfare in those instances when it could not be averted. Much more influential and eloquent voices were to take these ideas forward later in the war and in its aftermath. Nonetheless, one can see the seeds of something more significant beginning to crystallize: a vision of international relations predicated on a response to, and a rejection of, anything resembling *Realpolitik*.[45]

The Prussian Wolf and the English Lamb

The allegation that Britain was both hypocritical and delusional about its world role was not so easy to wish away as Muir hoped. The Indian philosopher, Sarvepalli Radhakrishnan, a future president of India, stated that *Realpolitik*, which has for its principle, "It is good when I steal your cow, and bad when you steal my cow," had been the governing force of European relations for centuries. India had been on the receiving end. "Self-interest is the end; brute-force, the means; conscience is taboo," he explained, and war was the penalty that Europe paid for its steadfast loyalty to a false ideal.[46]

Even as the nation mobilized itself for war, influential figures within the British Isles rejected the idea that *Realpolitik*, militarism, and even Junkerism were uniquely German sins—or that the Allies stood for the force of light over the force of darkness. In an October 1914 special edition of the *Hibbert Journal*, Field Marshal Earl Roberts, former commander in chief of the British armed forces, had offered a forthright and detailed exposition

of Britain's war aims as a response to German aggression. It was a decision reluctantly reached but Britain had concluded that it could not stand
by while the treaty it had signed guaranteeing Belgian independence was
destroyed. Thus Roberts cast Britain as the reluctant defender of order,
legality, and democracy, pulled into a fight it had not sought.[47]

In a series of articles for the *New York Times*, Roberts's arguments were
subject to a searing critique by George Bernard Shaw, a radical opponent
of the war. They were the work of a man "who can see things from his
own side only." Roberts's justification for war, said Shaw, was full of the
"usual nonsense about Nietzsche" and disingenuous British pretensions to
the "white man's burden." One thing that particularly irked Shaw about
English criticism of Germany was the idea that Germany had not developed
into a real democracy and was somehow stunted in its political growth.
The English often pointed to the continued dominance of the Prussian
aristocracy—the Junker classes, to which Bismarck belonged. Was Britain
so different? Did aristocrats not also predominate in English politics? The
British Foreign Office was nothing if not a "Junker Club." As for the idea
that Germany's political and intellectual leaders had radicalized German
society in preparation for war, Britain had suffered from its own "Jingo
Fever"–reflected in the bestselling invasion novels, *The Battle of Dorking*
(1871) or H. G. Wells's *War of the Worlds* (1897).

In Shaw's view, Britain was cursed with a failure to understand its own
history—a fatal intellectual laziness, "an evil inheritance from the time
when our monopoly of coal and iron made it possible for us to become rich
and powerful without thinking or knowing how." But that laziness had
become dangerous now that the monopoly was under threat from rival
nations:

> We got rich by pursuing our own immediate advantage instinctively; that
> is, with a natural childish selfishness; and when any question of our justifica-
> tion arose, we found it easy to silence it with any sort of plausible twaddle
> (provided it flattered us, and did not imply any trouble or sacrifice) ... we
> became fatheaded, and not only lost intellectual consciousness of what we
> were doing and with it all power of objective self-criticism, but stacked up a
> number of pious phrases for ourselves which not only satisfied our corrupted
> and half-atrophied consciences, but gave us a sense that there is something
> extraordinarily ungentlemanly and politically dangerous in bringing these
> pious phrases to the test of conduct. We carried Luther's doctrine of justifica-
> tion by Faith to the inane point of believing that as long as a man says what
> we have agreed to accept as the right thing it does not matter in the least what

he actually does. In fact, we do not clearly see why a man need introduce the subject of morals at all, unless there is something questionable to be white-washed. The unprejudiced foreigner calls this hypocrisy: that is why we call him prejudiced.[48]

In the course of her rise to power, Germany had learned much from Britain. Indeed, Shaw made the point that General Bernhardi's plan for German military glory—which had caused such consternation in England as the epitome of Prussian aggression—was partly inspired by the prec-edent of British imperial power. The British "were his grate [sic] masters in Realpolitik. . . . It is we who have carried out the Bernhardi programme; it is Germany who has neglected it." The only difference between the German and the British position was that Germans were prepared to be honest about their aims, whereas the British were in a deluded stupor about how they had reached their position as a global superpower. General Bernhardi's sug-gestion that circumstances alter treaties was "not a page from Machiavelli" but a "platitude from the law books" in England. Thus, urged Shaw, "let us have no more nonsense about the Prussian Wolf and the British Lamb, the Prussian Machiavelli and the English Evangelist."[49]

While the British had argued that German statecraft was ultimately self-defeating, Shaw turned that logic on its head in his criticism of the foreign policy of Sir Edward Grey. Grey's failure to see how Britain was perceived—or to understand the true foundations of British power—had been responsible for the disastrous drift to war. This had led him to talk in a gentlemanly way and to refuse to speak of anything but peace. By compari-son, at least Winston Churchill (the former home secretary) had been clear in his understanding of foreign affairs—"a straightforward holder of the popular opinion that if you are threatened you should hit out unless you are afraid to." If Churchill had been a German, Shaw asked, what would the English liberal press have made of such militaristic tub-thumping? Grey was a "charming man," incapable of telling a German "he intends to have him shot." But he had fallen between two stools. He "could not admit he was going to fight and, disastrously, persuaded Germany of the same."[50] Shaw's interpretation of the weakness of Grey's position is an eerie forerun-ner of debates about appeasement in the 1930s.

Shaw's critique did not go unnoticed in Germany. Friedrich Meinecke welcomed his "refreshing truthfulness" in highlighting the "brutal egotism and pharisaical superiority" of Britain. Like the majority of German pro-fessors and historians, Meinecke had become swept up in initial enthusiasm for the war.[51] He was conscious of the allegation that German politicians and academics—including historians like himself—had become "prey to a cult of power." It was true that Germany was pursuing a self-interested and assertive foreign policy. But so was every other major actor in the European scene. The difference was that Germany was not in a state of delusion about this reality. "Today we are one and all, friend and foe, pursuing a vigorous egotistic policy of imperialism," he wrote, "but the instinctive concealment of the uncompromising reality under sentimental illusions and dreams is stronger among our enemies than in our own midst." The English, as ever, were spouting "veritable cant." But the French were also guilty, in Meinecke's view, of accumulating a "wealth of high-sounding phrases which envelop every act of their imperialistic policy with a blinding aureole of culture and civilization." What the Western nations denounced as German mendacity was, in reality, brutal honesty: a form of "austere truthfulness, which pierces through every veil to the heart of things and scorns to parade itself in phrases."[52]

Meinecke was not the only German to make this case. At the outset of the war, the graphic artist Lewis Oppenheim produced a propaganda poster for the German government that addressed the notion that Germany was the nation of "barbarians." It included a table of figures showing that Germany spent twenty times as much as Britain on social support and three times more on schools, published four times as many books, put out six times more industrial patents, and had four times more Nobel Prize winners. Another poster, asking "who is the militarist?" noted that Britain had fought three times as many wars as Prussia since 1700 and was currently spending 50 percent more than Germany on armaments.[53]

Meinecke pinpointed a pamphlet written by a group of Oxford University professors in 1914, entitled *Why We Are at War*, as a typical example of English self-delusion. The book contained one chapter denouncing Treitschke and another proclaiming that the war was about a clash of two principles: raison d'état and rule of law. It was typical of the English to present their own policy as "a piece of furniture without veneer, as the massive wood of absolute legality and fidelity to treaties." As Meinecke put it, in a memorable phrase: "Their idea was that the new German theory said, 'Our interest is our right,' whereas the old, very old English theory was: 'Right is our interest.' "[54]

The will to power was not a German aberration of the twentieth century, so the argument went. It was an irreducible historical fact in the conduct of international affairs. Speaking at Freiburg in August 1914, Meinecke elaborated on this point, implying that Germany's behavior was nothing out of the ordinary. Every nation succumbed to "national egotism," a sense of destiny and self-assertion over circumstances.[55] Nonetheless, in making this case, Meinecke did offer some important qualifications. He warned against both over-exertion and overweening pride in foreign policy. He noted that Bismarck "observed a sharp distinction between a policy of national interest and one of national prestige, and even such a tolerant and broad-minded historian as Ranke managed to distinguish with accuracy the point at which a healthy, organic imperialism ended and a feverish over-exertion commenced."[56]

In other words, despite his own support for German imperialism, Meinecke was suspicious of the "radical and arrogant nationalism" he saw brewing in certain groups in Germany society—from entrepreneurs to army officers. Notwithstanding his own anti-Semitism and anti-Slavism, he complained about the notion of a German "master-race," "caste arrogance," and the "vulgar exploitation" of the ideas of Charles Darwin, Friedrich Nietzsche, and the racial theorist Arthur de Gobineau, who had popularized the idea of an Aryan master race. If Germany was to aspire to a global role, it must exhibit a less chauvinistic attitude to other peoples. Such "hard-hearted and loud-mouthed impetuousness discredits us not less than the parvenu attitude of the half-educated."[57] True *Realpolitik* understood that egotism and fanaticism could blind. But as with Rochau before him, these qualifications were difficult to maintain against the backdrop of the death of sixteen million people in the course of four years of war.

6

American Realpolitik

Of all the great powers, America was the last to discover *Realpolitik*. If Britain regarded itself as aloof from the naked Machiavellianism of Germany and other continental powers, the United States was farther away still, in ideological and geographical terms. While Germany's imperial ambitions were to be condemned, Americans were dubious about British pretensions to practice a superior, liberal model of imperialism. There was a certain irony in this. When Rudyard Kipling had written his famous poem about the "White Man's Burden" in 1899 he was actually addressing US colonization in the Philippines. Yet, for the most part, America saw itself as an anti-colonial power. Its sense of exceptionalism crystallized in an atmosphere of relative security from the zero sum survivalism that characterized European power politics.[1] Quite simply, the self-image of the United States was such that it had no desire to engage in such dastardly games.

It was in the period from 1900 to 1914 that America might be said to have awoken to the *Realpolitik* that was causing such a stir in Europe. Yet America's discovery of the notion was distinct from England's in a number of ways. First, Americans saw reason to be suspicious of all the major European powers, and Britain—for all its claims to hold itself to a higher standard—was certainly not exempt from the ways of "old world" diplomacy. Before American intervention in the First World War, British condemnations of Germany were treated with an element of skepticism. Second, partly as a consequence of this, from the moment it began to seep into the American public sphere in the 1910s, *Realpolitik* never had quite the same negative connotations as it did on the other side of the Atlantic. When America did eventually enter the war, the excesses of Prussianism became a discussion point and German *Realpolitik* was subject to a number of scathing critiques. Longer-term, however, the word more easily escaped these pejorative associations.

In this era, a small but influential portion of Americans began to articulate a new approach to international affairs. In arguing that the United States needed to engage with the rest of the world—in a more front-footed and assertive manner—there emerged what might be described as a new "realism" in American foreign policy debates, embodied by influential strategists such as Theodore Roosevelt and Captain Alfred Thayer Mahan. Building on both, it was the journalist, Walter Lippman, who was the first to urge his countrymen to adopt "a little realpolitik" in their own foreign policy. Thus was born an American version of realpolitik (lower-case and de-italicized). From its inception, this was clearly distinct from that associated with Germany. At the most basic level, what Lippman called realpolitik was in fact closer to what was later known as geopolitics. The Lippman version of realpolitik in fact owed more to traditional British than German ideas of strategy. It held that America had a broader interest in the stability of the international system and that the country must shape the world before the world imposed itself on America. It was, in essence, a form of robust internationalism, and it was to have a long legacy over the course of the twentieth century.

The White Man's Boredom

It was in this era that the United States established itself as a serious rival to the other superpowers on the international scene. This came about because of the convergence of a number of trends. Most important was the exponential growth in population and wealth that had occurred over the previous century. An ever-expanding trade empire led to ever-increasing expansionism and interference in Central and South America. In protecting its merchants and trading arrangements—and, by extension, gaining an interest in the stability and good governance of its neighbors—America began to project its power more ruthlessly to its immediate south.[2]

The Spanish–American War of 1898 has been seen as a watershed in American foreign policy, though the expansionist instinct went back further still. It would be a mistake to think that America was rebelling against its own isolationist past.[3] To extend its influence further and expand its trading empire across the Atlantic and Pacific Oceans, the prerequisite was for America to build a world-class navy. From the 1890s, the importance of sea power found an increasing number of advocates. The most influential naval strategist was Captain Alfred Thayer Mahan. Before 1900, however, it could be argued that Mahan had more influence outside his native country. He was courted in England, France, and Germany, and was read avidly in Japan. In London, he dined with the queen, prime minister, and first lord of the Admiralty in 1894, and was given honorary degrees in Oxford and Cambridge. In Germany, Admiral von Tirpitz was so impressed by Mahan's book, *The Influence of Sea Power upon History*, that he made it an official textbook for the German Navy and recommended it to the kaiser.[4] "I am just now not reading but devouring Captain Mahan's book and am trying to learn it by heart," said the kaiser. "It is a first class book and classical in all points. It is on board all my ships and constantly quoted by my Captains and officers." When he heard that Mahan would be one of the US delegates at the 1899 Hague Convention, he also described him as Germany's "greatest and most dangerous foe."[5]

Mahan was a critic of American isolationism, which he believed was implausible as a future strategy for the United States. Yet Mahan also knew that any successful foreign policy had to be based on a broad level of popular support, particularly in the United States, the most democratic of all the major powers. As he explained, in a passage with echoes of Rochau: "The sentiment of a people is the most energetic element in national action. Even when material interests are the original exciting cause, it is sentiment to which they give rise, the moral tone which emotion makes, that constitutes the greater force. Whatever individual rulers may do, masses of men are aroused to effective action—other than spasmodic—only by the sense of wrong done, or right to be vindicated."[6]

For Mahan, the defining feature of international politics was not ideological conflict but the struggle for power. Self-interest was an adequate motive in foreign policy. That said, Mahan believed that the two great Anglo-Saxon nations had something different to offer than other imperialist nations—an idea that had been picked up by Eyre Crowe in 1907. A global system based on a desire for trade with, rather than subjugation of, other peoples was more benign. Mahan was aware that this was a highly self-serving plea for Britons and Americans to make. But he did not see a fundamental problem with this. He famously remarked that "if a plea of the world's welfare seem suspiciously like a cloak for national self-interest, let the latter be accepted frankly as the adequate motive which it assuredly is."[7] Meinecke and Shaw would have at least applauded his honesty.

Mahan was not the only advocate of the argument that the United States must take a more active and assertive role beyond its immediate neighborhood. The most important was Theodore Roosevelt, president from 1901 to 1909. It was under Roosevelt that America had begun to enter the "great game," using some of the tactics that Mahan had described: flexing its muscles in securing the Panama Canal Zone in 1903; adding the "Roosevelt corollary" to the Monroe Doctrine in 1904 (which announced that the United States would intervene in conflicts between European and Latin American states); mediating in the Russo-Japanese War in 1905; and dispatching the "Great White Fleet" on a circumnavigation of the globe in 1907. While Roosevelt's policies—including his guiding mantra to "speak softly and carry a big stick"—still provoked a lot of domestic political opposition, they signaled America's growing ambitions.[8]

What Henry Kissinger later called "Rooseveltian grand strategy" was to transform American foreign policy forever, though this was not immediately obvious—partly because Roosevelt's views were not widely shared by his countrymen.[9] Just as German foreign policy had suffered from the loss of Bismarck, it was generally agreed that Roosevelt's successor from 1909 to 1913, William Howard Taft, was not so apt in these arts. In 1909, the *Spectator* magazine in England claimed that Taft's professed goal of achieving an "Open Door Policy" in China—in addition to an expanding role in South America—was reminiscent of "the Germanic method" of defining a nation's grand strategy. The similarities were only skin deep, however. German policy could be aptly described as *Realpolitik*, claimed the *Spectator*, in the sense that it seldom undertook anything without possessing the actual or potential means of accomplishing it. Taft's new policy, by contrast, was "unreal" because the United States did not have the power to enforce its new ambitions in the East in the way that it had recently done in protecting American investments in South America.[10]

In 1911, the British writer Sydney Brooks—whose writings often appeared in *Harper's Magazine*—expanded on the same theme in an essay on American foreign policy, asking whether America's approach to the Far East belonged "to the sphere of *Realpolitik*" or whether it should be described as diplomacy by bluff. Foreign policy, Brooks argued, to be effective beyond a certain range, rested on at least the implication of force. America had yet to understand that the other major powers in global affairs were engaged in a battle for survival. Alone among the great powers, it had a relatively secure position in its near-impenetrability from foreign invasion.

Europeans lived in a "powder magazine," whereas Americans "live in an atmosphere of extra-ordinary simplicity, spaciousness, and self-absorption, until from very boredom they are forced to make international mountains out of molehills, a diversion which by itself is proof enough of their unique impunity from the serious realities of *Weltpolitik*."[11]

Foreign policy was a second order in American politics. Brooks claimed that he could not recall a single well-informed debate in Congress about international affairs and that the American public was inclined toward isolationism. In his view, however, this was untenable in the long run. America was destined to be drawn into conflicts in Europe and the Far East. The United States' trading network had expanded so quickly that Americans were in for a rude awakening. Following expansion into Cuba and the Philippines, Americans had strewn the Pacific with stepping stones from Hawaii to Manila, just as the British had done in the Mediterranean.[12] Still, Brooks argued that the implications of America's accidental empire had yet to be grasped by Americans. They had an empire but had "not yet become Imperial" and were still beholden to the "precepts of an outworn past." They had fresh points of trading and diplomatic contact multiplying throughout the world but were still reluctant to abandon the "international aloofness" of the nineteenth century. "The white man's burden, so far as Americans are concerned, has become the white man's boredom," he joked.

There were signs, nonetheless, that the United States was awakening to these broader realities. Brooks cited two recently published books, written by Americans, that he saw as a welcome antidote to this naiveté. One was by Archibald Coolidge of Harvard, *The United States as a World Power*, published in 1908, and the second by Alfred Mahan, *The Interest of America in International Conditions*, published in 1910. Both tried to rouse Americans to a more accurate appreciation of the world in which they live. Both were attempts to remedy the greatest weakness in America's "international equipment"—the absence of a sober, sustained, and well-informed interest in foreign affairs among the American people. Both, reassuringly, had a spirit of cordiality toward Britain.[13] It was ironic that Brooks was later on board the SS *Tusciana*, a luxury liner carrying American troops to Europe, when it was struck by a torpedo from a German U-boat in 1918.

The assumption that Americans were ill prepared for the international game was, in truth, based on a rather shallow reading of American strategic culture. The rise to power of Germany, and the nature of *Weltpolitik*, did not go unnoticed in the United States. In 1907, the year of the Hague Convention, Amos Hershey, an American political science professor who had completed his PhD in Heidelberg—spoke of a "full-grown, united warrior-nation born in the midst of smoke and battle." He explained to his countrymen that German irredentism had its roots in the politics of *Realpolitik*. Those cognizant of the "Machiavellian principles (*Realpolitik*) practiced since Bismarck's day gave little credence to denials from Berlin about its true intentions."[14]

As in Britain, General Bernhardi's book, *Germany and the Next War*, also created a literary sensation in the United States when it was translated into English in 1914. It was sold as a cheap paperback edition in newspaper stands and hotel lobbies. The more alarming passages contained in the work of Nietzsche and Treitschke were also popularized in the press, alongside accounts of the massive drive for German naval armaments. As in Britain, scenarios of foreign invasion provided the fodder for a growing number of plays, novels, and even movies (such as the 1915 silent movie *The Battle Cry for Peace*, based on the bestselling novel, *Defenseless America*, by Hudson Maxim).[15]

In newspapers and periodicals, then, the nature of the discussion of German *Realpolitik* bore some similarities to what was going on in England at the same time. There was one significant difference, however. It was that a uniquely American version of realpolitik began to take shape. This, in turn, became a weapon in the debate between isolationists and pacifists and those who preferred something resembling the Mahan-Roosevelt approach to foreign affairs. The first sign of this was that Americans were willing to use the word in more favorable terms than most Britons. For example, in a discussion of the career of the former Ambassador to Britain, John Hay, the *New York Tribune* argued that his career—part of which had also been spent in China—proved that "the ideals for which this country stands in international relations may be the most enduringly successful Realpolitik as well."[16] In 1916, the *Chicago Daily Tribune* argued that it was "not shadowy" to be governed by self-interest. European principles may offend America's "sense of moral right," but if America rejected *Realpolitik* out of hand, it would be left with nothing but "a record of devotion to altruistic principles."[17]

As president from 1913, Woodrow Wilson's first goal was to keep the United States out of the European conflict. In some sections of the Republican press, the president was mocked as a pacifist with a naïve belief that the spread of virtue and prosperity could shape the international arena in lieu of force. In November 1915, the *New York Tribune* published a satire on Wilson's negotiations with the German ambassador in Washington, DC. It depicted Wilson sitting in the presidential office alongside his private secretary, Joseph Patrick Tumulty, and foreign policy advisor, Colonel Edward House. Before them, the German ambassador Bernstorff boasted of his *Realpolitik* and threatened to bomb the White House while telling the president that he had goodwill toward him.[18] The implication of this satire, two years before America entered the war, was that Germany was a direct threat to the United States. Before long, partly through the auspices of the League to Enforce Peace (a forerunner to the League of Nations), Wilson began to come to the same conclusion: that Americans were "participants, like it or not, in the life of the world." Liberal internationalism, he also came to realize, may require force behind it. One correspondent to the *New York Tribune* in 1916 took this as evidence that American statesmen were "converting a dream to Real-politik."[19]

In England, meanwhile, the *Spectator* described, with some relish, how America had now awakened to the true nature of German foreign policy following an outbreak of submarine activity on its coast in October 1916. Germany, "as they say in Texas, has taken the bridle off." America was finally asking the question that Britain had been posing for the previous decade: "What is Germany's game?" The answer was the one that readers of the English press were by now familiar with. The Germans were pursuing a policy of *Realpolitik* "wholly uninfluenced by moral considerations, or even by the thought of the public opinion of the world." Germany had a new card, the submarine, "therefore she will play it." The *Spectator* criticized what it saw as American equivocation about who had been the true aggressors at the start of the war. Until now, some had held "the conventional view that there were faults on both sides and merits on both sides." Nonetheless, Roosevelt and a number of the "best men" in America had understood the nature of the threat, and events had proved them right.[20]

The British government watched these debates closely. In the autumn of 1916, the British Foreign Office submitted a memorandum to prime minister Herbert Asquith, which raised the prospect of forming a League of Nations—following some of the recommendations of the League to Enforce Peace—but recognized that the United States would have to be centrally involved if it was ever to be effective. There were encouraging signs from America that "the more thinking people there are awakening to the fact that in the modern condition of things America can no longer cling to her position of splendid isolation."[21]

The First World War and the Birth of American Realpolitik

Before entering the war in 1917, America had begun to familiarize itself with the black arts of European statecraft. The first step in doing so was to understand how it was perceived by others. As Robert Osgood later described, "there existed during the long prelude to intervention a significant challenge to America's traditional attitude toward national security." A "new realism," which built on Roosevelt and Mahan—but took their ideas further—began to develop as the war raged in Europe.[22] The key intellectual protagonists behind it were a group of three young editors at the *New Republic*: Walter Weyl, Herbert Croly, and Walter Lippmann.

Walter Weyl had traveled throughout Germany and was well read in German writing about statecraft. From this experience, Weyl concluded that America's best policy in Europe was to present itself as the champion of "international law and morality." America had the advantage that it was comparatively free from the historical enmities that divided Europe. However, as the United States embarked on a program of re-armament, it had to be aware that European states watched its moves with interest and suspicion. Despite the fact that America disclaimed any selfish aims in Europe, it was not to be expected that "the astute gentlemen who conduct European foreign affairs will construe our motives with excessive charity or interpret our diplomacy in terms of our own history and primers." Europeans thought of US political leaders as "concrete, prescient, and ruthless, if heavy-handed statesmen." They pointed to American aggression toward Spain, Mexico, and Colombia, and to promises broken and treaties flouted, as well as the ease of American territorial expansion. "They ascribe to us more foresight than we possess, not realizing how often we have happily blundered into success, how often we have pursued *Realpolitik* in our sleep," Weyl wrote.

To illustrate the point, Weyl recounted a conversation he had had with a German academic about America's position, on a visit to Berlin: " 'We Germans,' a Berlin professor recently assured me, 'write fat volumes about *Realpolitik* but understand it no better than babies in a nursery; you Americans,' he added, I thought enviously, 'understand it far too well to talk about it.'" For that reason, Weyl argued that defensive armaments alone would not protect America. In fact, by alerting its enemies but not having a strategy of its own, it was courting disaster. America would be safer if the world had a clearer indication of its strategy and its goals. The fluidity of the international arena necessitated a willingness to shape it in one's own image, or be taken advantage of. Peace could not be secured by "embalming the world." You could not halt the rise and fall of nations like you could stop a watch. Some nations would grow faster than others. Trade routes would change, as would the techniques of production, patterns of consumption, and the source of supply of raw materials. This would require new demands and new alignments. Boldness was sometimes the safest course.[23]

Although Weyl was the first to use the term, it was his fellow *New Republic* editor, Walter Lippmann, who was to popularize realpolitik for an American audience. Lippmann, who left Harvard in 1910, later described how it was no longer possible "for an American in those days to be totally unconscious of the world he lives in" in that era. This explained something about his own intellectual journey. Just a few days after the assassination of Archduke Franz Ferdinand in June 1914, the event that triggered the war, he had set sail for Europe. On arriving in England, he spent a month in a summer school run by British socialists—among them George Bernard Shaw. Shaw's denunciation of British hypocrisy appeared in the *New York Times* the same month that Lippmann attended his lectures. It seems likely, then, that Lippmann took the word from Shaw, though he used it to very different ends.

In the last week of July 1914, Lippmann traveled to Belgium. He had planned to spend the summer walking across Germany, only for the border to be closed on the eve of Germany's invasion. Lippmann rushed back to London and was actually in the House of Commons lobby on 4 August 1914 when Britain declared war on Germany. For two years after that point, in common with the third *New Republic* editor, Herbert Croly, he "struggled with misgiving and reluctance to grasp our interest in the war." He later chided himself for not making a stand against the folly of the Washington Disarmament Conference and by 1917 had become convinced that America needed to enter the war.[24] Before long, Lippmann, two years short of his thirtieth birthday, was sought out and appointed by Wilson's

Secretary of War Newton Baker to "The Inquiry" to study possible ways to peace.[25]

As early as 1915, Lippmann had begun to build his case for America's entry into the theater of conflict, with the publication of *Stakes of Diplomacy*. He began by invoking Captain Mahan. Having sat at the feet of Bernard Shaw, too, Lippmann was far from sentimental about the nature of British war aims. To say that Great Britain was fighting for the small nations of the Continent was nothing but "the talk of English liberals who make a pious wish father to a pious thought." For our story, what was most significant about *Stakes of Diplomacy* was that Lippmann invoked the word realpolitik as a corrective to naiveté, isolationism, and pacifism. In a chapter called "A Little Realpolitik," he made the argument that peace could be secured if the great powers agreed to a humane and stable legal and administrative framework for governing unstable areas of the world. He derided pacifism and "peace-at-any-price propaganda" as entailing not the abandonment of force but its concentration in the least democratic empires. He also raised the prospect of "some coalition of the west" to secure international order in the future, on the grounds that liberal democracies tended not to go to war with each other. In an argument reminiscent of Eyre Crowe, he linked Western security to the stabilization of "backward countries," freeing up foreign trade. World commerce was inextricably tied to "progressive government."[26]

Seen another way, this was a case for robust internationalism. Yet, while a new era of international cooperation would be the long-term goal, the immediate situation required the United States to get its hands dirty. "If we are to grapple with the issues which distract the world, we have got to enter the theaters of trouble," Lippmann wrote. Investment and trade creation in backward countries would add weight to American diplomacy. But to be really effective, US foreign policy would "have to be weighted with armaments of sufficient power to make it heard by the Great Powers." Moreover, Americans would have to abandon their traditional dislike of European alliances. The country would have to work with those powers whose interests, and approach to politics, were closest to its own. The prospect of America embarking on a global policy of its own was not one that Lippmann took lightly. He knew that it was likely to provoke serious opposition. Indeed, he spoke of his own discomfort about the prospect. Ultimately, however, there was no viable alternative:

This is, I realize, a terrifying programme to most Americans. It terrifies me, and disturbs every prejudice of my training. We have all of us been educated to isolation, and we love the irresponsibility of it. But that isolation must be abandoned if we are to do anything effective for internationalism. Of course, if we wish to let the world go hang, we may be able to defend our coasts, and establish a kind of hermit security for ourselves. But even that security will be precarious in a world arranged as this one has come to be. Less and less is it possible to remain neutral, to stay out of the conflicts. Without the slightest intention of taking part in the great war we have several times almost been dragged into it. And though we may have escaped fighting, we have suffered tremendously because the dislocation of the globe affects all its parts.

Isolationism had become untenable, and America's only choice was between being the "passive victim of international disorder and resolving to be an active leader in ending it." There were costs in abandoning isolation, of course. But one thing was certain: America would be safer by surrendering it deliberately than by allowing itself to be dragged unprepared and surprised into the mêlée of the nations.[27]

It has been argued that the activist disposition of intellectuals like Lippmann undermined the tradition of pragmatic realism and anti-imperialism in American foreign policy. According to T. J. Jackson Lears, Croly, Weyl, and Lippmann "spoke a language pruned of hypermasculine excess, rhetorically pragmatic and tough-minded but as wedded to lofty purpose as ever." This "lofty purpose" was to use US intervention as a way to accomplish Wilson's larger goal to remake the world on the American model. The editors of the *New Republic* were particularly fond of arguing that the United States had yet to reach consciousness about the fact it had all the traits of an empire. For critics of American interventionism over the next hundred years, it has been argued that this "pattern of realistic rhetoric and unrealistic aims continued to characterize arguments for military intervention for decades to come."[28]

Many Americans were deeply uneasy about the implications of these new arguments, as Lippmann had predicted. Significantly, however, they did not reject to Lippmann use of "realpolitik" so much as his attempt to monopolise it. There were other visions for American strategy that did not depend on becoming embroiled in European affairs. This was the counter-argument put by Raymond Mussey, a professor at Columbia University, in New York at a May 1917 address to the National Conference on Foreign Relations of the United States. Mussey celebrated what he saw as

Walter Lippmann (1889–1974) was one of the most influential American journalists of the twentieth century. As an editor of the the *New Republic* at the time of the First World War, he introduced the notion of *Realpolitik* to an American audience and continued to have an important influence on foreign policy debates through the Cold War era. Library of Congress, Prints & Photographs Division, LC-H25-247207-T.

the tradition of "right-minded American diplomacy," which he contrasted with that of the old world. America's future was in the East. Improved relations with China and Japan would be sufficient to secure American interests in the Pacific region going forward. Thus Mussey drew a distinction between "old narrow" *Realpolitik*, which was to be found in Europe, and a "new broad" realpolitik, which he urged his country to adopt. "The failure of the old narrow *Realpolitik*, that saw but a part of the realities, is being written today in letters of blood on the battlefields of Europe," he wrote.

The Lippman vision for foreign policy promised more of the old. By forging new friendships in the Far East, America could create a new lifeline: a "rainbow arch" across the Pacific, based on mutual respect.[29] In just a few months, this dream was to be in tatters. It was into the dark heart of Europe that America was plunged.

Lessons from Germany's Collapse: The Failings of the Old *Realpolitik*

By 1917 Germany's stuttering war effort suggested that the country most beholden to the old version of *Realpolitik* had been rudely awakened to its limitations. To many in the United States, the failings seemed so obvious that they were a source of bemusement. The first and greatest misstep made by the Germans had been to make a mortal enemy of Britain, just before it went to war with France and Russia. Britain was deeply ambiguous about the necessity of intervening in the conflict on the European mainland. By violating Belgian sovereignty so flagrantly, however, the Germans had violated the terms of Britain's treaty commitment to preserving Belgian independence, and left it little choice.

To outside observers, such as the American historian Bernadotte E. Schmitt, writing in the *Nation* on 29 August 1914, it was extremely counter-productive to force one's enemies to join forces against you. "The *Realpolitik* so dear to German hearts, should have counselled moderation," he wrote. Yet even Germany's former chancellor, Prince von Bülow, had admitted that Germans did not understand the fine art of politics.[30] Tellingly, in the postwar period Schmitt campaigned against the opening up of diplomacy to greater public scrutiny—one of Woodrow Wilson's causes. Europe's drift to war in 1914 provided enough evidence of how public opinion could be "whipped up by governments" until it "assumed something of the shape of Frankenstein."[31]

The second catastrophic error was Germany's disastrous reading of American politics. Looking back at this period in the 1930s, the American historian Robert Binkley observed that "when the spirit of *Realpolitik* had once become a dogma of a foreign office, diplomats became incapable of understanding that any other spirit could exist." The example Binkley gave was an incident early in the war 1915 when William Martin, a Swiss journalist, visited

German foreign secretary Arthur Zimmermann in Berlin. The purpose of the meeting was to determine how likely it was that the United States would enter the war. Zimmerman told Martin that he believed that it was much more likely that America would enter the war against the British, on the same side as Germany (because of tension over Canada). In other words, Zimmerman's "mind worked according to rules that he thought universally true of political relations, and under these rules the desire for territorial expansion at the expense of neighbors was normal political motivation."[32]

Indeed, there was perhaps no better example of the self-defeating nature of German foreign policy than Zimmerman's famous telegram of January 1917, sent to the German ambassador in Mexico. In the event of the United States entering the war against Germany, Zimmerman offered a military alliance with Mexico. When British intelligence intercepted the message and decoded it, it caused a storm of indignation in America, which began the slide to war. Such was the recklessness of this move, in fact, that the apologists of Germany in the American press—such as the German American writer, George Sylvester Viereck—refused to believe that it was genuine. In 1910, after a year lecturing in Berlin, Viereck had written the bestselling *Confessions of a Barbarian* in which he expressed his strong sympathy for the German ideals of militarism and a strong state.[33] In February 1917, in a letter to the newspaper proprietor William Randolph Hearst on hearing about the Zimmerman telegram, Viereck decided that it was "obviously a fake." It was "impossible to believe that the German foreign secretary would place his name under such a preposterous document . . . the *Realpolitiker* of the Wilhelmstrasse would never offer an alliance based on such ludicrous propositions as the conquest by Mexico of American territory."[34]

It was in response to the rapid escalation of aggression against America that Wilson finally asked Congress to declare war on Germany on 2 April 1917. Suddenly, claimed the *Washington Herald*, the president had found a middle ground between old world diplomacy and the "Tolstoian" idealism of pacifists and isolationists. None of the European states had enough political wherewithal to anticipate the collapse of Russia's tsarist regime in 1917. To compound their errors, the Germans had now dragged America into the war: "How curious it is that these professors of realpolitik in European chancelleries, who lately saw nothing in the President but an academist, and nothing in his phrases but dreamy vaporings of the millennium, should be changing their tune at this time!" The European diplomats and militarists who dealt exclusively in facts could not see "much farther than their own noses." They lived in a circle circumscribed by their own intelligence. They had regarded such a thing as a Russian revolution, or an American intervention in the war, as a complete impossibility, until it had actually become a fait accompli. Wilson, by contrast, could see the day after tomorrow while his enemies could not escape today.[35]

While most Americans had ambiguous attitudes to the European powers, German machinations against the United States seemed to indicate that Berlin's intentions were considerably more mendacious. An April 1917 article in the *New York Tribune* made precisely this point—by comparing Germany's war aims to those of Britain. Treitschke and the other German professors had spoken about the civilizational power of war. The author contrasted this warlike disposition with the comparatively moderate statement of Britain's war aims, which Lord Roberts had made in 1914 in the *Hibbert Journal* (lampooned at the time by Shaw in the *New York Times*). True enough, the British were not entirely absolved from blame. It was also true that Roberts had written that war was "salutary, necessary and is the only national tonic" and Lord Kitchener too, another senior British general, had lamented the "rottenness of a long peace." But there was a crucial difference. For the British, war was still a last resort, come to reluctantly in the face of great provocation. On the battlefield too, the much-celebrated German military machine had also ground to a halt. The innovative German approach to technological warfare—with zeppelins and submarines—had failed to give it a decisive advantage. German statesmen and generals had talked sagely about *Realpolitik* "when in fact they were troubled with curious fragments of old illusions." They had babbled about a "place in the sun" because in reality they were afraid of the dark. At first they pinned their faith to a magic ship that sailed in the air (the blimp) and later to a magic ship that could sail under the water (the submarine).[36]

Mirroring the pattern in Britain, a series of new books appeared in the United States on the German psyche and Prussian political philosophy. Westel Willoughby, professor of political science at Johns Hopkins University, explored its inadequacies. Driven by a desire to rationalize their desire for conflict, the Prussians had developed a justifying political philosophy which, "though resting upon premises which are demonstrably false, and leading to acts which have horrified all the rest of the world, is nevertheless believed in as true."[37] Similarly, the *Nation*, edited by the idealist internationalist Oswald Garrison Villard, published an essay titled "The Real '*Realpolitik*,'" which described how there had been "a persistent indoctrination to hammer the theories into the heads of the people, to chloroform resistance, and blunt sensibilities." Now Germany was dying because it "accepted its disease as a virtue and a glory."[38] Even the *El Paso Herald* provided a helpful definition of Machiavellianism, which reflected the extent to which it had become bound up with perceptions of Germany: "Michiavellianism [*sic*]—pronounced 'mak-ee-ah-vel-eean-izm'. A term descriptive of unscrupulous diplomacy. Derived from the name of Machiavelli, a Florentine statesman . . . Michiavellianism has been revived by the Prussian military autocracy, and is called *Realpolitik*."[39]

By March 1918, the *Washington Herald* noted with some satisfaction how "eminent students" of *Realpolitik* had come to think rather less of their strategy as the war turned against them. For all the mockery of British hypocrisy, Germany again found itself without friends in the world, while Great Britain laughed in the background.[40] Seven days later, the German Spring Offensive began, in a desperate attempt to beat back the Allies before the full force of American military might was exerted on Europe. By April 1918, however, the Germans were on the defensive again, staring defeat in the face, as talk began to turn to peace.

In the prelude to intervention, Americans had mistrusted British denunciations of German *Realpolitik* as rather jaundiced and self-interested. When Germany became an enemy, attitudes in America began to echo those in Britain. The fight against the perceived sins of Prussianism provided a sense of common cause. There was also a shared recognition that German strategy was lacking in the very thing it had claimed to have a superior grasp of. The pretensions of German *Realpolitik* were mocked in America as they had been in Britain. Over the longer-term, however, it was the uniquely Americanized version of realpolitik that was to provide a better guide to United States foreign policy.

7

The Coming Peace
and the Eradication of *Realpolitik*

The allied leaders had framed their struggle as a war for democracy, fought for a Europe purged of Germany's brand of *Realpolitik*. In England, this idea had been used by the British government to mobilize national support even before Woodrow Wilson took the United States into the war. "We are not saints, we are not a nation of early Christians. Yet we are fighting for a great cause," wrote the academic Gilbert Murray, a friend of George Bernard Shaw, in a 1915 essay on the ethical problems of the war. This great cause included the observance of treaties, the recognition of mutual rights, and "the tradition of common honesty and common kindliness between nation and nation . . . the old decencies, the old humanities." The enemy had substituted these values "for some rule which we cannot yet fathom to its full depth." It was called *Realpolitik* and involved "the domination of force and fraud . . . organized ruthlessness, organized terrorism, [and] organized mendacity." Gilbert Murray's essay found its way into a 1917 collection, *The War of Democracy: The Allies' Statement*, edited by Lloyd George, who had become British prime minister in December 1916.[1]

As the prospect of victory against Germany grew, the question loomed ever larger of how to manage the peace that would follow. The issue of war guilt became one of growing importance as the Allies made gains on the battlefield. What had Germany's war aims actually been in 1914? And how much could the German people be held accountable for the mistakes made by their leaders? These questions fed into a deeper dilemma the Allies were preparing to tackle. What prospect was there of eradicating the practice of *Realpolitik*—and all its associated ills—from the international system? In Britain and the United States at least, there was growing optimism that if victory could be achieved, the very basis of the international system could be set on healthier foundations.

Some—such as the Anglo-American academic Sir Charles Waldstein—were deeply skeptical about the prospects of bringing Germany back to peaceful habits. Waldstein was born in New York, studied at Columbia University, and later took a position at Cambridge University. A classical archaeologist by training, he had also spent a number of years in Heidelberg. From his experience of Germany, where he had interviewed many senior statesmen, Waldstein argued that Germany's war aims were not simply those of the political elite but were held among "every section of the German people, every class, every occupation, every political party," including the Socialists. The whole basis of national and political principles was "clearly and confessedly amoral." The "terms *Real-Politik* and *Interressen-Politik* [interest-based politics] were constantly in the mouths of its leaders, from the Kaiser down to the political stump-speaker." The degeneration of public political discourse had begun in 1848. After this, rapid unification had undercut Germany's tradition of having many independent centers of thought (such as Heidelberg) and created a conformist intellectual culture.

The assault on Kantian idealism had been a deliberate political strategy, pursued from the top. Waldstein recalled meeting Prince von Bülow, the German chancellor, in 1904. In words reminiscent of Rochau, Bülow told him that the German people had required stiffening of their political fiber because they had been fed for too long on "the pabulum of romantic sentimentality and fantastic catchwords." According to Waldstein, Germany had no sense of respect for rules or honor in international politics. The will to power had created a rot in the German brain. This could be seen in the complete absence of any instinct for fair play or empathy. Thus Waldstein was deeply skeptical about the chances of re-integrating Germany into the community of nations. Until the Germans adopted the ideal of "the Gentleman in contradistinction to that of the Superman," there would be no understanding between Germany and the West.[2]

An even more uncompromising analysis of the German mind—and the implication of this for international relations—was put forward the same year, 1917, by Charles Sarolea, a Belgian professor at the University of Edinburgh. Before the war, Sarolea had written extensively on the Anglo-German problem and in 1915 he had traveled to the United States to raise awareness of German atrocities in the occupation of Belgium.

In a preface to Sarolea's book, *German Problems and Personalities*, the literary editor of the *New York Times* credited the author for being one of the first to highlight the true intentions of the Germans and for recognizing that the United States would inevitably have to confront them. In the introduction to his book, Sarolea complained that he had been dismissed by the English radical and liberal press in 1912, only to be proven right by the course of events.

In addition to the usual condemnation of *Realpolitik*, Sarolea also pointed to something even more poisonous that had been added to German political culture. He argued that the racialism of German nationalism—intermixed with a perverted application of Social Darwinism—had spilled into German theories of international affairs. Biological materialism was the equivalent of Marxist determinism in economics. It was the "same conception which has triumphed in the *Realpolitik* and *Weltpolitik*, and the elimination of the moral factor from the activities of high policy." The "tyranny of the race dogma" had permeated the thinking of a majority of the German historians and publicists from the early nineteenth century. These beliefs were to be found equally in the anti-Semitic, in the anti-Russian, and in the anti-French propaganda that existed throughout Germany. It had culminated in the "triple dogma of the superman, of the super-race, and of the super-State." As the umbrella term for this, German *Realpolitik* had aimed at the enslavement of Europe.[3]

By early 1918, as Germany began to recognize the likelihood of defeat on the Western front, a more emollient tone began to come out of Germany in its communications to the Allies (particularly toward the United States). But was this a new departure or a continuation of old diplomacy in a different guise? It was in response to these conciliatory noises that Arthur Balfour, the British foreign secretary, made the first mention of *Realpolitik* in the British parliament in February 1918. Specifically, Balfour addressed a recent speech the German chancellor, Count Hertling, had made in response to Woodrow Wilson, which indicated a softening of tone within Germany and a willingness to negotiate. For Balfour, it was important to remain on high alert. He was convinced that the speech was conceived "in that spirit of *Realpolitik*, which has been the true and dominating doctrine of every important German statesman, German soldier, and German thinker for two generations at least."[4]

By August 1918, after the failure of Germany's Spring Offensive, a peace communication was expected from Germany any day. But the *Spectator* warned that the German statesman was still "entirely possessed by the principles of *Realpolitik*."[5] In October, shortly before the armistice was agreed, the *Spectator* set out "to remind the world of the principles of *Realpolitik* which underlie the German diplomatic camouflage." Now that Germany was the underdog there would be plenty of appeals to sentiment. The reality, however, was that for the Germans, such abstract ideas as national honor, probity, and good faith did not exist. Insofar as they were used, this was to "entangle the legs" of its enemies.[6]

In attempting to define *Realpolitik*, the *Spectator* looked back to the famous example of the Melian dialogue, described by Thucydides in the fifth book of his *History of the Peloponnesian War*. During their war with Sparta, the Athenians attempted to force the small island of Melos out of its neutrality, demanding that it pay tribute or face the destruction of its city. When the Melians responded by stating their right to remain neutral and appealing to the humanity and values of the Athenians, the Athenian army responded by crushing them, killing every man or boy of military age, and enslaving the rest of the population. The Athenian warning to the Melians—that the strong do what they want and the weak suffer what they must—was regarded as one of the most profound historical examples of the realities of brute force and the primacy of power over justice.[7] Rather than accepting the German rediscovery of justice and sentiment at face value, the *Spectator* instead suggested that those dealing with Germany should remember Belgium, Serbia, Poland, and Alsace-Lorraine. These states might find justice "not poetic but real, in the doom and punishment of Prussian *Realpolitik*."[8]

Liberal Internationalism
and the Anglo–American Moment

At the end of 1914, the historian William Archibald Dunning, professor of history at Columbia University, published *The British Empire and the United States: A Review of Their Relations during the Century of Peace following the Treaty of Ghent*, under the direction of the American Peace Centenary Committee and the American Association for International Cooperation. The book contained an introduction by Viscount James Bryce, British Liberal politician, jurist, and recently retired ambassador to the United States.[9] Looking back at the last hundred years, Bryce took the line that

Anglo-American relations proved that two nations could keep a general peace if they worked conscientiously for it, even when their interests seem to clash.[10]

While there had been no rupture in one hundred years, Dunning explained that there had been many quarrels. The disarmament of the Great Lakes and the promulgation of the Monroe Doctrine had helped diffuse tensions after 1814. But then came the "roaring forties," the expansion of America westward and southward, and a whole series of new boundary disputes with Canada and quarrels over Mexico and Central America as well as controversy over British liberties taken with American ships in the name of the slave trade. Tensions peaked under President Polk and Prime Minister Palmerston in the middle of the century, but diplomats worked quietly behind the scenes to prevent the outbreak of hostilities.

At the time of the American Civil War, Britain had been presented with the opportunity to encourage the fracturing of the country in a way that suited its own interests. Yet, as Bryce pointed out, English liberals like John Bright and Goldwin Smith generally resisted the temptation to support the South, regarding the cause of anti-slavery as sufficient reason to stay out of the fight. That caricature of Prussian militarism, General von Bernhardi, mocked Britain's failure to seize the opportunity to support the Confederates in the war—and thereby dismember a rival—as evidence of the sort of Anglo-Saxon sentimental moralism that would be Britain's downfall. Addressing this argument in the *Times Literary Supplement* in January 1915, Sir Sidney Low, colonial historian at King's College London, argued that such a narrow "conception of *Realpolitik* has not been accepted by English statesmen." Indeed, viewed over the longer-term, Anglo-American relations provided a salutary lesson in how two nations could gradually diffuse the tension and rivalry between them. There were lessons in this relationship which might provide instruction for a "greater peace" to come out of the war.[11]

While a vague notion of "internationalism" and collaboration between nations had existed for many years—the idea of perpetual peace between nations could be traced back to Immanuel Kant—it was the gruesome reality of the First World War that gave it a new impetus and urgency. The idea that this was the "war to end all wars" reflected a hope that relations between nations could be put on a more solid footing. It held that each nation bore a share of responsibility for the outbreak of war because of their uncompromising pursuit of self-interest and willingness to trample on the right of self-determination of smaller nations. More problematic still was the way diplomacy was conducted—in secret, by elites, or those with vested interests, and with no democratic control or oversight. Indeed, it was no coincidence that the field of International Relations (as something thought to be worthy of academic exploration and greater scientific understanding) emerged in this period, out of the new internationalist impulse.[12]

The liberal internationalist movement was organized around the Union for Democratic Control (UDC), formed in 1914 by Charles Trevelyan, a Liberal government minister who had resigned in opposition to the declaration of war, and Ramsay MacDonald, who resigned as chairman of the Labour Party after it supported the government's war budget. The idea of a League of Nations—eventually founded in 1920, after many years of discussion—fitted with the UDC's campaign to take diplomacy out of the hands of elites and subject it to greater democratic scrutiny, and to uphold principles of national self-determination for smaller nations.[13]

Thus it was hoped that a greater peace could be achieved, which would address the deep flaws in the international system. The idea of a liberal international order—and perhaps even world government—began to take hold, though its exponents were divided on how this might be achieved.[14] Norman Angell, the Labour MP and one of the founders of the UDC, was one of the most influential exponents of the argument that Wilson's idealism could be the best antidote to the unraveling of international order that had led to the war. Angell later won the Nobel Peace Prize in 1933, the year that Hitler came to power. He has often been described as an archetypal idealist of the interwar period and a holder of naively utopian positions on international politics. This was an impression partly created by E. H. Carr, writing in 1939, and Hans J. Morgenthau, writing after the Second World War. In fact, it did not do justice to what might otherwise be called the realist core of his arguments.[15]

Seen another way, as Niall Ferguson has argued, Angell's famous "pacifist" text, *The Great Illusion*, can actually be classed as an argument for liberal imperialism. It ruled out using force against the colonies to subdue them but still held that the strength of the empire was "trade by free consent." It was to "English practice . . . and experience that the world will look as a guide in this matter," he wrote. The extension of the governing principles of the British Empire to European society provided the basis of a solution to the international problem. What was more, because these "principles of free human co-operation between communities" were, "in a special sense, an English development," it fell upon England to show the way. The argument was reminiscent of Eyre Crowe's memorandum of 1907. Belying its image as a paean to pacifism, Angell's work was widely praised by senior British naval strategists.[16]

Writing in the *North British Review*, a month after the United States entered the war, Angell described a theoretical British dinner party discussion among six people—with different political positions—as to what this might mean. The guests included an old Liberal (a former associate of the nineteenth-century Liberal prime minister William Gladstone), a young radical supporter of Lloyd George, a Foreign Office official, a Labour MP, a government official, and the host—an English banker who had spent many years trading in the United States. The banker began the discussion by suggesting that the cooperation of England and the United States, two liberal capitalist nations, would be "the real League of Peace in the future." The Foreign Office official criticized the United States for not obeying treaties while seeing themselves as the "unparalleled champions of arbitration." The Labour MP (who, one can assume, represented the views of Angell himself) threw up his hands and interjected: "Has not the failure of all your Congresses taught you anything? You talk as though your diplomatic, expert, *realpolitik*, foreign office settlements had brilliantly succeeded. But for the most part they have egregiously failed ... Can't we yet admit that the old methods have failed and that unless the war is to end in dreadful and tragic futility we must somehow apply new [methods]?"[17]

Angell was conscious of the argument that the new internationalism was regarded as naïve and utopian. For that reason, he was not shy to point out that American support for the League of Nations had a self-interested core to it as well. It was "to be explained not merely on humanitarian and idealist grounds, but on very tangible grounds of natural policy as well." Both British and American self-interests were tied up with a liberal international world order.[18]

Here one can see the synergy between the geopolitical awakening of the United States and the liberal internationalist movement of the era. In support of his argument, Angell cited editorials that had appeared in the *New Republic* by Walter Weyl, Herbert Croly, and Walter Lippmann, who, he added, were known to have close relations with the Wilson White House. In fact, just two months earlier, in February 1917, Lippmann had commissioned Angell to write for the *New Republic* in an attempt to win over the largely pacifist readership of the magazine. An article from Angell, "justifying America's entry into the war on liberal and internationalist grounds would be of immense help to us," Lippmann explained, raising the enticing prospect that there was "a chance by America's entry into the war to crystallize and make real the whole league of peace propaganda."[19]

In other words, the liberal internationalists were not shy of framing their claims in a way that resonated with nationalistic audiences in England and the United States. The very idea that victory could bring a greater peace was patriotic. In an article in the *Athenaeum*, titled "Nationalism and Internationalism," the Labour Party politician, Arthur Greenwood (who went on to become its deputy leader at the time of the Second World War) made the case that establishment of the League of Nations was the only victory worth of the sacrifices of war. The greatest enemies to the cause of democracy and peace were those who misread the lessons of the war and urged the people of Britain, the United States, and France "along the road of materialism and militarism." This was a policy of taking the "hair of the dog that bit us, to out-Prussia Prussia." Those who attacked internationalism might regard themselves as patriots, but Greenwood could not see how they differed "from the hated Germans of the *Realpolitik* school."[20]

The Limits of the Liberal Ideal

This Anglo-American moment was the backdrop to Wilson's announcement of "Fourteen Points" in January 1918, which laid out a policy of free trade, open agreements between states, and democracy and self-determination as the organizing principles of international relations. As David Kennedy has written, an important impetus behind Wilson's scheme for a "community of power", embodied in the League of Nations, was that it would replace the "time-tempered regime of *Realpolitik*, the regime of power and might."[21] Yet, following Hobson, some liberal internationalists predicted that the greatest obstacle to liberal internationalism would be vested interests within the Anglo-American world itself.

Among those to take this position was the anti-capitalist American economist, Thorstein Veblen. In 1915, Veblen had published *Imperial Germany and the Industrial Revolution*, which argued that Germany had suffered from an odd liaison between "advanced industrial technique, and quasi-feudal forms of social integration and an over-powerful bureaucratic state."[22] Writing in December 1918, Veblen argued that everyone bore a share of the blame for the breakdown of international order. Of course, there were important differences between Germany and the Allies. For example, the foreign policies of the democratic states were usually run by elected states-men, rather than counts and princes. Nonetheless, he argued, these policies were still managed for vested interests such as big business and corporations. Thus, even in the modern era, diplomacy still ran on the same lines of "sys-tematized prevarication" and a "medieval spirit" of self-interest: "All this run of national pretensions, wrangles, dominion, aggrandizement, chica-nery, and ill-will is nothing more than the old familiar trading-stick of the diplomatic power brokers who do business in dynastic force and fraud and is also called *Realpolitik*."[23] To truly change the system, the Allies would have to change their behavior, and their internal political systems too.

At the conservative end of the spectrum, there was a different type of skepticism. The *Spectator* could certainly acknowledge the appeal of the League of the Nations. It was better to aspire to a greater ideal, even if the effort ended in failure, than simply to revert to the patterns of prewar diplo-macy. The vision of peace by agreement and federation of nations had been around for centuries. To extinguish it entirely was impossible. As early as the Peloponnesian War, fought between the Greeks and the Spartans in 431–404 BC, "though the cynics and professors of *Realpolitik*, smiled at their simplicity," visionaries like Plato chose the larger hope. It would be disas-trous to make the aim of the League the "abolition of war in the abstract." It might just be possible to create an international system "so impossibly tedious for the ambitious demagogue or the cynical autocrat that he will not be able to lure the nation he deceives or compel the people he controls along the path of blood and iron." Prophetically, however, the *Spectator* sug-gested that Western diplomats were far more likely to "go snorting down the flowery meads" of impracticable idealism in their efforts.[24]

It was in the disintegration of this momentary alliance between liberal internationalists and the exponents of a more expansive "new" realism that the seeds of the failure of the League of Nations were sown. One problem was that the other European statesmen were not quite ready to buy into the logic of Wilsonian idealism in full. France's Prime Minister Georges Clemenceau archly noted, of Wilson's fourteen principles, that God had given us only Ten Commandments and we had broken every one. Another was that the liberal internationalist camp was wide, was eclectic, and lacked cohesion. The odd axis that had emerged among Wilson, Norman Angell, and Walter Lippmann—based on a temporary marriage of liberalism and realism—soon fragmented. Although they had been so important in the articulation of war aims, Croly and Lippmann broke with Wilson after the Treaty of Versailles because of his support for American involvement in the League of Nations. Formalizing American involvement in such a way, binding it into a system, was a step too far.[25]

Even more important than this, however, was how these events were viewed in Germany. In 1919, the English geographer Sir Halford Mackinder—discussed in later chapters, and sometimes referred to as the father of "geopolitics"—assessed the prospects of the League of Nations. Idealists were "the salt of the earth," he wrote, and without them society would soon stagnate and civilization fade. But the Treaty of Versailles was a victor's peace. He warned that the Germans regarded the collapse of the League as sooner or later inevitable. Indeed, he suggested that the cult of *Realpolitik* that had emerged in Germany before the war was much more embedded in the German national psyche than the Western nations had grasped. Large and intelligent sections of German society "acted under the persuasion of a political philosophy which was ... [not] less sincerely held because we believed it was wrong." [26] The argument had not been won, whatever the Allies wanted to believe. The West's hardest test was still ahead.

PART III

Interwar Realpolitik

What we require is to divest our diplomacy of cant metaphysics and the jargon of collective security, and to begin talking to Mussolini in the terms of Realpolitik.

(Prime Minister Neville Chamberlain, *Morning Post*, 1936)[1]

8

The Ingestion of Realpolitik

At the dawn of the twentieth century, Britain had the most to lose from a challenge to the international status quo. It was no coincidence that it was the first country to cry foul against the new methods practiced by those states—above all Germany—who wanted to challenge the structures established to preserve the existing order. By the end of the First World War, however, there was some acknowledgment that Britain was not so immune to these practices as its self-image would suggest. On one level, this was reflected in the diminution of what Friedrich Meinecke called the "pharisaical superiority" of the British, in an era when the certainties of British imperial identity had been severely undermined. On another level, a small but influential group began to suggest that a small dose of realpolitik—anglicized, de-italicized and shorn of its Teutonic connotations—might just be sprinkled onto aspects of British foreign policy. Before long, the word was to be found, with increasing frequency, in British diplomatic cables, memoranda, and high-level political discussions—and crucially, no longer just to describe the behavior of other states.

The idea that British diplomacy represented something distinct and superior to the diplomacy conducted by many other European nations, particularly Germany, was not jettisoned entirely. Behind the scenes, however, there was an acknowledgment that morally superior methods of British *Idealpolitik*, or anti-realpolitik, might sometimes have to be jettisoned. What might be called the creep of realpolitik began during the war itself. It could be used, without too much anguish, to justify short-term measures regarding peoples subjected to Ottoman rule, or within the boundaries of the Middle East, where British resources had been stretched. After the end of hostilities, however, a new set of problems presented themselves: the potential fragmentation of the British Empire, which came under severe strain in both India and Ireland; the unprecedented international challenge posed by the creation of the Soviet Union following the Russian Revolution of 1917; and the fragmentation of the liberal internationalist consensus described in the previous chapter. New challenges led to imaginative new justifications for the type of behavior that would have been condemned if others had been responsible. Unsurprisingly, the charge of Anglo-Saxon hypocrisy reared its head again.

The United States, meanwhile, further developed its own bespoke version of realpolitik (in which the word was used but with few references to its German origins). In the 1920s, it was not applied so much to Europe as to Latin America. The growing distance between the United States and the European powers, Britain in particular, weakened the liberal internationalist consensus that had existed at the end of the war. Without American involvement in the League of Nations, the mechanisms of liberal internationalism looked increasingly inadequate for the task of maintaining a general peace. In the Anglo-American world, a sense of idealism fatigue set in. Yet, in the dismantling of Wilsonianism, some of the broader foundations of Anglo-American realism were pulled down too.

By the early 1920s, it was clear that a number of influential opinion formers and statesmen in the West had ingested a significant element of realpolitik themselves. For the first time, the English began to use the word to justify their own behaviour. This was usually presented as a matter of necessity rather than design—temporary measures rather than a wholescale new approach. Nonetheless, it was significant that some of the staunchest and most articulate critics of German *Realpolitik*—such as the diplomat-scholar Sir James Headlam-Morley, or the prime minister, Lloyd George—came round to the view that "a little realpolitik" was perhaps necessary as a counterweight to a deluge of postwar idealism; and they used the term explicitly. These British examples of realpolitik were not intended to mimic the German precedent. Instead, they were seen as an antidote to what was perceived as the naiveté of Wilsonianism or pacifist internationalism. The spectre of Treitschke and Bernhardi began to fade in the Anglo-American world. What realpolitik increasingly came to imply was a reversion to tried and tested modes of statecraft that had existed in the nineteenth century. As the 1919 Treaty of Versailles was slowly undermined, British statesmen looked back to the era of the Treaty of Vienna one hundred years before, when a less sentimental, more realistic approach to foreign policy was thought to have been in the ascendant. This, they hoped, would provide a better guide.

Ironically, as Chapter 9 will show, it was the German theorists of state-craft who saw the potential strength of an Anglo-American alliance—a *pax Anglo-Saxonica*—at just the moment it began to disintegrate. Like all the major powers, Germany also underwent a process of intense self-examina-tion after 1918. *Realpolitik* came under scrutiny more than ever before. Some of the most original and powerful meditations on statecraft of the twen-tieth century emerged in this highly charged atmosphere—notably Max Weber's famous lecture, "Politics as a Vocation," and Friedrich Meinecke's book, *The Doctrine of Raison d'État*. Crucially, however, *Realpolitik* was not rejected in Germany but emerged in a revised, reformed, and even reinvigorated form. On the one hand, Treitschke was widely criticized by the postwar theorists of German statecraft. Yet this critique did not trickle down beyond the university professoriate. In its stead emerged a neo-*Realpolitik* for which—in its popularized form—a bastardized ver-sion of Treitschke once again provided the script. Once again, it exhibited the narrow racism that Meinecke had warned of as early as 1914. As an interesting subplot in the history of *Realpolitik*, some of the most effective attempts to articulate a different form of realism—one that would achieve national goals without succumbing to narrow self-interest or jingoism—came from German-speaking Jews and German-speaking Czechs, who were well versed German theories of state, but also able to see beyond their limitations.

In the West, in the vacuum caused by the failure of liberal international-ism—and in an increasingly dangerous international environment—one can see why a return to traditional diplomatic methods seemed appealing. At the signing of the Locarno Treaty of 1925, which aimed to normal-ize relations with Germany, foreign secretary Austen Chamberlain insisted that a portrait of Lord Castlereagh be hung overlooking the room. Citing Castlereagh's conciliatory approach to France after the defeat of 1815, he suggested that this was "not the end of appeasement and reconciliation, but its beginnings."[2] His brother, Neville Chamberlain, Britain's chancellor of the exchequer from 1931 to 1937 and prime minister from 1937 to 1940, followed a similar groove. The latter Chamberlain gorged himself on his-tories of nineteenth-century diplomacy.[3]

Ultimately, however, the reversion to old diplomacy was characterized by failures of perception and understanding of the contemporary world. This story is told in Chapter 10 (the final one in Part III). Those reading history as a guide for contemporary foreign policy came to think about the international arena in a rather perfunctory and mechanical way, as an arena in which states pursued their interests as rational actors. This left Britain, in particular, ill-equipped to understand the nature of the threat posed by fascism. It was the international arena, which did not succumb to preconceived patterns or general rules, that was to expose the limitations of this approach. But the learning curve was steep and perilous. In Britain, then, by the outbreak of the Second World War, realpolitik was to become—once again—a dirty word. There was a sense that it had been trialed but failed as a method of diplomacy. This time, however, it was not used to condemn "the other" but Britain's own statesmen and the policy of appeasement that they had pursued.

Britain's Slide toward Realpolitik

The internalization of the word realpolitik into British Foreign Office parlance at the time of the First World War can be credited to James Headlam-Morley, an academic who joined the Propaganda Department in 1914, before becoming assistant director of the Political Intelligence Bureau in the Department of Information (from 1917 to 1920). Headlam-Morley was part of the British Delegation to the Paris Peace Conference in 1919 and then became historical advisor to the Foreign Office in 1920, in which capacity he worked on an official history of British diplomacy before the war. Like Eyre Crowe, to whom he reported, Headlam-Morley had a German wife and a strong interest in Germany history and culture; he later wrote a life of Bismarck. Also like Eyre Crowe, he believed that Prussian militarism and German nationalism were the root cause of the war. A skilled propagandist, he was a regular contributor to the *Times* and the *Times Literary Supplement*, which explains the lengthy expositions on the concept that appeared in both.[4]

Unsurprisingly, it was in official reports on Germany, written by Headlam-Morley's team, that *Realpolitik* most often appeared. In December 1917, for example, as the Germans negotiated with the new Russian government at Brest-Litovsk, ministers were informed that the Germans were eager to take advantage of the Soviet collapse by imposing harsh terms—annexing significant chunks of Eastern Europe and the Baltic states. Germany's unforgiving strategy—in pushing home its advantage over the Russians and refusing to negotiate in concert with the other powers—was said to be typical of its whole approach to foreign policy. Thus, it was suggested that the eventual settlement of peace on the eastern frontier would be conducted "on the lines of *Realpolitik* and not on those of what the military people would regard as mere sentimentalism."[5]

For the most part, then, *Realpolitik* was still understood both in pejorative terms and as a flawed method. In August 1918, Headlam-Morley's Political Intelligence Department drew up a document for the cabinet on the likely angles of an anticipated peace offensive by the Germans. In suing for peace, Germany was playing a merely tactical game by silencing its hard-liners and talking of "peace by understanding." Looking back over the war, however, Headlam-Morley was struck by how counter-productive Germany's strategy had been to this point. Counted among its major errors were the invasion of Belgium (which forced Britain to enter the war), the under-estimation of Britain's fighting spirit, and the submarine attacks that had dragged the United States into the war. The sacrifice of five million British volunteers was a powerful rejoinder to the idea that the British were a nation of shopkeepers with no fight in their belly. The entry of the United States into the war also belied the idea that nations acted only in their immediate material interests. The submarine campaign and the Zimmerman telegram "may have seemed justifiable on grounds of near-sighted *Realpolitik*" but the intervention of the United States must be placed in the other scale of the balance.[6]

There was therefore no great desire to mimic German methods, especially as victory approached. Equally, however, there was a recognition that the practice of *Realpolitik* had spread throughout Europe. In particular, the collapse of Russia and the fragmentation of Eastern Europe meant that a number of new actors saw an opportunity to take advantage of the power vacuum. In the Balkans, a number of aspiring new nations believed that the moment had come to assert their own national claims. Any sense of unity between the Slavic nations was disintegrating fast. For example, Bulgaria, as one British official noted, had defied calls for unity of the Slavic peoples and was instead playing its own game of "Real-Politik."[7]

Second only to Germany, the greatest diplomatic challenge was presented by Russia, following the Bolshevik Revolution of October 1917. The first act of the new government had been to withdraw from the war unilaterally, thereby breaking all existing treaties with the Allies. Beyond this, however, it was unclear whether the new regime in Russia would last, and if it did, whether it would act in the name of narrowly Russian interests or revolutionary principles. This was partly because it was unclear whether Vladimir Lenin or Leon Trotsky would emerge as the leading political figure in the new Russia. During the Brest-Litovsk negotiations in January 1918, British officials hoped that Trotsky's Bolshevik idealism might frustrate the Germans in their efforts to cut a separate deal with Russia before settling with the Allies in the west. There was "no party in Russia less likely to abandon its principles than the Bolsheviks, and they [the Germans] must sigh for a Government that would be guided by notions of *Realpolitik* instead of socialist ideals." Indeed, for this reason British diplomats suggested that a Bolshevik government might, in the short term, be in the interest of the Allies, "however lavish the present rulers of Russia may be in their insults to all bourgeois and imperialist Governments." The ability of Trotsky to remain in control of negotiations, however, was far from clear due to the machinations that continued in St. Petersburg.[8]

Eventually, the Soviet Union adopted a realistic rather than a revolutionary approach to foreign affairs. The decision was taken to consolidate the position of the infant state against its enemies (internal and external) rather than actively promoting communist revolution elsewhere. As E. H. Carr later described, notwithstanding his own sympathy with the realist position, the opposition of Trotsky to this policy—which included the muzzling of the activities of the Comintern—left many socialists feeling there had been a "subordination of the interests of socialism and world revolution to a narrowly conceived *Realpolitik*." It was Josef Stalin who announced a policy of "socialism in one country" in 1924, but the trend had begun under Lenin, and the key moment had been Lenin's decision to enter into a trade agreement with Britain in 1921.[9] While Lenin did not deploy the word himself, a number of Marxist theorists in the 1920s, such as Georg Lukács, did use "realpolitik," approvingly, to distinguish Lenin's actions from Trostkyite utopianism.[10]

The Anglo-Soviet Trade Agreement of March 1921 was intended to reflect the realities of the new dispensation. For some American observers, however, it also conveyed a slippage back into the old habits beloved of European diplomats. America still refused to recognize the Bolshevik government. Even France, which had initially supported lifting the blockade against Russia, was critical of the deal on the grounds that it undercut the authority of the League of Nations. Indeed, the *New York Tribune* suggested that Britain had other selfish strategic interests at stake that went beyond a trading relationship. What the British really wanted was to stop Lenin from using anti-imperialist rhetoric to destabilize the British Empire in Afghanistan and India. It was, in other words, a return to the "great game" between Britain and Russia over Asia in the nineteenth century. In modern parlance, said the *Tribune*, it was "a flyer for what the Germans call *Realpolitik*. It is not idealistic."[11] Here was a new shorthand for an old imperial game.

The Unraveling of Internationalism

Britain faced serious challenges to the maintenance of its global empire after 1918. It was in response to these challenges that its government began to engage in tactics that it was prepared to justify as "realpolitik." An early case in point was the Armenian question that had begun to impress itself on Britain in the years before the war. There was great sympathy for the plight of the Armenians in Britain (and indeed in the United States) and their suffering within the Ottoman Empire, now accepted as having constituted genocide. Yet Britain's approach to the Armenian question reflected its traditional concern about the threat to British interests in the eastern Mediterranean caused by the disintegration of the Ottoman Empire. Another concern was that of pushing the Ottomans into the war on the side of the Germans (as eventually happened). Attitudes to Armenian concerns were seen primarily through this geo-strategic prism: so much so that Britain's Armenian policy has been portrayed as a model of realpolitik.[12]

Another example of this unsentimental logic was the Sykes-Picot Agreement of 1916—often condemned as a classic example of British hypocrisy and imperialism while it fought a war in the name of democracy and self-determination. This pact—named after the diplomats Sir Mark Sykes and François Georges-Picot, who struck the deal—carved up modern-day Iraq, Syria, and Lebanon into areas of British and French control. Before the outbreak of the war, a growing number of British Foreign Office officials (particularly the Arabists in the Cairo bureau, such as T. E. Lawrence) had argued for the creation of a non-Ottoman, Arab-led caliphate, with Mecca as the capital. By being the sponsor of such a scheme, Britain hoped to be able to secure its own interests in the region, which centered around unfettered passage through the Suez Canal and access to emerging oil markets. The chief obstacle to this plan was France, which, although Britain's most important ally in the European theater of war, was unwilling to give up its claim to Arab territories in Syria and Lebanon.

Going against Lawrence, Sykes prioritized the immediate gain of coming
to terms with France, thereby shoring up British interests in the Middle
East against a threatened German-Turkish incursion. In addition to the
perception that they had been betrayed, the Arabs were also infuriated by
British support for a Jewish homeland in Palestine contained in the Balfour
Declaration of 1917.

T. E. Lawrence condemned what he saw as the short-termism of
the move, denouncing Sykes as "a bundle of prejudices, intuitions,
half-sciences."[13] Crucially, however, Sykes had the support of the British
cabinet who also prioritized the successful prosecution of the war. It was on
this issue, in fact, that British officials used "realpolitik" for the first time,
not in a pejorative sense but as reasonable justification for their actions. As
a senior Foreign Office official explained in 1919, "the only 'real-politik'
for us is to take a line in the Near East that will keep [us] in with the French
(much as I dislike it) and the Jews, and not be too nervous of Arab suscepti-
bilities." They could not sacrifice the close relationship with France for an
Arab unity that might never materialize.[14]

Lloyd George, prime minister of Britain's wartime coalition government (in office from 1916 to 1922) and presiding over the Sykes-Picot deal
and the Anglo-Soviet Trade Agreement of 1921, was himself a lightning
rod for what might be called "British realpolitik." Like France's Georges
Clemenceau he was a skeptic about Wilson's internationalism and the
likely success of the League of Nations. His friend, C. P. Scott, editor of
the *Manchester Guardian*, noted at the time that the prime minister "savours
rather more of the 'real-politik' of Bismarck than Wilson's idealism which
we are supposed to share."[15]

Indeed, shortly after the Anglo-Soviet trade deal, Lloyd George also
signed the 1921 Anglo-Irish Treaty with Michael Collins of the Irish
Republican Army, partitioning Ireland and creating the Irish Free State
in the south. The deal had been preceded by a brutal counter-insur-
gency. At the time, Sir Horace Plunkett, the head of the Irish Dominion
League—which opposed partition in favor of a solution that kept Ireland
within the British commonwealth—wrote to the US diplomat and editor of *Foreign Affairs* Hamilton Fish Armstrong (himself a Wilsonian)
that "you must always bear in mind the *Realpolitik* of Lloyd George and
eliminate principle and substitute expediency as the determining factor."[16] A subtle but significant change was taking place in British political

The Sykes–Picot Agreement was a secret 1916 deal between Britain and France that carved up the Middle East into separate spheres of influence during the First World War. This was the first time that British officials described their own actions in terms of "realpolitik," having previously denounced the notion. From the National Archives (United Kingdom). Courtesy of Wikimedia Creative Commons. PD-US

discourse. From the Foreign Office to the prime minister, realpolitik was no longer regarded as something only Germans did.

The idea that the international system—and the conduct of diplomacy itself—could be transformed after 1918 had soon run into difficulties. The 1919 Treaty of Versailles was a case in point. The makers of the treaty had consciously aimed to break from the diplomatic practices of old. They had spoken of their desire not to repeat the mistakes made at the Treaty of Vienna of 1815. That treaty, which followed the end of the Napoleonic Wars, had been negotiated by Europe's elite, behind closed doors, with the aim of restoring Europe's prewar status quo. Among the criticisms made of the 1815 settlement was that it propped up discredited monarchical

British Prime Minister David Lloyd George, French Prime Minister Georges Clemenceau, and American President Woodrow Wilson at the Versailles peace conference in 1919. Despite the lofty idealism of Wilson, Lloyd George and Clemenceau were often accused of practicing their own brand of realpolitik. Photo by Hulton Archive/Getty Images.

regimes and trampled on the aspirations of liberals and nationalists. Yet was the Treaty of Versailles really superior to the Treaty of Vienna? The peacemakers of 1919 "would have nothing in common with the Congress of Vienna, with its secret debates and back-stairs intrigue" and "there would be no room for the selfishness and narrow views which had characterised the proceedings of the Powers in 1814–15," remarked the diplomatic historian William Alison Phillips shortly after the Versailles Treaty was concluded. He suspected that the world was preparing itself for serious disillusionment.[17]

In his 1914 history of European diplomacy, *The Confederation of Europe*, Walter Alison Phillips defended Castlereagh, the British foreign secretary in 1815, for having had far more insight into the true nature of foreign affairs than the peacemakers at Versailles a century later. In particular, he praised Castlereagh's foresight in creating a system of regular congresses between the great powers to keep the new international system preserved after 1815. His strategy had been to keep Emperor Alexander of Russia "grouped" within the international system so that he would not destabilize it from the outside. Here Phillip's choice of language was significant in that he invoked a specifically British tradition of "realpolitik." Castlereagh's aim in having international conferences did not come from an abstract faith in multi-lateralism but a desire to keep a check on Russia. It "represented a triumph of British *Realpolitik* over [Tsar] Alexander's dangerous idealism."[18] In this way, then, in the post-Versailles era, realpolitik was taken to mean a return to traditional nineteenth-century diplomacy—the tried and tested methods of the past, which had served the national interest long before the idea of "world government" had been concocted.

Headlam-Morley of the Political Intelligence Department personified a gradual change in the British official mindset. In 1918, he had optimistically declared that "the personal will of President Wilson is . . . one of the strongest forces in the world." Within five years, he moved away from strong support of the peace settlement and the League of Nations to become a critic of the Versailles Treaty and a skeptic about the League. Addressing the German complaint that the new world order was prejudiced in favor of Anglo-Saxon interests, he noted that the criticism was "not without justice." He was impressed by John Maynard Keynes's book of 1920, *The Economic Consequence of Peace*, which suggested that the harsh peace terms imposed on Germany were damaging Britain's economy because of the connections between the two. He also began to correspond with E. H. Carr and other like-minded intellectuals of a burgeoning "realist" school.[19]

In August 1922, Headlam-Morley produced a lengthy essay, "Realpolitik," which appeared in the *Times Literary Supplement*. The occasion for this was the publication of the first volumes of *Die Grosse Politik der Europäischen Kabinette*. This was a multi-volume collection of documents, edited by the Centre for the Study of the Causes of the War, a German government-funded think tank, that challenged the notion that Germany was primarily responsible for the war. Headlam-Morley criticized the collection and rejected German revisionism about the causes of the war. Yet,

another line of argument began to emerge. This was reflected in his concern about the excess of idealism in the postwar world: "men and women
outside the machine by which the world is governed, thinking and criticis-
ing and framing their plans for the Utopia of the future." On these grounds,
he displayed a colder rationale—typical of the weary official forced to
stand firm against the demos—which held that the independence of small
nations was perhaps not so important to Britain, or its core interests, as it
had seemed in 1918. In this, one can see the roots of the policy of appeasement. No "reasonable man" would suggest that it would be legitimate for
a country like France or England to imperil their major interests "for the
sake of a distant and alien peoples," he wrote, foreshadowing the logic that
saw Britain abandon Czechoslovakia to Hitler in 1938.[20] This thinking was
also transferred into a willful reappraisal of Germany. By 1925, Headlam-
Morley was stating that a "very genuine change of mind" had taken place
in Germany since 1918 and a large portion of the country had rejected militarism.[21] This assumption was to gain ground and exert an increasing influence on British foreign policy before 1933, when Hitler became German
chancellor.

The Death of Academic Idealism?

In the United States, realpolitik had never had the same pejorative connotations as it did in England. Germany had never played such an important
part in the American political psyche. In 1920, for example, the *New York
Tribune* referred to the recent "entente" between Czechoslovakia and
Yugoslavia as "a measure of *realpolitik* in the best sense of that much-abused
term—a policy founded on realities correctly gauged."[22] Likewise, when it
came to the growing ambitions of Japan in the East, it was felt that the problem could only be confronted on "realpolitik" terms.[23]

Americans stood aloof from the traditional practices of European diplomacy, epitomized by the Anglo-Soviet Treaty. Yet American relations
with Latin American countries underlined the potential tension between
the American self-image and the reality behind its growing power. On
the one hand, the Pan-American movement mimicked Wilsonian internationalism in its rejection of the "dark" arts of old world diplomacy. "Above
Pan American there is only panhumanism, to which it may lead some
day, bestowing upon all mankind the principles of law which are now the

privilege of a part of it and which we Americans theoretically and most times practically substitute for conquest and force," declared the Bulletin of the Pan-American Union in 1921. On the other hand, even an idealistic nation like the United States could, on occasion, behave in a renegade fashion characterized by "spells of disrespect for forms" such as international organizations and existing laws. This was "just as the followers of what was called *realpolitik* contributed so much to disparage an aspect of German thought before public opinion."[24]

The same logic played into the refinement of the so-called 1904 Roosevelt Corollary in 1928. Theodore Roosevelt's amendment to the Monroe Doctrine had decreed that the United States reserved the right to intervene in conflicts between European and Latin American states in order to enforce legitimate claims of the European powers, rather than having the Europeans do so themselves. In 1928, President Calvin Coolidge's undersecretary of state, Reuben Clark, prepared a memorandum on the original Monroe Doctrine, which argued that Roosevelt's corollary of 1904 was not justified by the original terms of the Monroe Doctrine. The document was made public in 1930 as the prelude to what became known as the "Good Neighbor Policy," by which the United States aimed to improve relations with Latin American states.

Clark reflected positively on early nineteenth-century British diplomacy. He quoted Castlereagh that "a steady and temperate application of honest principles is her [Britain's] best source of authority." Another powerful mantra of British foreign policy under Castlereagh was that the British self-interest in a peaceful and stable Europe was also consistent with the general good. America could play the same role in Latin America with her embryonic Good Neighbor Policy. To this end, Reuben Clark quoted from William Alison Phillips's *The Confederation of Europe*, discussed earlier in this chapter. In fact, Clark adapted Phillips's description of Britain's strategy for European affairs—"*Realpolitik* tempered by altruism"—as the ideal script for US policy in Latin America. It was in this document that the phrase "national security" was also first used to describe American strategy. Right from the inception, then, US national security was loaded with nineteenth-century British precedents.[25]

Throughout the interwar period, there remained an influential strand of Wilsonian idealism in the United States. In 1927, the American diplomat James McDonald argued that it was inevitable that the United States would be drawn back to the League of Nations in the long run and could not focus all its energies on Latin America. McDonald was chairman of the Foreign Policy Association in Philadelphia (previously known as the League of Free Nations Association). On the one hand, he warned his countrymen of the need for self-awareness, criticizing what he saw as "our complacent conviction that the United States in its foreign relations has been uniformly just, if not generous." US foreign policy had been motivated by self-interest as much as any other state. The American government "has preached lofty idealism, but more often has practiced *real politik*." Latin America, for example, provided scant evidence that the United States had "exercised our power with a benevolent, big-brotherly attitude." On the other hand, he retained providential faith in the United States as the reformer of world politics. In calling for a new code of international morality, McDonald believed that the first step toward this must be "a new understanding of what America really means." In his view, this should be "the adventurous America, which will dare out of its strength to try a new method in international affairs, based on a new philosophy, that will not merely preach, but will more and more nearly practice, the Golden Rule."[26]

Many saw the collapse of the peace movement, disintegration of the liberal order, and insipidness of the League of Nations as the ultimate rebuke to the supposed naïve idealism of the interwar years, embodied by Wilsonianism. The historian Adam Tooze has argued that this was the wrong lesson to learn. If anything, the restless search for a new way of securing order and peace was the expression not of "deluded idealism," but of a "higher form of realism," argues Tooze—what he calls "a Realpolitik of progress." Its failure was not inevitable and can be explained in two ways. The first was in the determination of revanchist (fascist and revolutionary) powers who mobilized every resource they had in an effort to escape the "chain gang" of nations marching behind the United States and its allies. The second, more important, reason was that the United States itself remained a reluctant Goliath. It was hamstrung in its attempt to construct a viable grand strategy by a strange anxiety about the fragility of its own polity. Thus Wilson was concerned that foreign entanglements with the "Dark Continent" of Europe or the "Oriental races" of Asia would corrupt the health and vigor of America's republic. At the hub of the rapidly evolving American-centered world system was a polity wedded to a conservative vision of its own future, preferring to sit aloof from the rapacious battles and power games played by the others, not quite at ease with its own recent tumultuous past, and still coming to terms with the fact that modernity had presented it with responsibilities it had never envisaged.[27]

In many ways, too, the liberal internationalism of the postwar years had grown out of a convergence of British and American ideas about international order. While Wilson had taken center stage in 1917—and taken things in the direction of the League of Nations—there were deeper foundations to this. It had arisen in the dialogue of men like Norman Angell and Walter Lippmann, Viscount James Bryce, and Theodore Roosevelt and on the shared strategic assumptions of men like Admiral Mahan and Eyre Crowe. However, the growing estrangement between Britain and the United States in the 1920s made this line of argument increasingly difficult to maintain. In both countries, proponents of the League of Nations expressed their disappointment. In 1924, Sir Esme Howard, British ambassador in Washington, DC, complained about what he saw as an inward turn by the Western powers. Their former commitment to the international order had been pushed aside "in favour of what the Germans call '*real politik*'—practical politics." It was to his eternal regret that international affairs were still governed by the notion of "do unto your neighbour as he thinks he would do unto you and do it first."[28]

Five years later, in 1929, in the year of the Wall Street Crash, Howard produced a memorandum on Anglo-American relations for Sir Austen Chamberlain, the British foreign secretary. It painted a pessimistic picture of relations with the current incumbent of the White House, Herbert Hoover, and expressed the hope that his successor might be more amenable to working more closely with Britain. In the United States, claimed Howard, "people move both under the influence of a generous but uninformed sentiment for peace and goodwill and under the influence of some powerful and wholly selfish national interest." What made this so disconcerting was that they "continually act from both motives" at the same time: "In one and the same breath they will declare for a reign of peace on earth, and also for maintaining American national interests by force." President Hoover was "nothing if not a 'realpolitiker,'" Howard wrote, wistfully turning his mind back to Wilson, "He cares more for efficiency than academic idealism."[29] Thus realpolitik had begun to corrupt the very states that had set out to destroy it just a decade before.

9

Postwar Germany
and the *Realpolitik* Revival

After World War I, Germany entered a period of soul searching and internal reflection about the path that had led to defeat. The country was faced with a bloc of Western nations in which the Anglo-Saxons predominated, with the French as a junior partner. To the German historian, Erich Marcks, it seemed like England was "the sole winner from this war, together with North America." He could see "an Anglo-Saxon world mastery rising on the horizon."[1] The notion of *Realpolitik*, which had become so important to the German self-image, underwent an autopsy at the hands of Germany's intelligentsia.

Ultimately, however, despite the trauma of defeat, *Realpolitik* was not entirely rejected or abandoned. The liberal critics of *Realpolitik*—the few who had opposed the war—were drowned out within Germany. It was a new, refined version that German statesmen and theorists hoped to articulate. Scholars such as Max Weber, Hermann Oncken, and Friedrich Meinecke instead tried to find a new and more effective formulation of *Realpolitik*. Their product was intellectually superior to what had gone before. Yet their subtle qualifications did not lodge themselves onto the popularized version of *Realpolitik* that was born anew, and fell, once again, into the Treitschkean trap of crude nationalism.

Weber's Critique of *Realpolitik* and the Limits of the New Realism

The birth of the Weimar Republic in 1919 injected new energy into German liberalism, at both the political and cultural levels. The spirit of a new humanism was captured by the work of Sigmund Freud and Thomas Mann, particularly the latter's 1924 novel, *The Magic Mountain*. Yet a residue of tough realism remained, despite the altered political circumstances. This was most famously articulated by Max Weber in his essay "Politics as a Vocation," which began life as a lecture given in Munich in January 1919, during the German Revolution. Weber, who opposed the revolution, urged young idealists not to fall into the trap of naiveté. He cautioned that those engaged in politics should practice an "ethic of responsibility," weighing social benefits against potential costs. A politician responsible for the common good also had to deploy power and "morally dubious means." Anything else was the behavior of the "political infant."[2]

Weber is regarded as one of the fathers of "realist" thought by modern theorists of international relations; "Politics as a Vocation" is taken as a foundation stone in that canon.[3] He had read Machiavelli's *The Prince* by the age of thirteen and has been credited with being the German thinker who came closest to achieving a synthesis of Hegel and Kant.[4] More specifically, Weber also occupies an interesting place in the story of *Realpolitik*. This was not least because his father had been a National Liberal politician in the age of Ludwig von Rochau. Leading National Liberals, including Friedrich Dahlmann and Treitschke, had stayed at his home.[5]

As a student in Berlin in the 1880s, Weber had attended the ageing Treitschke's lectures and had become alarmed by their tone and what he saw as a lack of scholarly objectivity and detachment in their content. Weber also saw Treitschke's popularity as a professor as an indictment of his peers and fellow students. Their lack of intellectual depth manifested itself in their tendency to revert to chauvinism or a cultish admiration for Bismarck. He observed with distaste "the frenetic jubilation that broke out in Treitschke's classes when he said anything that smacked of anti-Semitism." Recalling the way in which Treitschke could electrify a packed lecture theater, Weber suggested that this was "above all the audience's fault":

It is the same case with Bismarck: had the nation known how to deal with him, to oppose him firmly at the time he needed it most . . . they would have understood this from the beginning, but now it is too late—then the effects of his personal policy, so often destructive, would not have taken on the dimension that they have. And if my generation did not already worship militarism and similar monstrosities, the culture of so-called "realism," if they did not already despise all those endeavours that aspire to their goals without appealing to the evil side of man, especially to man's rudeness, then a mass of one-sided opinions often stridently so—the excitement of the battle against other opinions, and a predilection for what is now called Realpolitik that has arisen under the compelling impact of success would not be the only things that they take with them from Treitschke's class.[6]

This was a theme to which Weber returned on a number of occasions before the First World War. First, he thought *Realpolitik* was a rather lazy term that tended to be used, post facto, to describe simple common sense and to give it some intellectual gloss. "On the whole, people have the inclination to adapt strongly to those things that promise success or temporary success—in itself entirely understandable—not only in the means or the method by which they hope to achieve their final ideals," he wrote. In Germany, "people try to embellish such behaviour with the slogan 'Realpolitik.'" Thus Weber bemoaned that "type of 'satisfied' German for whom it was impossible not to support whatever was 'presently successful' with a breast inflated by Realpolitik." Other nations practiced self-interest but "do not chatter about it." The German, by contrast, "must turn Realpolitik into a slogan which he then embraces with all the ardour of feminine emotion."[7]

So Weber was conscious of what might be called the bastardization of *Realpolitik*. Yet, to what extent did he escape the trap himself? It has been argued, convincingly, that "Politics as a Vocation" bore a mild resemblance to Treitschke's work—not least in the "bleak Lutheran heroics" that Weber employed. Added to this was the sense of pessimism and despair that Weber felt about Germany's defeat in First World War. Weber was a fierce critic of the Treaty of Versailles, signed in July 1919, just a few months before he delivered his lecture. He was particularly critical of the way in which the Allies had aimed to apportion blame for the outbreak of the war—"searching like old ladies for the 'guilty one.'" Above all, Weber's realism was a realism of limits rather than possibility. He was inclined to dismiss something as utopian or unrealistic for the reason that he did not agree with it. Though his words were clad in "the rhetoric of realism," Weber in fact succumbed to the temptations of fatalism and despair.[8] This was a realism encased by the beholder's own immediate preoccupations.

The Faint Strains of *Idealpolitik* and the "Other than I"

Those who had opposed Germany's decision to go to war in 1914 were more willing to challenge *Realpolitik* at its foundations. Writing in the *Zürcher Zeitung*, a Swiss German paper, Dr. Hugo Ganz, an exiled Austrian publicist, expressed concern that German liberals were not using the moment of defeat to educate their country politically. For Ganz, the war, and the defeat that followed, was a product of "the inevitable consequences of the methods by which the empire had been created." The "blood and iron" approach had proved to be a fallacy. Instead, liberal ideals—such as international reconciliation, peaceful democratic development, good understanding with neighboring nations—were ultimately more realistic. Had the "impractical idealists" been listened to, Germany would be neither hated nor defeated. Her undoubted contribution to civilization would not be repudiated by a resentful world.[9]

Yet the case for a new internationalism was a difficult one to make in Germany after 1918. First, the new international system was predicated on German defeat and (as Weber had complained) an assumption of German guilt. Second, more fundamentally, the League of Nations looked weak from its inception because of the decision of the United States to remain aloof. This much was acknowledged by the exiled German pacifist and ethicist, Friedrich William Foerster. In a chilling irony, Foerster was the author of a 1920 memoir called *Mein Kampf*, which detailed his struggle against German militarism.

On the question of the League of Nations, Foerster was willing to concede that "Western pacifism has not displayed a genius equal to a world problem." It had "too much architecture, too little living soul." Yet, he asked his countrymen, did they really have an effective alternative? Over the past generation, their devotion to raison d'état had prevented Germans from seeing "the reality of the *other than-I*": "In spite, therefore, of all our talk of 'Realpolitik,' we have remained altogether incapable of assessing the surrounding world objectively, or of emerging from our own drunken egoism: and this especially because, in addition, a fundamentally false political philosophy has taught us to look upon egoism as the only true world philosophy."

What Foerster hoped for was a "league of culture," a greater interchange of ideas between nations. While he admitted that this might be "a dream for which the world is not prepared," he made the case that it was very much in Germany's self-interest to study and reflect on other cultures. The Romans, at their zenith, had been animated by a love of Hellenic culture. It was precisely its willingness to escape "from its one-sidedness, this self-development towards universality" that allowed Rome to become dominant. In the modern era, the respect that the English had traditionally had for German culture had served them similarly well. The Englishman also had a hard ego, but he was blessed with an understanding that there were others, and they must be reckoned with. In fact, Foerster went so far as to argue that a study of English culture might cure Germans of their "hallucinations of 'Realpolitik' " and a "conceited assumption that we are fundamentally superior to all others because in the matter of conquering we have made such great strides."

Germany's warmongering had also been based on a failure to appreciate the consequences of its own geopolitical position in the center of Europe. "We overlooked the fact that he who sits in the centre must ask for justice, not power," he wrote, "We called upon the earth god. He came and subjected us to his laws." Rather than invent a new *Realpolitik*, Germans should adopt the reverse course, regain confidence in their own idealism, and become "the prime movers among the genuine up-builders." The best course for Germany was to take the lead in world federation, as it had previously taken the lead in preserving European tranquillity through her own federal constitution. "The spiritual attitude of the centre, not that of the periphery, decides the fate of the world," wrote Foerster. Because of Germany's location and historic development its true destiny was to "play the part of mediator." The German "must emerge from the provincialism" of narrow nationalism and restore honor to the German name.[10]

Could theologians and ethicists save Germany from lurching back into the worst excesses of Treitschkean nationalism, or would nationalism trump liberalism in Germany once again? An interesting test case was Ernst Troeltsch, a prominent Protestant theologian and philosopher. Before the war, Troeltsch had been appealed to directly by a succession of English academics as a prominent professor who might exert a moderating influence in his homeland. He had expressed the view, for example, that a state need only expand as far as its interests demanded. When pressed, however, he had responded by claiming that German interests were in direct hostility to those of the British, that there was no hope of reconciliation, and that Germany's only choice was war.[11]

After the war, Troeltsch visited London and aimed to repair some of the damage. He denounced the theoretical fixation on the nation-state that existed in Germany and the tendency to regard compromise as weak. He also spoke of the "indestructible moral core" of the League of Nations and the potential for "communities of value."[12] Indeed, Troeltsch offered an ingenious diagnosis of what he saw as a contradiction at the core of the German mind. "Look at one of its sides, and you will see an abundance of romanticism and lofty idealism; look at the other, and you will see a realism that goes to the verge of cynicism and of utter indifference to all ideals and all morality; but what you will see above all is an inclination to make an astonishing combination of the two elements—in a word to brutalize romance, and to romanticize cynicism."[13]

Yet Troeltsch and others also returned to an earlier theme: Anglo-Saxon hypocrisy. He was one of a number of scholars—such as Hermann Oncken—who engaged in a lengthy debate about Thomas More's 1516 text *Utopia* in the decade after the war. On the one hand, More's idealism was beyond question—both in his vision of a commonwealth of men and in his martyrdom. On the other, he was an apparatchik of the court who enjoyed great personal wealth. Typically, More was known to be an exponent of mercantilism and a ruthless proponent of England's trading rights. He was therefore the perfect example of the English capacity to act with naked self-interest while casting these actions in a humanitarian light.[14]

These were rather niche arguments, of course. The effects did not trickle down beyond the heights of the academy. Writing about this period more than forty years later, one of Meinecke's students, Hajo Holborn of Yale, criticized the German historical profession in the interwar period for abdicating public and political leadership. The "ever-increasing specialization and professionalization of scholarship interfered with wide communication" and people began to look elsewhere for synthesis and narrative. They were presented with a new brand of populist writers—filling the hole left by Treitschke—who stressed, above all, the vitality of German *Kultur*. Chief among these was Oswald Spengler whose 1918 book, *The Decline of the West*, had actually been written in expectation of a German victory.

Spengler was at the heart of what Troeltsch called a "neo-conservative counterrevolution" in Germany, which aimed to purge the country of liberalism and capitalism.[15]

In this discussion, real *Realpolitik* (in its 1853 form) was never fully revived, even if Rochau himself was not entirely lost to view. In 1921, the first and only biography of Rochau was published in Heidelberg.[16] Significantly, it contained an introduction by Oncken.[17] Like Weber, Oncken was a critic of Treitschke and later became an opponent of Nazi Germany.[18] Yet he also shared with Treitschke an admiration for the *Realpolitikal Instinkt* that Rochau had instilled in German liberalism, and he believed it still had relevance to Weimar Germany.[19] Evidently, it was difficult to let go fully.

When applied at the level of policy, the reincarnated German *Realpolitik* also went in odd directions. In 1920, the *New York Tribune* alerted its readers to a new pamphlet by Captain Georg von Trapp, an Austro-Hungarian navy officer decorated for his role in Germany's submarine campaign (and the subject of *The Sound of Music*). For the previous quarter of a century at least, Germany's naval strategy had been directed, above all, against England's naval predominance. Now, Trapp suggested that Germany had made a grievous error. He absolved England from blame in the rivalry. He even called for a German National Assembly resolution denouncing the previous policy as "one of the most essential causes of the war" and committing to an alliance with England on every issue. To American observers, such an extreme change of position indicated an alarming tendency to swing from one extreme to another. "What . . . strikes anybody not a German is the utter unreality of the thing Captain Trapp talks, not politics, but the philosophy of either or," wrote a reviewer of Trapp's pamphlet in the *New York Tribune*. It was typical of "that lack of a sense for reality that characterizes the nation of *Realpolitik*." The true German "does not know or care as to what really is; he is coerced by the force of his assumed major premise, and such is the force of his logic that he frequently confounds 'ought' with 'is.'" The true German, it seemed, was "a sentimentalist parading as a logician."[20]

Germany had made terrible strategic mistakes; of that there was no question. But there was no consensus about what had gone wrong and plenty of self-serving revisionism about the events leading to the war. Traditional voices on the German right, for example, attempted to play down the suggestion that Germany had taken a fanatic course and had elevated racism and chauvinism to the platform of policy. The activity of the Pan-German

League, argued Dr. Otto Hammann, was confined "to an upper nationalistic stratum of people, with all the utter deficiency of half education in
political affairs and did not reach deep down into the people as a whole." In
this class, Hammann could admit, "the superman of a Nietszschian philosophy was embodied in its grossest form." These were men who imagined
themselves to be the true heirs of Bismarck even though they were completely lacking in the qualities of their hero. But while such views exerted
some influence on domestic affairs, Hammann claimed that they had no
impact on German foreign policy itself, which had still been run, in a sensible way, by traditional elites.

The danger of such revisionism was that it could become a tool of apo-
logia, seized on by those who aimed to play down the more mendacious
aspects of German nationalism. In some instances this was a deliberate ploy.
When his work was translated into English, Hammann was introduced
to American audiences as a "distinguished German publicist." It was not
mentioned that he had been director of the Press Section of the German
Foreign Office during the war, whose job it had been to offer positive views
of Germany to the rest of the world (particularly the United States). In the
1920s, Hammann was championed by the American historian Harry Elmer
Barnes, who later became infamous as a Holocaust denier. In a review of
a book on the Pan-German League in 1925, Barnes rejected the idea that
the First World War had been caused by Germany (blaming instead the
French and Russians).[21] The debate about the origins of the war was not
easy to settle. But, as Part IV will show, it was because of these precedents
that some historians—such as A. J. P. Taylor and Peter Viereck—were to be
so quick to raise the alarm at any sign of a new revisionism about German
history after 1945.

Meinecke and Pax Anglo-Saxonica

More subtle attempts to reinvigorate *Realpolitik* did exist among those
who had advocated it before 1914. Friedrich Meinecke began the next
evolution in his thinking by attempting to offer some explanation for
Germany's defeat. *After the Revolution*, published in 1919, suggested that
much of the blame for Germany's predicament lay with Kaiser Wilhelm
II, who had proved a disastrous heir to Bismarck's foreign policy. Above
all, he had dragged Germany into Bismarck's nightmare scenario: a war

on two fronts, against both France and Russia. The Kaiser's first mistake had been to give Grand Admiral Alfred von Tirpitz too much control over influencing naval strategy. The second was the failure to achieve *détente* where it was possible (above all with England). The third—going against Hammann—was to spend too much time listening to the Pan-German League, the ultra-nationalist pressure group that demanded the expansion of Germany eastward and the expulsion of Poles, Slavs, and Jews.[22]

It was in 1924, the same year that *The Magic Mountain* was published, when Meinecke came to the forefront, once again, in the history of *Realpolitik*. The occasion for this was the publication of his most famous work, *Die Idee der Staatsräson*, later published in English as *Machiavellism: The Doctrine of Raison d'État and Its Place in Modern History*. The book can be seen as an attempt to offer the most authoritative history to date of *Realpolitik*—a word he used throughout. The work was dedicated to his friend Ernest Troeltsch and it has been argued that both men were in some ways responding to Weber's "Politics as a Vocation."[23]

Meinecke also attacked the pacifist writer Friedrich Foerster. The key to political insight, Meinecke believed, was still historicism. Any discussion with Foerster was impossible because he did "not speak the intellectual language created by German historicism" in the tradition of Leopold von Ranke, but instead the language of "the old Natural Law of Christian and medieval times." Since he had "not eaten the apple of historicisim, he had not participated in the sinful Fall in which he regards all of us . . . as being entangled."[24] Despite this criticism of Foerster, Meinecke was prepared to concede that the message of Christian idealism should be viewed with respect "since it sharpens the conscience and draws attention to the shortcomings of mere relativism." Moreover, Meinecke took Foerster's point that Germany had become intellectually isolated, partly because of its departure from the natural law theories beloved of other Western nations. A system of thought based on a narrow pursuit of the national interest had also proved to be flawed. So while he did not abandon the foundations of his own thought, he did concede that there was a "profound need to carry out a self-examination of historicism." On such grounds, there might be possible a "new intellectual understanding between German historical thought and that of the Western peoples," though he suggested that this would take generations.[25]

Rather than simply revert to the tropes of pre-1914 German nationalism, Meinecke was attempting to make a serious new contribution to his countrymen's understanding of statecraft. Perhaps the most striking argument in the book was Meinecke's reassessment of the foundations of English power. He frequently quoted Edmund Burke (to whom Rochau also owed a debt), had read the "realist" novels of Sir Walter Scott (also admired by Karl Marx), and was well versed in British diplomatic history. Before the war, he had followed English commentary on Germany closely and had particularly enjoyed George Bernard Shaw's denunciations of English hypocrisy. English victory in the war had caused him to think again. What he and others like Treitschke had once denounced as "cant" in fact had a realist core to it. In a brilliant dissection of British power projection, Meinecke described how, having gained predominance through brute force and naval power, the English suddenly changed the script: they "showed an increasing tendency to change the sword of the naked power-policy, which the English always pursued, into the sword of the executor of the law—whether summoned to the task by God or by justice and morality." Thus they talked of the need to preserve international treaties and maritime laws while failing to mention that those laws had been crafted in their image, and in their interests.

The Anglo-Saxons were indeed hypocritical but were less naïve than Meinecke had once assumed. Hypocrisy, perhaps, was a useful tool in international affairs. What they practiced was, in fact, "the most effective kind of Machiavellianism, which could be brought by the national Will of power-policy to become unconscious of itself, and to appear (not only to others, but also itself) as being pure humanity, candour and religion." In other words, it was a useful self-delusion and something that had been missed by Germans who "yielded to the German tendency to call things by their proper names."[26] In their rage at English hypocrisy, German theorists of state had failed to understand this nuance. Treitschke, typically, thought and wrote in "imperatives." His statements were like decrees. For more than a generation he had been the leader of those who saw the nation-state as the giver of power and freedom. Through his influence, however, Treitschke had also become "the corrupter of those who prized desire more highly than thought, and now found in his inspiringly convincing statements and decrees a substitute for all their own intellectual endeavours." [27] In other words, German critical thinking had atrophied under Treitschke and slipped into absolutes.

For Meinecke, the First World War had seen the clash of two competing systems of political thought. Both Western and German political thought had demonstrated profound flaws. The West (by which he meant England, France, and America) had proved to be naïve about the nature of the international system and had failed to respond to those realities until it was too late. The profound shortcoming of the Western mode of thought was that "it did not affect the statesman deeply." It had hindered the rapid spread of raison d'état in international affairs, and "so it only took effect either in confused complaints or doctrinaire postulates, or else in hypocrisy and cant."

The failure of German political thought, by contrast, was to go too far in the other direction. This was reflected in the tendency "to excuse and idealize power politics" and even to accord to it "a superior type of morality," on the grounds that it was, at least, honest. The end result was the creation of a "crudely naturalistic and biological ethics of force." This had important implications for Germany going forward. Together with this "false idealization of power politics," he warned, "there must cease the false idealization of the State."[28] Before the war, Germans had greater confidence in "the beneficent meaning of power politics and in the warlike classes of nations." However, the negative aspects of this development received too little attention. As he now put it, "Power politics and *Realpolitik*, once freed of universal principles—and universal principles are basically ethical principles—could easily degenerate into a . . . politics of violence." The brutality of the late war made it all the more important to reconcile these competing notions. "Utilitarian and ethical motives must work in unison," he argued, and it was necessary to restrict the full excesses of state egoism. It was only by "restricting itself, purifying itself and suppressing the natural element in itself," that the national interest could be successfully pursued.[29]

Meinecke's view of the League of Nations was skeptical but not entirely hostile. At the very least, unlike Weber, he thought it a worthy experiment. Even if it was unlikely to succeed there was no alternative but to strive for its success "if one is not to sacrifice oneself to a boundless Machiavellianism." He confessed that before the war, he had regarded the idea of the League of Nations "simply as a cosmopolitan idea" that had put unwelcome restrictions on the autonomy of nations. After the war, he now believed that it was "a most sacred duty" to at least try to find another basis of international relations.[30] If the League of Nations should fail, as he expected it would, Meinecke wondered if another type of liberal order might be founded—one based on the dominance of Britain and America. The era of international conflicts might instead be brought to an end "not by a genuine League of Nations, but by the world-hegemony of the Anglo-Saxon powers, in whose hands the strongest physical powers of the globe are already concentrated." Such a *pax Anglo-Saxonica* would not be ideal by any means, but its strength lay in its being more endurable for those nations under it than many other forms of external dominance.[31]

If Meinecke's acceptance of Anglo-Saxon hegemony sounded fatalistic, others in Germany were rather more resistant to the new status quo. It was precisely such a prospect that Adolf Hitler railed against in *Mein Kampf*— his two-volume memoir published in 1925 and 1926—in which he even floated the idea of an Anglo-German alliance in its stead.[32] Meinecke's cautious meditations on the League of Nations and the dangers of chauvinistic nationalism were of little interest to Hitler and those who spoke of *Dolchstoßlegende* (a "stab in the back" by those who sued for peace). Writing in 1926, then, the German American academic Christian Gauss (whose father had fled Prussia in the nineteenth century) warned that German ultra-nationalists still constituted a powerful party and wanted to recover Germany's lost prestige. In fact, *Realpolitik* was only half the problem. Here Gauss made an all-too-rare distinction. The real danger was in fact *Machtpolitik* (an overwhelming commitment to the politics of force as the defining factor in international relations), which had as its aim the dismantling of the existing order. The increase in Franco-German tensions over the Rhineland in 1926 was a warning that old habits died hard.[33]

It soon became clear that there was more room for maneuver than Meinecke presumed in 1924. The weakness of the League of Nations opened up the international arena again—to new opportunities and new threats. In 1927, in the *History of the German-English Alliance Problem 1890–1901*, Meinecke returned to a theme he had first developed in *After the Revolution* in 1919. In it he emphasized the importance of intuition and creativity in statecraft. Foreign policy was an arena in which there was a greater sphere for movement and intelligence than a mere recognition of hard facts. He now distinguished between those who were adept at understanding raison d'état in foreign affairs and those who acted in its name but against its logic.[34]

Meinecke lived until 1954, making it very difficult to look at this work without viewing it through the prism of the rise of Hitler, Nazism, and the Second World War. In 1918, he had identified himself as a supporter of the Weimar Republic and was one of the founders of the German Democratic Party. Among his many influential students was Heinrich Brüning, the future chancellor of the Weimar Republic. Yet he was willing to reconcile himself to the Nazis, albeit grudgingly, after Hitler became chancellor in 1933. By November 1935, Meinecke found himself out of favor, and he was finally removed as editor of the *Historische Zeitschrift*.[35] He was privately critical of aspects of the regime but remained a virulent anti-Semite and supported the Nazi invasion of Poland in 1939. Meinecke's genius was in reading the context in which he operated, but he never quite escaped it. There was an important difference between being able to understand the political importance of *Zeitgeist*—as Rochau did—and being unable to see beyond it. Meinecke failed the second test.

Escaping *Realpolitik*: Liberal Zionism and Czech Nationalism

Despite the defeat of 1918, then, Germany refused to let go of *Realpolitik* entirely. Tellingly, it was those who had been on the receiving end of German nationalism who were most cognizant of its flaws and more willing to attack it at its core. Two subplots in the history of German *Realpolitik* reveal that some of the most imaginative attempts to transcend it—and to create a more sustainable basis for nationhood and security—came from two groups who had felt the blunt edge of German nationalism firsthand: German Jews and Czechs who spoke German but were not of German ethnicity.

Prominent among the first category was one of Meinecke's students—the Jewish theologian Franz Rosenzweig. In 1917, Rosenzweig (under the name Dr. Adam Bund) published an essay titled *Realpolitik*, written from the Macedonian front, where he was serving in an anti-aircraft unit. With the prospect of defeat looking more likely, Germany's "world historical mission" required it to depart from a narrow pursuit of the national interest. Bismarck's foreign policy had simply been based on an effective reading of the context in which he operated. The problem was that, since his death, *Realpolitik* had been celebrated as something sacrosanct: a value in itself. Such "calculating cunning," while sounding impressive, had actually left Germany directionless and in disarray, without a long-term strategy. Worse still, it had also fed into a narrow jingoism that undermined Germany's historical mission as a beacon of civilization and humanity.[36]

Early liberal Zionism took this argument further. Following in the tradition of Rosenzweig was the American rabbi and philosopher, Judah

L. Magnes, who had completed his PhD in Heidelberg and who arrived in Palestine in 1922. When he wrote of peace with indigenous Arabs, it was not just "a tactical . . . move in *Realpolitik*," Magnes insisted, at the time of clashes between Jewish settlers and local Arabs in 1928. Instead, he articulated a humanist vision of Zionist nationhood—shared by others such as Martin Buber and Ahad Ha'am—designed to transcend the limits of bourgeois culture and the chauvinism which so many European nationalisms had succumbed to. In its idealized form, this would "exemplify to the community of nations that national existence need not be fostered by militarism, *Realpolitik*, and chauvinism"—forces that these intellectuals held responsible for the First World War.[37]

Another iteration of this Jewish critique of German *Realpolitik* was the pacifist movement that emerged within Zionism at this time, evidenced by the "Jewish Society for International Understanding," formed in 1922 and led by Hans Kohn, a Czech-born, German-speaking Jew who immigrated to the United States before settling in Palestine in 1925. He was to become one of the most influential critics of totalitarianism in the interwar period. He wrote extensively about German history and, in particular, the malign influence of Heinrich von Treitschke. As a liberal nationalist, he looked to John Stuart Mill in England, Giuseppe Mazzini in Italy, and Thomas Masaryk, Prague philosophy professor, hero of Czech nationalism, and first president of Czechoslovakia from 1918 to 1935.[38]

The link between Jewish and Czech rejections of *Realpolitik* was not a coincidence, as the second subplot demonstrates. Despite the fact that Czechs were often on the receiving end of German chauvinism, there was also a strong element of Slavic anti-Semitism. Opposition to Czech chauvinism and racialism was one of the things that made Thomas Masaryk attractive to Kohn and others. He risked unpopularity among his countrymen by proving that the medieval manuscripts on which the Czech national myth was based were in fact forgeries. He also opposed the popular superstition of Jewish blood libel during the so-called Hilsner trials in Bohemia in 1899 to 1900. For Masaryk, aspiring nations should reflect individual ethics rather than naked self-interest. Also important was that Masaryk's strategy provided a practical alternative to narrow *Realpolitik*. He was a gradualist rather than an absolutist when it came to the question of Czech nationalism. Initially, he had called for reform within the Austro-Hungarian Empire rather than secession or independence. He was

the founder of the Realist Party in 1900, for which he sat in the Austrian
Parliament from 1907 to 1914, before becoming an advocate of Czech independence during the war. His strategy during the war was to convince the
Western nations—particularly the United States—of the need to support
the democratic self-determination of smaller states within Europe as something in the interest of the greater powers. This helped secure the independence of Czechoslovakia in 1918.

In 1925, a year after Meinecke published *Machiavellism*, Masaryk wrote
an essay titled "Reflections on the Question of War Guilt." This was in
response to what he saw as a German attempt to shift responsibility for
causing the war back on the Allies, thereby undermining the Versailles
settlement. Showing an awareness of the writings of Foerster, Troeltsch,
and Meinecke, he explored the distinction between Western political
thought and German theories of statecraft. In a now familiar script,
he argued that "German thought, beginning with Kant, took a wrong
road." From this point, the German universities "became the spiritual
barracks of . . . philosophical absolutism, which reached its consumma-
tion in the idea of the Prussian state and kingdom, deified by Hegel."
Prussian militarism and the racialism of the Pan-German League were
also thrown into the mix and the result was a headlong rush into war:
"Historical right was strengthened with the aid of Darwinism, through
the theory of mechanical evolution, guaranteeing success to the strongest. War and the making of war became divine institutions. Prussian
militarism . . . proclaimed the chief dogma of the so-called *Realpolitik*, the
notion that all right is born of might."

Masaryk rejected the idea that German philosophy was "entirely faulty."
On the contrary, it was "interesting and profound." "The savage and barbarian fight from original savagery; but in the World War, there were to be
found in the trenches disciples of Rousseau and Kant, Goethe and Herder,
Byron and Musset!" he wrote. At its core, however, German nationalism had proved to be "absolutist, violent, unjust to the greatness of free
united humanity."[39] Masaryk's condemnation of "so-called *Realpolitik*"
was also telling. While there is no evidence that Masaryk read Ludwig
von Rochau directly, one of his biographers has suggested that Masaryk's
political sensibilities were closer to the spirit of Rochau's "realpolitik" than
that of Bismarck himself.[40] Delivering a paper at King's College London
in 1930, Wickham Steed, foreign correspondent for the *Times*, who had

interviewed Masaryk in Prague, praised him on precisely these grounds. Masaryk held realism "to be the true aim of politics no less than of thought and of life." But there was a crucial difference. He taught that, "unlike the German notion of *Realpolitik*, realism in politics consists not of a cynical disregard of principles but of a scrupulous reckoning with facts, moral and material; that honesty is not only the best policy but the only safe guide in public as in private life; and that character, not astuteness or trickery, is the first requisite in a statesman." In Masaryk's conception of realism, the honest man was not "a simpleton nor a fool."

Crucially, Masaryk could claim successes to his name, just as much as Bismarck. Had he never been given the chance by the war to put his theories into action, he might still be thought an impractical moralist, "an ethical dreamer, who would be no match for politicians skilled in the art of blackmailing governments, hoodwinking the crowd, and coining catchwords that signify in practice something different from their ostensible meaning." However, as the leader of a "new school of political thought and an advocate of new diplomatic methods, he beat the old school, again and again, on its own ground." In this respect Masaryk was Bismarck's superior. Both of them were instrumental in founding new states, of course. But if Bismarck's version of *Realpolitik* made allowance for moral factors in politics, it did so unwillingly. Masaryk, by contrast, welcomed these "impalpable moral factors," gave them their full weight, and held them to be essential.[41]

Before 1930, one could argue that Masaryk's strategy was a model for what might be called a "liberal realism." One might even say that he was a much better exemplar of Rochau's original concept of *Realpolitik* than Bismarck. Yet ultimately his triumph in Czechoslovakia could not withstand the collapse of the European order in the 1930s. Confronted with the rise of Nazism, the liberal Western nations that had granted Czech independence in 1918 sold it back again to Adolf Hitler with the Munich Agreement of 1938. Writing in 1950, on the centenary of Masaryk's birth, A. J. P. Taylor praised him in a similar manner to Wickham Steed. "Unlike most nationalist leaders Masaryk understood power," Taylor wrote, but "he was more a realist than Bismarck for he knew the force of ideals." And yet, as Western and Eastern Europe became estranged again in the 1930s, the gains Masaryk had won looked increasingly vulnerable. With the prospect of German or Russian dominance befalling them once again, the Slavic races—Czechs, Slovaks, Croats, and Serbs—soon began to act like separate peoples, retreating into their own forms of chauvinistic nationalism. In Taylor's view, Masaryk was far too optimistic about these different groups being able to overlook centuries of conflict between them. There was in Masaryk's life a deeper lesson: "nationalism without humanism is harsh and destructive: humanism without nationalism is academic and barren."[42]

10

Realpolitik, Fascism, and Appeasement

By the final years of the 1920s, the humanitarian ideal by which some had hoped to recast international relations looked increasingly flimsy. In 1928, in an article on Italy's fascist leader, Benito Mussolini, the American philosopher William Kilborne Stewart reflected on the rise and fall of a "phantasmal and insubstantial" vision of world government. The experiences of the last decade had created a broken idol, embodied in the League of Nations. Europe was left fighting over the dead body. In his own country, the United States, Kilborne Stewart said that there was much to bemoan. He complained about corruption, partisanship, and mob politics. But the sickness in European politics ran deeper. It was manifested in the return of the creed of "realpolitik" across the capitals of Europe's leading states. Liberal internationalism had depended on an optimistic view of mankind. As such, it had been predicated on weak foundations. Europe's preference for realpolitik reflected its unique proclivity for pessimism in culture and politics. It was reverting to type, turning again to a long-established "philosophical tradition of disillusionment." In this context, it was no surprise to find that the writings of Niccolò Machiavelli were coming back into fashion again. Mussolini had led the way, celebrating Machiavelli as "the prophet of the pragmatic era in politics" and *The Prince* as "the statesman's supreme guide."[1]

Many other writers testified to this latest Machiavellian moment. The tradition was particularly strong in Italy for obvious reasons, of course. The Italian Catholic priest and Christian Democrat, Luigi Sturzo, who was exiled by Mussolini, traced the origins of fascism back to Machiavelli's concept of "effectual truth" (truth confirmed by success). Adapted by Cesare Borgia, Louis XIV of France, and then by Bismarck, this was "the politics of absolutism, of power without limits." In the international arena, it meant that treaties were to be preserved if they were useful and flouted if they were not. The effects of this logic had already been seen in recent history. When the Germans declared in 1914 that the treaty guaranteeing Belgian independence was a mere "scrap of paper," they had given the truest expression of *Realpolitik*.[2]

What had gone wrong? After the First World War, Machiavellianism had been censured as the "quintessence of Prussianism," observed the English theologian, Reverend J. C. Hardwick. By 1930, however, with democracy "more or less under a cloud for a variety of reasons; and being politically disillusioned," there was a tendency—once again—to "find Machiavelli's cynical realism very congenial." What was particularly dangerous was the way this cynical realism was combining with more recent ideas and trends. First were the arguments of those intellectuals who "tell us we are being swamped by mediocrity and ignorance"—and that democracy was effete and feminizing. Second were the theories of men of science (by which he meant the followers of Social Darwinism), "especially the biologists, whose utterances are accepted with a veneration as uncritical as that with which the dogmas of the priest were once received." The third trend was the decline of Christianity that had seen men casting elsewhere for the spiritual nourishment they had once sought in God.[3]

Worse still, these ingredients were mixed together in an atmosphere of almost constant political crisis. The result was a whole new set of putative "solutions" to Europe's ills. Fascism was unique in the way it combined elements of political theory from both left and the right. In 1930, Horace Friess, professor of philosophy at Columbia University and leader of the New York Society for Ethical Culture, argued that it grew out of an odd marriage between materialism and idealism in mid-nineteenth-century political thought. Karl Marx provided the most obvious illustration of this tendency in his attempt to offer a materialist analysis of history and society, while holding out "salvation" for mankind. Fascism had expanded the canvas on which grand designs were envisaged; Mussolini and those like him talked of imperial projects and a global game. The materialism that served them was that of the era of mass production, in which entire nation states could be mobilized for the attainment of national glory.[4]

Arguably the most insightful analyst of European fascism in the 1930s was Hans Kohn, a Prague-born German-speaking Jew who had spent five years in a Russian prisoner of war camp after fighting for Imperial Germany in the war. During the 1930s, Kohn wrote a series of prominent public essays that appeared as a collected volume, *Revolutions and Dictatorships*, published on the eve of the Second World War.[5] Kohn was insistent that those confronting the rise of these revanchist powers had to understand the ideological basis of their challenge to the postwar international system, rather than seeing fascism as an assertion of national interests alone. Germany, Italy, Spain, and Japan were revolting against "the established order of moral and intellectual values." In the second half of the nineteenth century, nationalism had increasingly been "stripped of all the implications of a cosmopolitan message." Concepts of equality and fraternity, as far as they were accepted, were strictly limited within nations and had never been transferred to foreign affairs. In his interpretation, fascism itself owed a hidden debt to biblical Messianism and was best understood as the "child of Prussianism married to Romanticism."

To say that all states acted with a clear-headed pursuit of the national interest was to miss the point. For Kohn, when fascists talked of *Realpolitik*, they did not mean "realism" or "realistic." It was a fatal mistake in Western capitals to see their actions in this way. What they really meant was *Machtpolitik* (the politics of force). This was something that they pursued with an ideological vigor that could not be bought off by reason.[6] The liberal democratic nations were paying the price for the failure to establish a robust international order. Kohn was no misty-eyed pacifist. He understood that "democracy, human solidarity, and 'high-sounding' moral phrases" were insufficient guarantees of international order. The will to peace was useless without a serious strategy for how peace was to be achieved. Fascism had fed off this self-doubt in the West. The defeatism and relativism of democracy in the face of counter-revolution was the most effective weapon in the hands of the followers of totalitarian ideals.[7]

Within Germany, too, many traditional nationalists saw something distinct in the creed of Nazism—an unhealthy departure from the *Realpolitik* of the Bismarck era. In 1933, the conservative political theorist Oswald Spengler argued in *Politische Schriften* that genuine *Realpolitik* ran completely counter to the racialism resorted to by the ultra-nationalists of the Nazi Party. In an echo of Ludwig von Rochau's *Foundations*, he argued that anti-Semitism was "petty, superficial, narrow-minded and undignified."[8]

To add to the confusion, the Nazis themselves were unsure about whether they wanted to associate themselves with *Realpolitik*. In some respects, it suited them to lay claim to the mantle. In 1939 the Nazi Party sponsored a study of the work of Moeller van den Bruck, the German historian and critic of Weimar Germany who created the phrase "Third Reich." Unwilling to give him any credit for the creation of National Socialism, the Nazis denounced him for not having Hitler's clear-sighted understanding of political success. Moeller van den Bruck was mocked for having an "unrealistic ideology which has nothing to do with actual historical developments or with sober *Realpolitik*."[9] Keener observers of German politics were not so easily swayed by this argument. They were aware, for example, of Hitler's disdain for the self-limiting nature of Bismarckian foreign policy.[10]

Following Hans Kohn, the German-American scholar Peter Viereck also warned that Nazi strategy was not as "realistic" as those confronting it might presume. On the surface, *Realpolitik* "by its very brutality and clear-cutness seems a pretty simple matter," he wrote. In practice, "few psychological motives of states and statesmen are more complex." Whereas Kohn had preferred to use the term *Machtpolitik* to describe the Nazi mindset, Viereck thought *Metapolitik* captured the essence of it. Nazism represented a "conscious force of anti-reason." As evidence for this, he quoted a passage from Hitler's *Mein Kampf* in which he dismissed Goethe and Kant as theorists of the Western mind, with nothing to offer modern Germany. They had put forward a view of civilization that elevated reason and rationalism above all else. In Hitler's view, the true patriot preferred to seek out the "life forces" and the irrational impulses of the heart. In Viereck's view, anti-Semitism and Teutonic racialism was an outgrowth of this. There was no self-restraint in Nazism. In the First World War, Prussian militarism was self-limited "by a stern Protestant sense of duty and by that genuine *noblesse oblige* which so often atones for snobbery." Those confronting Nazi Germany had to understand that any residues of Bismarckian restraint had gone. Hitler's true debt was to Richard Wagner with his "offensive grandiloquence, emotion to the point of hysteria" and vague and mystic ideas of "soaring and striving."[11]

Appeasement versus Confrontation

It was one thing to recognize that Nazism represented something new and dangerous; it was quite another to create an effective policy to counter it in the international arena. As early as 1933, in a debate on Germany in the House of Commons just a few months after Hitler had become chancellor,

Austen Chamberlain, the former British foreign secretary (1924–9) and Nobel Peace Prize winner, sounded a warning that Nazism was a reincarnation of Prussian imperialism but with "an added savagery, a racial pride."[12] Yet, ironically, it was Austen Chamberlain's younger half-brother, Neville, who was to become so closely associated with the policy of appeasement, as prime minister from 1937 to 1940.

The ambiguous nature of fascism posed a new type of dilemma for Western statesmen. In the domestic sphere, its revolutionary nature was beyond doubt. Much hinged on their reading of how this translated into international affairs. In this, there were some promising precedents. Despite the fact it was a revolutionary state, Britain had been able to deal with Soviet Russia on the basis of interests over idealism. If the fascist nations were simply asserting their national interests, then it was possible for the Western powers to accommodate themselves to these. Even if this meant undercutting the principle of collective security or international law, the history of diplomacy was full of examples in which strong nations cut deals in order to avoid war. On the other hand, if fascism actually represented something novel—and more ideologically driven—then sating its appetite by appeasement might not be so easy.

Some shared Kohn's analysis—that fascism was a revolutionary force in the international arena that fed off signs of weakness. *Realpolitik*, when emanating from Rome or Berlin, was not to be confused with "realism." As early as August 1933, Robert Vansittart, permanent under-secretary at the British Foreign Office, described how Germany, with Hitler as its newly appointed chancellor, demonstrated "a growing tendency to seize every opportunity and exploit every concession in order to push ahead with a truculent and aggressive *Realpolitik*." Vansittart can be credited with an early critique of appeasement. "So long as this mood prevails, the intervention of an honest broker ceases to act as a lubricant, and may easily become either a dangerous irritant or a general source of confusion and insecurity," he warned; "there are times when this delicate procedure can easily do more harm than good—and the period we are entering upon would seem to be one of them." At such moments, the only chance of "preventing a dictator situated like Hitler from committing himself irrevocably to a policy of foreign adventure and provocation is to pull him up sharp before his plans have crystallised," Vansittart advised, "and this sharp pulling up can be best and most painlessly done by joint action of the Great Powers."[13]

In England, this debate intensified considerably in the mid-1930s. Writing for the *Spectator* in 1935, foreign correspondent Francis Gower suggested that Mussolini was more "romanticist" than "realist." Italian policy was better characterized as *Wilpolitik* ("will to power" politics) than a rational pursuit of interests and resources. Italy's ambitions over Abyssinia were to be understood in this light. The justification that empire-building in Abyssinia was necessary to release population pressure on the Italian state was a prime example of the "affectation of realism." The only way to deal with Mussolini was with a will to peace, to match his will to power.[14] The will to peace, however, required a willingness to use force.

It would be wrong to suggest that the supporters of appeasement were completely naïve about the nature of what they faced. In 1935, the former British ambassador to Italy, James Rennell Rodd, now Lord Rennell, noted that "the pretext of Realpolitik" had often been used "as a mantle to cover action which the traditional practice of the society of nations would never endorse." Yet, while recognising the mendacious elements of fascism, there was still a presumption that a core of reason underlay it. "We have perhaps in this country been a little too prone to assume that moral values will influence international politics," Rennell suggested. When seeking to solve tensions with other nations it was "indispensable to look at the issue from the point of view of those with whom we are at variance," and to see whether there was any justification for their position, and whether there might be grounds to satiate their appetite. Thus, he could understand how the German people could hold reasonable objections to the Treaty of Versailles.[15]

The same logic informed British attempts to come to terms with Mussolini, despite the Italian invasion of Abyssinia in October 1935. Both the British and French governments were prepared to allow the partition of Abyssinia, thereby granting Mussolini the Italian colony in Africa he desired. Part of the logic behind this was to bind Italy to them, and thereby provide a stronger united front against Hitler. When details of the negotiations became public, there was public outcry at the attempt to buy Mussolini off, particularly after he had flouted League of Nations conventions by invading a fellow member state. It was during this crisis that Neville Chamberlain—then chancellor of the exchequer—came to the forefront of British policy. On behalf of the cabinet, Chamberlain bemoaned the fact that the British government had been hamstrung by the conventions of the League, and the British public's attachment to the notion of "collective security".

For our purposes, what is significant is not so much the government's policy itself as the way Chamberlain rationalized it. The words he chose were revealing. In an article for the *Morning Post*, written in May 1936, he complained that: "We are debarred by so-called collective security from striking with Mussolini a private bargain such as might, at one and the same time, preserve the peace, and protect our vital Imperial interests. We have gained none of the advantages of the new system and lost all the advantages of the old." In place of collective security, Chamberlain appealed to a different tradition entirely: "What we require is to divest our diplomacy of cant metaphysics and the jargon of collective security, and to begin talking to Mussolini in the terms of Realpolitik."[16] In this, there was a crucial distinction to be made. By realpolitik, Chamberlain did not mean the Germanic mode of statecraft but the traditions of nineteenth-century British diplomacy, associated with Canning and Castlereagh. It was these precedents he sought out, in his extensive reading of diplomatic history from the era of congress diplomacy.[17]

The danger with this Anglicized version of realpolitik was not that it was Prussianism reincarnated. It was that once France and Britain reverted to the methods of the "old diplomacy," the practice spread like wildfire. Giving up on collective security became a self-fulfilling prophecy, causing a further fraying of the international order. If the so-called defenders of the liberal international order played the game, smaller nations had little choice but to engage in it also. This had a domino effect—and British officials were quick to recognise it. Tellingly, once Chamberlain reintroduced the word, it began to be found more frequently in diplomatic cables. In Egypt in 1936, for example, the British signed a treaty with the popular Wafd Party—a hasty bargain that reflected British concerns about the looming challenge posed by Italian imperial ambitions in North Africa. Within a year, it was reported that the Egyptians were lobbying the British to assist them with a move toward Arab unity, just as they had done at the time of the First World War. If this were forthcoming, so Arabists in the Foreign Office hoped, it would mean that Italian penetration in the area could be resisted. Once again, the British would be the champions of the Arab cause. If not, one diplomat in the Cairo bureau warned, the Arabs would turn to Italy as a sponsor. Here one could see how quickly Chamberlain's "realpolitik" approach could spread. The Egyptians would "find it difficult to avoid

British prime minister Neville Chamberlain meeting Italian dictator
Benito Mussolini at the Munich Conference in 1938. Within a year, the policy
of appeasement was in tatters and the Second World War had begun. Federal
Archives, Bild 183-R99302, Hoffmann, Heinrich.

coming to some sort of terms with what may prove to be the rising power
from a 'Realpolitik' point of view in the Near and Middle East."[18]

It also became clear that the fascist powers had a sense of ideological
common cause that cut across narrowly defined conceptions of the national
interest. This was illustrated by the intervention of Germany and Italy on
behalf of General Franco's Nationalists in the Spanish Civil War. In fact,
the sense of common cause in the battle for the soul of Europe increased
at the moment that the British and French willingness to preserve a liberal
democratic order dissipated. Writing in 1937, the liberal German philosopher and constitutional expert, Karl Loewenstein—having been forced to
flee the country for America in 1933—warned that Europe's fascists shared

a "missionary urge" to counter Bolshevism, both within their own states and in confrontation with the Soviet Union. Again, the language he used was telling. This priority was elevated above "other distinguishing marks in program, ideology, and nationally conditioned premises of *Realpolitik*."[19]

For the critics of appeasement, Chamberlain's use of "realpolitik" to defend British policy came to symbolize two things. The first was a strategy that was anything but realistic and would fail, on its own terms, because it did not grasp the nature of fascism. By this stage, in fact, the British government believed war to be extremely likely and was in fact buying time to allow for rearmament. The second thing that "realpolitik" came to symbolize was perhaps even more important, however. It was a cheapening and moral degeneration in British foreign policy that brought shame just as it courted disaster.

To continue a core theme of this book then, the language of foreign policy remained extremely important. In April 1938, under the terms of the Easter Accords, Britain effectively turned a blind eye to Italian control over Abyssinia in return for an Italian agreement not to further disrupt the status quo in the broader Middle East and to uphold free access to the Suez Canal. Once again, this met with furious opposition in Parliament. Shortly after the Anglo-Italian deal, the leader of the Labour Party in the House of Commons, Clement Attlee, read out the passage from the prime minister's 1936 article in the *Morning Post* in which he had expressed his desire to apply "realpolitik" to Mussolini. "I should like to congratulate the Prime Minister on his candour in having made it abundantly plain where his real sympathies lie," he said, holding up the offending article from two years before. "There was all that talk about not taking sides with rival ideologies and not putting Europe into rival camps, but when the realist has spoken he has shown his admiration for Signor Mussolini and his regime." Chamberlain had "thrown over the principles of the League of Nations." But Attlee believed worse was to come. Machiavelli was "the natural teacher of Signor Mussolini" and Machiavellianism did not imply the politics of honor or trust. As soon as it suited him, Mussolini would make another deal with Hitler, and the strategy would be undone.[20]

The pinnacle of Chamberlain's version of realpolitik came in Munich in September 1938, when, along with France and Italy, he agreed to Hitler's annexation of the Sudetenland in Czechoslovakia. While Chamberlain famously declared that the Munich Agreement meant "peace in our time," there had been no place for Czechoslovakia at the table. For American observers, it seemed very much that Britain and France—previously defenders of the League of Nations and collective security—had given up on the international system entirely. Writing in the *Baltimore Sun*, Arno Dosch-Fleurot, an American foreign affairs reporter and son of a German immigrant to Oregon, believed Munich proved that Europe as a whole had relapsed into the same games that caused war in 1914. The starting gun had been fired by Hitler's territorial revisionism but others soon followed suit. "Pushed around by Hitler's ruthless racism as it was by Bismarck's policy of 'blood and iron,' Europe has slipped back into its old rut," he wrote. Even before Chamberlain flew to see Adolf Hitler in September 1938, the prime minister had declared his intention to "be a realist—in other words, to accept the rule of force." When France invited Germany's foreign secretary, Joachim von Ribbentrop, to Paris to sign a bilateral treaty with Germany, the French entered frankly, if resignedly, into "the ways of *realpolitik*." This wiped out the last vestige of the collective security that France had been so wedded to just a few months before. In the British and French foreign offices, they needed only go back to their archives for ample precedents on what to do next. Nonetheless, Dosch-Fleurot believed that "the present-day *realpolitik* is even more frank than in the last half of the nineteenth century."

Again, once the major powers reverted to type, it was inevitable that smaller nations would follow suit. Thus the Poles began to bully the Czechs over the disputed Teschen region, just as the Germans had done to them over the Sudetenland. József Beck, the Polish foreign minister, was, according to Dosch-Fleurot, "a *realpolitiker* if there ever was one," seeking to balance the Nazis and the Soviets against each other and again, circumventing the League of Nations. Faced with an accumulation of challenges to their survival, the Czechs had "thrown overboard their policy of the past twenty years, even throwing out literally the statues of the indisputably high-minded and patriotic President Masaryk along with it, in order to fall in line with the '*realpolitik*' of the day."[21] Masaryk had achieved Czech independence by understanding but bettering German *Realpolitik* and using the liberal internationalist moment at the end of the First World War to press forward the Czech right to self-determination. Now the Czechs were tangled under the wheels of great power politics once again, and another war was imminent.

Understanding the Twenty Years' Crisis

The two decades between the two world wars have traditionally been understood as providing the stage for the first of the three "Great Debates" that defined the practice of International Relations as an academic discipline. The collapse of interwar idealism, in the form of support for the League of Nations or the policies of collective security, is sometimes said to have culminated in a triumph for the "realist" view of international relations. In this interpretation, the publication of E. H. Carr's *The Twenty Years' Crisis* in 1939 represented an important moment for the triumph of the "realist" perspective, coinciding with the collapse of interwar liberal internationalism, on which realists had been proved right.[22]

The Twenty Years' Crisis has an important place in a history of English-language realpolitik. That is because it was a word that Carr was fond of using, as a term of praise. He did so in his defense of Lloyd George's Anglo-Soviet Treaty of 1921 and also in his support for Chamberlain's foreign policy in the 1930s. Carr was a professional diplomat and worked at the Foreign Office from 1916 to 1936, though he was also known as a formidable scholar. In *The Twenty Years' Crisis*, he discussed many of the individuals whose work has been addressed on these pages thus far—such as Machiavelli, Marx, Treitschke, Meinecke, Shaw, and Norman Angell. The main thrust of his argument was that academic and popular thinking about international affairs in the English-speaking countries since the First World War had failed to comprehend the role of power as the determining factor. This had led to flawed and utopian thinking about the international system and an alarming "rift between theory and practice." Carr rejected the type of criticism that Attlee had leveled at Chamberlain: that if only the liberal democratic order had been defended with sufficient vigor—sticking to collective security over shuttle diplomacy—it might have survived. For Carr, the premise was false. It was "meaningless evasion to pretend that we have witnessed, not the failure of the League of Nations, but only the failure of those who refused to make it work." Instead, the breakdown of the international system in the 1930s had been caused by the "bankruptcy of the postulates on which it was based."[23]

It should be noted that Carr inserted important qualifiers in his version of realism. While he argued for a "realist" approach to foreign affairs, he also warned about the limits of "pure realism." Realism, "if we attack it with its own weapons, often turns out in practice to be just as much conditioned as any other mode of thought." In politics, "the belief that certain facts are unalterable or certain trends irresistible commonly reflects a lack of desire or lack of interest to change or resist them."[24]

Nonetheless, it is somewhat surprising that Carr's book has such a totemic status among "realist" conceptions of international relations. For one, *The Twenty Years' Crisis* was not particularly original. It was the latest installment of a line of argument outlined at length in previous chapters. As others had done before him, Carr set out to highlight the contradictions, cant, and (unknowing) hypocrisy that characterized the Anglo-American worldview. He observed that British writers of the past fifty years had "been particularly eloquent supporters of the notion that the maintenance of British supremacy is the performance of a duty to mankind." In his view, theories of international morality were "always the product of a dominant group which identifies itself with the community as a whole, and which possesses facilities denied to subordinate groups." Thus, he made a nonsense of Winston Churchill's claim that the "the fortunes of the British Empire and its glory are inseparably interwoven with the fortunes of the world." In fact, he juxtaposed it with the observation from the German historian, Wilhelm Dibelius, that England was the only power that pursued a completely self-interested foreign policy yet told the world that it was fighting for order, progress, prosperity, and peace for all.

Continuing the theme, Carr gave a nod to George Bernard Shaw's comment that an Englishman "never forgets that the nation which lets its duty get on the opposite side of its interest is lost." He criticized Eyre Crowe's memorandum of 1907, in which Crowe warned of the danger from Germany, as "a curious instance of our promptness to detect the conditioned or purposeful character of other people's thought, while assuming that our own is wholly objective." Significantly, Carr also believed that the United States was just as guilty of self-serving hyprocrisy. He pointed to the American annexation of the Philippines and the "popular outburst of moral self-approval hitherto more familiar in the foreign policy of Great Britain than of the United States." Theodore Roosevelt was the greatest offender of all. He "believed more firmly than any previous American President in the doctrine *l'état, c'est moi.*"[25]

Unsurprisingly, then, Carr also made extensive use of the writings of Friedrich Meinecke, which had not yet been translated into English. Indeed, it was most likely from Meinecke that he lifted the concept of

Realpolitik. In the conclusion of his book, he even borrowed Meinecke's notion of *pax Anglo-Saxonica* to convey how others saw the international status quo. The *pax Romana* was the product of Roman imperialism and the *pax Britannica* was the product of British imperialism. A *pax Americana* would share the same traits. The "good neighbour" policy of the United States in Latin America was the epitome of "Yankee imperialism"; for it was only the strongest who could maintain their supremacy while boasting of being "good neighbours." Carr hit home his point by quoting an excerpt from *Mein Kampf* in which Hitler made his own claim for a *pax Germanica*. For Carr, Englishmen and the Americans could oppose the ambitions of Germany or Japan—and were well within their rights to do so. But the truth was that nations rose and fell over time. The idea of a *pax Germanica* or a *pax Japanica* "was *a priori* no more absurd than the conception of *pax Britannica* would have seemed in the reign of Elizabeth or of a *pax Americana* in the days of Washington and Madison."[26]

Carr is best understood as a creature of his time rather than a foreign policy sage for later generations.[27] More than anything, *The Twenty Years' Crisis* should be treated as an eloquent polemic against interwar liberal internationalism.[28] Sir Norman Angell, for example, was given unsparing treatment, while Woodrow Wilson, Clement Attlee, and Winston Churchill also came in for criticism.[29] A closer inspection reveals the extent of one-sidedness in Carr's argument. Moreover, Carr believed that Meinecke had offered the "best judgement by anticipation of the role of utopianism in the international politics of the period." As noted earlier, he quoted Meinecke's statement that the profound defect of Western liberal internationalism was that it "did not penetrate the consciousness of statesmen" and "led either to aimless complaints and doctrinaire suppositions or else inner falsehood and cant." In this instance he was guilty of selective quotation. For Carr did not include the comment made by Meinecke straight after this, that Germany's "false idealization of power politics" had been even more deluded.[30]

One could argue that Carr's version of realpolitik was in fact based on a rather crude regurgitation of Meinecke's arguments. It is worth noting that Isaac Deutscher, the Polish Jewish émigré and biographer of Leon Trotsky, argued that Carr was sometimes "carried away by his sound respect for Realpolitik and his contempt for illusion."[31] What is more, it was on the grounds of this version of realpolitik that Carr supported the policy of appeasement. At a number of points in *The Twenty Years' Crisis*, Carr favorably quoted Neville Chamberlain, the man most associated with the failures of that policy—siding with him against both Churchill and Attlee.[32] When at the Foreign Office, Carr himself had clashed repeatedly with Sir Robert Vansittart, whose early opposition to appeasement is discussed above. It was partly down to Vansittart that Carr resigned from the Foreign Office in 1936.

The version of realism presented by Chamberlain and Carr—in which realpolitik was explicitly evoked in defence of appeasement—was not the only one that existed in this period. In fact, it has been pointed out that those who are broadly considered to be "realists" were split over what to do about Germany in the 1930s—with Hans Morgenthau and Winston Churchill calling for strong opposition to Hitler; and Carr and Chamberlain in another camp with the American State Department diplomat George Kennan, who was working in Prague at the time. In a dispatch from Prague in October 1940, Kennan complained about the "irresponsible Czechs, both within and without the confines of the Protectorate" for contributing to the crisis.[33]

By the time of the Munich Agreement, as Paul Kennedy has argued, the appeasers were faced with an uncoordinated "pincer attack from the Right and the Left"—by self-styled realists, such as Churchill (who believed they had been hopelessly naïve), and by idealists (who regarded the Munich settlement as dishonorable).[34] This matters only insofar as it steers us away from a simplistic interpretation of the interwar years as a "great debate" between realists and idealists. This was a false paradigm created by later generations—many of whom looked back at the interwar years through the prism of Carr's book, and who mimicked the dichotomy that he created.[35] The story of the interwar years as one in which *"arriviste* idealism" was "beaten off by the atemporal tenets of realism" does not stand up to scrutiny.[36] Indeed, the story of the origins of the Second World War also raises questions about the utility of modern versions of realism. As Zara Steiner has written, all of the key statesmen were shaped by ideological assumptions. Personality, political beliefs, national and racial stereotypes and historical assumptions all played their part—as well as the strains and stresses of domestic politics. An obsessive concentration on the international environment only tells a small part of the story.[37] The Chamberlain-Carr version of realpolitik in the 1930s might be said to have fallen into a similar trap.

It has been pointed out that self-declared "realist" thinkers thrived in America after 1945, rising to a position of predominance in the academy, whereas "realists" in Britain remained in the minority. Some scholars have seen this as a product of Britain's declining relative power, suggesting that realism was, for the most part, a "philosophy of supremacy." Much more significant was the fact that realism had become somewhat sullied by its association with appeasement. The left-wing historian Arnold Toynbee, for example—whose writings Carr had attempted to debunk in *The Twenty Years' Crisis*—denounced the governing class of the 1930s for claiming the mantle of realism while "losing sight of . . . political realities." On the right of the spectrum too, Anthony Eden, Churchill's foreign secretary and an opponent of appeasement, suggested that the central flaw in 1930s realism was its fatalism. The West could not "content ourselves with a passive recognition of unpleasant facts. . . . Realism, so defined, becomes indistinguishable from defeatism." As George Orwell noted, Hitler and Mussolini had celebrated Machiavelli but had ultimately been smashed by the forces that their "own lack of scruple conjured up." If the West was to get out of the "pigsty" it was living in, the first thing to grasp was that " 'realism' does *not* pay."[38] Orwell, as a socialist, was no sentimentalist about British democracy or the British Empire. Unlike George Bernard Shaw at the time of the First World War, however, he held that "British democracy is less of a fraud than it sometimes appears." Yes, the British system was hypocritical—but, as Meinecke and others had realized only after the event—"hypocrisy is a powerful safeguard . . . a symbol of the strange mix of reality and illusion, democracy, and privilege, humbug and decency, the subtle network of compromises by which the nation keeps itself in familiar shape."[39]

A New Anti-Realpolitik?

Just as after the First World War, then, Britain moved into the period after the Second World War with a profound sense of the limitations of realpolitik. Once again, the word acquired deeply negative connotations in foreign policy debates. This time, however, realpolitik was not an alien creed, practiced by one's enemies. It had come to imply a moral degeneration in British foreign policy and, to compound the problem, one based on a flawed reading of reality. It was against appeasement that a reinvigorated version of anti-realpolitik asserted itself, and this was to have implications for British foreign policy after 1945.

Indeed, one could argue that it also helps explain Britain's comparatively aggressive stance toward the Soviet Union in the early stages of the Cold War—in which the Labour Party, having defined itself against Chamberlain's foreign policy, played a leading role. Addressing Parliament as leader of the opposition, on the occasion of Franklin Roosevelt's death in April 1945, Clement Attlee told the House of Commons that, in "facing . . . the problems of the world after the war we must be realists." Yet Attlee, who had been an advocate of collective security in the 1930s, also stressed his strong support for the establishment of the United Nations in 1945. As he told Parliament, just a few months before he replaced Churchill as prime minister, "the fact that we are realists does not prevent us from being idealists also."[40]

The idea that the nation had been engaged in a broader struggle for good—for a "New Jerusalem"—had been crucial to the whole war effort in Britain. British "grand strategy" had reflected this. "The base from which victory will arise is built not only of material resources or of military and industrial techniques, but also of social organization, religious ideals, methods of education and so forth, all of which must be maintained in times of peace," wrote two military strategists in 1942. Britain was "seeking also a fairer and more efficient form of nationalism for itself" and "trying to eliminate those weaknesses and injustices which have beset our past."[41] For some, of course, the idea of Western nations moving down the road of planned economies and state ownership was a dangerous path to take, in that it had echoes of the Prussian state or the five-year plans of the Soviet Union. Friedrich Hayek, in *The Road to Serfdom*, wrote in 1944 that if the West was to convince the Germans to change their ways, "it will not be by concessions to their system of thought. We shall not delude them with a stale reproduction of the ideas of their fathers which we have borrowed from them—be it state-socialism, 'Realpolitik,' or 'scientific planning.'"[42] When Churchill recycled Hayek's argument in the 1945 election campaign, Attlee dismissed this as the "second-hand version of the academic views of an Austrian professor."[43]

E. H. Carr regarded it as absurd that the Munich Agreement had been condemned as "immoral," and a matter of "shame" for Britain.[44] Yet the extent to which that notion lodged itself in the British political consciousness cannot be underestimated. Speaking after the war, the young Labour Party politician Richard Crossman argued that the "real road to appeasement . . . was the ambiguity and indecision of men who were defending an effete order." The so-called "guilty men" of Munich failed "because they had not the spirit without which the Nazi challenge could not be met." Indeed, Crossman—foreshadowing later debates—went further still and argued that communism also required a strong moral and ideological response. A "sterile military policy of containment is fatal ... if we are to defeat Communism, we need not merely strength—we do need strength—but a dynamic and creative idea through which we can organise our part of the world strongly enough to resist the challenge of that philosophy."[45] As the West faced a new threat after 1945, recent experience seemed to confirm that realpolitik—or, at least, the version that had been sold to them by Chamberlain and Carr—would not suffice.

PART IV

Realpolitik and the Tangled Roots of American Realism

With all of our shortcomings and failings, we will not accept the new science and follow the "will-o'-the-wisp" of *Realpolitik*. We will not abandon the faith we have lived by, nor deny the other nations the right to live in freedom without fear. Our commitments are to a world of free men working together in free nations. The democratic faith that lies at the base of everything we cherish is the overriding law of American policy both at home and abroad. We cannot surrender our belief in the equal dignity of little nations without, in the end, abandoning our belief in the equal dignity of men.

(Frank Tannenbaum, "Against Realpolitik," 2 October 1953)[1]

11

Geopolitics and the Ethics of American Statecraft

In 1918, world leadership had been offered, "by almost unanimous consent," to the United States, wrote E. H. Carr in 1939. The fact that it was then declined, he suggested, did not mean that it might not be grasped at some future time.[1] Yet in many ways the United States was a reluctant behemoth. Its rise to predominance was accompanied by a sense of unease and foreboding.

The 1930s and 1940s saw the further development of an identifiable "realist" tradition in American approaches to international politics—initially in the academy but with a number of prominent followers in the diplomatic world. Realism was set against the perceived ills of excessive utopianism, legalism, and sentimentalism, which, it was claimed, had characterized Woodrow Wilson's foreign policy. That tradition—embodied by academics such as the University of Chicago's Hans Morgenthau, the most famous realist scholar of the era, and diplomats such as George Kennan, Cold War realist par excellence—had an important influence on American foreign policy in the second half of the twentieth century. Yet the roots of American realism were in the pre-1945 period and reflected the sense of unease with which many Americans regarded taking the lead in world affairs, with all the moral dilemmas that this was likely to entail.

While most Americans remained reluctant to re-engage with the dark heart of Europe, the return of great power rivalry and the willingness of a growing number of states to use force to challenge the international status quo meant that Europe imposed itself on the American consciousness once again in the 1930s. In 1934, the Harvard political philosopher Francis Croker published a compendium of *Recent Political Thought* that discussed continental European concepts such as raison d'état,

Machiavellianism, and *Realpolitik* (along with the men presumed to be its chief exponents—Heinrich Treitschke, General Bernhardi, and Friedrich Meinecke). He noted how their writings had been revived in the era of fascism.[2] As we have seen, Ludwig von Rochau had long since faded from memory.

By the time the Second World War began, these concepts were sufficiently established in the American political lexicon to no longer need elaborate definition. In April 1940, the journal *American Speech* included *Realpolitik* in a list of "loan words" from Germany that had become increasingly prevalent in the American press in the preceding years, alongside some other imports: *Reich, Gestapo, and Putsch.*[3] Yet the word could also be used in a rather anodyne and generalized way. As Europe plunged into war, one movie critic called for an "awakened sense of *Realpolitik*" in the movie industry as a corrective to the "sugar-coated" endings that had seen cinema audiences decline since the Great Depression.[4]

In Britain in the interwar years, as we have seen, realpolitik had been used to denote traditional nineteenth-century diplomacy. It had also become associated with appeasement. In America, during the same period, it was used in ways specific to the context of US foreign policy debates. In contrast to Britain, it was invoked *against* appeasement, rather than as a justification for it. More specifically, it was used to counter the tendency toward isolationism in US foreign policy. Those who advocated "more realpolitik" in America called on their government to confront the danger posed by Germany, Italy, Japan, Russia, and other malcontents in the international system. This was a further development of the de-italicized, non-capitalized version of the concept that Walter Lippmann had used to argue for American intervention in the First World War.

To be more accurate, what was being advocated here was actually geopolitics—and the two words were used interchangeably. Translated into policy, this demanded that America must be on the front foot in the global power game—pre-empting and pushing back against the territorial ambitions of enemies and rivals. Geopolitics had an English-language heritage stretching back to the English geographer-strategist Sir Halford Mackinder. One might also categorize the ideas of Roosevelt, Mahan, and Lippmann in a similar way. But it was awareness of new Nazi theories of geopolitics (highlighted by German-speaking immigrants to the West) that gave the concept new impetus in the United States.

After 1945, however, realpolitik was to take on a different meaning again in America, and it became more laden with controversy. This was in the first decade after the Second World War—and in the early years of the Cold War—when those who described themselves as realists began to become more influential in American academia and diplomacy. For the most part, as Chapter 12 explains, the self-described realists of the early Cold War era eschewed the label. They understood that it carried negative baggage because of its Germanic origins. Those who had emigrated from Germany to the United States—from Morgenthau to Henry Kissinger—were understandably wary of being dismissed in this way. Nonetheless, the opponents of the realists—at the academic, diplomatic, and public levels—began to cry foul about what they saw as the internalization of un-American political notions in the making of the country's foreign policy. American realism, some claimed, originated from German *Realpolitik*.

The influence of German (or German-speaking) immigrants on American academia was profound across a number of fields—chemistry, physics, history, sociology, and international law. That there were some connections between German *Realpolitik* and the tradition of American realism is impossible to deny. But it is important to be precise about the nature of those links. One can draw a direct line between the original exponents of *Realpolitik* in Germany and some of the leading "realists" in America. A small number of them were aware of Rochau's original *Foundations of Realpolitik*. More often, their understanding of *Realpolitik* was mediated through their reading of Max Weber or Friedrich Meinecke. Weber's influence on the language of American realism was profound. Meanwhile, a number of Meinecke's students rose to influential positions in American academia, such as Hajo Holborn, the Yale historian who became the first foreign-born president of the American Historical Association. While this gives a genealogical spine to our story, one should avoid assuming teleology where it did not exist. Significantly, Holborn and other students, such as Felix Gilbert, offered criticisms of Meinecke—and the role of the German professoriate more generally—and none of them mimicked his work.

It is unfair to argue, as some were to do, that German *Realpolitik* was mischievously inserted into American discourse by these German émigrés and that this somehow subverted the basis of American thought on international affairs. If anything, the opposite is the case; many of these thinkers underwent a processs of Americanization. As early as October 1918, a young Protestant theologian called Reinhold Niebuhr—who was to become a key figure in America's realist tradition—submitted an article to Walter

Weyl of the *New Republic* on the "German-American problem."[5] Rather
than criticizing his fellow German Americans for dual loyalty, Niebuhr
in fact had argued that they did not have sufficient loyalty to the humanist
and idealist traditions of German thought—that they had forgotten their
heritage, had failed to uphold European traditions of liberalism, and therefore had left the path clear for the aggressive foreign policy of Germany in
this era.[6] The Germanic contribution to American foreign policy realism
was not some sort of alien imposition, then: whatever remained of it only
survived insofar as it resonated with existing strains of American political
thought.

By examining usages of the word "realpolitik," one can gain fresh
insight into the nature of realism in America after 1945, and the controversies around it. First, some of the critics of realism—such as Carl J. Friedrich,
Werner Stark, and A. J. P. Taylor—were well versed in the history of real
Realpolitik in Germany. Seeing similarities with American realism—not
least admiration for Bismarck—they warned that a cultish obsession with
realism over idealism could quickly morph into unhealthy cynicism, fatalism, or worse, if it was allowed to take over the state and the professoriate
unchallenged. Liberalism could become compromised by the insistent plea
of necessity over sentiment or reality over utopianism. This critique cannot
be dismissed as the work of ill-informed xenophobes as it was articulated
by German-speaking immigrants from Europe and by those most cogni-
sant of the story told so far in this book. Germany provided a warning.
They understood the dangers of the notion of "realpolitik" when taken
into the wrong hands, or misinterpreted or misapplied.

Against this, however, American realists were largely justified in object-
ing so strongly to being besmirched or caricatured as exponents of German
Realpolitik. In contrast to the militarism and chauvinism that had taken
over German nationalism, postwar American realism was a discourse of
restraint and responsibility, skeptical of adventurism, formed under the
shadow of potential nuclear war. A feature of this period was the conflation
of "realpolitik" with broader notions of realism. This was misleading and
reflected the increasingly polemical nature of debates about foreign policy.
Despite the academic setting, much hung upon semantics. In truth, realists
and their critics caricatured each other. They also developed a tendency to
talk past each other in a manner that continues today.

In the final analysis, despite some crucial differences, Chapter 12
will argue that American realism did not entirely rid itself of traits that

characterized the type of German *Realpolitik* associated with Bismarck and Meinecke. It was a different creed but one with some commonalities with the original—not least a strong dose of Weberian pessimism. It was also similar in that it was shaped by the outworking of an internal moral and philosophical angst about the health of the nation and the challenges of modernity. This gave realist discourse a rather exasperated, impatient tone—reflected in its belief that the odds were stacked against it, or that the politicians in charge simply did not see what the realists could see. In a burgeoning academic field of International Relations, realist contempt for the illusions of others saw some of its proponents adopt an increasingly theological or, in some cases, pseudo-scientific stance. They spoke of the need for nothing less than a "reformation" of American foreign policy. In search of this reformation, they also organized themselves into categories and schools. Oddly reminiscent of fissiparous Protestant sects, these categories orbited around certain prominent scholars, institutions, or key texts.

Chapter 13, the final one in Part IV of the book, moves away from the debates among theorists of international relations. It argues that some of the most enlivening debates about real *Realpolitik*—by those who understood its origins with Rochau and the nature of its association with Bismarck—took place in the historical profession. It is important to stress that this was not an academic sideshow. Policy makers mostly preferred history as a surer guide than theory. Renewed admiration for Bismarck in the United States during the Cold War had implications at the level of policy. In a story that is further explored in Part V of this book, some influential figures—such as George Kennan—held him up as a model of statecraft. It was suggested that the Bismarckian approach to foreign affairs provided a better model for America than the British precedent of the nineteenth century. Indeed, the question of "Bismarck or Britain" was to outlast the Cold War itself.[7] Against this, however, others—such as A. J. P. Taylor—warned of the dangers of a cult of Bismarck emerging in the United States and stressed its malignant role in German history. It was thus that a new strand of anti-realpolitik asserted itself again in the English-speaking world. To the frustration of a number of realists, Anglo-American approaches to foreign policy remained resistant to theories of statecraft lifted from continental Europe, from Machiavelli through to Bismarck. The realist reformation of Anglo-American foreign policy never came.

The Second Wave of Geopolitics

As America re-engaged in global politics in the years leading up to the Second World War, it did so with the help of other concepts lifted from German strategic thought. A starting point for this reorientation was the publication, in April 1933, by Frederick Schuman at the University of Chicago, of *International Politics: An Introduction to the Western State System*. In a later article, "Let Us Learn Our Geopolitics," Schuman was to introduce the term "geostrategy" into American politics, a translation of the German *Wehrgeopolitik*, as used by the German strategist Karl Haushofer, whose work had a profound influence on Nazi visions of expansionism.

In *International Politics*—published, significantly, just after Hitler became chancellor in Germany—Schuman claimed to be offering a new approach to the study of international affairs. This broke from narrow diplomatic history or international law and attempted to incorporate both, as component parts of a larger design. In the introduction to the book, he described his approach as that of "*Realpolitik*, characterized by Machiavellian detachment and an earnest effort to delve beneath phraseology to underlying realities." In Britain, Neville Chamberlain had rationalized his foreign policy in very similar terms. Yet here one can see an important difference. In Schuman's view, the opposite to E. H. Carr's, Chamberlain's policy of appeasement flew in the face of realpolitik. "In terms of *Realpolitik*, the consequence of the irresponsible diplomacy of the 1930s has been a constant enhancement of the fighting capacity of the 'dynamic,' 'unsatiated' States and a corresponding diminution of the relative power of France, Great Britain, the USSR, and the United States," he wrote in the introduction to the second edition of the book, in April 1937.

For Schuman, a new status quo had been allowed to develop in recent years, one that depended on a highly unstable balance of power. To accept it also meant passive acceptance of the Japanese conquest of Manchuria, the re-armament of Germany, the Italian conquest of Abyssinia, the remilitarization of the Rhineland, and the triumph of fascism in Spain. In calling on Western nations to confront this threat, Schuman invoked Machiavelli's dictum that "the prince who contributes toward the advancement of another power, ruins his own." At some point the respective enemies of the fascist powers must offer armed resistance or lose their independence. "No amount of evasion, irresponsibility, 'neutrality' or desperate hopefulness in London, Washington, or Geneva will alter this result," he warned in 1937, predicting that a war between the major powers would almost certainly break out before the time arrived for a third edition of his book. Referring back to the murder of Archduke Franz Ferdinand in Sarajevo in 1914, the event that sparked the First World War, Schuman wrote that the power game had "reverted to its pre-Sarajevo pattern, characterized by unprecedented competition in armaments, by periodical diplomatic crises, and by complex manoeuvring for favourable strategic position for attack or defense."[8]

A second influential figure in this American geopolitical awakening was another German speaker, the Austrian émigré, Robert Strausz-Hupé, founder of the Foreign Policy Research Institute in Philadelphia. His 1942 *Geopolitics: The Struggle for Peace* built on the ideas of the English geographer Sir Halford Mackinder, much as Lippmann had built on the work of Captain Mahan in his *Stakes of Diplomacy*. Strausz-Hupé made an important distinction between *Realpolitik* and geopolitics, which Schuman had failed to explain. In fact, geopolitics, practiced by one's enemies, was perhaps even more of a threat. What seemed like fascist megalomania had a geostrategic rationale. Geopolitics was not—as had been widely assumed—a "theory of power politics, or even of *Realpolitik*, as these terms were understood in the nineteenth century," wrote Strausz-Hupé. It was an interpretation of world politics that denoted "everlasting struggle" in which the frontiers of states are merely the expression of a situation of transitory power.[9]

The return to fashion of Mackinder told a story in itself. In 1942, a new American edition of Mackinder's 1919 book, *Democratic Ideals and Reality*, was published with an introduction by Edward Mead Earle of Princeton University. As noted previously, Mackinder had used the book to warn Western leaders about the potential limits of the League of Nations, in its attempts to end the machinations of the defeated nations after 1918. German irredentism was likely to rear its head again, he had warned. In particular, Mackinder had emphasized the crucial role that the map played in German *Kultur* and the German strategic mind. "His Real-Politik lives in his mind on a mental map," Mackinder had written, of the archetypal German statesman, as early as in 1919. The only antidote to this was for those in the West to develop a global strategy of their own. One map image of world politics had to be confronted with another.[10]

Twenty years later, on the eve of the war, it seemed that Mackinder's predictions had been proved right. The predominance of Karl Haushofer in shaping Nazi strategy—and the fact that Hitler had clearly articulated a desire to end Anglo-American strategic hegemony—meant that Americans had to wake up to the threat. Liberal states would have to gird themselves for the coming challenge.[11] The three-pronged nature of the challenge from Germany, Italy, and Japan—added to concerns about the long-term intentions of the Soviet Union—underlined the global nature of the challenge at the level of government too. In a letter to the *New York Times* on 7 March 1939, former secretary of state Henry L. Stimson articulated the growing consensus that American foreign policy could not, with safety, be "limited to a defence of this hemisphere or of our own continental boundaries."[12]

This realization—reluctantly reached—had strong echoes of the argument made by Walter Lippmann in his 1915 *Stakes of Diplomacy*: that America needed to ready itself to project its power beyond its immediate neighborhood, for its own self-preservation. Indeed, the continuity was underlined by the interjection of Lippmann into the debate with his 1943 book, *US Foreign Policy: Shield of the Republic* (which sold half a million copies within months of publication). Here, again, Lippmann explained the strategic rationale for US intervention in the war. If Great Britain and France fell and were no longer able to hold Western Europe or Western Africa, America would become, for the first time in its history "insecure and vulnerable" on its Atlantic flank.[13]

Yet there were important differences between the fifty-four-year-old Lippmann of 1943 and the twenty-seven-year-old Lippmann of 1915. Despite his involvement with the Fourteen Points, he had abandoned Wilsonianism after 1918. Now he was highly skeptical about a renewed discourse of "one-worldism," which he expected to follow the latest war. World peace depended on great-power cooperation rather than international law and transnational parliaments. So Lippmann called for a policy of "realism" based on "national interest" rather than abstract concepts.[14] "We shall no longer exhort mankind to build castles in the air while we build our own defences on sand," he wrote in *Shield of the Republic*, using Ludwig von Rochau's favorite metaphor (also deployed by Treitschke and Meinecke). America must become at last a "mature power."[15] To this Lippmann added an important caveat. His geopolitical conception of American safety was limited to the Atlantic basin. He believed that the US was much less vulnerable in the Pacific. This meant that he was skeptical about later interventions in Korea and Vietnam, and was also more willing than many to allow for the existence of a Soviet sphere of influence in Eastern Europe.

Institutional Training and Superpower Readiness

While Lippmann's work was directed at a popular audience, it was in the 1930s that the new science of geopolitics—and it was consciously more scientific—embedded itself in American academia. The two most important institutions in this development were the University of Chicago and Yale University.

At Chicago, where Schuman had written *International Politics*, the steering hand was provided by Quincy Wright, professor of international law, who was known for his decade-long study on the causes of war, completed in 1942. Wright addressed the age-old dialectic between the "sentiment of humanity" and the "reason of state." Despite the best efforts of the peacemakers of 1919, Machiavellianism was an irreducible factor in international politics. Not for the first time, it was suggested that Machiavelli was the father of raison d'état and all the notions associated with it. "The medieval idea of chivalry and of a universal order both temporal and religious was in large measure scrapped by the *Realpolitik* of Machiavelli," he wrote. Despite the best efforts of the peacemakers of Versailles, however, nothing had yet had been found to replace it.[16] Again, we see how the concept was understood in a different way in the United States than it was in the United Kingdom. Most Americans who used the term urged a robust stance against the revisionist powers. Thus, when Robert Kaplan attributes "a *Realpolitik* view of national security" to Wright, he means that Wright was willing to countenance overseas intervention to preempt threats to national security. In keeping with this, Wright lent his efforts to the Committee to Defend America by Aiding the Allies, an anti-appeasement and anti-neutrality organization.[17]

A similar set of geopolitical assumptions prevailed at the Yale Institution of International Studies (YIIS) formed in 1935. Its two guiding lights were the Dutch American scholar Nicholas Spykman and Arnold Wolfers, a Swiss lawyer who had worked in Berlin before arriving in America in 1933 as visiting professor.[18] In 1940, Wolfers published a study of British and

French foreign policies in the interwar years that demonstrated how their competing strategies for peace were shaped by their different geostrategic circumstances. This also helped explain why they had failed to work together for the preservation of the Treaty of Versailles. While stressing the limitations of liberal internationalism, Wolfers attacked appeasement and stressed the importance of preserving a "balance of power" in world affairs.[19] Again, when Kaplan describes Yale as another "academic bedrock of *Realpolitik* thinking," he means this in contrast to the vocal isolationist movement that also existed at the university in the 1930s (a product, according to Kaplan, of its upper-class ethos).[20] This was also the meaning implied by Raymond L. Garthoff, a State Department diplomat in the Cold War era, who later wrote that the greatest influence in his thinking was "Arnold Wolfers's exposition of Realpolitik."[21] Again the word was used in a way that was thoroughly Americanized. From Lippmann through to Wright, Wolfers, and Spykman, it became a rhetorical tool. Realpolitik was deployed like a bucket of cold water, to be poured on the heads of isolationists and pacifists.

Spykman's 1942 book, *America's Strategy in World Politics*, represented a further outworking of this theme.[22] In keeping with most of the American advocates of geopolitics, he believed that the "basic power aspect of international relations" had received insufficient attention in his new country. He called for an American foreign policy that reflected the fact that each nation made self-preservation its first and foremost aim. It should be noted that Spykman's conception of realism did not solely focus on power. International affairs were also influenced by "love, hate, charity, moral indignation, material gain, psychological abnormalities, and emotional afflictions."[23] The book sold ten thousand copies within three months.[24] It has been said to contain within it the seeds of the containment strategy toward the Soviet Union.[25]

The emergence of Chicago and Yale as hubs of foreign policy expertise also reflected the growing sense that the United States needed to equip itself for the responsibilities and demands of its role as a global superpower. To service this need, an array of new specialist courses on other countries and regions was created. Spykman believed that there was no region of the world too remote to be studied in expectation of American power reaching there. This was something deemed more urgent because of the decline of the British Empire. American distaste for the British Empire was widespread. However, the resolutions of a YIIS conference in March 1945 included the suggestion that it was in America's interest to prop up Britain for the foreseeable future and maintain a balance of power in Europe. To do so, it was made clear, America had to engage in what one resolution called the "dirty game of power politics."[26]

The long-term importance of YIIS was reflected in the number of alumni who went on to serve at the highest levels of government in the postwar period, including Cyrus Vance (future deputy secretary of defense and secretary of state), William Bundy (future assistant secretary of state), and McGeorge Bundy (national security advisor to President Kennedy).[27] It has also been pointed out that institutions like YIIS existed at the nexus between big business and government. Funding came from huge business-oriented philanthropy (the Ford and Rockefeller Foundations, in particular) which, in turn, opened the door to high-level political influence. The result, argues one scholar, was a "self-serving realpolitik" favored by the state, philanthropists, and university professors. It was in this spirit, for example, that Spykman reported to the Rockefeller Foundation how students who saw the study of international relations as a function of "Christian peace building" were shocked by "the rather realistic approach to the subject" as it was taught at Yale.[28]

In terms of the spread of this worldview—and the desire to prepare the nation's next generation of diplomats for geopolitical responsibilities—one must also acknowledge the influence of Princeton's Edward Mead Earle, who had edited the 1942 edition of Mackinder's work described above. As the director of the American Committee for International Studies from 1939, Earle coordinated classes on war strategy that ran at the University of California–Los Angeles, Northwestern, the University of North Carolina, and the University of Pennsylvania, as well as at Yale and Princeton.[29] His view of American national security requirements necessitated an activist foreign policy backed up by military force. He also believed that the American people could be educated to understand the necessity of this military interventionist stance.[30] In 1943, Earle also published the *Makers of Modern Military Strategy from Machiavelli to Hitler*, co-edited by two historians of Germany, Gordon Alexander Craig and Felix Gilbert, a student of Meinecke.[31]

It is important to be clear about the difference between the pre-1945 proponents of American geopolitics (who used the word realpolitik favorably) and the postwar realists (who did not). The distinguishing mark of the former was the great importance they put on a global military reach;

Spykman and Earle advised the geopolitical section, which was set up within the Military Intelligence Service in the War Department in June 1942. The second was the inclination toward interventionism created by such a conception of geopolitics. The whole planet was increasingly understood as an American strategic environment.[32]

To explain the Korean or Vietnam wars as arising out of the new geopolitics in Chicago and Yale would be teleological. It would fail to do justice to the complexities of the post-1945 international environment, or the role of the key decision-makers themselves. Yet it might be said that modern American realists sometimes have the wrong target when they set out to assail the ghost of Wilsonianism, as the root cause of American meddling abroad. It was the exponents of geopolitics who set the conceptual terms for these interventions, beginning with the Second World War.[33] It was Meinecke's student, the Jewish German émigré historian Felix Gilbert, who co-edited *The Makers of Modern Military Strategy* with Edward Mead Earle, who best encapsulated the new intellectual consensus that underpinned America's entry into another world war. As he explained, it was crucial that this should happen "not for Wilsonian idealistic reasons, but for reasons of *Realpolitik*" such as national security.[34] This confirmed that American realpolitik had taken on a life of its own and a meaning distinct from that which existed in Germany (associated with the Bismarckians) and even England (with Chamberlain and Carr), as the Second World War began.

The Ethical Foundations
of American Realism

Geopolitics was just one ingredient in a broader re-envisaging of America's world role in the 1930s. Versions of Wilsonianism—and the belief that the country had an ethical mission in world affairs—still existed, though they were usually girded with a more tough-minded rationale about national security. In 1937, Hamilton Fish Armstrong, the editor of *Foreign Affairs*, published *We or They*, which argued that authoritarian and non-democratic states were incompatible with the liberal democratic system, and that long-term security depended on protecting and preserving democracy. In *Ideas and Weapons*, Max Lerner, editor of the *Nation*, took the Nazi-Soviet pact of 1939 as evidence for the need for democracies to bind themselves together in the name of global security. As in 1917, it was leading liberal journals, the *New Republic* and the *Nation*, which had begun to make the case for American intervention in the war.[35]

One did not have to be a Wilsonian to recognize the great moral responsibility that was attendant on America's rise to superpowerdom. It was a self-declared realist, Reinhold Niebuhr, who did more than any other to articulate the ethical dilemmas that this presented. "We need something less circumspect than liberalism to save the world," Niebuhr wrote in *Moral Man and Immoral Society* (1932), reflecting his own disillusionment with Wilson's ideals, with which he had initially been sympathetic.[36] Significantly, however, Niebuhr inserted an important caveat. He rejected what he saw as excessive realism, which led to cynicism and pessimism.[37]

The development of Niebuhr's thinking on international politics over the course of the 1930s reflected the fact that foreign policy belied neat ethical and philosophical formulae. An early test case was Japan's invasion of Manchuria in 1931. Whereas his brother Richard Niebuhr—also a theologian—urged American non-intervention, Reinhold took a more robust line and urged the assertion of US diplomatic weight against Japan. He was quick to recognize the substantively different nature of both Japanese imperialism and European fascism. In Niebuhr's hands, the notion of balancing in international relations took on an ethical dimension too. The worst excesses of human nature could only be checked by competing assertions of interest—a sort of morally conditioned geopolitics.[38]

At a number of points in *The Twenty Years' Crisis*, E. H. Carr expressed his admiration for Niebuhr. For the most part, however, their relationship was one of unrequited love. Niebuhr, unlike Carr, was a vocal critic of appeasement. If anything, the development of Niebuhr's position in the 1930s was closer to that of Winston Churchill. Churchill also criticized the naiveté of those who clung to the League of Nations long after its impotence had been demonstrated. Yet he refused to succumb to the fatalism he saw in appeasement. An effective foreign policy required credibility and capability, and "principled and prudential" statesmanship. In a similar way, Niebuhr made the opposite journey to a number of so-called realists in the 1930s, insisting that there were still transcendent values in a world of necessity. His was "sober, not somber realism" with a modest faith in human progress at its core.[39]

The Niebuhrian worldview was grounded in theology and therefore distinct from the putative science of geopolitics. This also meant that it drew on a different lexicon. Niebuhr's view of Machiavellianism—invoked by Schuman and other exponents of American geopolitics—was strikingly different. Speaking at Oxford University in 1939 he proclaimed that it was a "terrible heresy to suggest that, because the world is sinful, we have a right to construct a Machiavellian politics or a Darwinian sociology as normative for Christians."[40] Indeed, Niebuhr's verdict on Schuman's book, *Soviet Politics at Home and Abroad*, further underlines the distance between these two strands of realist discourse. While Schuman has been held up as a paragon of a tough-minded Cold War mentality, he was known to be leftwing and later came under investigation by the House Un-American Activities Committee for perceived communist sympathies (which he denied).[41] In Niebuhr's view, *Soviet Politics* had failed to synthesize Schuman's liberal ideals with the methods he prescribed. He had "the bewildering habit of ascending to the most rarefied heights of constitutional idealism and then descending to the depths of *Realpolitik* without giving the poor reader a chance to adjust himself to the different levels."[42] Niebuhr was asserting that such polarities were not always helpful.

This position—which rejected both Wilsonian liberal internationalism and pessimist isolationism—was also held by Max Lerner.[43] In *Ideas for the Ice Age* published in 1941, a year after Niebuhr's *Christianity and Power Politics,* he also discussed the return of Machiavellianism in the international arena. While Machiavelli had been widely rejected during the Enlightenment, he had come into fashion again from the mid-nineteenth century in the age of the new nationalism. The Germans, in particular, "took from him the concept of *Staatsräson*—opportunism justified by reasons of state policy; and in the field of foreign affairs, *Realpolitik*." But these notions soon spread. In almost every country, the rediscovery of Machiavelli had made a profound impact. In England, for example, H. G. Wells's 1911 novel *The New Machiavelli*, evoked a state that blended Machiavellianism with English Fabianism.

Lerner believed that it was folly to reject Machiavelli entirely. "Let us be clear about one thing," he explained, "ideals and ethics are important in politics as norms, but they are scarcely effective as techniques." Likewise, Machiavelli was useful in helping to distinguish "the realm of what ought to be from the realm of what is." He rejected the first for the second. Nonetheless, there was a third realm, Lerner argued. This was "the realm of what can be." Here Lerner, following Niebuhr, called for something more than Machiavellianism, a "humanist realism" to re-frame America's approach to the world: "We can start with our democratic values, and we can start also with Machiavelli's realism about tough-minded methods," he explained, "[and] we may yet find an effective pursuit of democratic values is possible within the scope of a strong and militant state and unsentimental realism about human motives."[44]

In other words, from the outset, exponents of "ethical realism" in American foreign policy warned of the dangers of undiluted Machiavellianism. The existence of German *Realpolitik* had shown its limitations. Even the exponents of geopolitics, such as Spykman, while more consciously scientific, had cautioned against overly mechanistic readings of international politics that left no room for personality and passion. These caveats, however, were sometimes lost sight of in the course of subsequent debates in the 1950s and 1960s. Here an intriguing parallel with the early history of *Realpolitik* begins to emerge. Ludwig von Rochau's original concept had left room for ideas, abstractions, and morality. In the hands of others, his notion had been made more rigid and inflexible, and used as an intellectual stick with which to beat one's opponents.

Without rejecting realism, Niebuhr and Lerner understood that it was important to give a higher purpose to American foreign policy. As Niebuhr put it, in May 1944, both action and inaction—intervention and non-intervention—contained within them the possibility of good and evil: "we cannot do good without also doing evil . . . we cannot defend what is dearest to us without running the risk of destroying what is even more precious than our life . . . we cannot find moral peace in any of our virtues even as we can have no security in the ramparts of our boasted civilization."[45]

After 1945, these dilemmas multiplied in the setting of the Cold War. With America's position of global predominance came more responsibilities and new dilemmas. "We never dreamed that we would have as much political power as we possess today," Niebuhr elaborated in 1952 in *The Irony of American History*, pointing to a "vaster and vaster entanglement of other wills and purposes, which made it impossible for any single will to prevail, or any specific goal of history easily to become the goal of all mankind."[46]

Containment: Between Theology
and Geopolitics

The various Cold War strategies that are often lumped under the banner of "containment" had elements of the new geopolitics and the ethical realism reflected in the theology of Niebuhr.[47] A fusion of the two was evident in George F. Kennan's legendary 1946 "Long Telegram," on "The Sources of Soviet Conduct," which appeared (in an adapted form) in *Foreign Affairs* in 1947.[48] It is worth noting that Kennan's essay has some resemblance to Ludwig von Rochau's analysis of German politics and society in *Foundations of Realpolitik*. Kennan had spent a number of years in Germany between the wars. In the summer of 1926 he was in Heidelberg, and then in 1929–30 and 1930–31 he was in Berlin, where Rochau had worked and Friedrich Meinecke taught. More important in terms of the comparison with Rochau, Kennan's analysis of the Soviet system aimed to achieve a feat of analytical detachment and synthesis similar to that of Rochau in *Foundations of Realpolitik*. Kennan's essay also offered an attempt to understand the relationship between socioeconomic conditions and ideas as guides to political behaviour (helped by Kennan's mastery of Russian). In a Rochau-esque phrase, he regarded the character of the Soviet regime as the "product of [both] ideology and circumstances," even quoting Vladimir Lenin on the unevenness of economic and political development.[49]

Kennan's perspective was also shaped by the language of contemporary American Protestantism (particularly Niebuhr).[50] While arguing for more restraint on the international arena, Kennan also described his "gratitude to a Providence which, by providing the American people with this implacable challenge, has made their entire security as a nation dependent on . . . accepting the responsibilities of moral and political leadership that history plainly intended them to bear." Indeed, he later compared the Long Telegram to "an eighteenth-century Protestant sermon."[51] The description was a revealing one, and one might argue that it applied to a number of other famous texts on international affairs that appeared after the war.

In Kennan's view, American foreign policy had to be placed in a harness to prevent it running away with itself. In 1948, he gave a series of lectures at the University of Chicago that formed the basis of his book, *American Diplomacy*. Mindful of past failures, he warned that the idealism of Woodrow Wilson "runs like a red skein through our foreign policy."

Wilson had lurched from isolationism into a philosophy of total victory. His mistake had been to assume that others could be made to think, talk, and walk like Americans. In particular, Wilson had declared war on German *Realpolitik*. This had informed his view that "Prussian militarism had to be destroyed to make the way safe for the sort of peace we wanted." In a memorable metaphor, Kennan described American democracy as a prehistoric monster with a huge body and a brain the size of a pin: "he lies there in his comfortable primeval mud and pays little attention to his environment; he is slow to wrath—in fact, you practically have to whack his tail off to make him aware that his interests are being disturbed; but, once he grasps this, he lays about him with such blind determination that he not only destroys his adversary but largely wrecks his native habitat."[52]

On the one hand, Kennan's position illustrated the fundamental differences between the type of *Realpolitik* associated with Germany's rise to power and that of postwar American realism. The former was born of striving, a fear of others, and a sense that national destiny meant the attainment of great power. The latter was born out of an assumption of great responsibility, and wariness about the damage that one could do to oneself as much as others. On the other hand, however, Kennan's criticism of Woodrow Wilson and post-1918 attempts to rid the world of Prussian militarism were revealing in another way. His deep skepticism about grand schemes of world government—and his admiration for Bismarck—placed Kennan firmly against those of the anti-realpolitik tradition described thus far in this book. Unsurprisingly, even if Kennan did not use the word, others saw an Americanized version of realpolitik in his writing. Writing in the English liberal newspaper, the *Manchester Guardian*, the French philosopher Raymond Aron suggested that Kennan "defends what the Germans call Realpolitik or, if you prefer, a less distasteful expression, traditional diplomacy."[53]

Notably, it was in his own country that Kennan's approach was treated with most suspicion, as the internalization of European methods that Americans had long ago rejected. "He would accept the world as a jungle rather than as a potential society," objected the *Washington Post* in 1952. "Idealism would thus be eschewed and realpolitik would be the god." The *Washington Post* declared itself a convert to Niebuhr's argument that America needed a "reorientation of the whole structure of our idealism." But it rejected the cure that Kennan was offering. The "return to an undefined and undefinable national egotism," it declared, "did not correspond with the volition of history, let alone the civilization of which we are heir."[54] For here was a countervailing theology—a sense of manifest destiny that was closer to that expressed by Harry Truman when he had declared that America was "now faced with what Almighty God intended us to be faced with in 1920 . . . the leadership of the free peoples of the world."[55] Superpowerdom had been handed to America by Providence. For some, this great responsibility created a feeling of wariness and foreboding; for others, the sense of destiny could inspire.

12

German Émigrés
and American Realism

In the 1930s there was a large influx of German scholars—both humanities and sciences—into American academia. Many of them were exiles from Nazism but nonetheless brought with them methods, ideas, and traditions learned in German universities long before Hitler's rise to power. Rather than subverting American intellectual traditions, it was more often the case that their output bore the imprint of their new home and its preoccupations. Morever, the German influence on American scholarship predated the arrival of many of these émigrés. There was deep admiration for German culture and religion and a long tradition of scholarly exchange that stretched back to the nineteenth century. American sociology was particularly indebted to German precedents—with Lester Ward, Albion Small, Robert Park, and Arthur Bentley building on the work of German predecessors such as Ludwig Gumplowicz, Gustav Ratzenhofer, and Franz Oppenheimer. Through these connections, it has been argued, American sociologists imbibed an element of spiritual despair and nihilism. It has even been suggested that American sociology owed an unwitting debt to Leopold von Ranke, Heinrich Treitschke, and General Bernhardi.[1]

One field where the influence of new German scholars was pronounced was in the historical profession.[2] In fact, one can trace a direct line from some of them back to Ludwig von Rochau, either through their work on nineteenth-century German history, or in their education in the 1920s by the great German theorists of state, such as Meinecke. The most influential of Meinecke's students to arrive in the United States was the aforementioned Hajo Holborn, who was awarded his doctorate in 1924, the same year that Meinecke had published *Die Idee der Staatsräson*. Just as Meinecke had discovered Rochau through Treitschke, so Holborn discovered Rochau through Meinecke.[3] As his wife was Jewish, Holborn was forced to flee the Nazis, first to Britain and then to the United States, where he was appointed to the faculty at Yale in 1934. During the Second World War, he served in the Office of Strategic Services as special assistant to another Yale historian, William L. Langer (a second-generation German himself, and an admirer of Bismarck). After the war, Holborn returned to Yale as a senior professor.

Another student of Meinecke who became prominent in the United States was Felix Gilbert. Gilbert recollected his time in Meinecke's seminar class at the University of Berlin in the 1920s alongside Holborn, where they would read and discuss excerpts from Machiavelli. Gilbert cited Meinecke's *Cosmopolitanism and the National State* as an important influence in his intellectual progression. He also cited the longer-term influence of Meinecke's friend Ernst Troeltsch on his work.[4]

These scholars did not regard themselves as uncritical disciples of what they had learned in Germany. When presenting the work of Meinecke to a later generation, they often did so with a health warning. In an introduction to his 1970 edition of Meinecke's *Cosmopolitanism and the National State*, Gilbert criticized aspects of his former tutor's work. On grounds that Ludwig von Rochau would have recognized, he suggested that Meinecke did not sufficiently link the study of intellectual trends to the social forces they represented.[5] There was plenty that was worthwhile exploring in these German intellectual traditions. But it was also important to recognize the limitations.

Historians felt they had a particular responsibility to treat such notions with a critical eye. Holborn bemoaned the role that German historians had played in public debate both before and after the First World War. Treitschke was the most famous example but others had followed his precedent. In the late nineteenth century they had become, with very few exceptions, self-appointed guardians of the Bismarckian Empire. "History to them was exclusively the struggle of states, and only political history a legitimate field of study," Holborn wrote. This meant they had failed to contribute to great moral and social questions of the day. The First World War had failed to shake them out of their stupor. To give Meinecke his due, Holborn suggested that his former tutor had gone further than most in confronting the true reasons for defeat in 1918. Meinecke had recognized the demonic potential of power politics and insisted on the absolute validity of universal ethical norms.[6] Yet the rise of the Nazis had proved that he and the rest of the professoriate had not gone far enough.

Holborn's own student, Otto von Pflanze (a second generation German American and future biographer of Bismarck) suggested that Holborn's debt to Meinecke was more personal and professional than philosophical. If Holborn had a hero it was not Ernest Troeltsch or Friedrich Meinecke but Leopold von Ranke, the preeminent historian of the nineteenth century, in whom he saw not "scientific history" but a historian of "scientific temperament" (guided by a spirit and ethic of objective inquiry—and a broader universalism that linked German history to European history as a whole). One might even argue that Holborn was more influenced by the original writings of Rochau; he was arguably closer than anyone to the original spirit of *Foundations of Realpolitik*. Holborn's most original contribution to the historical method was his insistence on the need to relate ideas to social movements—an idea that Rochau had pioneered. "Social history is the necessary complement to the history of ideas," he wrote in a 1953 *Festschrift* to Meinecke, mildly criticizing his teacher for failing to take this into account.[7] In his own *History of Modern Germany*, Holborn made use of Rochau's *Foundations of Realpolitik* on a number of occasions—particularly those sections that addressed the importance of ideas and societal forces.[8]

As preeminent historians, Holborn and Gilbert understood the true origins of *Realpolitik* perhaps better than any scholars of international relations in the same era. Given this, it is significant that they did not seek to convert an American audience to it. Even the most refined version of German *Realpolitik*, articulated by their former teacher, was subject to criticism. Rather than treating the intellectual traditions of the New World as somehow naïve and immature, they saw them as having inherent strengths of their own. At the start of his history of Germany, Holborn said that his "transformation" into an American had given him a better perspective on his former country.[9] Likewise, Gilbert went on to produce work on early American foreign policy, in addition to his earlier work on Machiavelli and Renaissance diplomacy.[10]

The fact that both men served in the Office of Strategic Services (OSS)—the precursor to the Central Intelligence Agency—during the war was a pointed example of the rapid integration of this community. They were joined by more German émigrés such as the left-wing Jewish scholars Franz Neumann, Herbert Marcuse, and Otto Kirchheimer. Between 1942 and 1944, these three founding members of the Frankfurt School were recruited from posts in American academia by General William "Wild Bill" Donovan, head of the OSS. They were asked to provide their view on "possible patterns of German collapse" that would allow the Allies to hasten Hitler's defeat and, crucially, plan for the invasion and reconstruction of Germany after the war. The overriding theme behind all of their reports was their conviction that class structures were the determining factor in Nazi Germany. These scholars rejected the idea that there was something inherent in German political culture that made it more susceptible to Nazism, such as Prussian militarism or what Neumann called the "Teutonic urge for domination." Instead, at the core of Nazism was the support and acquiescence not of Prussian Junkers but the industrial bourgeoisie. Nazism was built around technocratic efficiency and was, as such, highly modern, embodied in the rise of men like the famous Nazi architect Albert Speer.[11]

Again, the faint echoes of real *Realpolitik*—going back to the original *Foundations*—were evident in the reports produced by these men. Like Rochau, they analyzed social structures, the distribution of power, and the role of ideas, and aimed to demonstrate the relationship among them. Also like Rochau, they did so with an emphasis on the importance of retaining a sense of analytical detachment. These were historical methods applied to a pressing foreign policy problem. They looked beyond governments and dug deeper into the state in question. Both the methods and the culture of the OSS provide an interesting contrast to the increasingly polemical debates in the field of international relations after 1945, in which jurists and theorists held more sway.

Hans Morgenthau and the Moral Dignity of the National Interest

Of all the German immigrants to the United States, the man to whom the label "realpolitik" was most often appended was the jurist and international relations theorist Hans Morgenthau. Indeed, it has been said that Morgenthau "brought the German *Realpolitik* discourse to the United States in the late 1930s."[12] He was born in Coburg in Germany to a Jewish family in 1904. He taught law in Frankfurt and Munich before he was forced to flee Germany. He moved to France, then Spain, before arriving in the United States in 1937 as a thirty-four-year-old, where he soon established himself at the University of Chicago. In 1946 he produced *Scientific Man versus*

Power Politics, which set the tone of his postwar work with its essentially pessimistic view of human progress and the limits of "liberal rationalism."[13]

Morgenthau had begun his academic career as a theorist of international law rather than an expert on international history.[14] Earlier in his career, Morgenthau had considered writing a book on raison d'état in history, but he gave up on the venture because he felt Meinecke's *Die Idee der Staatsräson* could not be much improved upon. As a student, he was taught by Hermann Oncken. As well as being an expert on Bismarck and the Franco-Prussian War of 1870-1, Oncken had also written about Rochau. There is no evidence that Morgenthau ever read Rochau. But he was very much aware of the evolution of the concept of *Realpolitik* in Germany after him. For Morgenthau, the concept was ever associated with Bismarck's foreign policy. He described how, when he was a student of Oncken's, he had first felt "the impact of a coherent system of thought," through a "distillation of Bismarck's *Realpolitik*."[14]

Morgenthau wrote three books in Germany before arriving in the United States. He began his career with some optimism about the potential of international law as a tool of conflict resolution, but his early idealism began to wane over the course of the 1930s. Thus, it has been argued, Morgenthau gradually imbibed some of the pessimism—and, more controversially, illiberalism—associated with many theorists of politics in interwar Germany, such as Carl Schmitt, whom he had initially set out to oppose. This fed into the belief that the international arena was an "unending struggle for survival and power," as expressed in *Scientific Man versus Power Politics*. There were also echoes of Max Weber in his observations about "the tragic sense of life, the awareness of unresolvable discord, contradictions, and conflict which are inherent in the nature of things and which human reason is powerless to solve."[15]

For all this, Morgenthau's English-language work must also be understood in its Anglo-American context. He regarded himself as the latest exponent of a tradition of Anglo-American realism, following on from others such as E. H. Carr.[16] In keeping with this, he repeatedly stressed the ethical value of prudential statecraft over any cult of national interest.[17] Published in 1948, Morgenthau's *Politics Among Nations* was to become a key text in postwar American realism. "Realism maintains that universal moral principles cannot be applied to the actions of states," he wrote. The national interest must be the organizing principle in a nation's foreign policy. In keeping with this, he emphasized the importance of balance and equilibrium in international politics. Morgenthau's sense of balance in international relations grew out of his understanding of how the most successful and stable states (chiefly the Anglo-Saxon ones) achieved *internal* equilibrium. In America, this insight went back to the Founding Fathers and the *Federalist Papers*, which emphasized the need to ensure that inerests were balanced within the structures of the state.[18]

Morgenthau's writings soon won the attention of George Kennan, then director of the Policy Planning Staff, which Kennan had created at the State Department. The two were introduced at Chicago in 1948 and struck up a friendship. Kennan told Morgenthau that his work was "being read with attention and respect by many who have responsibility for the conduct of foreign policy."[19] Yet in their early conversations, one gets a glimpse of a different Morgenthau—a man with a strong conviction in the unique power of the United States, even prepared to celebrate the name

Hans Joachim Morgenthau (1904–1980) of the University of Chicago, one of the most influential figures in the study of international politics in postwar America. Photo by Ralph Morse/The LIFE Picture Collection/Getty Images.

of Woodrow Wilson. Moreover, he saw American idealism as much more robust and resilient than the traditions of German idealism (represented by such thinkers as Goethe), which had been trampled in the last hundred years.

In a strikingly idealistic plea, Morgenthau expressed a hope to Kennan that America could lead the unification of Europe in a way that mirrored its own federal polity. He saw the whole history of American foreign policy, from George Washington's Farewell Address through the Monroe Doctrine and the Marshall Plan, as demonstrating the favorable popular response with which momentous decisions in American policy were received if they were presented to the American people in frank and morally relevant terms. Morgenthau knew that Kennan was familiar with German history, having studied there. Yet it was on the grounds of American exceptionalism that he made his appeal. If German idealism and humanism had been trampled over, the same could not be said for the United States. Thus Morgenthau referred to Friedrich Nietzsche's comment that Johann Wolfgang Goethe was "an accident without consequences" in German history. He knew the same could not be said of Washington, Abraham Lincoln, Woodrow Wilson, Franklin Roosevelt, or George Marshall, the recently retired secretary of state.[20]

While *Politics Among Nations* was the richest of Morgenthau's books, it was his 1951 *In Defence of the National Interest* that projected him to greater fame and sparked a controversy that went much further than academia. More baldly polemical, it would play a significant role in shaping what was to become known as the second Great Debate in the field of international relations (following on from that of the interwar years).[21]

According to Morgenthau, there were four great evils in American foreign policy thinking that needed to be confronted: utopianism; sentimentalism; legalism, and neo-isolationism. No nation could "escape into a realm where action is guided by moral principles rather than by considerations of power." The second strand of his argument was that a canon of realist thinking already existed in the English-speaking world. His concern was that the English-speaking peoples would forget their own realist heritage.

Relying heavily on the work of English diplomatic historians of the 1910s and 1920s (such as Charles Webster, Harold Temperley, and William Alison Phillips) Morgenthau made an argument that had become commonplace in 1930s Britain. This was that there was more wisdom to be found in the 1815 Treaty of Vienna than in the 1919 Treaty of Versailles.

Typically, he praised Lord Castlereagh, in particular, for his ability to understand the "distinction and relationship between ideology and power politics" and his "consistent refusal to be swayed by ideological preferences or animosities into embracing policies which can contribute nothing to the national interest of one's country." Others in this realist tradition included Alexander Hamilton, George Canning, John Quincy Adams, Benjamin Disraeli, Lord Salisbury, and—of more recent vintage—Dean Acheson. This time, Abraham Lincoln, Woodrow Wilson, Franklin Roosevelt, and George Marshall—celebrated in Morgenthau's first letter to George Kennan as heroes of American idealism—did not make the cut. More controversial was Morgenthau attempt to claim Winston Churchill for this version of the realist tradition, by including excerpts of his speeches in the appendix to the book.

Morgenthau warned that America must avoid "well-intentioned folly" and focus on its national interest rather than vague liberal internationalist fantasies. At the same time, he rejected the argument that he elevated the "national interest" above moral or ethical considerations in statecraft. On the contrary, in keeping with what has been said about Kennan and Niebuhr—whom Morgenthau also counted as a friend—there was an irreducible ethical core to his argument. Morgenthau emphatically rejected what he called the "equation of political moralizing with morality and of political realism with immorality." In fact, there was a strong "moral dignity" to the national interest, not least because it demanded great caution in the exercise of power.[22] Once again, the idea of restraint remained the distinguishing characteristic of American realism.

The Return of Anti-Realpolitik: The Reaction against Morgenthau

Despite his best efforts, Morgenthau could not escape the imputation that he was trying to convert America to some form of *Realpolitik*—a hardline vision of statecraft that was somehow alien to the United States. Even a relatively sympathetic review in the *Economist* declared *In Defence of the National Interest* to be the latest addition to the now "considerable American library of sermons based on the theology of *Realpolitik*."[23] When it came to winning followers, Morgenthau was not necessarily helped by his trenchant style of argument.

Tellingly, some of the severest criticisms of Morgenthau (and Kennan, by association) came from other German-speaking émigrés. One of the most unforgiving reviews of his work was by Frank Tannenbaum, an Austrian-born historian, sociologist, and professor at Columbia University. In the *Baltimore Sun*, Tannenbaum warned that "the advocates of *Realpolitik* would sweep away all our old beliefs and foolishness, [as] sentimental and moralistic." They would have Americans build their foreign policy on the balance of power and a false "science" of the national interest. "With all of our shortcomings and failings, we will not accept the new science and follow the 'will-o'-the-wisp' of *Realpolitik*," he protested, or dispense with "that sense of human integrity and national morality which is part of the substance of our very being."[24]

An even more influential German American critic was the Harvard political theorist Carl J. Friedrich. An expert on totalitarianism, he graduated from the University of Heidelberg in 1925, after studying under Alfred Weber, Max Weber's older brother. In the *Yale Review* of 1952, Friedrich reviewed *In Defence of the National Interest* alongside Kennan's *American Diplomacy*. He ventured that those who counted themselves in "that rising school of foreign-policy analysts who call themselves 'realists' were essentially survivalists," who exhibited deep unease about the nation's future. They were inclined to think that America's "unprecedented rise to its position of world power is the work of incompetent 'moralizers' without any sense of 'realities.'" Their position, which could be traced back to Machiavelli, was "an American version of the German *Realpolitik*, stressing as it does military potential and natural resources." Given his origins, Friedrich felt he was in a position to recognize the real thing when he saw it.

Rather than dismissing the realists out of hand, Friedrich was prepared to concede that the arguments of this new school provided a "valuable check on excess enthusiasm" and utopianism. Against this, however, he regarded them as overly dogmatic. Morgenthau's exasperation with "moralizing" was so intense that it became "oppressive." He asserted three times on one page in *In Defence of the National Interest*, "in slightly different words—that it is wrong to equate moralizing with morality and political realism in terms of national interest with immorality." Friedrich was quite happy to accept that Morgenthau and Kennan did not want to repudiate morality. But in his view, they had still failed "to show how moral and other considerations of interest are to be blended." Nor did they ever adequately define what the "national interest" meant in practice. The very idea of the national interest had always been endowed with conflicting meanings.

Moreover, Friedrich argued that the self-styled realists were creating a caricature of the supposed "legalistic-moralistic" position they were setting themselves up against. There were a number of points in Morgenthau's book where the position of those who would urge the importance of moral factors in politics was "so misstated as to make it into a strawman," such as the "ever-repeated statement that the 'sentimentalist' sees foreign policy in terms of a struggle of 'virtue and vice.'" One might well agree with Morgenthau's remark ("trite" as it was) that a successful foreign policy "must be commensurate to power available to carry it out." But did it follow, as Morgenthau also argued, that all moral objectives in foreign policy were essentially irrelevant as they were subjective? When General Dwight Eisenhower described the Second World War as a "crusade" (in the title of his memoirs), he was obviously falling short of the standards set by the realists, commented Friedrich. But this type of statement was kindled by a moral enthusiasm that, "even when it overshoots the mark, cleans up a lot of places." Who was to say that Americans were better placed to adopt "the old-world tradition of defining national interest purely in terms of either enhanced national power or survival?" Why were the American people obliged to look on their foreign policy "merely as a shield, and not as a sword or an arrow?" Thus, Friedrich suggested, the Truman Doctrine—by which President Truman committed America to resisting communist expansionism globally—was understood and supported by the majority of Americans, despite the fact that a number of realists, Kennan included, had criticized it.

Finally, Friedrich argued that the problem confronting America's foreign policymakers was how to balance the country's "interests *and* aspirations" with its resources, both material and moral, in such a way that success can be achieved. In his mind, this called "for a vigorous insistence upon the broad and ideal goals that are part of the American heritage." This was not simply for idealistic reasons but because they provided a better guarantor of long-term success. Only these goals could provide a firm ground for alliances and friendships. In a classic reworking of the anti-realpolitik tradition described in previous chapters, he argued that "the logic of power cannot, in the long run, be divorced from the logic of justice and right."[25]

Similar debates had already been worked through in Britain in the 1930s. Thus, a different set of criticisms were aimed at the American realists by British historians whose perspective was shaped by the failures of appeasement. They were particularly resistant to the notion that there was superior wisdom in nineteenth-century diplomatic methods. Who wanted to live in a world where all the nations made national self-interest the sole criterion of policy, asked John Roberts, a British historian of nineteenth-century Europe? Here was what such "real politics" meant in practice. Morgenthau evoked a world in which "nothing but cold facts are permitted to intrude, where nations, unlike civilized man, cannot safely take thought of morals and are not restrained by any sort of self-discipline or community thinking, beyond what is purely selfish." Roberts himself had no problem with expediency. A pointed example he gave was the wartime alliance with Russia, which he fully supported. Nonetheless, he argued that any attempt by the realists to completely divorce American action from American idealism was a denial of realism itself. If America could not fight for a better world, however difficult that might be to attain, it would not fight at all.[26]

The criticism that stung Morgenthau most was that offered by another British historian, A. J. P. Taylor, writing in the *Nation*. Taylor began his review by conceding that most historians and political observers would agree that power is the determining factor in international relations. But it was dangerous to define power too narrowly. Ideas were also a form of power, and the national interest was best secured by having them on one's side. In particular, Taylor claimed that Morgenthau's admiration for Count Metternich demonstrated the weaknesses of his argument. Pointing to the 1848 revolutions, he noted that it was "ideas that brought Metternich down." Taylor argued that as the Cold War took shape a century later, it was the "best form of realism to have superior ideals." Morgenthau, like Metternich, was "a system-maker." Foreign policy would not satisfy him unless it followed a script or a pattern.[27]

That Morgenthau took the time to reply to Taylor—of all his reviewers—demonstrated the extent of his irritation with this criticism. In his response, he expressed surprise that his book had provoked such a hostile reaction. Rather than offering a new theory of international politics, he reiterated that he simply intended to recover the "lessons of the past," as exemplified by the foreign policies of Washington, Hamilton, John Quincy Adams, and William Pitt, Castlereagh, Benjamin Disraeli, and Lord Salisbury. He denied any admiration for Metternich whom he had never mentioned in the text (though Metternich had been put on the blurb of the book by the publisher). Moreover, it was absurd to suggest that realists believe in systems. The opposite was the case, he argued. From Pitt and Castlereagh through to Disraeli and Bismarck to Churchill, "all the realists have been blamed by their opponents as being opportunists, devoid of principles, without a system."[28] Again, the realists and their critics were talking past each other. The fact that they all believed Churchill was in their own camp was a case in point.

It is striking that those who knew most about German iterations of *Realpolitik* were so anxious that the notion should not be allowed to lodge itself on American soil. This applied to the German-American historian and poet, Peter Viereck, whose previous denunciations of Treitschke have already been discussed. In a new 1953 book, *The Shame and Glory of the Intellectuals*, Viereck now expressed concern that American foreign policy realists were resuscitating the very ideas that had been defeated by Western idealism. To do so after victory was perverse. In the era of the Holocaust, he made a counterplea "for the material necessity of more idealism, for the economic necessity of more than economics, and for a road back from *Realpolitik* and brutalization."

In particular, Viereck baulked at the idea that Churchill could be claimed for a "realist" tradition, citing four instances when he had opposed the prescriptions of realists such as E. H. Carr: his call for intervention against Bolshevism in Russia in 1918; his opposition to the appeasement of Hitler; his warning of postwar dangers from Russia during the Second World War; and his famous speech of 1946, at Westminster College in Fulton, Missouri, when he introduced the term "iron curtain" to describe the division of Europe. During the 1930s, the West had "dawdled and disarmed" while its enemies grabbed half the globe. To the self-styled realists of the postwar era, Viereck objected that it was no good "telling us with a superior, bored patience—that concepts like 'ethics,' 'absolutes,' 'human dignity,' 'tragedy,' and 'death' are incorrect, amateurish semantics."[29]

Viereck's point was an important one that goes to the heart of this book. The language of the foreign policy debate did matter. To insist on the preeminence of rationality and reason, or to reject sentiment and morality, was to cheapen one's discourse. It reflected a poverty of ambition about the world. The West could be hypocritical, of course. By and large, however, it was better when it believed it was right.

Between Theology and Science: Realism
and the Failed Reformation

Given the fierce reaction to their arguments, one can see why the realists felt under siege. This partly explains their tendency to huddle together and to self-identify as a "school" of thought, despite differences between them. The connection between Kennan and Morgenthau has already been noted. Morgenthau also kept up a correspondence with President Truman's secretary of state, Dean Acheson—by then out of office—who described himself as "a follower of the Morgenthau line" in 1953.[30] There was also a burgeoning friendship between Morgenthau and Walter Lippmann in the same period. Lippmann's version of realism had developed, moving from his support for American intervention in both world wars to a realism of restraint. An early clue had been provided by his *Shield of the Republic*, in which he had argued that America's aggressive confrontation of threats should be limited to the Atlantic basin. After 1945, he cautioned against America's confrontation with the Soviet Union and argued that the United States should accept Russia's dominance in Eastern Europe.

Morgenthau sought out such connections because he believed that the case for a realist foreign policy could not simply be fought within academia. He wrote to Lippmann in August 1950, expressing admiration for his journalism at the *New York Herald Tribune* and the "public spirit, courage and insight, which will assure you a place in history as one of the great mentors of our time, regardless of whether your advice will be heeded or not."[31] The two would meet at the Cosmopolitan and Cosmos Clubs in Washington and compare notes on critical reviews of their work.[32] Morgenthau would also send Lippmann suggestions for books to read.[33]

In Morgenthau (the scholar), Kennan (the diplomat), and Lippmann (the journalist) one sees three important strands of postwar American realism. To a lesser extent, one could also add Niebuhr (the theologian) and Acheson (the statesman) to this group, though they kept a greater distance. Niebuhr operated in a different intellectual space, and Acheson, Lippmann, and Kennan clashed on the details of Cold War policy. Nonetheless, Morgenthau's hope, as expressed to Kennan, was that this broad grouping could influence not just "academic" but "public thinking" on foreign affairs.[34]

These men felt they were pushing against the tide of prevailing ortho-
doxy in the academy, in policymaking circles, and in the public sphere.
Thus Morgenthau went to Kennan with his concerns about the editorship of *Foreign Affairs* under Hamilton Fish Armstrong, complaining
about the "difficulty people of my persuasion have in making their views
known to the general educated public by way of articles." *Foreign Affairs*
enjoyed a "virtual monopoly in the field and speaking with great authority to virtually the whole segment of public opinion which takes an intelligent interest in American foreign policy." However, it was dominated by
Wilsonians and what Morgenthau saw as a bias "against a realistic approach
to American foreign policy." In fact, he believed that Tannenbaum's
attack on his work, discussed above, had been deliberately commissioned
by Armstrong in order to counteract what he saw as a "nefarious trend of
thought." Meanwhile, Morgenthau felt forced to take any opportunity he
had to express his views, by writing for comparatively obscure journals
that "reach only small fractions of that segment of public opinion." He
contrasted this with past debates on American foreign policy that had been
carried out on the pages of one journal: such as Alexander Hamilton versus
James Madison in the *Gazette of the United States* and Captain Mahan versus
Norman Angell in the *North American Review*.

In Morgenthau's grievance with *Foreign Affairs*, two things stood out.
The first was Morgenthau's belief that the odds were stacked against
him—a recurrent refrain. The second was an increasing absolutism in his
position. "If you scan at random the table of contents of a number of volumes of *Foreign Affairs*," he explained to Kennan, "you will indeed find a
number of articles by authors of official standing, such as yourself, which
implicitly deviate from the legalistic-moralistic position. You will, however, not find a single article which takes explicitly issue with that position." In other words, rather than restraining idealism, Morgenthau's goal
was to dismantle its philosophical foundations. Rather than acting as a
check on Wilsonianism, he believed that it was necessary to overturn it
entirely. A few articles from Kennan or Lippmann were insufficient for
the purpose. The whole editorial line had to be debunked. "It is my whole
point that the journal which has a virtual monopoly both in circulation and
authority is, at least surreptitiously, dominated by what I believe to be an
obsolescent philosophy of foreign affairs," he explained.[35] Kennan's more
wily reply urged Morgenthau not to be too discouraged. He described his
own, rather less absolute goal—a gradual approach, which meant chipping

away at the prevailing status quo: "Yours is one of the few clear and sober voices speaking on these subjects in our country today, and the need is tremendous. I think that a dent has now been made in the traditional schools of thought on international affairs in this country, but it will be a long time before people can be shamed into refraining from writing and teaching high-sounding nonsense."[36]

For Morgenthau, this was no less than a battle for the soul of the American worldview. In an odd way, then, the precise details of foreign policy were of secondary importance to its theological premise. Thus Morgenthau was eager to cast the postwar debate on American foreign policy as the most significant that had ever taken place in the history of international relations (as a field of study). In a 1952 article entitled "Another Great Debate" he argued that foreign policy debates of the past had been about tactical choices: interventionism and non-intervention in the 1890s; expansion versus status quo in the Mexican War; intervention versus abstention in the 1930s. The one occurring in the 1950s was about the "philosophical" basis on which the nation would conduct its foreign policy.[37]

One might say that American realism set itself an unrealistic task—of flushing Wilsonianism out of the American mind and the American political system entirely. In its efforts to do so, it also began to develop something of an identity crisis—stuck between a theology and a putative science. Some of its leading exponents stressed its ethical component; the echoes of Weber and the influence of Niebuhr have already been noted. Yet, in rejecting naïve liberal interpretations of the nature of international politics—as E. H. Carr had done—they also claimed to offer a superior understanding of the functioning of the international system.

To understand the moral parameters of human action, one first had to paint a compelling picture of the world as it was, rather than the world as one would like it to be. As an example of this, in his 1957 book, *Ethics and American Foreign Policy*, the Yale theologian Ernest Lefever set out to reconcile his religious belief and personal faith in humanism with his realistic interpretation of international affairs. He cited his debt to Niebuhr, Kennan, Lippmann, and Morgenthau's student, Kenneth Thompson. In a telling phrase in a foreword to the book, Morgenthau praised Lefever for creating "another stone to that bridge of understanding which, from opposite sides of the valley, theologians and political thinkers have been building." It showed that the "religiously committed and morally sensitive person can reflect on foreign policy in relevant terms."[38] To be clear,

Morgenthau did not see himself as a theologian or a scientist but as an expert on the "technical aspects" of politics—or, as he put it, "the rules of political art."[39] Nonetheless, the idea that they had a more scientific grasp of international politics was to become increasingly important to the self-image of some realists. An important moment in this was the 1954 Conference on Theory, sponsored by the Rockefeller Foundation, convened with the express aim of achieving a scientific understanding of world affairs.[40]

Another important moment was the 1959 publication of Kenneth Waltz's *Man, the State and War*, one of the foundational texts in so-called structural or neo-realism. Specifically, Waltz—a political science professor at Columbia University and a veteran of the Korean War—set out to defend the concept of "realpolitik" from writers like Frank Tannenbaum who had argued that it was passé and out-dated. He rejected the idea that it implied pessimism about the nature of man. For Waltz, realpolitik was a "loosely defined method" in an international arena defined by a state of anarchy.[41] Yet his own definition, which held up Machiavelli as its founding father, was indicative of the way in which the notion had become confused with other trends of political thought. There was no appreciation of the context of its origins and changing meanings. The same criticism can also be made about Waltz's use of other concepts such as the "balance of power." A balance of power was long regarded as something that nineteenth-century British statesmen had preferred to maintain in Europe. When used in scientific theories of international relations, however, time-bound vistas were being elevated to the position of rules, or doctrines.[42]

On the one hand, *Man, the State and War* was a highly original piece of scholarship. It offered an entirely new theoretical lens through which to look at international politics. On the other hand, it fitted within a long-established tradition of of realist philosophy. Waltz himself was quite clear that his work sat within the mainstream tradition of Continental European political thought. As well as using Machiavelli, Waltz drew on familiar German precedents in the form of Ranke, Metternich, and Bismarck. There was no doubt about where his sympathies lay. What Waltz offered was, in fact, a critique of the anti-realpolitik tradition that had emerged in the early twentieth century (as described in Part II of this book). Thus, Waltz described how Anglo-American liberal internationalism grew, in part, out of English liberal distaste for German approaches to statecraft. In Waltz's view, anti-realpolitik was a discredited tradition. Its exponents had tried to apply the supposed methods and sanctions of internal governance—such as judicial settlement and public opinion—to affairs among states. But they had failed to comprehend the fundamental truth that each state "pursues its own interests, however defined, in ways it judges best." Force was an inevitable part of the international arena because there was no consistent, reliable process for reconciling the conflicts of interest that inevitably arose among states in an anarchical system. A foreign policy based on this image of international relations was "neither moral nor immoral, but embodies merely a reasoned response to the world around us."[43] This version of realism did not need to defend itself against allegations that it was immoral because—its exponents claimed—it was founded on scientific truth.

Weber, not Treitschke: The Last Remnants of German *Realpolitik*

While Waltz espoused a more scientific or structural approach to international relations, his conscious invocation of the German tradition of *Realpolitik* demonstrated that a tangible connection between it and postwar American realism did remain. For good reasons, Morgenthau was always more squeamish about addressing this fact head-on in his published work. Yet his private correspondence is more revealing, particularly an exchange he had with Dr. Gottfried-Karl Kindermann, a Far Eastern research specialist at the German Council for Foreign Relations in Freiburg. Kindermann was greatly enamored with Morgenthau's work and hoped to publish excerpts of it in German. He sent Morgenthau a list of questions about the basis of his political theory.[44] Morgenthau's responses demonstrated that American realism was a different creed, but that it was perhaps more entangled with German *Realpolitik*, and admiration for Bismarck in particular, than his published work would suggest.

First, it was clear that Reinhold Niebuhr was the starting point for any discussion of American realism. Asked by Kindermann whether he saw any fundamental differences between his overall approach to research and that of Niebuhr, Morgenthau answered in the negative. Asked if he saw any difference between Niebuhr's understanding of the basic factors of politics and his own, Morgenthau replied that there was only a difference in emphasis. While Niebuhr stressed "the moral and philosophic aspects of politics," Morgenthau was more interested in its technical aspects and the details of statecraft. Second, the idea that America must come to political maturity was a major theme. Morgenthau concurred with Kindermann's definition of the realist position as holding that "the political culture of a given nation can be measured by the degree of its awareness of the nature of power and its ability to translate this awareness into action, in a manner that provides domestic security."

What, if anything, remained of his German intellectual heritage, asked Kindermann? Here Morgenthau readily acknowledged his debt to Max Weber. But when asked to comment on comparisons that had been made between his work and that of Heinrich Treitschke, he was understandably irritated. "This is a complete misunderstanding of my position," he wrote: "Treitschke was an ideologue of the nation state of Bismarck, and of power. I am an analyst of the nation state and of power and have emphasised time and time again their negative connotations."[45]

To compare Morgenthau to Treitschke was absurd. This extreme version of *Realpolitik* had no appeal to him. In truth, however, he shared more of an admiration for Bismarck than he cared to admit in this instance. While his English-language work mainly focused on English-language statesmanship, he did exhibit a certain hankering for the unsentimental ways of nineteenth-century European statecraft. In a letter to Dean Acheson in 1963, he expressed despair at the "dearth of men who are capable of thinking in political terms" in Washington. "Reading 19th century history, as I do from time to time for intellectual stimulation, I am struck by the political isolation of Bismarck and Cavour whose most brilliant and successful moves were understood by hardly anyone at the time and were actively opposed by those who were to benefit most from their success," he wrote.[46]

Morgenthau's wistfulness about the past betrayed something else about postwar American realism. This was the fact that it was more idealistic than its self-image would suggest. Something that united the realists was a tendency to hanker after some lost era of statecraft. During the 1960s, Niebuhr, Lippmannn, Morgenthau, Kennan, and Acheson expressed growing discomfort about the direction of American politics in general. In addition to their work on foreign policy, they all contributed to a large corpus of cultural criticism. There was a melancholy tone to their work, with grumblings about the effects of technology and the disproportionate concentration of wealth in the West. Kennan, for example, complained about motorcars, became interested in environmental protection, and spoke of an almost Arcadian vision of the past.[47] While the context was American, this did reflect a sort of Weberian angst about modernity. It was redolent of what the German-American Jewish scholar Fritz Stern—who married Niebuhr's daughter, Elisabeth Sifton—had called "the politics of cultural despair" when writing about German nationalism.[48]

In their efforts to debunk Wilsonianism, legalism and moralism, the American realists longed for a reformation that never came. Writing in memory of Morgenthau just after his death in 1980, Robert Osgood (director of research at Johns Hopkins Foreign Policy Institute in Washington, and a mentee) attempted to capture the realist mindset Morgenthau represented. On the one hand, Osgood wrote, Morgenthau had "expounded the gospel of *Realpolitik* and exorcised the moralistic illusions nurtured during the nation's isolation from the mainstream of international politics." He had been right to make the case that there was a moral dignity in the national interest and the responsible use of power. On the other hand, in a shrewd observation, Osgood also noted that Morgenthau "was more of a critic than a prophet." [49] Like many other realists, he was a critic inspired by a mission that was never fulfilled. Realism had become something of an ideology in its own right. It was more bound up with its immediate surroundings than its chief proponents were prepared to admit to themselves.

13

The Bismarck Debate

In the 1950s in the United States, there had been a growing tendency for scholars and theorists of international affairs to identify themselves as belonging to certain schools of thought. Attempting to evade such categorization was not easy, partly because of the nature of the academic patronage network. An important and underrated attempt to do so was Robert Osgood's 1953 *Ideas and Self-Interest in America's Foreign Relations*. If one insists on such labels, Osgood—who later worked for Henry Kissinger on the National Security Council staff during Richard Nixon's first term and then as an advisor to Ronald Reagan—should be put in the realist category, though his influence extended beyond it.[1]

In the introduction to his 1953 book, Osgood thanked both McGeorge Bundy, his supervisor at Harvard, and Hans Morgenthau, who helped him with publication with University of Chicago Press. Above all, Osgood indicated his desire to find some sort of compromise between what he saw as unhelpful polarities in the Great Debate of the postwar era. The utopian, "anxious to assert the claims of idealism and impatient with reality," or the realist, "exasperated by the inability of utopians to perceive the reality of national egoism" had created a false dichotomy. In very few situations were statesmen faced with a clear choice between ideals and national interest; more often they were faced with the task of reconciling the two. To recognize the points of convergence between self-interest and supranational ideals was one of the "highest tasks of statesmanship."[2]

In fact, Osgood went out of his way to rescue so-called idealists from the allegation that they did not understand the national interest. What really distinguished him from other realists was that he told a story of gradual maturation in American foreign policymaking over the last fifty years, "from fitful adolescence to self-possessed maturity." In doing so, he made much use of Walter Lippmann's early work, at the time of Woodrow

Wilson's presidency, when he had urged America to play a part in the restructuring of the international order. By becoming the leader in this process, and projecting itself as the champion of democracy, the United States had expanded its reach and power. The mistake made by Wilson with the League of Nations had been to confuse what was desirable with what was attainable. Nonetheless, Osgood shared the view that the internal health of the Republic depended on its behavior abroad. Unless Americans "constantly relate their pursuit of national security to a hierarchy of universal values, they undermine those moral qualities that were "as indispensable to national welfare as character is to personal welfare." This was "no academic proposition," for as America's foreign relations grew more complex, there would be a natural tendency to resolve moral dilemmas "by ignoring them or rationalizing them out of existence."

Osgood was a supporter of limited containment and argued strongly against an anti-communist crusade in American foreign policy. Yet he also added a warning about the increasingly uncompromising tone of the self-described realists. Unless contemporary realists fully grasped the interdependence of ideals and self-interest in international relations, they would "spread little enlightenment by opposing one kind of oversimplification with another." No great mass of people was Machiavellian, he explained, least of all the American people.[3]

Osgood's use of Lippmann's early writings touched a nerve with the veteran journalist, now sixty-four and having long since distanced himself from the Wilsonian tradition in US foreign policy. Osgood had suggested that the young Lippmann, as a journalist at the *New Republic*, had had a large share in Wilson's Fourteen Points. Writing to Morgenthau, Lippmann felt the need to explain that six of the Fourteen Points dealt with specific territorial settlements in Europe and he had had nothing to do with them. These were entirely Wilson's work, though it had become Lippmann's job at the Armistice Conference to "make an interpretation of those abstract points which might be reasonable and practical for negotiation with the Allies." More substantively, he also explained that the Fourteen Points were, in part, designed as an answer to the secret treaties just published by the Bolsheviks—including the Sykes-Picot Agreement—which exposed the machinations of the Allied powers. This was America's way of distinguishing itself from the imperialist nations. In effect, Lippmann was explaining the broader strategic rationale behind the Fourteen Points, as part of a battle for world opinion. As he put it, this had "a bearing upon the general question of the realism of the underlying foreign policy at the time."[4] Yet it could be argued that this clarification bolstered Osgood's overall argument rather than undermined it. It underlined the fact that there was more to Wilsonianism than utopian naiveté and that America was a much more mature actor on the world stage, and had been for some time, than many of its critics would acknowledge.

Osgood's point about gradual maturation also struck a chord with those charged with articulating the aims of American foreign policy outside academia. Indeed, the suggestion of some realists that America had to "grow up" or transform the whole basis of its foreign policy was rather irritating to some. Being talked to like a child was not particularly well received by the public. William Lee Miller, the chief speechwriter for Democratic presidential nominee Adlai Stevenson in 1956—and self-confessed follower of Niebuhr—expressed exasperation with "the rather familiar indictments of our 'legalistic-moralistic' approach" which seemed to imply that the country should "somehow exhibit a degree of political sophistication never seen on land or sea." Wilsonianism had become something of a phantom and a straw man in the realist critique. As Miller argued, the so-called Wilsonian tradition that the realists were so determined to debunk was "just a coloration and not a consistent picture." In his view, it was better to err on this side of the divide than to go to the other extreme, a "cynical, utterly pessimistic, and thoroughgoing *Realpolitik*."[5]

Beyond Bismarckism

Left in the hands of theorists of international relations, the notion of realpolitik had lost some of its original meaning, along with a sense of the context in which it emerged. It was in the historical profession, where trenches were not dug so deep, that a true sense of real *Realpolitik*—one that was cognizant of its origins in mid-nineteenth-century Germany—was kept alive. Appropriately, some of the most enlightening discussions about its strengths and weaknesses coincided with a revival of interest in the careers of both Otto von Bismarck and Friedrich Meinecke.

The spark for this debate was lit by the English historian A. J. P. Taylor's biography of Bismarck, published in 1955. Taylor picked up on what he regarded as a worrying intellectual trend—a creeping admiration for Bismarck among foreign policy strategists in Britain and America.

Taylor used his biography of Bismarck to challenge the idea, popularized by Heinrich Treitschke, that Bismarck was a political genius. Accident and fluke, as much as anything else, had characterized the unification of Germany. One reason for the distortion of Bismarck's reputation was his self-serving 1898 memoir, *Reflections and Recollections*. In Germany, admiration for Bismarck had actually increased after defeat in the First World War. After 1918, a number of German historians (Meinecke among them) had returned to the archives of the Bismarck era to absolve him of blame for the catastrophe. As Taylor described, they argued that Kaiser Wilhelm's *Weltpolitik* had been an aberration and a break with the Bismarck tradition of pursuing a realistic foreign policy and avoiding encirclement by one's enemies. But the revival of Bismarckian hero worship had also had poisonous effects. It had created the impression that Germany need only return to his ways to re-establish its dominance in Europe. This had contributed to the undermining of any support for multilateralism and international law in the country after 1918.

By wrapping themselves up in this comfortable narrative, German intellectuals had failed to confront the ills of extreme German nationalism. This had helped create the environment in which Nazism was able to flourish. When the Weimar Republic fell, the Bismarckians (the Junkers and traditional nationalists) got their way. But it was the Nazis who inherited the state. Soon the Bismarckians lost control of the army, the foreign office, the administration, and even the universities. Even Meinecke lost the editorship of the *Historische Zeitschrift* in 1936 for refusing to include a section on anti-Semitic history. A few Bismarckians, such as the conservative historian Hans Rothfels, left Germany for a new home in the United States (once he failed in his application for honorary Aryan status). Others lay low in Germany, waiting for their moment. They did not know how to oppose the regime from the outside so they tried to intrigue against Hitler from within, or to steer him on a saner course. But Hitler completely outmaneuvered them, time and time again.

It had taken another world war, and another crushing defeat for Germany, to finally rid Germans of these illusions about the genius of Bismarckian *Realpolitik*. Meinecke was one of the first academics to confess the error, in his 1945 book, *The Great Catastrophe*. As Taylor described, a final few "unrepentant Bismarckians still praised *Realpolitik* and even contended that there would have been nothing wrong with Hitler if he had left the Christian Churches alone and not persecuted the Jews." But the vast majority of professors in Germany would no longer propagate this myth. They came to understand that "the academic world had been seduced by Bismarck's success," that they "should have admired ethical values more, and worldly power less," that Gilbert Murray, the famous classicist and humanist public intellectual, and not Treitschke, was the true example of what a university professor should be.

Why was this important in the Cold War era? By 1955, Taylor saw another danger. He was more concerned about the return of Bismarckian hero-worship in the West than he was about its revival in Germany. A significant portion of the Anglo-American elite had imbibed the Bismarckian myth in the interwar years. "Many causes combined to win sympathy for Germany in England and the United States," Taylor wrote, in an analysis of the intellectual origins of appeasement: "Sentimental regrets at victory counted most; the complaints of economists against reparations for something. But the name Bismarck counted too." Nazism was such an aberration that the governing classes in England and the United States spoke wistfully of a return to the days of Bismarck, thereby parroting what many had said when the kaiser had dismissed Bismarck in 1891. "Now they came to believe that Realpolitik was right after all," Taylor explained—or, at least, superior to the doctrines of William Gladstone or Woodrow Wilson.

Even Winston Churchill had fed this narrative, albeit unintentionally, by praising Konrad Adenauer, West Germany's first postwar leader, as the best chancellor since Bismarck. But it was in the United States that a new cult of Bismarck had really taken hold. Specifically, Taylor highlighted the work of the German American historian, William L. Langer (professor at Yale and leading figure in the Office of Strategic Services), in restoring Bismarck's reputation in the United States. Through his work, Taylor claimed, "Realpolitik was taught to a generation of students who were to determine American policy after the Second World War—not the least of Bismarck's victories."[6] Langer offered an English language version of a now familiar argument—Bismarck was a wise practitioner of diplomacy whose carefully constructed system had been ruined by the megalomania of Kaiser Wilhelm and Adolf Hitler.[7] As discussed in the next chapter, a similar argument was made in George Kennan's book, *The Decline of Bismarck's European Order: Franco-Russian Relations, 1875–1890.*[8] It was also to be challenged by Henry Kissinger.

Another striking continuity was that Langer was influenced by the work of Otto Hammann. As noted earlier, Hammann was the chief propagandist

"Dropping the Pilot" was a cartoon by Sir John Tenniel, which appeared in *Punch*, an English political magazine, on 29 March 1890, in response to Bismarck's dismissal by Kaiser Wilhelm II. The Bismarck debate echoed through the Cold War, and the British historian A. J. P. Taylor warned against a cult of Bismarck re-emerging in the West after 1945, as it had done in Germany after 1918. But Bismarck continued to have influential admirers, including George F. Kennan. Courtesy of Wikimedia Creative Commons. PD-old.

for the German state before the First World War. In his book, *The World Policy of Germany, 1890–1912*, he emphasized the difference between Bismarck's foreign policy and more extreme forms of pan-German nationalism. Langer reviewed it favorably in *Foreign Affairs* in 1924.[9] Taylor was particularly critical of the aforementioned Hans Rothfels as one of the few remaining unrepentant German partisans of Bismarck. In 1948, Rothfels had published an essay on the centenary of the 1848 revolutions—one that actually mentioned Ludwig von Rochau but went on to present Bismarck as the exemplar for any aspiring statesman. The same year Rothfels also published a book on the German opposition to Hitler, which celebrated those army officers who attempted the 20 July 1944 plot against Hitler.[10]

Not everyone swallowed this revisionism about Bismarck, of course. A telling example was Hajo Holborn, who worked under Langer at both the OSS and Yale. In his history of Germany, Holborn noted how many Bismarckian conservatives had condemned the Nazis for their "herd character, mass oratory, and lack of *Realpolitik*."[11] Yet, just as he had criticized Meinecke, Holborn did not follow the Langer line. In fact, he offered a different interpretation entirely. He argued that Bismarck, rather than being the arch pragmatist, was much more ideologically driven than had previously been assumed. It was true that he took the national interest as the guiding star of policy. Nonetheless, he held strong convictions about the ultimate moral goals of statecraft, derived from his strongly held Protestant faith. This caused him to think of himself as a creator, rather than just someone who responded to events.[12]

This was an argument further expanded by Holborn's student, Otto von Pflanze, who, it is worth noting, was also familiar with Rochau's original work.[13] Indeed, Pflanze attempted to offer a fuller definition of *Realpolitik*, as he understood it in historical context. On the one hand, it implied a "particular conception of the realities of political life," and on the other, "techniques of achieving positive results in view of these realities." The notion of Bismarck*ism* was itself a false construct, Pflanze argued. To think of Bismarck as having created some sort of science of politics was to miss the point entirely. Bismarck's genius was in his use of a "strategy of alternatives," by which he always gave himself a back-up option to minimize risk. Indeed, Pflanze quoted Bismarck's own statement to a Bavarian journalist to underline his point: "There is no exact science of politics, just as there is none for political economy. Only professors are able to package the sum of the changing needs of cultural man into scientific laws."[14] In other words, while expressing admiration for Bismarck's talents, Pflanze was just as cautious as Taylor about the notion that Bismarck bequeathed any great insight for later generations.

Thus historians were able to offer a fuller exposition of real *Realpolitik* than theorists of international relations. The latter often used it inaccurately or to serve polemic ends; the former aimed to place it in context. Over the long sweep of time, the danger of *Realpolitik* was its capacity to metastasize and take on other forms. This was argued by the American historian John Snell in his history of diplomacy during the Second World War. It was now well known that Hitler's policy had been based on zeal and ideology rather than the pragmatism associated with Bismarck. Yet the rot had started long before, with the very idea that Germans dealt in fundamental truths about politics while others (chiefly the English) dealt in cant. Even in Bismarck's time, "many Germans who wrote and talked of *Realpolitik* were thinking in terms more illusory than realistic," corrupting the concept by seeing it as synonymous with the politics of force, and failing to distinguish between ends and means. Since that time, German policy had been based on doctrinaire fixations rather than a calm assessment of the international arena. In the 1930s too, Japan and Italy also succumbed to the same "gambling that passed for *Realpolitik*" with the same fatal effects. Here Snell also commented on the strengths and weaknesses of the anti-realpolitik tradition in the West. In the 1930s and the 1940s, the Allies and their leaders—Franklin Roosevelt, Harry Truman, and Churchill foremost among them—had learned an important lesson. "If preoccupation with force distorts *Realpolitik*," he explained, the refusal of a global power to accept global responsibilities and to maintain military power to uphold them was just as certain a formula for "the transmogrification of idealism into appeasement and surrender." The best asset that the West had was "reason."[15]

Reason was superior to simple idealism, on the one hand, and narrow rationalism and materialism on the other. This idea was increasingly important to those who sought to give liberal internationalism a sounder foundation than it had had in the interwar years. A year after Snell's book, in 1963, Richard Rosecrance produced *Action and Reaction in World Affairs*, which warned of the dangers of regressing to old diplomatic methods—such as summit diplomacy, bilateralism, and appeals to narrow self-interest—in the Cold War environment. The book was introduced by Carl J. Friedrich, the Harvard-based expert on totalitarianism who had been so critical of Morgenthau and Kennan. Rosecrance warned that to play the Bismarck game was to court disaster over the long term. Contrary to the arguments of the realists, the Bismarck approach had not signaled "a new age by virtue of its nonideological character." In fact, it had consisted of the application of every means possible to serve the ideological goal of unification under Prussia. As practiced by Bismarck, it had also had "the mark of conservative desperation." Fraudulent reformism and revolutionary militarism, stage-managed by Bismarck and his followers, could only ever be a short-term strategy. Bismarck's *Realpolitik* depended on a "controlled unleashing of what otherwise might become an unchecked chain reaction."[16] It achieved many political successes within a limited window. But whether through folly or misunderstanding, it had unraveled over time and proved to be a dangerous tool in the hands of others. In any case, a political method that depended on a high degree of individual genius and ingenuity was not fit for the nuclear age.

Significantly, it was in the Bismarck debate of this era that the dying embers of Ludwig von Rochau's original concept were to be found. And here lay the most pointed critique of Bismarck of all which takes us back to the start of this book. It was that Bismarck had failed by the original terms of Rochau's *Foundation of Realpolitik*.

It was in 1972 that the prominent German historian Hans Ulrich-Wehler produced the only modern edition of Rochau's *Foundations*.[17] Wehler's own criticisms of the limitations of Bismarckism were lifted straight from Rochau's work. Bismarck had delivered successes but these were largely short term and limited. He had resisted rather than embraced the political implications of economic modernization, as Rochau had urged. The fact that Bismarck subscribed to a "vision of conservative utopia" had seen him react to a period of rapid development by repressive and diversionary measures, "whereas a truly realistic *Realpolitik*, keeping in step with industrial growth and the process of democratization, should have had as its starting point the political and social process of emancipation, and should indeed have sought to further this process."[18] Wehler's critique of Bismarck made little or no impact on Bismarck's English and American admirers. Yet its genius lay in the way it condemned Bismarck for failing on the very terms for which he was so admired by later generations—that is, failing in *Realpolitik*.[19]

Anglo-American Versus Continental Thought

In 1957 the first English-language version of Meinecke's *Die Idee der Staatsräson* was produced. It was edited and introduced by Werner Stark, an atheist of Czech Jewish origin, who had fled the Nazis in both Prague and Vienna, before eventually moving to England and serving in the British army in the Second World War. Stark's introduction of Meinecke to an

English-speaking audience was both a subtle and sympathetic portrayal of the development of his thought over the course of his career. Yet this laid the ground for a brilliant critique that was also designed to dent contemporary American realism. Stark's trick was to point out the lack of realism in Meinecke's *Realpolitik*. It was to subject him to the same test as Wehler had done to Bismarck—that is, to challenge a hero of *Realpolitik* on his own terms.

Stark argued that Meinecke had been more driven by religious belief than his reputation as a realist suggested. More specifically, his understanding of historical development was based on his religious conviction that the given circumstances of the world were the reflection of providence. This was a form of pantheism: the idea that God and the world established by God are one and the same. Throughout his career, Meinecke's understanding of good and evil had failed to transcend the prevailing circumstances in which he wrote. At first, before 1918, "evil was to him no more than a step toward good, a cost item as it were, which, in due course, will pay in terms of profit." Thus he could justify certain acts—on the part of Germany's leaders—so long as they were undertaken in the name of the national ideal. Between 1918 and 1933, Meinecke, succumbed to fatalism. During this phase of his career, he accepted the existence of evil as "a fact of nature which it would be as vain to try and stop as it would be to arrest the movement of the stars or the coming and going of the tides." This spoke of a desire to escape his existing surroundings—to postpone or steer clear of individual responsibility on ethical matters. After the rise of the Nazis in 1933, as Stark put it "evil was indeed bemoaned, but at the same time pushed away to the far horizon of that metaphysical haven or heaven in which our philosopher-historian had built the residence for his declining years."

The potency of Stark's critique of Meinecke was in his ability to identify, understand, and even sympathize with Meinecke's conception of *Realpolitik*—that is, to enter its bloodstream and to subvert it from within. Stark regarded Meinecke as a brilliant analyst of the world around him. He saw things that other theorists missed. Yet Stark also aimed to show that Meinecke was a prisoner to the structures around him—and that he struggled to see beyond his immediate horizon. Thus, he concluded, it was "as a realist that Meinecke failed his whole life."[20]

However many truisms the German theorists of statecraft had identified, and however many admirers they had outside Germany, there was a natural resistance to the complete incorporation of their ideas in the West. It was a prominent exponent of geopolitics—Arnold Wolfers of Yale, who had studied in Berlin and Munich—who recognized that there remained a firewall between continental European and Anglo-American political thought on international affairs. In a co-edited collection, published in 1956 with his Yale colleague Lawrence J. Martin, Wolfers collated reflections on statecraft from a list of Anglo-American thinkers—beginning with Thomas More, ending with Woodrow Wilson, and including Hobbes, Burke, Hamilton, Jefferson, Mill, Mahan, and Hobson. First, this was because the continental European authors (Machiavelli, Grotius, Spinoza, and Kant, for example) had historically received more scholarly attention. Second, Wolfers believed that an analysis of Anglo-American thinkers would help explain some of the peculiarities of the British and American approach to world affairs, which "often puzzle the foreign observer and lead him either to praise the special virtues of Anglo-Saxon policy or condemn what he considers its hypocritical wrappings."

Wolfers did not go so far as to claim that all continental thought had been Machiavellian in its understanding of international politics. In fact, Wolfers cited Meinecke's *Die Idee der Staatsräson* as evidence that, since the publication of *The Prince*, there had always been a robust debate between the Machiavellians and the anti-Machiavellians. Yet even Meinecke's book proved that the continental debate mostly centered around the idea of "necessity of state." As continental political philosophers saw it, the main problem presented by foreign policy was the conflict between morality and raison d'état. This was in line with the historical experience common to all continental countries, which, in the face of external threats to their existence, believed themselves exposed to the impact of forces beyond their control. There was always a feeling that these nations were "puppets in the hands of demonic forces, with little leeway if any to rescue moral values from a sea of tragic necessity."

Meanwhile, English and American thinking on statecraft had followed a different trajectory over the last three centuries. The Anglo-Americans were not blind to the exceptional freedom of choice their insularity gave them. "Long before the science of geopolitics," Thomas More, Viscount Bolingbroke, and Thomas Jefferson acknowledged "the privileges offered by their respective countries and the fact they had the luxury to remain aloof from many international struggles, and therefore moral conundrums." The Anglo-Americans began their meditations on foreign policy with a philosophy of choice rather than a philosophy of necessity. From More to Woodrow Wilson, the recurrent topics of concern and debate were questions such as the right of self-defense and its limits, the right and duty to intervene or not to intervene in the affairs of others, or the extent to which colonial rule and territorial expansion were justified.

Whereas the politics of necessity tended to lead to "resignation, irresponsibility, or even the glorification of amorality," freedom of choice could lend itself to "excessive moralism and self-righteousness." There was a self-correcting mechanism in Anglo-American political thought, however. This was the recognition that freedom of choice should not come at the expense of self-preservation. Nations were not advised to sacrifice themselves on the altar of humanity or human liberty or to set the general interest above the national interest of self-preservation, explained Wolfers. As Meinecke had understood, there was room for hypocrisy in this argument.

On the whole, however, Wolfers noted that the Anglo-American moral philosophers, rather than posing as apologists of a national mission, "placed themselves in the creditable role of serving as the conscience of the nation, reminding statesmen of the dictates of justice and reason." Even among the exponents of what Wolfers called the "power political school of thought"—in which he included Thomas Hobbes, Francis Bacon, Alexander Hamilton, and Alfred Thayer Mahan—there remained a strong ethical core that distinguished them from the continental tradition. Thus, wrote Wolfers, "pessimists and optimists, realists and idealists," all emphasized the moral aspects of political choice. They rejected the German line of argument, for example, that competition for power, conflict, struggle, or war could be regarded as signs of national health or heroism.

Yet there was a catch. As an exponent of geopolitics, Wolfers warned that the world was changing in a way that would test Anglo-American theories of foreign affairs more than ever before. In matters of expansion, or intervention in other people's wars, there would still be significant room for maneuver and ethical debate. Gone, however, was the insular security in which these ethical codes had been developed. With the advent of air power and nuclear weapons, the international arena contained existential threats to survival and now looked more similar to how it had appeared to the continental theorists.

There was a choice facing the Anglo-American powers in how they conducted their foreign policy in the future. One option was to swing over to the continental approach in its most extreme form, which would mean the acceptance, without qualification, of a philosophy of necessity. By this road, all major decisions in foreign policy "would then be conceived as dictated by external circumstances beyond human control, statesman and people alike being absolved as a consequence from all responsibility." The danger, however, would be to fall into the trap of fatalism—to use the excuse of compulsion to argue that "what was considered evil when undertaken by others was no longer evil when done by oneself."

For Wolfers, this was the wrong path. Anglo-American foreign policy should keep faith with the traditions that had served it thus far rather than turning itself over to the continental tradition in strategic thought. Even under the shadow of nuclear war, there remained freedom of choice between more or less moderation, more or less concern for the interests of others, more or less effort to preserve the peace, more or less respect for justice, more or less of a sense of responsibility for the whole of mankind. The essence of Anglo-American political thought—and the formula that had served both countries well for so long—was to aim for a wise interpretation of the national interest that could also "conform with the principles of morality, reasonably applied, and to the broader interests of mankind."[21] In the search for a realistic approach to the world, the English-speaking nations had enough in their armory that they did not need to seek guidance from Bismarck, Machiavelli, and Meinecke. They were also more mature and self-aware than some wise men would have them believe. They should remain alert and alive to the changing environment but there was no need for a wholescale reformation of the worldview that had served them so well so far.

PART V

Practical Realpolitik

This word conjures up images of tough leaders and armed forces. The term has come to imply a certain amorality and immorality in action, choosing a course that may be the most effective but not one overly concerned with what is right or proper. Realpolitik has been used in many ways, some for purely self-serving political interests and others for mere intellectual debate. Regardless, realism (as realpolitik is alternately known) has been a guiding influence in policy-making across the national capitals of the world as well as within the ivory towers of academia.

(Frank Wayman and Paul F. Diehl, *Reconstructing Realpolitik*, 1994)[1]

14
Realpolitik before Détente

Having been bounced back and forth between academics and foreign policy theorists, the term realpolitik became embedded in the language of government and the policymaking world in the last third of the twentieth century. The debates about US foreign policy described in previous chapters had taken place in the press and public sphere, in the historical profession, and in the expanding field of international relations. Increasingly, the categories and concepts that were introduced seeped into the discourse of those responsible for the *practice* of foreign policy as opposed to its theorization. A rare early mention came in 1945 in discussions about China. Then, in the 1950s and 1960s, the word realpolitik began to be used with greater frequency at the Department of State and the Central Intelligence Agency (CIA). It began to appear in reports, reviews, memoranda, and policy statements, much as it had in Britain after the First World War.

Significantly, however, the term was still regarded with some suspicion in the 1950s and 1960s—as a foreign creed and therefore alien to the traditions of American diplomacy. When it appeared in the realm of official discussions of foreign policy, it was normally in descriptions of the behavior of other states. This was encouraged by the fact that the representatives of other states used the word in their dialogue with the United States. Among those to do so was János Kádár, the leader of the Hungarian Communist Party, when suggesting a normalization of relations between Hungary and the United States. Perhaps more significantly, even important allies, such as Britain and France, also used the same language with increasing frequency. These two nations, had traditionally stood against German *Realpolitik* and were in the vanguard of internationalism after both world wars. Yet they were left with increasingly less room for maneuver to pursue a more idealistic foreign policy as they attempted a managed drawdown from imperial commitments. In Suez and elsewhere, the dam was leaking and resources were stretched.

Confronted by a world where others rationalized and explained their own actions in terms of realpolitik—from close allies to enemies—it was difficult for the United States to remain immune to such practices forever. Yet this was a conclusion reached with some reluctance. In those instances where US officials used the concept to rationalize their own actions, they usually did so with misgivings. An example was US policy toward Iran in the early 1960s, when the dilemma arose over whether to continue to support the shah of Iran—put in place by a 1953 coup co-engineered by the CIA and the British secret service—or to encourage Iran down a more democratic path. This was the first time US officials had used the concept to explicitly justify their own actions. It had striking echoes of the British state's first use of it to justify its own behaviour, at the time of the Sykes-Picot Agreement in 1916. As ever, realpolitik reared its head first in the Middle East. Justified as a last resort, it still left an unpleasant taste in the mouth.

In the 1970s, the floodgates opened. As Chapter 15 explains, the usage of realpolitik became ubiquitous. It was one of the most frequently deployed words in debates about American foreign policy through the presidencies of Richard Nixon, Gerald Ford, and Jimmy Carter. Its use proliferated in diplomatic correspondence, official government documents, and in Senate and congressional hearings in this era, as well as in the media. In fact, by the early 1970s the word had become so entrenched in the American political lexicon that it was used as a rhetorical weapon in a range of controversies—on rapprochement with China, détente, human rights, and democracy promotion.

This was by no means inevitable. It occurred for two main reasons. The first was that American foreign policy came under the stewardship of a new generation, educated in the 1950s and early 1960s. Many of these policy-makers had been through the schools of foreign service—Chicago, Yale, Princeton, Harvard, Johns Hopkins, and Georgetown—at the time of the Great Debate described in the previous section. They were well versed in the key texts of American realism discussed earlier. If nothing else, their understanding of these debates provided them with a shared lexicon and set of organizing concepts. There was a certain irony in this development. While policymakers used the language learned in universities, a growing number of the professoriate became disillusioned with the overall direction of American foreign policy. This polarization began over the Korean War but the biggest escalatory factor was the Vietnam War. In the short term, this situation created an odd synergy between realist and radical critics of the country's foreign policy.

The second explanation for the proliferation of the word's use in this era was its association with the foreign policy of Richard Nixon, who became president in 1969, and then, just as important, the reaction against it under Jimmy Carter after 1976. In this, as in much else, Henry Kissinger (Nixon's national security advisor and then secretary of state) provides a crucial bridgehead. In popular perception, the Kissinger-Nixon approach to foreign affairs became synonymous with realpolitik. Kissinger's German origins—and probably his Frankish accent too—meant that the association was an easy one to make. It was not necessarily in a negative way that the connection was made. Some welcomed the "Europeanization" of American foreign policy in this era, as a sign of greater maturity. Favorable accounts of Kissinger's time in office describe him as holding a pessimistic worldview, "strongly influenced by his German provenance," and, by association, of being the last in a line of great European diplomats (Lord Castlereagh, Count Metternich, Otto von Bismarck, and late nineteenth-century British prime minister Lord Salisbury).[1]

Yet the assumption that Kissinger represented the epitome of this creed is misleading in a number of respects. First, Kissinger retained an acute sense of the limitations of German *Realpolitik*, which one can see when reading his scholarly work. This was reflected, for example, in his appreciation of the limitations of Castlereagh, Metternich, and Bismarck—to whom he was so often compared. Second, having moved from the academy to the world of the practitioner, Kissinger offered a mild—but nonetheless profound—critique of the type of realism that had taken hold in the academy. Not only did he make the point that *Realpolitik* had turned in on itself in the age of Bismarck; he also identified what he saw as a trend toward absolutism and academic escapism in elements of American realism (chiefly in Kennan and Morgenthau). Many of Kissinger's critics missed these nuances but so, it should be noted, did many of those who celebrated his approach to foreign policy as the implementation of a realist blueprint.

In mainstream political discourse, realpolitik became understood in one of two ways in the 1970s. For some, it was a pejorative term—an unwelcome import from the dark heart of *Mitteleuropa* that went against the grain of more noble Anglo-American traditions. For others, it was an accoutrement of sophistication—an antidote to hubris and a sign of maturity, historical literacy, and wisdom. To its critics, the word denoted cynicism and pessimism—and, in some cases, dastardly deals or backdoor diplomacy. To its defenders, it was a badge of honor—a corrective to naiveté and utopianism. Chapter 15 goes on to describe how the semantics of such divisive foreign policy debates could cause difficulties when it came to the implementation of policy.

Chapter 16, the final one in Part V, charts the various usages of "realpolitik" in the late stages of the Cold War, and beyond. In the 1980s, the presidency of Ronald Reagan showed the inadequacies of these categories and the need for a new foreign policy lexicon. Reaganism, as it came to be called, was a time-specific and somewhat accidental formulation. One of its distinguishing characteristics was that it defied the usual categories offered by realists and their critics. Some Reaganites saw his foreign policy as an antidote to the pessimism associated with realpolitik, whereas others regarded Reaganism as the next stage in its evolution. That left a rather ambiguous legacy that was still working itself out during George W. Bush's presidency from 2001 to 2009.

If the Reagan years broke the mold of these familiar categories, it was the end of the Cold War—and a shift to a unipolar international arena—that ground them into the dust. After the fall of the Berlin Wall, realpolitik seemed to go out of fashion. Even so-called realists (such as secretary of state James Baker) talked of a future age, or new world order, in which it would not be needed at all. In Britain, foreign secretary Robin Cook announced that Britain had adopted an "ethical foreign policy" that would have no place for realpolitik. As British prime minister, the famously ahistorical Tony Blair put Bismarck in history's dustbin. Ultimately, such hopes were confounded. Over the course of the 1990s, the word began to creep back into Anglo-American political discourse in a series of debates over military intervention—in the Balkans, Africa, and the Middle East. By 2005, it became common to talk, once again, about the "return of realpolitik." But the notion was further removed than ever before from Ludwig von Rochau's *Foundations*. It is to Rochau's original work that the conclusion of the book returns.

The Intellectuals and Foreign Policy

University professors provided the conceptual framework, and the vocabulary, for America's rise to the position of the world's greatest superpower. While there was no uniformity of opinion among the teachers, or their students, there were commonalities of language and understanding. The predominance of certain institutions in the postwar era meant the predominance of distinct worldviews. The Yale Institute of International Studies, created in 1935 with a Rockefeller Foundation grant of $100,000 over five years, was nicknamed the "Power School." An estimated eight hundred students majored in international relations between 1935 and 1945; many of whom went into senior government positions. The diffusion of the "realist paradigm" was also evident in Chicago, Princeton, and other major universities.[2]

For all the ambiguities surrounding the term realpolitik, what is beyond doubt is that this next generation was extremely familiar with the word. It appears in many of the interviews of former diplomats and State Department officials contained in the Library of Congress's Frontline Diplomacy Archive (dealing with the postwar era through to the present day). In many of these cases, the interviewees linked the notion back to specific faculties and professors. One diplomat, John W. Holmes, describes being taught by a young Kenneth Waltz at Columbia University, who left him "with an abiding bias towards a 'Realpolitik' view of foreign policy."[3] Georgetown's School of Foreign Service was also said by students in the 1960s—when Bill Clinton attended—to propound a "Realpolitik view" of international affairs.[4]

The role of certain textbooks was also particularly important because they were shared across different institutions. The original model for this was Frederick Schuman's 1933 *World Politics*.[5] Morgenthau's *Politics Among Nations* also aimed at a similar synthesis of international history, with lessons for the contemporary era. "All of us who taught the subject after him, however much we differed from each other, had to start with his reflections," noted Henry Kissinger. While not everybody agreed with him, "nobody could ignore him."[6] *Politics Among Nations* was also the dominant text at the University of Southern California, where, one diplomat noted, both the School of International Relations and the history and political science departments "prided themselves on their realpolitik orientation"—adding that they "sincerely felt they were not ideologically orientated, but, in fact, they really were."[7] So great was Morgenthau's influence that some officials talked about being influenced by his work when they were still in high school. One future diplomat at the State Department, when explaining his own opposition to the Vietnam War as a teenager, insisted that he "opposed it for reasons of realpolitik . . . for the same kinds of reasons Hans Morgenthau opposed it, because I didn't see it being in our core national interests."[8] Morgenthau was not the only individual for whom this was true. Frederick A. Becker, a career diplomat who was at Berkeley in the early 1960s, describes coming of age while reading Kissinger's 1957 *Nuclear Weapons and Foreign Policy*, and being influenced by the "realpolitik school of international politics," which, for him, also included Morgenthau and Kennan.[9]

Far from being delighted at the spread of their influence, some of the leading realists more commonly expressed disillusionment that the next generation of practitioners was not up to the task. In a 1963 letter to Dean Acheson, Morgenthau complained about "the dearth of men who are capable of thinking in political terms." This was not so much a question of evaluating specific problems like the recent Cuban missile crisis. What Morgenthau found disheartening was "the congenital inability to bring political categories to bear upon these issues." It was "as though people were to judge paintings not in view of their intrinsic aesthetic value but in terms of, say, the costs of their production, the chemical composition of the paint, or their physical relations to each other." Morgenthau confessed that he felt "ambivalent longing at trying my hand at doing better what is being done so badly."[10]

Acheson's reply demonstrated greater appreciation of the difficulties faced by those in office. "One would love to get one's hands on the levers of control; and yet one would hesitate if asked to do so," he conceded. Taking responsibility was "so more hellishly difficult than 'comment'—that foul word—or criticism." The young men in charge had much to be said for them. Nonetheless, Acheson also wondered whether they had planned "beyond the next play or two." The problem was their obsession with finding immediate solutions. Had they thought outside their own time, he asked? "But this is, no doubt, too modest a goal for a Grand Design," he joked. " 'What big words you have, Grandmama!' said little Red Riding-Hood."[11]

The timing of this letter was significant. Between 1961 and 1963, under Kennedy, America began to build up increasingly large numbers of troops in Vietnam. After 1963 President Johnson further escalated the campaign, with formal combat units deployed in 1965. Acheson's complaint about the "young men" and their "grand designs" foreshadowed that in David Halberstam's famous 1969 book, *The Best and the Brightest*—an excoriating critique of the supposedly brilliant advisors and academics around Presidents Kennedy and Johnson, whose policies were responsible for the Vietnam War.[12]

Disillusioned Realists and the New Left

Vietnam drove a huge wedge between the American foreign policy establishment and the professoriate. In this process of disillusionment and distancing, some prominent realists found themselves in unusual company. In 1965, Morgenthau expressed public support for the radical "teach-in" movement, convened on university campuses in protest against the Vietnam War. When he did so, he received a letter, in German, from fellow émigré and Marxist agitator Herbert Marcuse, asking what "might have driven the theorist of Realpolitik to transcend Realpolitik critically." To Marcuse, surprised to find a kindred spirit in Morgenthau, it was "ever more clearly apparent that moral imperatives are not just mere ideology, but real forces." By "denying that morality, we ceased to be human, so we must fight for it."[13] The radicals, in other words, saw something ideological and ethical in the realists.

Marcuse was the leading figure of the New Left movement of the 1960s in the United States and an inspiration for many student radicals of the era. He was known for emphasizing the humanist rather than the simply rationalist dimensions of Marxist thought.[14] He also argued that the Soviet Union and the United States were already engaging in an early, tacit form of détente in the Vietnam era. Their power games were played out at the expense of the weaker and poorer nations. In fact, there was an unspoken cooperation between the Soviet Union and the United States that went beyond "temporary *Realpolitik* and seems to correspond with the wholly un-Marxian theory that there is a community of interests of the richer nations in opposition to the poorer nations, one which overcomes the distinction between capitalist and socialist societies and individuals."[15]

One historian, expanding on this idea, has even argued that the origins of détente can be explained by the desire of the elites in both the Soviet Union and the United States to stabilize their internal polities in the face of popular protest and unrest.[16]

While coming from different perspectives, Morgenthau and Marcuse arrived at a similar conclusion. Morgenthau believed that it was the task of the intellectual to challenge the philosophical basis of existing policy. Marcuse believed that the intellectuals should be in the vanguard of popular protest, as a moral imperative. The Marcusian approach was embodied by the influential MIT linguistics theorist Noam Chomsky, in his 1969 book *American Power and the New Mandarins*. In Chomsky's view, the very idea of a foreign policy elite—even one based on knowledge—was dangerous. The role of the professors and their students was to challenge the establishment rather than train it for governance. What grounds were there for supposing that those whose claim to power was based on knowledge would be more benign in their exercise of power than those whose claim was based on wealth or aristocratic origin, he asked. On the contrary, "one might expect the new mandarin to be dangerously arrogant, aggressive and incapable of adjusting to failure, as compared with his predecessor, whose claim to power was not diminished by honesty as to the limitations of his knowledge, lack of work to do or demonstrable mistakes."[17] The temporary coalescence of realists and radicals was further underlined by Chomsky's use of excerpts from both Morgenthau and Walter Lippmann in his critique of American capitalist imperialism, and opposition to the Vietnam War.[18]

This unexpected alliance would not last forever, of course. What was more, it rested on a rather fanciful role for academics as the protectors of truth and justice. In August 1965 in *Encounter*, the writer Irving Kristol—who became known as the "godfather of neo-conservatism"—contrasted responsible critics of the Vietnam War, such as Lippmann and Senator William Fulbright, with the academics and radicals of the "teach-in movement," of which Marcuse was a key protagonist. "Unlike the university professors," Kristol wrote, "Mr. Lippmann engages in no presumptuous suppositions as to 'what the Vietnamese people really want'—he obviously doesn't much care—or in legalistic exegesis as to whether, or to what extent, there is 'aggression' or 'revolution' in South Vietnam." Lippmann's view, noted Kristol approvingly, "is a *realpolitik* point of view; and he will apparently even contemplate a *nuclear* war against China in extreme circumstances."[19]

In *American Power and the New Mandarins*, Chomsky picked up on this criticism. In fact, he used it to condemn Kristol as an exponent of realpolitik, on the grounds that Kristol had used the term to describe Lippmann in comparatively favorable terms.[20] In fact, this did not reflect the complexity of Kristol's position, which was to develop over the 1960s and 1970s. Kristol had written critically of the role of Machiavelli in what he had called the "profanation" of politics. Everyone knew that politics was a dirty business, but Machiavelli had fulfilled the role of a "pornographer" of this idea, brazenly announcing that the statesman should only be judged by success. It is also significant that Kristol was in the small minority of commentators who had read Friedrich Meinecke's work on Machiavellianism, and the criticisms of unadulterated Machiavellianism (exhibited by Treitschke, for example) contained therein.[21]

So, while Kristol wanted to distinguish the Lippmann position on Vietnam from the one held by Marcuse, that did not mean he shared it himself. In 1967, two years after his *Encounter* article on the anti-Vietnam protests, Kristol developed his ideas further in a famous article in *Foreign Affairs*, in which he offered a broader critique of the role of American intellectuals in foreign policy. Significantly, he singled out aspects of the realist case for scrutiny—not least the notion that the United States has "unthinkingly accepted world responsibilities which are beyond its resources." For Kristol, echoing Fritz Stern's work on the "politics of cultural despair," such a view was symptomatic of "the tortured connections between the American liberal ideology and the American imperial republic." In a memorable phrase, he called this a "crisis of the intellectual class in the face of an imperial destiny." By and large the American public had come to terms with their new superpower status. But this "resigned acceptance of great-power responsibilities by the American people has been accompanied by a great unease on the part of the intellectuals." It was among American intellectuals "that the isolationist ideal is experiencing its final, convulsive agony," he wrote. It was entirely understandable that contemporary policymakers found this responsibility a terrible burden. Yet the intellectuals were "bemused by dreams of power without responsibility, even as they complain of moral responsibility without power."[22]

While many intellectuals complained about their marginalization in the 1960s, Kristol's riposte was that they were doing a pretty good job of isolating themselves. In his 1963 letter to Acheson, Morgenthau had bemoaned the failure of the policymakers to think in terms of "political categories" and instead become too focused on details. By contrast, Kristol believed that such categories were almost meaningless. Indeed, it was "the peculiarity of foreign policy that it is the area of public life in which ideology flounders most dramatically." There was no left-right spectrum on foreign policy. There was no great radical or conservative text on the conduct of foreign affairs. These were false polarities. What texts there were—from Machiavelli and Hugo Grotius through to Kennan and Morgenthau— were "used differently by all parties as circumstances allow" (as Chomsky's co-option of the latter had demonstrated). In fact, from the writings of Thucydides onward, "political philosophy has seen foreign affairs as so radically affected by contingency, fortune and fate as to leave little room for speculative enlightenment." This left the intellectuals floundering. It was only when politics was ideologized that intellectuals played a pivotal social and political role. But this simply did not apply to foreign affairs.

To be good at coping with expediency and contingency, one did not have to be an intellectual. In fact, Kristol noted, "it may even be a handicap." No modern nation had ever constructed a foreign policy acceptable to its intellectuals—a point he may have gleaned from his earlier reading of Meinecke. What was more, Kristol pointed out what he believed were "extraordinary inconsistences of intellectuals on matters of foreign policy, and the ease with which they can enunciate a positive principle, only in the next breath to urge a contrary action." He quoted Charles Frankel, President Johnson's assistant secretary of state for education, to the effect that intellectuals were missing the point of their role when they sought to theorize about foreign policy. Frankel had written that international affairs were "peculiarly susceptible to galloping abstractions" and that intellectuals had "the power to create, dignify, inflate, criticize, moderate or puncture these abstractions." Yet, argued Kristol, the intellectuals rarely moderated or punctured but were "diligent in inflation." The idea of a realist theory of international politics was one example of this. As Kristol wrote: "Abstractions are their life's blood, and even when they resolutely decide to become 'tough-minded' they end up with an oversimplified ideology of Realpolitik that is quite useless as a guide to the conduct of foreign affairs and leads its expounders to one self-contradiction after another." His point was not that intellectuals were always wrong on matters of foreign policy: "they are not, and could not possibly be, if only by the laws of chance." What was more damning was that they were "so often, from the statesman's point of view, irrelevant." It was their "self-definition as ideological creatures that makes them so."[23]

For all this, however, Kristol's criticism of this "oversimplified ideology of Realpolitik" did not cause him to dismiss the concept altogether. This was an important distinction. From 1969, it meant that he was to be found in the camp of President Nixon and Henry Kissinger, Nixon's national security advisor. For Kristol, the approach adopted by Nixon and Kissinger was markedly different from the theories of foreign policy realism found in the universities. It denoted historical depth and an intuitive understanding of the uselessness of simple categories, and cautiousness about the need for self-definition. As Kristol's fellow neo-conservative thinker Norman Podhoretz later wrote, "During the Nixon administration Irving was a great defender of *Realpolitik*, applauding the 'Europeanisation' of our foreign policy under Kissinger." It was only later, Podhoretz claimed, that he was able to persuade Kristol "that ideology was and should be a central element of America's relations with other countries."[24]

Eventually, the neo-conservatives were to set themselves up against Nixon and Kissinger over the policy of détente. The neo-conservative critique was to reflect, much as postwar realism had done, the outworking of internal anxieties about the moral and political state of the American republic. To a certain extent, these were a hangover from the domestic political upheaval of the late 1960s. As late as 1974, Kristol observed that Kissinger was a "much admired and much distrusted" secretary of state. Yet he also noted that there was a certain "anxiety as to the meaning of Kissinger [that] pervades the entire political spectrum—right, left, and center." There was, Kristol later wrote of Kissinger, a "dim nagging recognition that he has a new conception of American foreign policy."[25]

American Diplomacy and Realpolitik Before Détente

Before Nixon came to office, those within government and policymaking circles did not know what to make of realpolitik when they came across the word. One reason for this was a lag of time before those trained in international politics in the 1950s took up senior positions in office. For those in government in the postwar period, realpolitik still denoted something a little exotic. As it was practiced by other states, and had contributed to another world war, most American policymakers were programed against realpolitik. Yet its existence in the international system was something they could not escape, as the Cold War took shape. Before 1968, one can see the tension between these two inclinations—a desire to leave the old practices behind and an acknowledgment that they were an irreducible feature of the international game. Whether one liked it or not, the fact was that others kept playing the same record.

The gentleman-diplomat classes of the middle part of the twentieth century—of which Dean Acheson is the best example—viewed their trade in a way that did not sit easily with the idea of pursuing naked self-interest. The only mention that Acheson ever made of realpolitik, for example, reflected the view that honor and trust were the foundations of the diplomatic art. In the early period of the Second World War, Britain had readily shared nuclear secrets with the United States. By the end of the war, America was far ahead in the nuclear game but some within the US government were expressing reluctance to return the favor with a full information exchange. "Grave consequences might follow upon keeping our word, but the idea of not keeping it was repulsive to me," Acheson wrote: "The analogy of a nation to a person is not sound in all matters of moral conduct; in this case, however, it seemed to me pretty close. Even in *realpolitik* a reputation for probity carries its own pragmatic rewards."[26]

A major theme in postwar American foreign policy was a desire to prevent a repetition of the perceived failures of Woodrow Wilson after the First World War. There remained hope and desire that international affairs could be put on a more stable footing—and that the United Nations could provide a more sustainable source of international arbitration than the League of Nations had done. Nonetheless, if geopolitics had taught anything it was that more was needed to preserve stability than legal structures. In particular, it was understood that other major powers—chiefly the Soviet Union—had to be prevented from gaining hegemony in areas important to US interests; to accomplish this the United States had to push back to create a balance against them. On this matter, it was felt that there needed to be more room for what officials increasingly came to label realpolitik.

In August 1946, the US ambassador to China, John Leighton Stuart, wrote to then secretary of state James Byrnes about the difficulties caused by growing Soviet influence in the region. The United States was heavily involved in the reconstruction of Japan, yet Japan had been almost destroyed as a serious military power in the region. This created something of a vacuum of power, into which the Russians had entered. They had designs for dominance over Manchuria, were slowing down China's industrial development, and were supporting the communist insurgency. "Let us admit at once that this question leads us into the field of *Realpolitik*, which we in this postwar world had hoped to abandon in favour of a system of mutual cooperation," the ambassador wrote. He believed it would be remiss for the United States not "to take into realistic account the effects of the Soviet policy on a region which we have traditionally regarded as important."[27]

Meanwhile, America assumed unwelcome burdens in the Middle East and Asia, as its main allies—Britain and France—retreated from their imperial commitments. Here again, America was confronted with behavior that was often rationalized as realpolitik. For example, Britain's failed 1956 attempt to seize control of the Suez Canal—which caused a rupture with Washington—was condemned in the British parliament as "a hundred years out of date as a piece of realpolitik."[28] Yet Britain had everdiminishing capacity to pursue a different course. After the Suez debacle, this meant coming to terms with the new regime of Colonel Gamal Nasser in Egypt. As Jo Grimond, the leader of the British Liberal Party told the House of Commons, the government would have "to face the fact that it is simply in our national interest to come to some sort of arrangement." In the end, this "must be regarded as an exercise in realpolitik."[29]

As in the 1930s, this type of logic could have a domino effect across Europe. The desperation that characterized British policy was further fuelled by its alienation from Europe. The rise to power of General de Gaulle as president of the Fifth Republic in France in 1959 was greeted with alarm in the British cabinet, which was warned that de Gaulle's foreign policy was a "blend of Realpolitik and empiricism."[30] De Gaulle's reorientation of French policy toward an alliance with West Germany, explicitly presented as a counterbalance to Anglo-American dominance, signaled a further fragmentation, as did his decision to withdraw the French Mediterranean fleet from the North Atlantic Treaty Organization (NATO). Further afield, France's withdrawal from Indochina was the prelude to disastrous American attempts to fill that vacuum.

For the most part, then, America was confronted with realpolitik in the behavior of other states. A striking example was provided by a 1960 conversation between American diplomats and János Kádár, the general secretary of the Hungarian Socialist Workers' Party, who had been installed follow-ing the Soviet suppression of the Hungarian rebellion in 1956. On a visit to New York, Kádár suggested that since the events of 1956, there had been a lot of "childish (*gyerekes*) things going on between our two countries." Both the US government and the Hungarians had "been acting like a cou-ple of kids," by periodically expelling each other's diplomats. In exploring the possibility of an understanding and improved relations, Kádár made the following plea: "I don't like the Germans (I mean Adenauer's Germany) but to illustrate my feeling on this subject, I would use the German word 'Realpolitik' to describe the way this matter should be treated. We do not hate the Americans. After all, let us be realistic: Who are we? We are only a 'little louse' . . . in this big world. However, the prerequisite for normal rela-tions is a willingness on the part of the U.S. Government to recognize the hard facts. The People's Republic of Hungary is an accomplished fact. It is here today. It will stay here tomorrow. All you have to do is to recognize this fact. The rest is simple."[31] American officials were not immune to such arguments. Before long, they also adopted elements of the same diplomatic language when pursuing policies that fell into a similar bracket. For exam-ple, some diplomats described American efforts to detach Yugoslavia's leader General Tito from Moscow as a "success of a kind of realpolitik."[32]

In the West, there were many who countered—on the basis of past expe-rience with Nazism—that mere pragmatism would not suffice. The ideo-logical and international threat from communism required an ideological response to match it. In the past, "we have tended to look at these in 19th century terms of *Realpolitik*, national interests, and balance of power," one speaker told the Inter-American Defense Board, convened by the CIA in 1958. But the challenge of the "ideological empire of communism, which calls itself a 'commonwealth,' requires that we ourselves find some new form of ideological unity within which we can draw our politics and eco-nomics closer together." Communism was "making a bold appeal for the loyalties of the masses of humanity, offering a promise of material, cultural and even spiritual betterment." This must be countered with a "positive reaffirmation of our higher values, and a resolute effort to give them life and meaning."[33]

Throughout the 1960s realpolitik was usually used, by those working in the American government, to describe the actions of other nations. In most cases, it was used to denote instances of pragmatism elsewhere. Similar to the State Department archives from this period, most of the 146 references to realpolitik in the CIA files at the American National Archives appear in discussions of others states' intentions. In keeping with the Hungarian precedent, one notable theme in CIA reportage was that states within the communist bloc repeatedly prioritised their own national interests above those of ideological communism. This, in turn, was a potential area of exploitation. In trying to assert their influence in China, for example, the Soviets clearly were losing ground on the matter of "doctrinal purity" by the early 1960s. Moscow pointed, somewhat accusingly, to "the *realpolitik* behind the Chinese positions," reported the CIA in 1963.[34]

Yet the primacy of national interests could work in other ways. For example, India's relationship with the United States came under strain because of the importance Washington placed on Pakistan as an ally. A 1962 telegram from the US embassy in India to the State Department noted the "danger of a realpolitik argument that Americans being largely indifferent, India had better make up with the Chinese."[35] When India established its own nuclear weapons capacity in 1972, officials observed that the country's leaders seemed "to relish newly proven skills in realpolitik" by striking out on an independent course from the West.[36]

In those rare instances where US officials did consciously invoke the concept to rationalize their own actions, they did so with marked reluctance—and usually with the caveat that it was only a temporary measure. In fact, it seems the first time the word was used to explain or justify an aspect of American policy was in 1962, in internal discussions of US policy toward Iran. A decade after the overthrow of the democratically elected prime minister of Iran, Mohammad Mosaddegh, in which the CIA and British had a hand, the Kennedy administration was being questioned about its policy there. Bobby Kennedy, the attorney general, was under pressure from Supreme Court Justice William Douglas, a vocal critic of US policy and a strong supporter of democracy in Iran.

A policy paper produced by Robert W. Komer of the National Security Council staff for McGeorge Bundy, the president's national security advisor, examined the potential alternatives. Propping up the shah of Iran was clearly not ideal. There had been suggestions that the United States could help push him aside, or encourage the formation of a new government. For the moment, however, there was "no contender worth considering (though we're keeping eyes peeled)." Here was an early statement of what was to become the classic dilemma in US Middle East policy: "While we could slough off the old regime in Iran, we'd just be out of the frying pan into the fire. We'd have no way of assuring that we could protect our interests satisfactorily in the chaos likely to ensue. Indeed the odds are that, in the absence of even the modest source of stability the monarchy and army now provide, we'd have less leverage with whatever regime eventually emerged. Would it at least be a stronger, more satisfactory regime from the American standpoint? I doubt this too."

While Komer claimed the paper was his alone, he did believe that it roughly approximated the consensus of "those around town" who saw current Iran policy as inadequate but also found it "too pat to say let's back another horse . . . (when we don't see one running yet)." In the absence of any viable alternatives, the status quo would have to do. Radical solutions such as encouraging regime change or backing the Islamist or secular opposition against the shah were too risky. Here was the rub, contained in the very last line: "We stick with realpolitik."[37] As noted earlier, this had echoes of the first time the British used the word to justify official policy, at the time of the Sykes-Picot Agreement of 1916. There was no relish with which these policies were adopted and not a little shamefacedness. But the Middle East, more than any other region, had a tendency to expose the least flattering aspects of Anglo-American foreign policy.

This subtle change in American foreign policy discourse should be presented as a conversion to the ways of British imperialism. Self-interest in policy toward the Middle East was nothing new and was often most apparent when oil resources were at stake. What one can see is that the "best and the brightest" trained in the postwar era—such as Komer of Harvard, and McGeorge Bundy of Yale—were using a new foreign policy lexicon. Thus, deputy assistant secretary for International Affairs Bill Bundy wrote to under secretary of state George Ball in 1963, arguing that the case for foreign aid had "suffered through not having the hard-headed political interest and policy of the U.S. constantly expressed." This "tended to obscure the often completely persuasive Realpolitik of particular programs."[38]

For all this, America could not quite rid itself of the sense in which realpolitik was something exotic. Mindful of the idealistic disposition of the American people, many of those in the foreign establishment remained cautious not to imbibe the notion fully, even at the height of the Cold War. In 1967, John Badeau, professor of modern Arabic studies at Columbia University and recently American ambassador to the United

Arab Republic, called for a change of foreign policy in the Middle East, moving away from Israel and toward the Arab regimes. The Soviet Union was gaining an advantage because it practiced an effective brand of realpolitik in the region. The only way to counter this was for the United States to adopt a similarly unsentimental approach, "estimating conditions for what they are, differentiating between interests and desiderata, appraising accurately the forces in the Arab world and not viewing them simply in the light of a popular or traditional image." Yet Badeau also suspected that his was a losing argument. He recognized that most Americans were suspicious of the connotations of what he regarded as a "sophisticated" foreign policy. To many Americans, "sophistication is suspect; it suggests deception, specious argument, a wily course of action without principle or consistency," he wrote.[39] Even if the diplomats wanted to pull a certain way, the American people had a harness on them.

15

The Kissinger Effect

In the late 1960s, a full tilt toward realpolitik seemed highly unlikely. For most Americans, even those in government, the word still stuck in the gullet. For this reason, the new departure in US foreign policy under Richard Nixon and Henry Kissinger created something of a shock wave, both within and outside the apparatus of government, which left its mark on American political discourse for years to come.

When one speaks of realpolitik in the modern era, the name of Kissinger—President Nixon's national security advisor from January 1969 to November 1975 and secretary of state for Nixon and then President Ford, from September 1973 to January 1977—usually follows close behind. During Kissinger's tenure in office, usage of the word realpolitik spread throughout the governmental machine. It also became popularized, more than ever before, in the public sphere. There was a widespread fascination with the Kissingerian mind among followers of foreign policy. Not for the first time, it became common to juxtapose contemporary American foreign policy with nineteenth-century European diplomacy. As the historian Walter Laqueur described in *Commentary* magazine in 1973, one of the side effects of Kissinger's rise to eminence was a sudden revival of interest in Lord Castlereagh and Count Metternich, triggered by Kissinger's 1957 book, *A World Restored.* Political commentators, "not previously known for their expertise in the intricacies of early 19th-century European diplomacy, have been eagerly leafing through the pages of this book, expecting to find some useful leads—if not the master key—to Kissinger's grand design for the 1970s. Nowadays no article, and few columns, seems complete without a quotation or two about the Metternichian system or Bismarck's *Real-politik.*"[1]

At the simplest level, one can see an obvious connection that links our story together. Kissinger was a German-speaking immigrant to the United

States from Bavaria, and he wrote about nineteenth-century European diplomacy. Yet when one digs a little deeper, the picture becomes more complex. For one, realpolitik is a label that Kissinger himself regards as unhelpful. In an interview with *Der Spiegel* in 2009, he commented: "Let me say a word about realpolitik, just for clarification. I regularly get accused of conducting realpolitik. I don't think I have ever used that term. It is a way by which critics want to label me and say, 'Watch him. He's a German really. He doesn't have the American view of things.' "[2] "The advocates of a realist foreign policy are caricatured with the German term *Realpolitik*," he added in 2012, "I suppose to facilitate the choosing of sides." [3]

Stanley Hoffmann, a Harvard professor and contemporary of Kissinger, claimed that Kissinger's career was "a quest for a realpolitik devoid of moral homilies," but this is to paint a caricature.[4] Kissinger's intellectual formation bore the imprint of an eclectic range of influences and experiences. From inception, it also included a strong dose of what has been described so far as anti-realpolitik. Much has been made of the time he spent in his native Germany, returning as an American soldier, in the final stages of the Second World War, under Fritz Kraemer—a fellow German American, who recognized his intellectual talents—with the 84th Division in Bensheim.[5] Kraemer later broke with Kissinger in the détente era because of his belief that the moral component to the Cold War had not been emphasised sufficiently during Kissinger's tenure, though the two were reconciled and Kissinger spoke at his funeral oration.[6]

It was also significant that Kissinger—educated at the Government Department at Harvard, outside the main hubs for the study of international affairs at Yale or Chicago—did not bear the imprint of a particular theory of international relations, and perhaps evaded some of the rhetorical grooves associated with these. Rather than structures or systems, his initial interest was more the history of ideas. One of his professors at Harvard, Sam Beer, later recalled that Kissinger "had an intuitive grasp of the importance of ideas in world affairs," particularly religion. German refugees, Beer added, had "firsthand experience of the effect ideas can have in the world." The journal that Kissinger ran at Harvard, *Confluence*, sought contributions from a wide range of prominent thinkers and public intellectuals, all with different perspectives. Alongside contributions from Reinhold Niebuhr and Hans Morgenthau were essays by Hannah Arendt, McGeorge Bundy, Enoch Powell, and Paul Nitze.[7]

Kissinger was no follower of a single line. Hans Morgenthau briefly taught at Harvard in 1951 and Kissinger later called him "my teacher," in that he subscribed to the basic principles of *Politics Among Nations*. He should not, however, be classed as a disciple of Morgenthau, with whom he differed on a number of issues.[8] He spent more time under the tutelage of William Yandell Elliott, who steered him toward other traditions in the history of ideas such as the writings of Homer, Baruch Spinoza, and Georg Wilhelm Hegel. It was for Elliott that Kissinger wrote his undergraduate dissertation, "The Meaning of History." This explored the writings of Immanuel Kant, Oswald Spengler, and Arnold Toynbee—three thinkers who stood firmly on the side of anti-realpolitik. As we have already seen, Kant was denounced by the German exponents of *Realpolitik*, and Spengler regarded them as hopelessly naïve. Toynbee was a liberal internationalist and a delegate to the Paris Peace Conference in 1919. More significantly, perhaps, Kissinger's dissertation rejected narrow empiricism and the idea of pure reason, arguing that the role of history should be to grasp "the totality of life, not just its appearances."[9]

Another influence was Carl J. Friedrich, a German-born scholar who had been at Harvard since 1926. It has been claimed that Friedrich steered Kissinger away from two prevailing trends in American intellectual life favored by some realists—naturalism and pragmatism, which had little room for the spiritual or supernatural components of intellectual life.[10] Friedrich, as noted earlier, was a strong critic of both Morgenthau and Kennan, whom he accused of expounding an "American version of the German *Realpolitik*."[11] Kissinger does not necessarily see Friedrich as a foreign policy thinker, though he does acknowledge his influence.[12]

In addition to the history of ideas, Kissinger was as much interested in statesmen and statesmanship—and the role of the individual in managing and mitigating trends in international relations.[13] This was reflected in *A World Restored*, based on his doctoral thesis. A study of the diplomacy of Count Metternich and Lord Castlereagh in the period after the defeat of Napoleon, it set itself against a "scholarship of social determinism" that "reduced the statesman to a lever on a machine called 'history.'" The test of a statesman, argued Kissinger, in a phrase Ludwig von Rochau might have written, was "his ability to recognise the real relationship of forces and to make this knowledge serve his ends."[14]

It has been pointed out that Kissinger's subjects in *A World Restored* were tragic figures, and that—following Weber perhaps—the expectation of tragedy is something which lurks behind his work. Metternich and Castlereagh both fell into the "abyss" of their age. Castlereagh killed himself in 1822 and his policies were denounced by later generations; Metternich fell in 1848 and the balancing act by which he had attempted to preserve the Austrian Empire lurched from crisis to crisis. Yet, on closer examination, Kissinger's interpretation of this period was far from fatalistic. It allowed for the triumph of wisdom and smart statecraft to mediate danger and steer a steady course.[15] It can be said that Kissinger shared the Weberian notion of an "ethics of responsibility" with Niebuhr, Morgenthau, and Kennan. But again, it is a mistake to assume that this was simply the preserve of self-described realist thinkers.[16]

Another mistake is to assume that Kissinger has certain historical "heroes" whom he hoped to emulate. He has dismissed as "childish" the notion that he personally identifies with Metternich.[17] Of greater significance was his interjection into the Bismarck debate of the 1950s and 1960s (described in Chapter 12). It has often been observed that there was "something Bismarckian" about the grand strategy of Nixon and Kissinger after 1968.[18] Yet it is worth subjecting the Bismarck comparison to greater scrutiny as it provides a clue to much else besides.

In fact, Kissinger's assessment of Bismarck's political strategy shows an acute awareness of its limitations. In 1968, shortly before his appointment by Nixon, Kissinger published his own reflections on Bismarck (which he had been unable to include in his original PhD thesis). In Kissinger's view, what Bismarck had practiced was a policy of "self-restraint on a philosophy of self-interest." But he had built a system that was dependent on his genius, which was extremely dangerous when inherited by those with less skill and caution: "In the hands of others lacking his subtle touch, his methods led to the collapse of the nineteenth-century state system." One of the weaknesses of the Bismarckian state was its authoritarian nature, which encouraged "the emergence of courtiers and lobbyists, but not statesmen." What was more, Germans had also learned the wrong lessons from him. "They remembered the wars that had achieved their unity" but forgot "the patient preparation that had made them possible and the moderation that had secured their fruits." German nationalism, he wrote, "unleavened by liberalism turned chauvinistic." The exclusion of the liberals was also damaging. Liberalism without responsibility "grew sterile." This combination of forces had created the space for the rise of Nazism. Here Kissinger ended with a telling quotation from Bismarck's friend General

Albrecht von Roon, who wrote: "No one eats with impunity from the tree of immortality."[19]

Kissinger's interpretation of Bismarck was closer to A. J. P. Taylor's critical 1955 biography than William Langer's attempt to resuscitate the Prussian statesman for an English-speaking audience in the 1930s. It was also markedly different from the version of Bismarckism celebrated by George Kennan, leading to a revealing discussion between the two. Kennan's 1981 book, *The Decline of Bismarck's European Order: Franco-Russian Relations, 1875–1890*, had Bismarck as its hero.[20] After publication, Kissinger wrote to Kennan: "I have enjoyed your book greatly. Not that it fails to be depressing. If even Bismarck could not prevent what he clearly foresaw, what chance does the modern period have? That is the real nightmare." Kennan's reply was that "Bismarck did all that he could, in his outwardly rough, but essentially not inhumane way." In Kennan's view, the greatest danger was the failure of the current generation, "with the warning image of the atomic bomb before it," to learn from Bismarck's example.[21] Yet Kissinger always had a sense of the need to keep a rein on Bismarckism, based on his understanding of its after-effects in Germany. In his 1994 book *Diplomacy*, he offered as resounding and unambiguous a criticism of it as any that appeared in Britain before 1914. As he put it, "the unification of Germany caused *Realpolitik* to turn in on itself, accomplishing the opposite of what it was meant to achieve."[22]

Kissinger's mild critique of Kennan—for whom he had much admiration—follows similar lines to the criticisms of American realism made in Part IV of this book. He saw in Kennan's later writings an unwillingness to "manage nuance" and accept ambiguity as irreducible components of political life. In a *New York Times* review of John Lewis Gaddis's 2011 biography of Kennan, he used his own version of Bismarck against Kennan. The challenge of statesmanship was "to define the components of both power and morality and strike a balance between them." This was not a one-time effort but required "constant recalibration." It was "as much an artistic and philosophical as a political enterprise" and demanded "a willingness to manage nuance and to live with ambiguity." The practitioners of the art must learn "to put the attainable in the service of the ultimate and accept the element of compromise inherent in the endeavor." Bismarck defined statesmanship as the art of the possible. Kennan, as a public servant, had been celebrated for his penetrating analysis of the international order. Yet his career was stymied, Kissinger argued, by his "periodic rebellion against the need for a reconciliation that could incorporate each element only imperfectly."

As Kissinger argued, there was an absolutist tendency in American realism. This had created an ever-greater distance between the self-described "realists" and those responsible for the exercise of power. In fact, realism had taken on the form of an ideology in its own right, just as it had done in Bismarck's Germany: "The irony of Kennan's thought was that his influence in government arose from his advocacy of what today's debate would define as realism, while his admirers outside government were on the whole motivated by what they took to be his idealistic objections to the prevalent, essentially realistic policy."

What was more, Kissinger argued that Kennan's view of international affairs was an externalization of a uniquely American understanding of politics. Kennan's vision of peace "involved a balance of power of a very special American type, an equilibrium that was not to be measured by military force alone." More specifically, it reflected the "culture and historical evolution of a society whose ultimate power would be measured by its vigor and its people's commitment to a better world." In his famous "X" telegram, of course, Kennan had called on his countrymen to meet the "test of the overall worth of the United States as a nation among nations." Significantly, Kissinger contrasted Kennan, the idealist and philosophizer, with Dean Acheson, the craftsman. The growing distance between the two men in the postwar era reflected Acheson's greater aptitude as a practitioner, and Kennan's rather wistful retreat into scholarship and history. It took Acheson "to translate Kennan's concept [of containment] into the design that saw America through the cold war."[23]

Kissinger's relationship with Hans Morgenthau might be viewed the same way. Kissinger retained great admiration for Morgenthau and spoke at his funeral in 1980.[24] Yet the two men disagreed over the Vietnam War, which Nixon inherited from President Johnson in 1968. On 22 October 1968, Morgenthau wrote to Kissinger directly, just as Kissinger was about to take up his position as national security advisor, to denounce him for not coming out strongly enough against the war or signaling his intention to bring it to an end.[25] He was also extremely hostile to the bombing of Cambodia in 1970, as part of the Kissinger-Nixon strategy to extricate the United States from the war without being seen to surrender; writing to

Reinhold Niebuhr—another Vietnam War opponent—Morgenthau said, "The incompetence and pathology is really shocking."[26]

Morgenthau's objection was not so much to the details of policy in Vietnam, as the fundamental premise on which it rested. In portraying American strategy as "pathological," his target was the whole philosophical basis of foreign policy. In fact, the text of his 1968 letter to Kissinger, and his 1970 letter to Niebuhr, appeared almost verbatim in an article he produced in 1976 on "The Pathology of American Power." This pathology was characterized by four "intellectual defects shared by all": first, obsolete modes of thought and action; second, "demonological interpretations of reality," or primitive answers to complex problems; third, denial of reality though illusory verbalizations; and fourth, faith in worldwide social reform. Typically, the only remedy was a "reformation" of the basis of American foreign policy. This reformation was "predicated upon the performance of the intellectual task of laying bare the roots of American failure and upon the moral resolution to act upon the political insights gained by this re-examination."[27]

Thus Kissinger's defense of the administration's Vietnam policy was markedly distinct from such absolute categories. Having negotiated the Paris accords that ended the war, he argued for meaningful financial and military aid for Vietnam in 1974, partly because 50,000 Americans had died fighting there, though this request was rejected by Congress. As he wrote in his memoirs, in one of his few uses of the word, "the thrust of my appeal was to such unfashionable concepts as 'honor' and 'moral obligation,' not to realpolitik as our critics had it."[28] Writing a decade after Kissinger had left office, the historian Michael Hunt made the case that both Nixon and Kissinger had a profound sense of America's unique world role—a perception heightened by the Cold War paradigm. Their insistence on maintaining prestige and credibility over Vietnam spoke to a longer tradition in American foreign policy stretching back at least as far as the 1890s. Thus Hunt argued Kissinger acted in a way more redolent of Alexander Hamilton than a classic European diplomat.[29]

To this day, there is a strong element of American exceptionalism running through Kissinger's writings, in which the legacy of Theodore Roosevelt is the touchstone.[30] David Mack, former deputy assistant secretary of state for Near East Affairs in the early 1990s, who had taken Kissinger's classes at Harvard, saw his "realpolitik perspective" as uniquely American rather than European. "He saw the United States as the last best hope of the world, even if we could use a greater dose of cynicism and reality."[31]

Britain over Bismarck: Nixon's Grand Strategy

As Kissinger also pointed out on many occasions, he was no puppet master behind the president. Nixon was his own man with an independently formed worldview, and their working relationship was not always smooth.[32] Nixon's intellectual and political journey in the foreign policy field reflected different experiences gained over the previous decade and a half: on the side of the prosecution in the Alger Hiss trials, as Eisenhower's vice president (as Eisenhower was often ill), and during his temporary political exile in the mid-1960s, which he used to travel the world. He made his name as a staunch anti-communist, which was one reason his shift toward a policy of détente was to become so enraging to previous supporters such as William F. Buckley.[33]

In 1967, Nixon announced that the United States should seek rapprochement with China to weaken the communist bloc. This preference for détente was linked to a consciously new conception of US foreign policy, in which "reciprocity" and "balancing" were to be cornerstones. Nixon's defining contribution, he claimed with hindsight, was to make Americans think about the entire international picture rather than dealing with events episodically, crisis by crisis. "Our tendency to become preoccupied with only one or two problems at a time had led to a deterioration of policy on all fronts," he wrote in his memoirs.[34]

Meanwhile, Nixon spoke of his desire to seek a middle path between "hawks and doves" on what action to take in Vietnam.[35] By that point he had inherited a war in which 31,000 Americans had died. The conundrum was how to extricate half a million troops without complete humiliation and the routing of South Vietnam by the North. He believed that any opening to the Chinese or the Soviet Union depended on a demonstration of American strength. In this, he disappointed widespread expectations that his presidency would bring a swift resolution of the war. "Peace with honor" was the aim; "Vietnamization" and the "quarantining" of the conflict were the means to the end. What this meant, in practice, was that the

South Vietnamese would have to bear the burden of the fighting on their own but the communists would be prevented from expanding their campaign further, such as into neighboring Cambodia. So, while American troops began to return home in their thousands, US Air Force planes were sent in ever-increasing numbers in the opposite direction to take part in what became the biggest aerial bombardment in history. The attacks were timed to coincide with talks with the North Vietnamese to bring the war to a close and to get the Chinese and Russians to reduce their support for the Viet Cong. They set the background to Nixon's celebrated visit to China in February 1972 and the release of the Shanghai Communiqué, which created the basis for normalization of relations. This, in turn, set the basis for the summit between Nixon and Soviet leader Leonid Brezhnev in Moscow that enabled the signing of the first Strategic Arms Limitations Treaty (SALT I) in May of the same year. The idea behind such "triangular diplomacy"—as it was to be known—was to put the United States in

An example of realpolitik in practice? President Nixon's famous visit to China in February 1972, which ended twenty-five years of alienation between the People's Republic and the United States. From the US National Archives and Records Administration. Courtesy of Wikimedia Creative Commons.

the position of power broker between the world's two great communist powers.

This approach was not inspired by German but by British precedents. As Nixon described it, in an excerpt released from recordings of his private conversations in the White House, the aim was to assume the "position the British were in in the 19th century when among the great powers of Europe they'd always play the weaker against the stronger."[36] This was a tale told, of course, in Kissinger's *A World Restored*, when Castlereagh had been the master of British foreign policy—balancing tsarist Russia against Napoleon to ensure his defeat and then balancing defeated post-Napoleonic France against the tsar after 1815.[37] Here, in the most explicit terms, was a precedent for American foreign policy based on a British rather than a Bismarckian script.[38]

In other words, the Nixon-Kissinger approach owed as much to Anglo-Saxon precedents as it did to continental traditions of statecraft. Nixon, for example, compared himself with Winston Churchill, suggesting that Churchill's years in the wilderness had made him the great man he would become in 1940. He spoke of how he had once regarded Neville Chamberlain, declaring "peace in our time" on his return from Munich in 1938, as a hero. In retrospect, he came to think that "Chamberlain was a good man" but "Churchill was a wiser man."[39]

Setting aside debates about the strength of the "special relationship," what one can see here, once again, is a shared Anglo-American worldview. At a speech given at the Royal Institute of International Affairs in London in 1982, Kissinger noted how, at the end of the Second World War, many American leaders condemned Churchill as "needlessly obsessed with power politics, too rigidly anti-Soviet, too colonialist in his attitude to what is now called the Third World, and too little interested in building the fundamentally new international order towards which American idealism has always tended." At that time, the British saw the Americans as "naïve, moralistic, and evading responsibility for helping secure the global equilibrium." Over the course of the 1960s and 1970s, this situation had been turned on its head. It was the Americans who were accused of being too obsessed with power politics and the balance of power. For all this, Kissinger argued, "Britain had a decisive influence over America's rapid awakening to maturity" in the second half of the twentieth century. Above all, it had bequeathed to America "a convenient form of ethical egoism" which held that "what was good for Britain was best for the rest."[40]

President Richard Nixon and Henry Kissinger, his national security advisor and then secretary of state, at the White House in 1973. From the Central Intelligence Agency. Courtesy of Wikimedia Creative Commons.

From Détente to the Human Rights Crusade

Such subtleties did not always trickle down the system. Kissinger generally eschewed the term, and Nixon never used it; but many of those working under them did interpret their directives as deriving from something they understood as "realpolitik." One can see this in the testimony of foreign service personnel in this era. In a typical example, Samuel R. Gammon III, a career diplomat at the State Department who was to be involved in the Paris peace negotiations, described the impact of Kissinger's arrival in government in these terms: "Henry introduced a healthy dose of realpolitik into American foreign policy. Foreign policy has never gotten away from this necessity, but we are, to our credit, a country of amiable, good-natured people who want to do the right thing! We have a heavy cargo of ideals and it's to our credit. But that cargo can work to our disadvantage in the cold, cruel world sometimes. And Henry is nothing, if not a practitioner of Real- and Macht politik, with a healthy dose of central European pessimism."[41] This was an impressionistic analysis. To continue a motif of earlier chapters, for example, it made no distinction between *Realpolitik* and *Machtpolitik*.

Nonetheless, one can see that the mood music of foreign policy was perceived to matter to these professionals. The words used helped provide some sort of delineation. More agile officials were quick to adapt themselves to what they saw as subtle changes in emphasis. One example was Maurice Williams, who made his name as an expert on international development. As the role of USAID (US Agency for International Development) came under scrutiny—and Congress began to question the budget for it—Williams drew up plans for a bifurcation of aid into two programs: one for security assistance in support of American foreign policy objectives; a second to address basic human needs to support longer-term American objectives. "Perhaps the way I framed the proposal was helpful," he reasoned, "for it appealed to the realpolitik of President Nixon, and to the strong moral tradition of American foreign policy as well."[42]

This was more than semantics. Existing initiatives were consciously repackaged in a way intended to resonate with the prevailing mood. Winston Lord, who was a special assistant to Kissinger when he was national security advisor and then became director of policy planning at the State Department in 1973, described how this worked. He encouraged colleagues in the Bureau of African Affairs, who wanted to do more to tackle South African apartheid, to remember when framing their proposals that Kissinger was a "balance of power, realpolitical type." This meant placing an emphasis on building up American influence in the region, rather than simply focusing on the question of human rights.[43]

For others, realpolitik became more associated with détente—the policy of limited rapprochement with the communist powers. Seen in this context, it did not seem like such a new departure. To state the obvious, there was a considerable degree of continuity in US policy. The idea of establishing a bilateral relationship with China had been in the ether for much of the previous decade. As the American vice-consul in Kunming in China later recalled, "I think in terms of foreign policy or realpolitik the feeling was that this was a regime that was entrenched, it was going to be there for the foreseeable future, and that we were going to have to deal with it."[44] Used this way, there was little to distinguish realpolitik from basic common sense. This certainly resonated with messages coming from capitals east of the Iron Curtain. Following the Nixon-Brezhnev summit of 1973, the Bulgarian news agency, for example, stated that the United States was finally coming to terms with the realities of the international order. These hard facts

Richard Nixon welcomes Leonid Brezhnev, general secretary of the Communist Party of the Soviet Union, to Washington on 19 June 1973, as part of the policy of détente. Courtesy of Wikimedia Creative Commons.

had "induced the governments of the most powerful nations in the West to embark on a course of realpolitik in international relations."[45]

Speaking in October 1973, Kissinger attempted to deal with some of the controversies that had arisen in the course of the previous four years of the Nixon administration's foreign policy. On the one hand, "purely pragmatic policy provides no criteria for other nations to assess our performance and no standards to which the American people can rally." On the other hand, he argued that "when policy becomes excessively moralistic it may turn quixotic or dangerous." The policymaker, he had concluded, "must strike a balance between what is desirable and what is possible."[46]

Many of the bitterest controversies related not so much to the overall tone of strategy as the second-order tactics required to make it a success. For example, sensitivity over negotiations with the Soviet Union was heightened by the fact that they were mediated through Pakistan and Romania, two unrepentant dictatorships with poor human rights records. The broader goal of Nixon's foreign policy was to stabilize the world in a way that was more likely to ensure peace between the major powers. But the path to this end goal was full of perilous and ugly compromises. "Now our interest in Romania was that we certainly wanted to encourage independent tendencies in Eastern Europe, not just as a narrow realpolitik approach, but really as part of a long-term process of gradually encouraging greater diversity to unfold in the Soviet Union itself, and in Eastern Europe," claimed one diplomat involved in the policy. This was "not just a narrow anti-Soviet thing, but it was part of a policy of change throughout the area," and it came with the recognition that "this was a pretty horrible regime internally." [47]

Likewise, a US diplomat serving in Romania at the time was prepared to concede that the "excessive attention we lavished on Ceausescu" hurt America's reputation. But he also argued that there was always a recognition that such arrangements could only be temporary and were likely to drain foreign policy of legitimacy over the longer-term. Realpolitik was a useful descriptor but not when it was used in a caricatured way. "Yes . . . Kissinger and Nixon were both very Realpolitik kind of guys. But eventually even Kissinger, if you read his book *Diplomacy* . . . concluded that for the United States, straight Realpolitik, no chaser, is not a possible policy, [as] it'll never be accepted by the American people. The American people insist that there must be some human rights or moral element, some idealistic input, into their foreign policy." It was not the case that the ambassador to Romania at the time, Harry Barnes, simply said "let's ignore human rights and just focus on Realpolitik." The embassy did retain some contact with dissidents, but this was before the human rights "crusade" hit US foreign policy.[48]

That so-called crusade began to gather momentum in 1974. As Arthur M. Schlesinger described in his book *Cycles of American History*, there were two components to the reaction against the approach of Kissinger, Nixon, and Gerald Ford, who became president after Nixon's resignation in August that year. The first came from those within the Wilsonian tradition of internationalism who were naturally inclined to a more liberal, rights-based foreign policy. The second came from those in the school of Franklin D. Roosevelt, a more tough-minded approach that nonetheless put forward the argument that there was a "moral vacuum" at the heart of US policy. It was through this pincer movement that Congress was used as a way to put pressure on the executive. An early example of this pressure was requiring the State Department to release annual reports on the state of human rights in more than a hundred countries. Kissinger had already requested these reports for internal consumption, but Congress now demanded they be made public.[49]

Another issue on which Congress exerted considerable pressure was the matter of emigration from communist countries—particularly involving political dissidents and Jews. In January 1975 President Ford signed a trade agreement with Romania that incorporated the Jackson-Vanik Amendment (co-sponsored by Henry "Scoop" Jackson of Washington State in the Senate and Charles Vanik of Ohio in the House of Representatives).[50] This introduced a provision into US federal law that restricted American trade relations with those countries that suppressed freedom of emigration and other human rights. One diplomat who worked under Jim Wilson, the assistant secretary of state for Human Rights and Humanitarian Affairs at the State Department, later described the strain that the refugee issue put on the administration, "when secretary of state Kissinger was being strongly criticized that we were practicing too much 'realpolitik,' or power politics, and not paying enough to attention to things like human rights, which, after all, reflected basic American values."[51] Kissinger himself came to view Senator Jackson as the greatest opponent of détente. He "sought to destroy our policy, not ameliorate it."[52]

With the increased emphasis on human rights, the controversies of the era spread beyond the immediate requirements of détente. Policies that had previously slipped below the radar became ever more controversial. Before the military junta that ran Greece fell, in 1974, the chief of the State Department's Office of Greek Affairs suggested that geopolitical considerations trumped other concerns in the case of Greece and Turkey (which invaded Cyprus that year): "Mr. Kissinger was Mr. Realpolitik. That's it. Balance of power, we've got to support the Greeks, we've got to support the Turks, because that's what holds the southern flank together. That sort of thing."[53] Likewise, in 1975–6, US support for General Pinochet's regime in Chile became increasingly controversial. Ambassador Thomas Boyatt, who was minister-counselor at the American Embassy in Chile at this time, later described the difficulty: "we had a sort of realpolitik from the executive branch, and human rights driven pressures from the legislative branch, and the media, and so on. And we were in the middle." [54]

In October 1974, the State Department produced an internal memorandum on Policies on Human Rights and Authoritarian Regimes. This was an attempt to adjust to the changing terrain. Recent events in four countries—the restriction of civil liberties in Chile and the Philippines, the tightening of authoritarian rule in South Korea and the behaviour of the military junta in Greece—had brought these questions to the fore.

The charge that the government was insensitive to human rights hindered the creation of a domestic consensus on foreign policy. It was necessary for the State Department to come up with "a more systematic way of thinking, planning and speaking about human rights issues." Here was the key point. The "moral factor" was now having a direct bearing on "the pragmatic success or failure of our foreign policies and . . . is therefore as real as any other factors that are normally included in realpolitik calculations."[55] In other words, the image of US foreign policy had a direct bearing on its efficacy.

Jimmy Carter and the New Anti-Realpolitik

The reaction against the foreign policy of the Nixon and Ford administrations amounted to more than Wilsonianism redux. In 1976, when Andrei Amalrik, the Russian émigré writer, received the annual award of the International League for Human Rights in New York, he addressed the American people in terms of both their idealism and their realism: "And now, in appealing to you, I am appealing to the American revolutionary spirit. I appeal to your desire to sow the seeds of a new revolution, not to your desire to live undisturbed, paying for your tranquility with credits, wheat and Pepsi-Cola. I appeal to the spirit of Jefferson and not the spirit of Kissinger! I am a better realist than the exponents of so-called realpolitik. You shall never feel safe while you compromise with violence instead of fighting against it. The battle has been thrust upon you and you will not succeed in dodging it."[56]

Jimmy Carter's 1976 presidential election victory was expected to herald a demonstrable shift in US foreign policy. Carter's promised focus on human rights during his campaign was deliberately intended to convey this. Donald McHenry, who served as a member of President Carter's transition staff at the State Department before joining the US Mission to the United Nations, described Carter's foreign policy in precisely these terms. "We had been in a period of realpolitik, and in our zeal to be anti-Communist, we had actually aligned ourselves with some pretty unsavory characters."[57] Likewise, in one of the first changes made by the new administration, the US Information Agency (USIA) was reinvigorated with the goal of "reacting against the *Realpolitik* and the strategic priorities of the Kissinger-Nixon era."[58]

The words one chose to describe oneself, or one's enemies, signaled broader intentions. The language of the foreign policy debate had become ever more important, as we have seen. The difficulty was implementing this at the level of policy. A general desire to promote and protect universal human rights was not a grand strategy in itself. Almost immediately, the loose coalition that had united against aspects of the Nixon-Ford foreign policy—from ideologically inspired anti-communists to neo-Wilsonians—began to fracture.[59] In the former camp was Irving Kristol who accused Carter of seizing the human rights issue "as a way of mobilizing, in an America thirsty for self-affirmation, the latent electoral appeal of Wilsonian idealism against Henry Kissinger's version of *Realpolitik*." The problem was not that a human-rights based policy had no meaning. It was that it was so vague.[60]

These finer points of language broke down at the point of delivery. In 1977, the historian Walter Laqueur explained the problem in *Commentary* magazine. "The exponents of Realpolitik [by which he meant the partisans of the last Republican administration] do not doubt the commitment of President Carter to the cause of human rights," he observed. But they suspected that his priorities were not seen as quite so important to some of his staff. When it came to relations with the Soviet Union, for example, they were unlikely to act in a way that undermined détente. Laqueur predicted that there would be "no sudden back down" by the Democratic administration. But there would be a gradual "slump in idealism" on the question of human rights, which would soon "fade into the realm of rhetoric." Laqueur himself still believed that the struggle for human rights was "not a lofty and impractical endeavor, divorced from the harsh realities of world affairs, but itself a kind of Realpolitik, one with a direct bearing on international security." But he did conclude that the Carter administration was already showing signs of confusion and a loss of nerve.[61]

Just two months into the Carter presidency, in March 1977, these difficulties were addressed in another internal State Department memorandum. It was written by Anthony Lake, who had left government in 1970 in protest over the bombing of Cambodia. In *Foreign Policy* magazine in 1971, Lake had written an exposé of the campaign, to illustrate what he called the "human reality of Realpolitik."[62] When Carter won the election, he returned to government as director of policy planning, reporting to Warren Christopher, the deputy secretary of state. The aim of the document was to pull together the administration's "general approach on human rights." As Lake described, the Carter administration had "moved fast to establish its bona fides on human rights." But obstacles were beginning to present themselves. By and large it was felt that the policy was "what most on the Hill want," which meant that Carter was unlikely to meet the same legislative resistance faced by Nixon and Ford. Yet Lake himself raised concern that the focus on human rights was dangerously vague. "Our strategy for Congressional relations on the human rights question need not be so much a 'strategy' as an attitude," he reasoned. The key facet of this approach would be to work with Congress in a way that alleviated too much pressure.[63] This was a matter of procedure and presentation rather than a transformation of the overall policy.

On the other hand, some State Department officials complained that both Cyrus Vance (the secretary of state) and Warren Christopher (as his deputy) were "almost ideological purists" on human rights. This did not lend itself to coherent policymaking. Ronald J. Neitzke, special assistant to the director of the Policy Planning Staff, described a meeting chaired by Christopher about what arms should be sold to an unnamed Latin American state (most likely Chile) with a poor human rights record. Following "endless debate and moral hairsplitting of an almost Jesuitical nature," it was decided that the government in question could receive arms but not bullets. This was emblematic of an attitude, "which may have emanated from Carter himself, that when it manifested itself in concrete, yes or no, foreign policy decisions could appear naïve, wildly unrealistic, or just unworkable." Meanwhile, Carter seemed much less inclined to apply the same scruples in Middle East policy. It was as though "they drew a circle around the whole oil-producing area and exempted it."[64]

Africa was another region laden with controversy and where the human rights emphasis could be tested to breaking point. Here criticism came from Chester Crocker, who had previously worked for Kissinger at the National Security Council. Crocker was prepared to concede that the United States was "inevitably going to be somewhat Wilsonian because of who we are." On Carter, however, he was scathing about what he saw as a "great deal of showboating, talking the talk, identifying with a kind human rightsy approach to Africa," without due consideration of strategic realities.[65] When the Cold War did impose itself, human rights slipped down the agenda. In 1978, when President Mobutu was facing a rebellion in Zaire, the United States offered logistical support, along with France and Belgium, to prop him up. Despite his horrific personal record in

office, Mobutu was deemed worthy of support because he had aligned himself with the United States in the Cold War. When it came down to it, "the
realities of American national interest and realpolitik considerations led the
Carter administration to oppose the fragmentation of Africa."[66]

Even some of those who had welcomed the arrival of Cyrus Vance as
an antidote to Kissinger came to the conclusion that the pendulum had
swung too far the other way. Theodore S. Wilkinson served in a number of US embassies in Europe and Latin America, in NATO, and at the
UN, and later became head of the Foreign Service Association. By 1976,
he claimed, officials were ready for Cyrus Vance "because Kissinger had
been so cynical in his approach, that the idea of having a man who was
palpably and demonstratively honest and open and straightforward was a
welcome change." Yet he came to the conclusion that neither Vance, nor
the president himself, was "as clever as architects of relationships and foreign policy as Kissinger was."[67] Nor could the foreign policy machine be so
easily turned in the oppositie direction. As one career diplomat put it, it was
"very easy for the Political Appointees to come in and want to accomplish
great things versus the realism of the career people and cynicism perhaps
who saw nothing but apple carts to be upset."[68]

As in many administrations, tensions between senior officials mud-
died the water further. Vance clashed with Zbigniew Brzezinski, Carter's
national security advisor, partly because Brzezinski urged a more robust
line on human rights in American dealings with the Soviets on arms control. Brzezinski owed something of his understanding of, and opposition
to, totalitarianism to the anti-realpolitik tradition of Carl J. Friedrich.
Like Kissinger, he had worked under Friedrich at Harvard and published
Totalitarian Dictatorship and Autocracy with him in 1956. Yet he also bore the
imprint of the geopolitical approach of Nicholas Spykman, which saw him
approach the international system as a "grand chess board" of moves and
countermoves against the Soviet Union (something which was to partly
explain his role in Carter's strategy of supporting the Afghan mujahedeen
in 1979).[69] These were long-established strategic traditions in American
foreign policy making, though they bore the inflections of European
thought.[70] Ultimately, they provided a surer guide to strategy than the
growing obsession with language and labels that had characterized this
period.

A final side note, but an important one, is that Carter's foreign policy
received a sneering response by those in Europe, particularly America's

two old allies, France and Britain. Warren Zimmermann, a diplomat, who had spent time in Moscow, Paris, and Vienna, noted that Carter's emphasis on human rights was regarded as rather naïve and was beginning to risk stability in places like Iran. The French in particular "saw it as a kind of childish approach to the adult game of diplomacy which had to do with things like the balance of power and realpolitik and Machiavelli and God save us not Thomas Jefferson and people, fuzzy thinkers like that."[71] Even a left-wing Labour government in Britain could concede a sneaking preference for the Kissinger-Nixon approach, and a "more sophisticated Realpolitik approach to things." These were the words of Labour Prime Minister Harold Wilson, who had once hoped to distance himself from Nixon in 1969 but came to think Nixon's policies preferable to the Carter approach.[72]

Such comments were oddly reminiscent of Georges Clemenceau's and David Lloyd George's privately dismissive remarks about Woodrow Wilson at Versailles in 1919. In Europe, it seemed, Americans were damned if they did, and damned if they didn't.

16

From Cold War to New
World Order

During the 1970s, the controversies around American foreign policy had become increasingly bitter and ideologically charged. This had been reflected in the growing importance of the language used by the participants. On 10 April 1980, speaking to the Annual Convention of the American Society of Newspapers, Henry Kissinger bemoaned what he saw as the tendency to frame the US foreign policy debate in terms of absolute dichotomies, particularly as a new presidential election loomed. "We are at the beginning of another of our quadrennial debates over foreign policy," he said. The party in office claimed "that it has inherited a debacle and by a near-miraculous effort has raised our prestige to new heights" and the party out of office "assails the current debacle and promises a radically new start." This courted dangers at home and abroad. For the American public, it created the impression that the foreign policy of the United States reflected "only the idiosyncrasies of whoever is incumbent" when—in reality— the national interest of the United States did not change in years divisible by four. For other nations, the controversy was "profoundly unsettling, whether they are foes watching in bewilderment or friends observing in dismay."[1]

There was more continuity between administrations than might be assumed by the pendulum swings in rhetoric. It is simplistic to portray the Nixon-Ford years as some sort of transformation in American foreign policy to unsentimental and ruthless pragmatism. The same way, one should be careful about a simplistic depiction of the Carter years as the polar opposite of their predecessor. On certain issues, Carter behaved like an unsentimental realist. On Iran, for example, he continued with the policy of his predecessors in calculating that the regime of the shah was preferable to the alternatives. In December 1977, during a visit to Tehran, he famously said, "Iran, because of the great leadership of the Shah, is an island of stability in one of the more troubled areas of the world," paying tribute to his host's leadership and noting the "respect and the admiration and love which your people give to you."[2] As the regime began to crumble over the course of the following year, Carter's national security advisor Zbigniew Brzezinski reassured the shah that the United States would "back him to the hilt." This was a much stronger line than the Kennedy administration had taken in the early 1960s, when they had resisted the temptation to push the shah aside. Another controversy was Carter's decision to back the Afghan mujahedeen against the Soviet Union. The CIA even went to lengths of arming them with Russian-made weapons, obtained from other countries, in order to disguise the US role. The aim, according to Brzezinski, was to "make the Soviets bleed for as much and as long as is possible."[3]

In May 1980, as the presidential election campaign gathered pace, Brzezinski offered a rationalization of the administration's foreign policy to date. In his view, it could be explained by an attempt to blend the two conflicting strands in American thinking about the world. On the one side

President Jimmy Carter with the shah of Iran in December 1977. As early as 1962, during the administration of John F. Kennedy, American officials described their policy toward Iran, and the propping up of the shah, as an example of "realpolitik" in practice. © Bettmann/CORBIS.

were those who emphasized the primacy of power, and were "subsumed with the word *Realpolitik*". He defined this as "a hard-nosed, realistic, foreign policy," embodied by Nixon and Kissinger. On the other side were the Wilsonian idealists, who were suspicious of the idea that power was the key determinant in international politics. Carter's emphasis on human rights, Brzezinski claimed, reflected an effective blend of the two. It borrowed the best assets of both without falling into the same traps. One of the positive effects of the approach was an improvement of the image of the United States in Latin America. Its growing prestige had also helped it play the role of arbiter and contribute toward peace in the Middle East.[4] The partisans of the Carter administration chewed this message down further for public consumption. Thus, Jennifer Seymour Whitaker, associate editor of *Foreign Affairs*, wrote in the *New York Times* that the human rights initiative had helped make America make strategic gains. Rights had become realpolitik.[5]

This version of American strategy had been gradually etched out over the course of the first term—and it never saw a second. The Carter era ended with the election of Ronald Reagan in November 1980. Would realism provide the script for a Republican administration once more? In truth, those within the realist school seemed to be at something of a crossroads. Morgenthau's disappointment with almost everyone in office had seen him further alienated in the 1970s. Even Nixon and Kissinger had failed to deal with America's foreign policy "pathology," he complained.[6] Such exasperation knew no bounds. By the time Morgenthau died in 1980, his old mentee, Robert E. Osgood, was an advisor to Ronald Reagan. Yet Osgood demonstrated no desire to turn the clock back or revive the Morgenthau line. Like Kissinger, he bemoaned "the inveterate national habit of oscillating between the neglect and affirmation of power as we rediscover the gap between our interests and power in each successive crisis." Osgood felt Morgenthau was a critic rather than a prophet. His work would not provide a script for what was ahead.[7]

Meanwhile, alternative versions of realism had taken hold in parts of the academy. One of the most important texts was Kenneth Waltz's *Theory of International Politics*, published in 1979, which expanded on his 1959 *Man, the State and War*. In Waltz's view, states behaved according to general laws.[8] The criticism of such structural or neo-realist theories was twofold. First they de-contextualized the concepts used, such as "realpolitik." Second, they depended on a selective and overly mechanized view of the international system. This failed to recognize its fluidity and how much depended on perception.[9] An elegant defence of "classical" realist thinking was Kenneth Thompson's 1984 *Traditions and Values in Politics and Diplomacy*, which held that it was "illusory to think that politics can be free of values." Any notion of a value-free science of international affairs was flawed. Structural realism would never win the day. Americans had choked on the idea that international affairs could be incubated from morality. Again, the language mattered. As Thompson described, the Watergate scandal and the other controversies of the the Nixon era had left a mark on a people "who earlier had tended to see American political virtue as uncontaminated by comparison with European realpolitik."[10]

Taken together, one can see that there was wariness about the false polarities that had characterized the foreign policy debates of the 1970s. There was also a desire to avoid destabilizing pendulum swings from one foreign policy script to another. The existing categories and dividing lines in the foreign policy debate were in flux. New coalitions were coalescing. One factor that was underestimated, and which was to take on great significance during the rest of the decade, was the force of personality.

In Search of the "Reagan Doctrine"

The presidency of Ronald Reagan, which began in January 1981, brought new controversies, and a new set of tropes and doctrines, to the American foreign policy debate. In the first instance, Reaganism took its cue from the critics of détente, such as Paul Nitze, a key advisor, and George P. Schultz, his secretary of state from 1982 to 1989. They stood in a tradition of those who had always had a more overtly hawkish posture on the Cold War, dating back to the 1940s.[11] Added to this was a pronounced skein of ideological anti-communism. This was chiefly, though not exclusively, associated with neo-conservatives, such as Norman Podhoretz and Irving Kristol.[12] Also in the Reagan ranks were a number of supporters and staffers of Democratic senator Henry Jackson, such as Jeane Kirkpatrick and Richard Perle (once a student of Hans Morgenthau). This group rowed in behind the president, feeling that they no longer had a viable home in the Democratic Party.[13]

In the 1970s, *Commentary* magazine had been the main incubator for this loose coalition. It offered both a critique of détente under Nixon and Ford, and of what was seen as a vague and half-committed emphasis on human rights under Carter. Jeane Kirkpatrick, then a professor at Georgetown, declared that a "realistic foreign policy that pursues 'national interest' without regard to morality, ultimately founders on its lack of realism about the irreducible human concern with morality." Her famous essay of November 1979, "Dictatorships and Double Standards," won her the attention of Reagan, who hired her on its strength. It made a distinction between *authoritarian* regimes and the *totalitarianism* of the Soviet Union. Kirkpatrick argued that the United States should generally promote the liberalization and democratization of other states. That said, it should not do so in a way that destabilized those authoritarian regimes that were friendly to the United States, particularly if this meant that they fell into the hands of communists.[14]

This mix of ideological self-confidence and ruthless power politics set the tone for much that came after. It became crucial to the neo-conservative conception of foreign policy. Robert Kagan, who started writing for *Commentary* as a twenty-two-year old in 1981, defined the approach as one that "combines an idealistic moralism, and even messianism, with a realist's belief in the importance of power."[15] Irving Kristol, the figurehead of this group, rejected utopianism and bemoaned the naiveté of the human rights lobby. Yet he also insisted that "Realpolitik a la Disraeli" (Britain's famously pragmatic Conservative prime minister of 1874–1880) was unthinkable in America. American foreign policy needed more ideological sustenance to sustain itself.[16]

Ironically, neo-conservatism shared one striking similarity with postwar American realism. Both held foreign policy to be an indicator of the general state of the nation and the health of the American republic. The two were indivisible. As noted earlier, Kristol had initially been favorable to the "Europeanization" of American foreign policy under Kissinger and Nixon. In part, he viewed this as an antidote to what he saw as the vapid internationalism of the country's intellectual elite in the 1960s. Yet his despair at the state of the American middle classes took him in a different direction in the late 1970s and early 1980s. In his view, American bourgeois culture had lost some of its moral and religious fiber. A realist foreign policy was a symptom of a broader sickness. It represented the "the vulgar substitution of expedience for principle," and it had "no part of the American political tradition." A similar point was made by Jeane Kirkpatrick. She argued that the notion that foreign policy "should be orientated towards balance of power politics, or realpolitik," was totally alien to the American way of life.[17]

It was Norman Podhoretz, a longer-term critic of Nixon's foreign policy, who claimed to have convinced Kristol to come round to his way of thinking on this issue. For Podhoretz, writing in 1981, the failed war in Vietnam had proved—more than anything else—the hopelessness of pursuing a foreign policy without a convincing moral rationale, behind which the nation could rally. In the 1970s, the Nixon, Ford, and Carter administrations had robbed the conflict with the Soviet Union of its moral and political dimension. In Podhoretz's view, this policy was doomed. A "strategy of containment centered on considerations of *Realpolitik* would be unable to count indefinitely on popular support" and would ultimately head toward isolationism.[18]

Podhoretz expanded on this argument in a long review of Kissinger's White House memoirs, *Years of Upheaval*, in *Commentary* in 1982. In *Years of Renewal*, it is worth noting, Kissinger had actually praised Podhoretz for offering the "subtlest" critique of détente. In return, Podhoretz, like Kristol, expressed his admiration for Kissinger. Nonetheless, he objected to what he saw as an element of ideological relativism on which détente was predicated. The Kissinger approach was based on a long view of history that held that "Communist China was not all that different from Tsarist Russia, the facts of geography, history, and ancestral culture being far more decisive than the ideas of Marx and Lenin."[19]

Was history so important after all? In complete contrast to Nixon's, Reagan's foreign policy was largely—one might even say defiantly—ahistorical. This is what surprised Kissinger more than anything else about the Reagan administration. He described, with some wonderment, how Reagan presided over an "astonishing performance—and, to some academic observers, incomprehensible." A president who "knew next to no history" and who had "the shallowest academic background," developed a foreign policy of "extraordinary consistency" and effectiveness.[20]

To class Reagan as a neo-conservative would be misleading; he is perhaps better described as a "hard-line romantic."[21] Nonetheless, there were important points of convergence between neo-conservative discourse and the administration's foreign policy. A clear statement of intent from the Reagan administration came in January 1981 in the testimony of secretary of state-designate Alexander Haig before the Senate Foreign Relations Committee. As Soviet spending was outstripping American spending,

Haig signaled his desire to break from the arms limitation treaties of the 1970s. While Haig did not last long in office, his choice of language before the committee was significant. It seemed to herald an idealist turn in Republican foreign policy: "An American foreign policy of cynical real-politik cannot succeed because it leaves no room for the idealism that has characterized us from the inception of our national life," he stated. Foreign policy was the "ultimate test of our character as a nation."[22]

As ever, statements of intent were not always translated into policy. In fact, in pushing back against some Carter administration policies—in Latin America, for example—the Reaganites actually found themselves revert-ing to positions that were more characteristic of the Nixon-Ford years. The ambassador to Bolivia, Samuel F. Hart, claimed that within a matter of weeks of Haig's appointment, the new secretary of state wanted to release him and bring an end to the existing policy—which had been to lean on the mili-tary junta to force it to either reform or leave office. Instead, it was felt that Haig wanted to "throw the policy of supporting democracy out the window,

Before the Senate Foreign Relations Committee, 9 January 1981, secretary of state nominee Alexander Haig rejected "cynical realpolitik" as a basis for American foreign policy. While Haig lasted only eighteen months in office, this seemed to signal a new approach to international affairs on the part of Ronald Reagan's administration. Courtesy of Wikimedia Creative Commons.

and to go back to something approaching a Cold War realpolitik in Latin America."[23]

From the outset, Reagan's foreign policy juggled these competing instincts. Despite their increasing prominence, the neo-conservatives were not always happy with the direction of policy in the administration. Again, like the realists perhaps, they were hard to satisfy. In a 1986 group profile in the *Bulletin of the Atomic Scientists*, it was suggested that many of them—including Kristol, Podhoretz, and George Will—were "not policy practitioners by nature; they tend to be conceptualizers, opportunists and pamphleteers." They were critical of both George P. Schultz (who replaced Secretary Haig in 1982) and even Paul Nitze—notwithstanding his reputation as a hard-liner—for the suggestion that the United States was prepared to engage in a "live and let live" approach to the Soviet Union. Nonetheless, they had "shaped the terms of the political debate" in Washington, even if they did not always get their way on arms control and other issues.[24]

Any attempt to put a name on Reaganism is fraught with difficulty then. The notion of a "Reagan doctrine" was put forward by the conservative commentator Charles Krauthammer, of the *New Republic* and *Time* magazine, to denote the policy of supporting anti-communist movements across the world in Africa, Asia, and Latin America (also, in fact, known as the Kirkpatrick doctrine). In a famous 1986 essay, "The Poverty of Realism," Krauthammer argued that the goal of American foreign policy was not just security but "the success of liberty." This meant a foreign policy that was "universal in aspiration" but also "prudent in application."[25]

Like many foreign policy doctrines, the Reagan doctrine seemed more coherent with the benefit of hindsight. In the 2004 Irving Kristol Lecture at the American Enterprise Institute, Krauthammer described it as "democratic realism." Unlike some Reagan partisans, Krauthammer did not reject the American realist tradition at its core—he even praised Hans Morgenthau. Instead, he suggested that Reaganism was the next stage of its evolution. Realism was a "valuable antidote to the woolly internationalism of the 1990s," but it lacked a fundamental goal. Its basic problem lay in the narrow way in which Morgenthau had defined the national interest. Accoding to Krauthammer, Morgenthau postulated that what drives nations was the will to power. For most Americans, this "might be a correct description of the world—of what motivates other countries—but it cannot be a prescription for America. It cannot be our purpose." Ultimately,

America "cannot and will not live by realpolitik alone." US foreign policy must be driven by "something beyond power."[26]

In some ways, however, this was a post facto rationalization of Reaganism, viewed through the prism of victory in the Cold War. In fact, if one returns to the mid-1980s, Krauthammer's version of the Reagan doctrine was much more haphazard and selective. It was less a grand strategy than a posture or an attitude—one in which hard-nosed and unsentimental military and political maneuvers were to be celebrated as proof of virility and power. At the simplest level, it was enough to remind the world that America was as ruthless as it was powerful—that it, too, could play rough with the best of them.

Thus, in the midst of the Cold War, Krauthammer was quite willing to celebrate instances of naked realpolitik. In 1985, for example, he praised the administration for its willingness to deal with Iraq's Saddam Hussein, an old enemy, in the Iran-Iraq war. The rapprochement with Iraq showed that Americans "can play as cool a game of *Realpolitik* as anyone. . . . And who can blame us? . . . We must take our allies where we find them," he wrote in the *Washington Post*.[27] In 1988, when the Iran-Iraq War ended with Saddam in the ascendant, Krauthammer argued that it was time to tilt back toward Iran, and against Saddam, for precisely the same reasons. Iran was "no less odious a place today" than it was during the Iran-Iraq conflict. It was "only more useful," he wrote.[28]

Power projection was the single most important factor in this understanding of foreign policy. It was the old realists who tended to urge restraint and probity. In an article in *Foreign Affairs* in late 1985, which defended the legacy of the realist tradition from attacks by Reaganites, George Kennan made the familiar point that "in national as in personal affairs the acceptance of one's limitations is surely one of the first marks of true morality."[29] Against this was set an interpretation of the national interest in which virility and self-confidence were paramount. What was really at issue here were two contending versions of American nationalism, both born at home and tested abroad.

Gorbachev's Turn to Realpolitik

For those watching in other countries, the changing language of American foreign policy was carefully scrutinized. The reaction in Europe was varied. After the eye-rolling Carter's perceived naiveté generated in some quarters, some feared that the Reagan administration would be a source of instability. "We are living in a world that is governed by the principle that realpolitik is dangerous," speculated the British Labour Party MP, Bruce George, a strong supporter of NATO and a pro-American voice, in the House of Commons in 1981. "However, a world governed by—I am not sure whether my next word exists—idealpolitik would be even more dangerous in which to live."[30]

Others repeated the familiar trope that the Americans were naïve about world affairs. They did not expect Reaganism would amount to much because of its lack of historical depth. Notable here was the view of Régis Debray, the former Marxist intellectual who once stood alongside Che Guevara in the 1960s. By 1984, he was acting as special advisor to the socialist President Mitterrand of France on foreign affairs. Debray was no sentimentalist. He explained that he had little faith in traditional conceptions of socialist foreign policy, such as international arbitration, collective security, and disarmament. "What you can call Realpolitik is simply the converse of this ineffective idealism," he told the New York Times. What better defined the notion for him was an acute sense of national interest, a willingness to look at the long term, and an understanding that strategy could never be decoupled from historical realities. In his view, American foreign policy under Reagan still failed on these terms. Too dependent on power, it was "modern in its means and retrograde in its spirit" and "short, flat and simple."[31]

A better measure of the effectiveness of Reagan's foreign policy was its impact in Moscow. Above all, it prompted a more pragmatic and conciliatory approach on the part of the Soviet Union itself. An early glimpse of this had come in Mikhail Gorbachev's visit to Britain in December 1984, four months before he was officially appointed as the new leader of the Soviet Union. As British foreign secretary Geoffrey Howe later reported, Gorbachev had shown glimpses of a growing "appreciation of realpolitik." In conversation with the British Prime Minister Thatcher, the Soviet leader had even used one of the favourite quotes of Anglo-American realists. This was the mantra of nineteenth-century British foreign policy, made famous by Lord Palmerston, that nations have "no permanent friends and no permanent enemies but only permanent interests."[32]

A week later, Thatcher visited Reagan at Camp David. She reported that Gorbachev was demonstrating more flexibility than past Soviet leaders and talking in less ideologically charged language. Crucially, according to Thatcher, Gorbachev was not only worried about the weak Soviet economic performance but was also feeling the pinch of Reagan's Strategic Defense Initiative.[33]

Thus, from the middle of the decade, both sides began to recalibrate and reshape the language they used about the Cold War. Realpolitik was pushed back into the lexicon but this time it had come from the Soviets, eager to return to détente. Just four months after Thatcher's visit, in April 1985 the CIA's special assistant for warning produced a forecasting report that was intended to predict the state of the international arena in the year 2000. For the most part, it proved to be wildly inaccurate. Among other things, it predicted a "diffusion of world power, a decline of America's relative economic and political influence" and a shift from a bi-polar to a multi-polar international system. The Soviet Union would "not experience anything approaching a genuine systemic crisis before the year 2000" and had "sufficient reserves of social and political stability to enable the regime to ride out the economic stagnation and civic malaise of the late 1970s and early 1980s." What was significant, however, was that the CIA also picked up on the new realism that seemed to be emanating from the Kremlin in the face of Reagan's tougher line. Referring to the long-term tradition of Bismarckism in Europe, the report suggested that the Soviets were now the true "inheritors of the European tradition of *Realpolitik*."[34]

After years of misuse in the partisan debates of US foreign policy, the word was now deployed with greater precision. The Soviet leaders evoked realpolitik because they recognized that they had little other choice. Once the Berlin Wall fell in November 1989, the existing structures of the international system began to dissolve. In July 1990, following a meeting with Germany's Helmut Kohl in Russia, Gorbachev agreed to remove any remaining barriers to German unification and to accede to German membership in NATO. Reconciling himself to the new dispensation, the Soviet leader told the world's media that the discussions had been conducted in "the spirit of that well-known German word, 'realpolitik.' "[35] Not for the first time, the word echoed back and forth between East and West and, one could argue, provided a plank between.

After meeting Germany's chancellor Helmut Kohl in July 1990, Soviet leader
Mikhail Gorbachev told the world's media that their negotiations had been
conducted in "the spirit of that well-known German word, '*realpolitik*.'"
Gorbachev had used this word in previous visits to the United Kingdom.
POOL/EPA/LANDOV.

Old Diplomacy and New World Order

The uncompromising ideological stance of Reagan had played an important role in hastening the end of the Cold War. For Americans, this was not
a victory that could be explained by realpolitik. Initially victory seemed
to herald greater certainty and confidence on the part of the United States
about its world role. In this spirit, George H. W. Bush's State of the Union
address of 31 January 1990 famously invoked the prospect of a new world
order, an idea he returned to at various points during the year.

Two months later, in March 1990, Bush's secretary of state James
Baker informed the World Affairs Council at Dallas of the Bush administration's desire to adopt a "democratic foreign policy." For an individual
often taken to be a realist, his language was surprisingly bold: "Let me
put it this way: Beyond containment lies democracy . . . a task that fulfills
both American ideals and self-interests." Quite explicitly, Baker rejected
the proposition of those "who argue for a realpolitik that has a place only

for our economic or military or political interests and leaves our values at home."[36]

Almost immediately, however, the Bush administration came under criticism for not following through on Reagan's victory or making good on its own rhetoric. When Bush sought improved relations with Deng Xiaoping of China, the move was condemned in the *Washington Post* as a reversion to the old habits of the détente era. At the time of Bush's visit to Beijing earlier that year, Deng Xiaoping had given little hope for any democratic or human rights reforms by stating that "the need for stability" overrode anything else in China. The *Washington Post* complained that the Bush administration would present this visit as "the very essence of *realpolitik*—a tough-minded power play that puts America's long-term strategic interests above morality." In practice, it entailed ignoring the concerns of Chinese Americans about China's human rights record, and failing to support the growing democracy movement within the country. To "sophisticated foreign-policy analysts in Washington or New York" it might seem natural to deal with the powers that be. But recent history suggested that such an approach was shortsighted.[37]

Significantly, some Reaganites believed that it was necessary for the United States to pause for breath after the fall of the Berlin Wall. In 1990, for example, Jeane Kirkpatrick predicted a period of retrenchment or disengagement. The Cold War had given foreign policy "an unnatural importance" in American life. In the *National Interest*, she argued that it was time for America to return to being a "normal nation."[38] Others, however, like Elliott Abrams, assistant secretary of state under Reagan, expressed disquiet about the return to summit diplomacy under Bush, seen in his dealings with Deng Xiaoping and Gorbachev. Such "excessive personalization of foreign affairs" came at the cost of overall strategic direction. The administration had "borrowed from 'realpolitik' an evasion of principle, but has substituted personalized diplomacy for the concrete approach realpolitik demands."[39]

The greatest challenges to Bush's foreign policy were not to come from China or Russia but the Middle East. There was a strong consensus behind the decision to repel Saddam Hussein's Iraqi army out of Kuwait, following its invasion in August 1990. But the first Gulf War sparked a new debate about the potential of American power in a unipolar world. After a swift victory in forcing Saddam Hussein out of Kuwait, Bush's decision not to topple his regime—by marching farther into Iraq—was taken by some as a failure to capitalize on American capabilities and to fulfill its moral mission.[40]

Victory over Saddam had been followed by a dire humanitarian crisis, as the regime undertook brutal reprisals against the Shi'ite-dominated regions in the south, and Kurdistan in the north, which had risen up against it in expectation of an American invasion. In April 1991, two months after the end of US military operations in the First Gulf War, the *Wall Street Journal* ran an editorial titled "The Realpolitik of Morality," which held that, in the era of twenty-four-hour television coverage, it was likely to be increasingly difficult for American statesmen to ignore such humanitarian questions. There was a danger that the "sentimental moralism that often failed to distinguish good from poor policy during the Carter years will emerge again in the current reassessment of realist thinking." Nonetheless, the *Wall Street Journal* warned that foreign policy was "not so readily separated from national values, from a country's common idea of itself."[41]

The English writer Christopher Hitchens pursued much the same line in an excoriating critique of the failure of the United States to do more to liberate Iraq. Having protected its immediate financial interests by securing Kuwait's oil supplies, it had left Iraqis to their fate. "The word concocted in the nineteenth century for this process—the shorthand of Palmerston and Metternich—was 'realpolitik,'" Hitchens wrote. Maxims of "cynicism and realism—to the effect that great states have no permanent friends or permanent principles, but only permanent interests—became common currency in post-Napoleonic Europe." In presenting Metternich and Palmerston as paragons of the realpolitik tradition, Hitchens was slightly misguided. But his broader point was that a certain mentality had returned to fashion again. There was not "a soul today in Washington who doesn't pride himself on the purity of his realpolitik."[42]

The triumph of the United States in the Cold War meant that the old pleas of necessity and narrow national interest were more difficult to maintain. If America's rise to superpowerdom had come with great responsibility, unipolarity made those responsibilities even more difficult to shirk. This problem was to play itself out in the debates over humanitarian intervention that were to define the 1990s, into which the old Western allies, Britain and France, were also drawn.

Intervention and Non-Intervention

On 1 November 1992, two days before the presidential election between George H. W. Bush and William Jefferson Clinton, the *New York Times* produced the most elaborate definition of realpolitik to have appeared in the mainstream American press since the writings of Walter Lippmann at the time of the First World War. In fact, this was the only mention of the word to refer back to the true origins of the concept and its coinage by Ludwig von Rochau in 1853. In the modern era, it had come to imply "international diplomacy based on strength rather than appeals to morality and world opinion." But, with America triumphant in the Cold War, such a philosophy of necessity seemed less important. If Clinton won the presidential election, there would be no return to realpolitik. Instead, it was likely that Anthony Lake, who had served in the Carter administration as director of policy planning, would be brought in as national security advisor. Lake, of course, was the man who had been tasked with crafting the anti-realpolitik policies of the Carter government.[43]

Again, while the rhetorical pendulum shifted, the substance of policy did not. Herman Cohen, assistant secretary of state for African Affairs from 1989 to 1993, suggested that despite a "tendency to look at the morality side of issues rather than the realpolitik side," there were no dramatic changes under Clinton.[44] Two relatively minor operations, in Somalia and Haiti, demonstrated the difficulties of adventurism overseas, despite the extent of US military reach. The Battle of Mogadishu in October 1993, triggered by the downing of US Black Hawk helicopters, saw the Clinton administration become more wary about risking American lives for second-order priorities. Despite the relative success of Operation Uphold Democracy in Haiti (from September 1994 to March 1995), it left senior officials with little appetite for getting entangled in imbroglios elsewhere. Thus, according to James Dobbins, American ambassador to the European Community in this period, the experience of Somalia and Haiti saw the administration revert to "more pragmatic realpolitik" by the end of Clinton's first term.[45]

On the other hand, as the *Wall Street Journal* had predicted, the difficulty in evading the question of intervention was also demonstrated by events in the former Yugoslavia. From 1992 to 1995, the violent breakup of the country provided a unique challenge to the Western conscience. Here was a violent civil war and ethnic cleansing taking place within Europe itself, on a scale not seen since the Second World War. Typically, those who opposed intervention appealed to "realpolitik."[46] Meanwhile, the word realpolitik was used, in a pejorative sense, to denounce the cynicism of those who opposed intervention.[47] Old descriptors were being revived to serve new polemics.

The debate over intervention was particularly intense in the United Kingdom. This was partly due to the proximity of the conflict and partly because of a growing sense that the end of the Cold War had opened up more room for Britain on the international stage. The "conservative pessimism" of John Major's Conservative government—and its opposition to intervention—came under severe criticism before its emphatic defeat by Tony Blair's Labour Party in the 1997 general election.[48] This was the issue on which Blair carved out a distinctive foreign policy of his own. Initially, he had the full backing of his colleagues in the Labour Party in this endeavor. Shortly after victory, Blair's foreign secretary Robin Cook proffered a new foreign policy doctrine. This he called an "ethical foreign policy." It was intended to support human rights, civil liberties, and democracy around the globe, with the overall intention of improving Britain's global standing by making it a "force for good" in the world. "It supplies an ethical content to foreign policy and recognises that the national interest cannot be defined only by narrow realpolitik," Cook explained.[49]

Cook's "ethical foreign policy" was one of the clearest iterations of the anti-realpolitik described at various points in this book. As such, he consciously distanced himself from episodes in the history of British foreign policy that had fallen foul of these standards. This not only included the Major government's failure to act over Yugoslavia, it went further back to the betrayal of Czechoslovakia in the name of appeasement in the 1930s. Exactly a year after he announced the new policy, Cook spoke before the House of Commons and recounted a conversation he had recently had with the foreign minister of the Czech Republic. "If your entire history is about being the victim of foreign policy realpolitik," he explained, "you respect a Government who are prepared to follow foreign policy on the basis of principle."[50] It seemed the ghost of Neville Chamberlain was finally to be exorcised.

Two inconvenient truths were to undermine Cook's ethical foreign policy doctrine almost immediately. The first, now clear with the benefit of hindsight, was the extent to which the United Kingdom's much vaunted ethical approach to the world depended on the global predominance of the

United States—at least its acquiescence and more often its military capability. The second was that Blair himself took Cook's doctrine in a different direction. Blair was more active and interventionist than any British prime minister since the Second World War. The United Kingdom engaged in five wars in six years: joining the Clinton administration in the bombing of Iraq in 1998 (Operation Desert Fox), leading the NATO operation in the Kosovo War in 1999, and conducting a brief expeditionary operation in Sierra Leone in 2000, before the wars in Afghanistan in 2001, and Iraq again in 2003.[51] The last was the moment of rupture. Cook became the most senior member of the government to resign in protest against the invasion of Iraq.

In truth, even before Cook left the Foreign Office in 2001, a new Blair doctrine was subsuming Cook's. In the midst of the Kosovo intervention, Blair delivered a famous speech, in Chicago in April 1999, in which he went beyond Cook to articulate a new "doctrine of international community." Again, for the sake of our story, the historical echoes were profound. Here, once more, was a piece of anti-realpolitik, predicated on a classic British rejection of Bismarckism. "Bismarck famously said the Balkans were not worth the bones of one Pomeranian Grenadier," observed Blair. "Anyone who has seen the tear stained faces of the hundreds of thousands of refugees streaming across the border, heard their heart-rending tales of cruelty or contemplated the unknown fates of those left behind, knows that Bismarck was wrong." Instead, the prime minister argued for "a more subtle blend of mutual self-interest and moral purpose in defending the values we cherish."[52]

British foreign policy was being crafted in the space created for it by the predominance of its most important ally. It was ironic then, that when it came to the question of liberal intervention, the United Kingdom was much bolder and more self-assured. As Blair's chief of staff, Jonathan Powell, pointed out, the critics of the Chicago speech included Condoleezza Rice, who was George W. Bush's foreign policy advisor during the 2000 US presidential campaign.[53] At the 2000 Republican Convention, Rice had warned that America's armed forces were "not a global police force . . . [and] not the world's 911."[54] The contours of a potential Bush foreign policy were further laid out in an article by Rice in *Foreign Affairs*, in which she also acknowledged a scholarly debt to the ideas of Hans Morgenthau.[55]

Bush's foreign policy team, collectively known by the nickname "the Vulcans," encompassed a range of contending perspectives, from traditional

Cold War realists through to Reaganites and neo-conservatives. These were mediated through figures such as Donald Rumsfeld, Dick Cheney, Colin Powell, Richard Armitage, Paul Wolfowitz, and Rice. As a group they bore the imprint of some of the major debates of the Cold War era and the experience of the Gulf War of 1990–1. Before the terrorist attacks of 11 September 2001, the balance of forces within the George W. Bush foreign policy team gave little cause to expect that Bush would adopt an activist, interventionist foreign policy.[56]

In its initial response to the September 11 attacks—declaring war on the Taliban regime in Afghanistan—Bush was able to enjoy an almost unprecedented level of public consensus for his foreign policy. That consensus began to break down following the 2003 invasion of Iraq. Outside the administration, realist critics of the war evoked the spirit of Hans Morgenthau against the venture.[57] Within the administration, there was no realist rebellion. Iraq did put a strain on the existing balance of forces within it, however. Writing in the *National Interest*, Richard Lowry, then editor of the *National Review*, cautioned against simplistic labeling of the administration's foreign policy. Familiar terms of identification were more blurred than ever. In the first instance, he rejected what he called the "falsity of the academic realists" as essentially redundant. A policy rooted in "amoral calculations of power and interest—grand strategies associated with Richelieu, Metternich, Kissinger and others" would never sustain public support. Next, he noted that almost any supporter of the Iraq war had been "lumped in with the neocons." This was also "a slippery label" and it had never been the dominant strain of thinking in the Republican Party, notwithstanding flashes of neo-conservatism in Bush's rhetoric. Instead, Lowry thought it more accurate to identify a tension between traditional Reaganites and neo-Reaganites. The former supported the war but were more cautious about intervention and democracy promotion abroad. The latter had built a myth around Reagan and an over-ideologized version of his foreign policy.[58]

To complicate matters further, some individuals straddled these boundaries. Indeed, some of the administration's self-declared realists moved between them—the most famous example being Condoleezza Rice. In doing so, they took the language of realism with them but deployed it to different ends. This gave birth to the idea of a new, higher version of realism, in which the spread of democracy was raised from a loose preference to a goal in itself. Democratization was now seen as a key component of stability and security. This idea was captured by Rice's speech in Cairo in

June 2005 when she famously repudiated aspects of America's Cold War strategy in the Middle East for being too focused on a short-term view of stability. "For 60 years, my country, the United States, pursued stability at the expense of democracy in this region here in the Middle East—and we achieved neither. Now, we are taking a different course. We are supporting the democratic aspirations of all people."[59]

For the architects of the Iraq War, it was important to stress that realist and idealist motives were in operation at the same time. "In my nine years as Prime Minister I have not become more cynical about idealism," Tony Blair wrote in 2006, "I have simply become more persuaded that the distinction between a foreign policy driven by values and one driven by interests, is wrong." Globalization begat interdependence and interdependence begets "the necessity of a common value system to make it work." Thus, he wrote, "Idealism becomes realpolitik."[60] This was a hard case to make against the backdrop of Iraq's slide into civil war, combined with growing difficulties in Afghanistan. It became common to argue for a return to realpolitik as an antidote to the Bush-Blair approach. Those who *truly* understood realpolitik, it was argued, would never have undertaken a pre-emptive war, or an ideologically driven effort at regime change. Realists had been dismissed as "sad sacks" and "party poopers" but, once again, their more prudential approach seemed to return to fashion.[61]

As early as 2004, in fact, it was claimed that Condoleezza Rice was re-engaging with her former realist mentors, such as Brent Scowcroft, whom she had been distanced from over the war. Bush and Rice began to talk of a "balance of power that favors human freedom"—a careful attempt to reconcile the Kissingerian and Reaganite traditions in the Republican Party.[62] The 2006 *Iraq Study Group Report* led by James Baker III and Lee H. Hamilton was said by some to herald the moment that America's Middle East policy would revive realism and the traditional goals of stability, in its recommendations of phased withdrawal and dialogue with Iran and Syria.[63] Unexpectedly, its proposals were largely rejected by the Bush administration in favor of an alternative plan—a massive troop surge that began in 2007, with the goal of stabilizing the most tumultuous areas.[64]

In terms of military strategy, Bush had resisted the full tilt of the pendulum swing over Iraq. In terms of rhetoric, it had already set in around him and would envelop any successor. Those charged with the conduct of foreign policy in the era after Bush and Blair would seek a new intellectual armoury; or, more accurately, they would return to the certainties of the old. There would be a return to realpolitik but what form would this take? In 2008, former French foreign minister Hubert Védrine, a supporter of the 1998 intervention in Kosovo, suggested that after the end of the Cold War, the old methods had been too hastily rejected. He called for a new form of "Smart-Realpolitik" which was more likely to preserve humanitarian objectives in the long term.[65] In 2009, Robert J. Art put forward a different conception. This was a grand strategy based on "selective engagement," also called "realpolitik plus." The basic goal would be to keep the United States secure and prosperous, but Art's vision went beyond those classic realist goals to "nudge" the world toward the values that America itself held to—democracy, free markets, human rights, and international openness.[66] Circumspection, caution and restraint were to be the new watchwords.

Niebuhr's Return

In the mid-1970s, Arthur Schlesinger had observed the tendency of American politics to follow cycles. In the field of foreign affairs, the effect of such cycles could be disorientating. In 2005, the eighty-nine-year old Schlesinger wrote an article for the *New York Times* in which he urged Americans to rediscover Reinhold Niebuhr. As Iraq's sectarian civil war reached its peak, Schlesinger rejected Niebuhr's warnings about the dangers of pre-emptive war and our "inability to comprehend the depth of evil to which individuals and communities may sink, particularly when they try to play the role of God to history." Schlesinger ended his article with an excerpt from Niebuhr's 1952 book, *The Irony of American History*. "If we should perish, the ruthlessness of the foe would be only the secondary cause of the disaster," Niebuhr had written. "The primary cause would be that the strength of a giant nation was directed by eyes too blind to see all the hazards of the struggle; and the blindness would be induced not by some accident of nature or history but by hatred and vainglory."[67]

Less than two years later, in 2007, Barack Obama, then a candidate for the Democratic presidential nomination, told the *New York Times* that one of his favorite philosophers was Niebuhr. On the one hand, Obama noted, Niebuhr recognized "the compelling idea that there's serious evil in the world, and hardship and pain," though he thought that "we should be humble and modest in our belief that we can eliminate those things." On the other hand, however, Niebuhr has also believed that we should not use this as an excuse for cynicism and inaction. Obama took away from Niebuhr "the sense we have to make these efforts knowing they are hard, and not swinging from naive idealism to bitter realism."[68] Following on from this, the president's Nobel Peace Prize acceptance speech of 2009 was an attempt to articulate a liberal realist worldview.[69] Borrowing from Niebuhr, he sought a third way, between the misadventures of the Bush years and the temptations of isolationism and fatalism.[70]

The president also announced his desire to move beyond the dichotomies of the past. This remained a constant refrain throughout his two terms. In an interview given in 2015 he bemoaned the tendency to categorize people in certain camps. If you were an idealist, "you're like Woodrow Wilson, and you're out there with the League of Nations and imagining everybody holding hands and singing 'Kumbaya' and imposing these wonderful rules that everybody's abiding by." And if you were a realist, "then you're supporting dictators who happen to be our friends, and you're cutting deals and solely pursuing the self-interest of our country as narrowly

A return to realpolitik? President Obama's foreign policy has been described by his former chief of staff, Rahm Emanuel, as "more realpolitik, like Bush 41." Both American and British foreign policy have undergone pendulum swings in recent years. From the Official White House Photostream. Courtesy of Wikimedia Creative Commons.

defined." "I just don't think that describes what a smart foreign policy should be," he said.[71]

The desire to articulate a worldview—to seek some sort of reconciliation between one's ideals and an understanding of the limits of morality in the political sphere—is nothing new, of course. For the statesman, the defining question is not whether one can articulate a cogent worldview, even one wrinkled with irony and nuance (as Niebuhr undoubtedly provides). What matters, for those charged with the responsibility of governance, is whether it is functional or not, at the point of delivery. We have been here before. As Niebuhr observed himself in 1953: "The definitions of 'realists' and 'idealists' emphasize disposition, rather than doctrines, and they are therefore bound to be inexact." Ultimately, it "must remain a matter of opinion whether or not a man takes adequate account of all the various factors and forces in a . . . situation."[72] A "smart foreign policy," therefore, can be assessed only on the grounds of its successes and failures, rather than its coherence or intellectual lucidity. The difficulties faced by the Obama administration in foreign affairs have not been conceptual ones.

Today, the invocation of realpolitik tends to denote a posture or a general intuition, and a suspicion of grand schemes. Those who use it know what they stand against. Arguably, they are less sure-footed about an alternative strategy of their own. But the original concept, as articulated by Ludwig von Rochau, was a means of analysis—a way of understanding power and politics—rather than a meditation of the responsibilities that come with it. Unlike Niebuhr's work, Rochau's does not offer a theology of statecraft, and addresses the mechanics rather than metaphysics of politics. Nonetheless, if we want to understand political situations better—particularly in the field of foreign affairs—we would be well served by a return to the original *Foundations of Realpolitik*.

Conclusion

A Return to Foundations

This is true, that the wisdom of all these latter times in princes' affairs is rather fine deliveries and shifting of dangers and mischiefs when they are near, than solid and grounded courses to keep them aloof.

(Sir Francis Bacon, as quoted by Ludwig von Rochau in *Foundations of Realpolitik*, vol. 1, 1853)[1]

So what now for realpolitik, born in 1853, and today more than a century and a half old? One of the themes of the previous chapters has been that discussions of international affairs are too often dominated by stark dichotomies that do not necessarily shed much light on the world around us, or the individuals involved. Another has been that our foreign policy debates follow cycles, in which policymakers declare themselves more idealistic, or more realistic, depending on which way the political pendulum swings.

Language does matter in the Anglo-American foreign policy debate. Yet it can also confuse and mislead. Labels such as realpolitik can change so much over time as to lose much of their meaning. Thus former secretary of state James Baker could publicly and explicitly reject "realpolitik" in 1990 but be heralded, as the co-chair of the Iraq Study Group, as the man to restore it to a flailing Bush administration in 2006.[2] What is more, the tendency to huddle in groups, or to put those with different opinions into rival categories or schools, stifles debate and encourages territorialism. So many of our foreign policy debates are taken up with the mischaracterization, and even caricaturing, of our opponent's position. Self-definition seems to take up almost as much of our energies. To define oneself as standing for or against something remains a natural human inclination, as does seeking reconciliation between one's morals and the nasty, brutish world. Yet it is also an activity better suited to moral philosophy or theology than to foreign policy analysis.

In recent times, there have been profound failures in the Anglo-American world's ability to anticipate, understand, and to come to terms with complex problems it has encountered in other countries or regions. Some of the failures of policy are not, in the first instance, due to bad analysis; they can be more accurately attributed to flawed political leadership and poor strategy. A deeply textured understanding of a province in Afghanistan (its power relationships, cultural sensitivities, anthropology, history, and topography) will not necessarily advance the goal of overall policy if that policy is misconceived or breaks down at the point of delivery.[3]

These shortcomings have contributed to a sense of lost control, being at the mercy of events, and a general loss of authority in world affairs. To take only one region on which energies have been focused over the last two decades—the modern Middle East—it has become clear that the West (the United States and the United Kingdom in particular) is often caught on the hop, forced to respond reactively because of a failure to anticipate what is round the corner. Even when we have a sense of the broader picture, we tend to perform the same trick on others as we do to ourselves: that is, to impose artificial categories of analysis—such as "moderate" or "extremist"—or fail to appreciate the social and economic foundations on which political forces are based. An ability to "read the runes" has to be the basis of any successful foreign policy.[4]

Calling for a "reformation" of our foreign policy or a new grand strategy is beyond the scope of this book. In fact, it has shown just how futile such attempts at reformation have been in the past. But it does end with a humbler call—for a return to the *Foundations of Realpolitik*. Ludwig von Rochau's work is valuable today because it reminds us of the messy business of politics and all the tributaries that flow into it. Rochau looked at the mechanics of states and societies—and the nuts and bolts that made them up—rather than the physics of the international system. He sought to analyze and synthesize what he saw before him—to dig down below the surface but not at the expense of painting an overall picture. *Foundations of Realpolitik* began with an emphasis on the importance of history in setting the circumstances for any political situation. But it did not accept that the development of history was pre-determined to follow a certain course. It offered an attempt to anticipate, and therefore shape, the future.

This book ends, therefore, with eight recommendations, inspired by the original *Foundations of Realpolitik*, but also building more recent historical experience on top of them. Real *Realpolitik*—that is, its Rochau vintage—remains superior to many versions of foreign policy realism that have come since. Yet it should come with a health warning. There have been many bastardized versions of realpolitik—some malign, and some well-intentioned—which should warn us against drinking too deeply of the draught. In fact, the final recommendation is that there are also lessons to learn from the tradition of anti-realpolitik, to which realpolitik has been juxtaposed throughout this book. Anti-realpolitik provides a hidden clue to Anglo-American strategy that we dismiss at our peril. It points the way to a higher realism, albeit one with its own weaknesses. This has served us well in the past, and may well do so in the future.

1. Real *Realpolitik*, as articulated by Ludwig von Rochau, offers a simple but sensible formula for approaching most foreign policy dilemmas

Rochau's most useful legacy lies in the method of political analysis he bequeathed. This was to consider any given situation on three levels: the existing distribution of power within a state (*Herrschaft*); the socioeconomic structures of society; and the cultural and ideological setting of the time. He synthesized these to provide a general assessment of the specific historical context and the parameters for political action within it. This provides a basic four-part script. While it is far from perfect, this is a good place to start when confronted with most problems in the realm of foreign policy.

- Who holds power in any given circumstances (as distinct from who claims sovereignty or the right to hold power)?
- What are the social and economic conditions that underlie the political system and how are they changing the distribution of power?
- What is the prevailing cultural context and what are the most important ideological undercurrents of the society in question?
- Considering all these things together, what is the room afforded for political action to forward one's interests or one's ideals, and what are the risks?

2. Real *Realpolitik* is an enemy of "habitual self-delusions" and "naively accepted catchwords" from wherever they come

"Formless ideas, impulses, emotional surges, melodic slogans, naively accepted catchwords . . . [and] habitual self-delusions"—these were the main targets that Rochau had in mind when he wrote *Foundations of Realpolitik*. Rochau castigated his fellow liberals for dreaming up "castles in the sky" and failing to understand the foundations of political power. Woodrow Wilson, modern-day realists have long argued, built "castles in the sky" in the form of his Fourteen Points and support for the League of Nations. Yet Rochau would have been equally unimpressed with those versions of realism in which the critical faculties have atrophied—anything that resembles a knee-jerk reaction or that responds to idealism with a roll of the eyes and retreats to its own set of tropes and doctrines.

Realpolitik was not a theology or a science of statecraft. It did not follow rules. Above all, it did "not entail the renunciation of individual judgment and it requires least of all an uncritical kind of submission," Rochau wrote. It was more "appropriate to think of it as a mere measuring and weighing and calculating of facts that need to be processed politically." What Rochau offered was not a strategy in itself as much as a *way* of thinking. In challenging the arguments of others, one had to be prepared to confront one's own presuppositions and assumptions. *Realpolitik* was always alert to "the misguided pride which characterizes the human mind." Approaching foreign policy problems with a pre-prepared script, or with unshakeable faith in one's "methods," falls foul of this basic rule.

3. *Foundations of Realpolitik* helps us understand political possibility in the age of modernity

Many theorists of foreign affairs, and some practitioners, use history as a guide. And yet, as Paul Schroeder has argued, this has also encouraged a tendency "go at a history like a looter at an archaeological site, indifferent to context and deeper meaning, concerned only with taking what can be immediately used or sold."[5] Likewise, as David Runciman has written, too many participants in the world of contemporary politics think they need only to read Machiavelli's *The Prince*, or Sun Tzu's *Art of War*, in order to understand the nature of the game they are playing.[6] Rochau wrote in an era that more closely resembles our own than that of Machiavelli or Sun Tzu. He wrote after the European Enlightenment in an age of industrialization and great power rivalry. His understanding of modernization was similar to ours.

Rochau himself needs to be understood in context. Indeed, one could argue that one of the weaknesses in his analysis was his assumption, common to many liberals, that economic modernization begat political liberalization. Another mistake was to assume that social and ethnic conflict would be easier to mediate because of the rise of nationalism—something the subsequent history of his own country was to emphatically disprove. On the other hand, Rochau did not believe in a single path of historical development— that Germany must follow the precedent of Britain and France. Thus, while liberalism had the force of history behind it, he did recognize that rapid industrialization and social and political change could be destabilizing. He also understood that liberalism and other ideas of freedom would not simply triumph on their own. They needed protecting and nurturing, and they required actual political force behind them. In this respect, *Foundations of Realpolitik* does address some of the quintessential problems of modernity.

In the twenty-first century, reading Rochau cannot tell us what to do about global markets, energy interdependence, climate change, or the sphere of cyberspace. *Foundations of Realpolitik* does, nonetheless, remind us of the need to take such things into account—that is, to craft our political analysis around, and to anticipate, changing circumstances. Today's policy analysts need not predict the future; but they might do more to consider recent developments in technology, or emerging economic, social, ideological, or climatic phenomena. An excellent example here is the work of the Spanish sociologist, Manuel Castells, whose work, *The Information Age*, looks at social movements, class structures, identity, ideas, political legitimacy, and technology on a global scale.[7] While such a broad perspective was beyond Rochau himself, this is the spirit of *Foundations of Realpolitik*.

4. *Foundations of Realpolitik* emphasizes the importance of ideas and idealism as forces of change and transformation

For Rochau, ideas mattered. This was not a soaring insight in itself. Very few theorists of statecraft argue anything but. What *Foundations of Realpolitik* really helps us do is to understand which ideas matter, how they do so, and why some ideas matter more than others. In the first instance, Rochau believed that the "feeble self-conscious opinion of the day is not entitled to claim political consideration." But the more "consolidated it becomes, and the more it transforms itself into a firm conviction, the more important it becomes for the state." Powerful ideas usually have social and economic weight behind them. The purity, elegance, or symmetry of an idea is no indication of its political force.

Indeed, it was as a theorist of public opinion that Rochau was at his most original. The most important expression of public opinion was the *Volksgaube* (popular belief), which should always be treated with "care and protection, not blandishment." While the popular belief was the highest peak of popular opinion, the *Zeitgeist* was its broadest foundation. The *Zeitgeist* was the "consolidated opinion of the century as expressed in certain principles, opinions and habits of reason." Anyone who tried to go against it was likely to get mangled in history's wheels.

Rochau was a critic of utopianism, not idealism—a crucial distinction, often missed by those who claim the mantle of realism today. He understood that ideology played the "role of a harbinger and trailblazer of events." Indeed, he believed his approach "would contradict itself if it were to deny the rights of the intellect, of ideas, of religion or any other of the moral forces to which the human soul renders homage." What mattered was the political power of an idea rather than its "rationality." It was common that "the most beautiful ideal that enthuses noble souls is a political nullity." When it came to "phantasms" like "eternal peace," or international fraternity, with "no will and no force" behind them, "*Realpolitik* passes by shrugging its shoulders." On the other hand, "the craziest chimera" could become the most serious matter. One could not ignore "those latent forces of habit, tradition and sluggishness" such as "poverty, lack of knowledge, and prejudice" and even "immorality." Real *Realpolitik* appreciated that the customs and habits of a people—even if they appeared atavistic or immoral—were more than a mere "pudendum"; they were a crucial part of the living organism of any state or society.

5. *Foundations of Realpolitik* asks us to consider power, ideas, economics, and society at the same time, and to identify the junctures and connections between them

The first and most important task in politics, argued Rochau, is to understand where power resides in any given situation. But power and sovereignty are not simply understood as military force or political authority; they are a reflection of the balance between social, economic, and cultural forces within society and state. What is most important is the ability to identify where power, socioeconomic conditions, and ideas overlap and converge.

Real *Realpolitik* emphasized the importance of thinking synthetically and holistically, based on an assessment of all the information before us. This may sound like basic common sense. In truth, however, it is something that we could be better at. Too often we assume that political developments will follow a certain trajectory, only to leave us floundering when events do not follow the groove we anticipated. Again, the recent history of the Middle East provides many such examples. An effective foreign policy is better served by a more textured analysis—a sense of patterns, interactions, and connections—than by new theories. Such an approach to the Arab spring, for example, would have told us to examine the specific circumstances in each country where it was taking place—but not to dispense with a sense of the connections between each. It would have helped us to distinguish between pure and elegant ideas of freedom—that resonated with our own, or appealed to our sense of symmetry—and those with real social weight and revolutionary force. Rochau would have asked us to consider the social force and political power of ideas we regard as impure, irrational, or arcane. He would have asked us to take these ideas seriously, even if they seemed deeply unappealing to us. He would have cautioned us against thinking that one political system could supplant another overnight, or that people would always act in their own interests.

This is not a recipe for status quo politics, however. Nothing could have been further from Rochau's mind. Authoritarian regimes were inherently unstable, particularly in the age of democracy. More specifically, such regimes were "anachronistic." *Foundations of Realpolitik* asks the reader to look first at the power relations within a country, but also to think beyond those power relations, and to understand how quickly they can break down under the pressure of modernity (demographic change, technology, and the spread of transnational ideologies). It tells us that some political structures are weaker than others because they are predicated on weak socioeconomic foundations, and that others are more resilient than we might otherwise have assumed. Applying such an approach at the onset of the crisis in Syria would have asked us to consider the regional, social, and ideological basis of the Assad regime and the anomalies therein (such as a relatively quiescent Sunni merchant class in Damascus and the surrounding area). In all these instances, Rochau would have advised us, as Marx did in the *Eighteenth Brumaire*, to distinguish between town and countryside and between different social classes. He would have reminded us, as Edmund Burke did, to reflect on the balance achieved in our own political systems, which is organic and uneven, and a product of specific circumstances.

Looking further back, such an approach would have looked beyond Kremlinology (an obsession with high politics, statesmen, and personalities) to *glasnost*, demography, economics, ideological resistance, and ethnic and national identity within the Soviet bloc. As one scholar wrote in 1993, given that so many experts were taken off guard by one of the most far-reaching political transformations in history, it was "time to loosen one's grip on words such as 'obviously' and 'of course.'"[8] Indeed, real *Realpolitik* may not only have provided a better predictor of Soviet collapse. It may also have provided a better indication of the forces that would eventually fill its void. It would not have seen human history in terms of the development of legal and political structures, but as a struggle between ideas, peoples, and interests in which atavism, sectarianism, and racism were an unavoidable part of the picture.

6. Real *Realpolitik* is ecumenical in the tools it chooses for political analysis and is suspicious of those methods of analysis that claim to offer a science of politics, or to be innately superior to others

Rochau's basic approach is one of historicism and empiricism, before anything else. An analysis of any given situation begins with an understanding of how it arrived at a certain point in time and what has come before. As he put it, one had to contend, first of all, "with the historical product, accepting it as it is, with an eye for its strengths and weaknesses, and to remain otherwise unconcerned with its origins and the reasons for its particular characteristics."

After wedging the door open with historicism, there are many other tools to deploy in search of political insight. It does not matter whether these methods derive from the left or right of the political spectrum. Rochau combined French positivism, the organicist conservatism of Edmund Burke, and an understanding of socioeconomic forces and class (and class consciousness) provided by Marx and Engels. He wrote as a journalist rather than a jurist but his analysis was arguably more incisive because of this. He witnessed the political conditions in a number of European countries firsthand (Germany, France, Italy, and Spain) and read widely about England and America. He was not given to one narrative of political change. He did not see the superiority of one political system over another, but believed that they were a reflection of the given historical circumstances of each. This also taught him that to follow one model of political philosophy (either as a method of analysis or as a theory of change) was self-limiting.

This holds a lesson for today's foreign policy analysts. They can have their cake and eat it. They can use both Marx and Burke at the same time rather than restricting themselves to one method, or following the teachings of a "school." They might well add some literature if it improves their understanding of intellectual or cultural context and the role of ideas. Just as both Karl Marx and Friedrich Meinecke read Honoré de Balzac and Walter Scott, those in the profession of security studies would be well-served by Joseph Conrad's *Secret Agent*, a novel about radical politics, anarchism, and a terrorist plot in late nineteenth-century London.

Today, the *real Realpolitik* tradition—which eschews narrow obsessions with definitions, methodology, or academic territorialism—is perhaps best embodied in the work of Walter Russell Mead. To understand politics and history, Mead urges students of foreign affairs to begin with Thomas Carlyle's *History of the French Revolution* or the novels of Anthony Trollope. As Mead puts it, we need leaders trained to "lead and to choose—and to do that under conditions in which neither they nor the specialists will have a full understanding of the forces at play and the risks in the system." For this, what is required is an education system that "promotes non-conformity, originality, courage and sacrifice."[9]

To this end, one could do worse than channel the spirit of the wartime Office of Strategic Services, in which a few of the scholars who understood the real history of *Realpolitik*—such as Hajo Holborn, William Langer, and Herbert Marcuse—played a significant part. As the philosopher Raymond Geuss writes, the great achievement of the OSS was the "toleration of intellectual deviancy," in which Marxists such as Marcuse could be harnessed in the defeat of Nazism and in the reconstruction of Germany. This is something that stands in contrast to the "politics of myopic intellectual conformism" of today and the territorialism of academia.[10]

7. Real *Realpolitik* should be distinguished from a cult of the national interest and avoid the traps of fatalism, absolutism, and pessimism that have infected some versions of realist thought

History tells us that we should be wary about those who are convinced that they are the the the torchbearers of realpolitik. The story told in this book is full of instances where those who claimed to have a superior grasp of reality made major strategic mistakes. The insistence on asserting "reality" against utopianism has repeatedly slipped into forms of absolutism and theologizing. This is anything but realistic. Heinrich von Treitschke's malformation of Rochau's concept provides an obvious fable here. We have also seen how quickly *Realpolitik* got conflated with *Weltpolitik, Machtpolitik,* and *Wilpolitik*; and how it got infected with chauvinism and anti-Semitism, despite Rochau's warnings.

There are good reasons why *Realpolitik* should be treated with care, then. In the wrong hands, it has been shown to be a degenerative notion, quick to fall into misuse, and encourage fatalism or extremism. Some of the wiser "realist" thinkers have noted this flaw. Henry Kissinger observed the tendency of *Realpolitik* to turn in on itself, beginning in Bismarck's Germany. Max Weber was unsettled by the way his fellow Germans boasted so loudly about their *Realpolitik*. He felt that his countrymen had their "breasts inflated" by the word, turning it into a "slogan" that was embraced "with all the ardour of feminine emotion." As Weber added, those nations that pursued a genuinely realistic foreign policy tended not to "chatter about it" so much.[11]

8. Anti-realpolitik has been the default setting of Anglo-American foreign policy for many years, and will most likely remain so. While this can seem hypocritical or naïve, it obscures a "hidden" or "higher" realism that has been a major strategic asset to both nations

The anti-realpolitik tradition described at various points in this book also has many flaws. From Woodrow Wilson to Jimmy Carter to George

W. Bush and Tony Blair, it has been associated with naiveté and adventurism. Yet anti-realpolitik has also performed a number of very important
functions in the past. The first has been to provide hazard lights at crucial
points in history. The first example of this came from the German critics
of Rochau, who warned that, by casting their lot in with Bismarck, the
National Liberals were making a fatal compromise with authoritarianism.
One could also point to the interjection of Clement Attlee, leader of the
Labour Party in 1938, warning Neville Chamberlain that the deals he had
entered into with Hitler and Mussolini—justified on the grounds of "realpolitik"—would make a mockery of the very notion.

This book has aimed to dust off the original concept of *Realpolitik*, to
deconstruct it and reconstruct it, and to protect it from inaccurate usage
and blandishment. So to oppose any new exponent of realpolitik as a
potential Treitschke is absurd. One can understand Hans Morgenthau's
fury when this suggestion was leveled at him. Equally, however, those who
have set themselves against realpolitik also deserve more serious consideration than they have sometimes received at the hands of realists. To dismiss
the anti-realpolitikers as naïve or utopian is to miss a hidden clue to Anglo-
American foreign policy. Here we might recall the conversation that *New
Republic* editor, Walter Weyl, had with a Berlin professor in 1916. Germans,
said the professor, "write fat volumes about *Realpolitik* but understand it
no better than babies in a nursery." Americans, he observed, with a hint of
envy, "understand it far too well to talk about it."[12]

Anglo-American foreign policy has remained strikingly resistant to the importation of certain ideas from continental Europe, from
Machiavellianism to Bismarckism and *Realpolitik*. Expressions of outrage
and horror about the existence of such notions can sound rather pompous
and pious, as countless exasperated realists point out. E. H. Carr and Hans
Morgenthau were two who could never reconcile themselves to the cant
and hypocrisy they heard around them in the Anglo-American world.

Yet there is more to this anti-realpolitik than meets the eye. As Meinecke
came to understand, the Anglo-Saxons were indeed hypocritical, but were
less naïve than was assumed. They expressed outrage about the "profanation"
of politics but they were more adept at playing the game than first seemed.
In fact, they practiced "the most effective kind of Machiavellianism," albeit
one which dare not speak the name. They pursued their interests with great
rigor, but in the name of "humanity, candour and religion," and the promise that everyone could share in the spoils. If it was a self-delusion, it was a

highly useful one, and it propped up an Anglo-American world order. In the midst of the Second World War, George Orwell also recognized that this "strange mix of reality and illusion"—hypocritical as it was—was the thing that girded the British nation at its darkest hour and was superior to the boasted realism of Hitler's Germany and Mussolini's Italy. In 1982, speaking in London, Henry Kissinger described this as Britain's greatest gift to the United States in foreign policy: a "convenient form of ethical egotism" which held that what was good for us was good for the rest.[13] There was, in other words, a rational kernel in the mystical shell.

In many cases, Anglo-American idealism has been vapid or self-deluding. And yet, it has given Anglo-American foreign policy more coherence, direction, and purpose than it might otherwise have had. A little realpolitik can serve a higher purpose, as this book has argued. It gets us closer to the true nature of politics. But one should always be wary of an overdose, lest we forget our greatest asset of all.

Acknowledgments

The writing of this book was made possible by two research awards, for which I am extremely grateful. The first was the Henry A. Kissinger Chair in Foreign Policy at the John W. Kluge Center at the Library of Congress, which I was lucky enough to hold in 2013–4. The second was the award of a Leverhulme Foundation research fellowship which enabled me to take a sabbatical from King's College London and to travel to the United States to complete my research at the National Archives at College Park, Maryland.

At the Library of Congress, I was fortunate to work with Dr. Carolyn Brown, the recently retired director of the Kluge Center, and her dynamic team. I would particularly like to thank Travis Hensley, JoAnne Kitching, Mary-Lou Reker, Deneice Robinson, Jason Steinhauer, and Dan Trullo for their assistance on a range of matters, and their good humor. It was a particular pleasure to get to know the Librarian of Congress, Dr. James Billington, who made sure that I got the most out of the library's unrivaled resources (particularly the manuscripts division and digital collections). It was thanks to the Kissinger Chair Committee, particularly Alan Batkin, that I was able to meet Dr. Kissinger and discuss this book with him, as well as a shared interest in Lord Castlereagh. Thanks to Jason Cowley, my editor at the *New Statesman*, I also had the privilege of interviewing President Carter, giving me two very different perspectives on past foreign policy controversies. While at the library, I was delighted to host Robert Kagan of the Brookings Institute for a public conversation on realpolitik in the modern world, and to have a fascinating discussion with Eliot Cohen of Johns Hopkins about the work of Robert E. Osgood (which helped guide this book). I owe a major debt to Ambassador Mitchell B. Reiss, who has been a mentor for many years, and to Sir Nigel Sheinwald, former British ambassador in Washington, for his professional encouragement.

When in Washington, I was lucky to have some close friends for company and many dinners. I would like to thank Matt, Danielle, Stan, Becky, Scott, Kate and Bella Perl, Andy and Kelly Polk, Gary Schmitt,

Tom Donnelly, Marty Sieff, Michael Barone, and Michael McDowell. Ryan Evans, editor-in-chief of *War on Rocks*, deserves a special mention for reading this manuscript from start to finish and for apprising me of his concept of "ecumenical realism." Ryan also introduced me to Jacob Heilbrunn of the *National Interest*, who published two of my essays during my time in Washington—though I had escaped by the time my defense of Lord Cornwallis appeared. Thanks also to Adam Garfinkle for giving me the opportunity to write for the *American Interest* and to build on some of the themes dealt with in this book. Very early into the project, I was able to test some of the ideas in a paper delivered at Yale, an opportunity organized by Alexander Evans (a former Kissinger Chair) and hosted by John Lewis Gaddis. Charlie Laderman, a graduate of the grand strategy program there, has also been a very helpful interlocutor. This book partly grew out of a UK–US dialogue. Over the last few years, I have had a series of enlivening conversations on this topic with many others, such as Frank Gavin, William Inboden, George Seay, Jeff Engel, Ted Brommund, Walter Russell Mead, Andrew Roberts, Dean Godson, and James Ellison.

At the Department of War Studies at King's College London, two heads of department, Mervyn Frost and Theo Farrell, have been consistently supportive of me in this project, and much else besides. This also applies to a former head of department, Sir Lawrence Freedman, whose book, *Strategy*, sets the tone for so much of what our department is, and does, and Michael Rainsborough, who is a brilliant sounding board. I have had many interesting discussions about the ideas in this book with other colleagues including Rudra Chaudhuri, Jan Willem Honig, Ned Lebow, David Betz, Walter Ludwig, Alex Meleagrou-Hitchens, Shiraz Maher, Peter Neumann, and David Martin Jones. Thomas Rid deserves a special mention, having read *Foundations of Realpolitik* in the original German and shared my enthusiasm for it. I must also acknowledge the excellent work of Hannah Ellerman, a native German speaker, who translated significant chunks of Rochau's original work from the nineteenth-century German. My former student Gabriel Elefteriu gave the whole book the most thorough attention, and cast an honest and critical eye on every line. His honesty was much appreciated and he is a star in the making. Another, Nina Musgrave, helped with the bibliography. Any mistakes in the text are mine alone.

This book bears the mark of ten years spent in Cambridge where I was trained, guided, and helped in every possible way by Jon Parry. It also bears the imprint of Brendan Simms, who advised on an earlier draft and will no doubt recognize many of the themes contained therein. Another former colleague, Magnus Ryan, also read Rochau's work in the original and offered brilliant insights on it. I hope to return to *Foundations of Realpolitik* to work on a more sustained treatment of Rochau's work with him in the near future. My close friend, Martyn Frampton, has probably heard more about this book than anyone, so I salute his patience. In the latter stages of the work, I was lucky enough to discuss some of the core concepts with Adam Tooze, who provided me with a preview of an unpublished essay on Max Weber. The book exists at an odd juncture between intellectual and international history. In this respect, the work of David Armitage of Harvard was a useful guide, and I also owe an intellectual debt to scholars such as Duncan Bell, Jonathan Haslam, and Mark Mazower, whose work I have admired from afar. I should probably go to more conferences.

My nearest and dearest will be sick of hearing about realpolitik—a word that seems to pop up in the most unlikely places, from *Game of Thrones* to sporting strategy. This applies to my mother and father, grandmother, and my not-so-long-suffering wife, Jo, who lived with this book more than anyone. I fear it also applies to my agent Georgina Capel and Timothy Bent, a most conscientious and patient editor. Thanks also to Alyssa O'Connell, for sourcing images and dragging me through the final stages before publication.

The book is dedicated to my mother, Greta Jones, whose own book, *Social Darwinism and English Thought*, provided a model for this one, who read and commented on every chapter of this, and who has the great virtue of never saying anything predictable or *bien pensant*.

Notes

INTRODUCTION: THE RETURN OF *REALPOLITIK*

1. Robert Kagan, *The Return of History and the End of Dreams* (New York: Vintage Books, 2009); Robert Kaplan, *The Revenge of Geography: What the Map Tells Us about Coming Conflicts and the Battle against Fate* (New York: Random House, 2012).
2. John Bew, "The Real Origins of Realpolitik," *National Interest* (March–April, 2014).
3. Perhaps the nearest previous attempt to provide a history of *Realpolitik* was by Friedrich Meinecke in 1924: *Machiavellianism: The Doctrine of Raison d'État and Its Place in Modern History* [1924], edited by Werner Stark and translated by Douglas Scott (New Haven, CT: Yale University Press, 1957),
4. For two prominent examples in Britain and America, respectively, see Jonathan Powell, *The New Machiavelli: How to Wield Power in the Modern World* (London: Random House, 2010); Philip Bobbitt, *The Garments of Court and Palace: Machiavelli and the World That He Made* (New York: Atlantic, 2013). See also Corrado Vivanti, *Niccolò Machiavelli: An Intellectual Biography* (London: Routledge, 2013) and Marco Cesa, ed., *Machiavelli on International Relations* (Oxford: Oxford University Press, 2014).
5. Michael Ignatieff, "Machiavelli Was Right," *Atlantic*, 20 November 2013.
6. The phrase "Machiavellian moment" is from J. G. A. Pocock, *The Machiavellian Moment: Florentine Political Thought and the Atlantic Republican Tradition* (Princeton, NJ: Princeton University Press, 2003).
7. For Castlereagh's "return to fashion," see J. Bew, *Castlereagh: A Life* (Oxford: Oxford University Press, 2012) and Christopher Meyer, *Getting Our Own Way: 500 Years of British Diplomacy* (London: Weidenfeld and Nicolson, 2009). For Metternich, see Alan Sked, *Metternich and Austria: An Evaluation* (London: Palgrave Macmillan, 2007).
8. Henry A. Kissinger, *A World Restored: Metternich, Castlereagh and the Problems of Peace, 1812–1822* (London: Weidenfeld and Nicholson, 1999).
9. For the best recent biography, see Jonathan Steinberg, *Bismarck: A Life* (Oxford: Oxford University Press, 2011).
10. John Lewis Gaddis, *George F. Kennan: An American Life* (New York: Penguin, 2011); George F. Kennan, *The Decline of Bismarck's European Order: Franco-Russian Relations 1875–1890* (Princeton, NJ: Princeton University Press, 1981).

11. Henry A. Kissinger, "The White Revolutionary: Reflections on Bismarck," *Daedalus* 97.3 (Summer 1968): 888–924.

12. Henry Kissinger, *World Order* (London: Allen Lane, 2014). For Clinton's review, see *Washington Post*, 4 September 2014.

13. Peter Viereck, *Metapolitics: From Wagner and the German Romantics to Hilter* (New York: Alfred A. Knopf, 1965), pp. 189–208.

14. Quoted in Peter Baker, "Obama Puts His Own Mark on Foreign Policy Issues," *New York Times*, 10 April 2010.

15. Gregor Peter Schmitz, "Unlikely Heir: Obama Returns to Kissinger's Realpolitik," *Der Spiegel*, 22 May 2013.

16. Douglas Hurd, *Choose Your Weapons: The British Foreign Secretary: 200 Years of Argument, Success and Failure* (London: Weidenfeld and Nicolson, 2010), p. 163. For Neville Chamberlain's reading of Castlereagh and George Canning during the 1930s, see Bew, *Castlereagh*, pp. xi–xii, 5, 178, 181, 409, 488.

17. A. J. P. Taylor, *The Italian Problem in European Affairs, 1847–1849* (Manchester: Manchester University Press, 1970 [first edition 1934]), p. 1.

18. Henry Kissinger, "The Limits of Universalism," *New Criterion*, June 2012.

19. Henry Kissinger, *Diplomacy* (New York: Simon and Schuster, 1994), Chapter 6, "Realpolitik Turns on Itself."

20. Quoted in Black Hounshell, "George H.W. Obama?" *Foreign Policy*, 14 April 2010.

21. See, for example, Kenneth Waltz, *Theory of International Politics* (New York: McGraw-Hill, 1979), p. 117.

22. Lucian M. Ashworth, "Did the Realist-Idealist Great Debate Really Happen? A Revisionist History of International Relations," *International Relations* 16.33 (2002): 33–51.

23. For the classic statement of this position, see Quentin Skinner, "Meaning and Understanding in the History of Ideas," *History and Theory* 8.1 (1969): 3–53. For the application of the Cambridge school to international affairs, perhaps the most important scholar is Duncan Bell. See Duncan Bell, "Political Theory and the Function of Intellectual History: A Response to Emmanuel Navon," *Review of International Studies* 29.1 (January 2003): 151–160. See also Duncan Bell, ed., *Political Thought and International Relations: Variations on a Realist Theme* (Oxford: Oxford University Press, 2009).

24. Quentin Skinner, *Liberty before Liberalism* (Cambridge: Cambridge University Press, 1998), pp. 116–119.

25. Jonathan Haslam, *No Virtue like Necessity: Realist Thought in International Relations since Machiavelli* (New Haven, CT: Yale University Press, 2002), pp. 184–185.

26. In many theories of international relations, these concepts have been presented as one and the same. See, for example, Kenneth Waltz, *Theory of International Politics* (New York: McGraw Hill, 1979), p. 117.

27. For a convincing take on the Anglo-American worldview, see Walter Russell Mead, *God and Gold: Britain, America and the Making of the Modern World* (London: Atlantic Books, 2007).

28. Terry Nardin, "Middle-Ground Ethics: Can One Be Politically Realistic without Being a Political Realist," *Ethics and International Affairs* 25.1 (Spring 2011); Richard Little, "The English School's Contribution to the Study of International Relations," in *European Journal of International Relations* 6.3 (September 2000): 395–422; Joseph Nye, "Toward a Liberal Realist Foreign Policy: A Memo for the Next President," *Harvard Magazine* (March to April 2008). See also Anatol Lieven, *Ethical Realism: A Vision for America's Role in the World* (London: Pantheon Books, 2006).

29. Reinhold Niebuhr, *The Irony of American History* (Chicago: University of Chicago Press, 1952); William Inboden, "The Prophetic Conflict: Reinhold Niebuhr, Christian Realism, and World War II," *Diplomatic History* 38.1 (2014): 49–82.

30. "Remarks by the President at the Acceptance of the Nobel Peace Prize," 10 December 2009, http://www.whitehouse.gov/the-press-office/remarks-president-acceptance-nobel-peace-prize. See R. Ward Holder and Peter B. Josephson, *The Irony of Barack Obama: Barack Obama, Reinhold Niebuhr and the Problem of Statecraft* (Ashgate: Farnham and Burlington, 2012).

31. For a recent defense of classical realism against neo-realism, see Sean Molloy, *The Hidden History of Realism: A Genealogy of Power Politics* (Houndsmill: Palgrave, 2006). See also Kenneth W. Thompson, *Traditions and Values in Politics and Diplomacy: Theory and Practice* (Baton Rouge: Louisiana State University Press, 1992), pp. 135, 189–194 and Kenneth W. Thompson, *Morality and Foreign Policy* (Baton Rouge: Louisiana State University Press, 1980).

32. Paul Schroeder, "Historical Reality vs. Neo-Realist Theory," *International Security* 19.1 (Summer 1994): 108–148 and Karl-Georg Faber, "Realpolitik als Ideologie," *Historiche Zeitschrift* 203.1 (August 1966): 1–45. See also Paul Schroeder, "The Nineteenth Century System: Balance of Power or Political Equilibrium?" *Review of International Studies* 15.2 (1989): 135–153 and Ernest R. May, Richard Rosecrance, and Zara Steiner, eds., *History and Neo-realism* (Cambridge: Cambridge University Press, 2010), pp. 129–154.

33. See, for example, Joel Isaac and Duncan Bell, eds., *Uncertain Empire: American History and the End of the Cold War* (Oxford: Oxford University Press, 2012).

34. Felix Gilbert, *The End of the European Era: 1890 to the Present* (New York: W. W. Norton, 1970), p. xi.

35. Arlette Farge, *The Allure of the Archives*, translated from the French by Thomas Scott-Railton, with a foreword by Natalie Zemon Davis (New Haven, CT: Yale University Press, 2013).

36. Franco Moretti, *The Bourgeois: Between History and Literature* (New York: Verso, 2013). For a discussion of this approach, see Valerie Sanders, "The

Bourgeois: Between History and Literature by Franco Moretti," *Times Higher Education Supplement*, 27 June 2013.

37. Skinner, *Liberty before Liberalism*; David Runciman, *Political Hypocrisy: The Mask of Power, from Hobbes to Orwell and Beyond* (Princeton, NJ: Princeton University Press, 2008); Greta Jones, *Social Darwinism and English Thought* (Brighton: Harvester Press, 1980).

38. Perry Anderson, *American Foreign Policy and its Thinkers* (London and New York: Verso, 2015).

39. Raymond Williams, *Keywords: A Vocabulary of Culture and Society* (London: Fontana/Croom Helm, 1976), pp. 9–24, 216–221.

PART I: REAL *REALPOLITIK*

1. Ludwig von Rochau, *Grundsätze der Realpolitik, Angewendet auf die staatlichen Zustände Deutschlands*, vol. 2 (Heidelberg: J. C. B. Mohr, 1868), preface, pp. i–x.

CHAPTER 1. ORIGINS

1. See Andrew Whitehead, "Eric Hobsbawm on 2011: 'It reminds me of 1848,'" 23 December 2011, http://www.bbc.co.uk/news/magazine-16217726; Anne Applebaum, "Every Revolution Is Different," *Slate*, 21 February 2011; Kurt Weyland, "The Arab Spring: Why the Surprising Similarities with the Revolutionary Wave of 1848?" *Perspectives on Politics* 10.4 (December 2012): 917–934.

2. Christopher Clarke, *Iron Kingdom: The Rise and Downfall of Prussia, 1600–1947* (London: Allen Lane, 2006).

3. A. J. P. Taylor, *The Course of German History: A Survey of the Development of German History since 1815* (London: Methuen, 1961), p. 69. For a critique of this view, see Clark, *The Course of German History*, pp. 500–504.

4. Rochau is briefly discussed in a number of books on mid-nineteenth-century German liberalism. For example, see Andrew Lees, *Revolution and Reflection: Intellectual Change in Germany during the 1850s* (The Hague: Martinus Nijhoff, 1974); James J. Sheehan, *German Liberalism in the Nineteenth Century* (Chicago: University of Chicago Press, 1978); Peter Uwe Hohendahl, *Building a National Literature: The Case of Germany, 1830–1870* (Ithaca, NY: Cornell University Press, 1989); Dieter Langewiesche, *Liberalism in Germany* (Princeton, NJ: Princeton University Press, 2000).

5. For an important recent exception, see Jonathan Haslam, *No Virtue like Necessity: Realist Thought in International Relations since Machiavelli* (New Haven, CT: Yale University Press, 2002), pp. 184–185.

6. Hajo Holborn described it as a "strange concoction of French sociology and a perverted Hegelian philosophy," in *A History of Modern Germany, 1840–1945* (New York: Alfred A. Knopf, 1969), pp. 117–118, 151.

7. For a recent study of German involvement at the battle of Waterloo, see Brendan Simms, *The Longest Afternoon: The 400 Men Who Decided the Battle of Waterloo* (Harmondsworth: Penguin, 2014).

8. Auguste Comte, *Système de politique positive, ou Traité de Sociologie instituant la Religion de l'Humanité* (1851–1854), vol. 1. (Paris: Carilian-Goeury, 1880). For the influence of French positivism on, for example, Engels, see Etienne Balibar, *Cinq Etudes du Materialisme Historique* (Paris: Maspero, 1974), p. 85.

9. The most detailed discussion of Rochau's life in the English language is an unpublished dissertation by Johanna Margarette Menzel, "August Ludwig von Rochau: A Study on the Concept of Realpolitik" (MA dissertation, University of Chicago, August 1953). For a brief German biography of Rochau, produced in 1921, see Hans Lühman, *Die Unfange August Ludwig von Rochau, 1810–1850* (Heidelberg, 1921). The best account of his political thought is by Natasha Doll, *Recht, Politik und "Realpolitik" bei August Ludwig von Rochau (1810–1873): Ein wissenschaftsgeschichtlicher Beitrag zum Verhältnis von Politik und Recht im 19. Jahrhundert* (Frankfurt am Main: Vittorio Klostermann, 2005). For a recent Italian study of Rochau, see Federico Trocini, *L'invenzione della "Realpolitik" e la scoperta della "legge del potere." August Ludwig von Rochau tra radicalismo e nazional-liberalismo* (Bologna: Il Mulino, 2009). Biographical information about Rochau in this section is mainly taken from the work of Menzel (chapter 1, in particular) and from Doll's book, except where other references indicate.

10. Ludwig von Rochau, *Grundsätze der Realpolitik, Angewendet auf die staatlichen Zustände Deutschlands* [*Foundations of Realpolitik*, vol. 2 (Heidelberg: J. C. B. Mohr, 1868), preface, pp. i–x.

11. L. B. Namier, *1848: The Revolution of the Intellectuals* (The Raleigh Lecture on History), *Proceedings of the British Academy*, vol. 30 (London, 1944), pp. 1–20, 31–40.

12. Namier, *The Revolution of the Intellectuals*, pp. 1–20, 31.

13. Michael Burleigh, *Blood and Rage: A Cultural History of Terrorism* (London: Harper Collins, 2008).

14. Karl Marx, "The Eighteenth Brumaire of Louis Napoleon" [first published in *Die Revolution*, 1852], in Karl Marx, *Collected Works*, vol. 11 (New York: International Publishers, 1976), pp. 103–116. Also published as *The Eighteenth Brumaire of Louis Bonaparte* (Moscow: Progress Publishers, 1977).

15. Marx, *The Eighteenth Brumaire*.

16. E. H. Carr, *The October Revolution* (New York: Alfred A. Knopf, 1969), pp. 58–61.

17. Karl Marx, *The First International and After*, edited by David Fernbach (Harmondsworth: Penguin, 1974).

18. *New York Tribune*, 23 October 1852.

19. Peter Uwe Hohendahl, *Building a National Literature: The Case of Germany, 1830–1870*, translated by Renate Baron Franciscono (Ithaca, NY: Cornell University Press, 1989), pp. 60–69; Michael Stolleis, *Public Law in Germany, 1800–1914* (Oxford: Bergahn Books, 2001), pp. 255, 263.

20. Ludwig von Rochau, *Geschite Frankreichs von 1814 bis 1852* (Leipzig: Nizel; London: Williams and Morgate, 1859).
21. *The British Quarterly Review* (July–October, 1859), pp. 268–269.
22. Ludwig von Rochau, *Wanderings in the Cities of Italy in 1850 and 1851*, translated by Mrs. Percy Sinnett, 2 vols. (London, 1853), vol. 1, pp. iii–vi, 27–29, 31–35.
23. Doll, *Recht, Politik und "Realpolitik,"* p. 10.

CHAPTER 2. FOUNDATIONS

1. Ludwig von Rochau, *Grundsätze der Realpolitik, Angewendet auf die staatlichen Zustände Deutschlands*[*Foundations of Realpolitik, applied to the current state of Germany*], vol. 1 (Stuttgart: Karl Göpel, 1859), p. 23.
2. The version that is used for all direct citations from volume one is the second edition, which was published in 1859. It was identical to the original apart from a new preface from Rochau on "The Present Crisis." See Ludwig von Rochau, *Grundsätze der Realpolitik: Angewendet auf die staatlichen Zustände Deutschlands*, vol. 1 (Stuttgart: Karl Göpel, 1859), hereafter referred to as Rochau, *Realpolitik*, vol. 1. The only modern edition of the book was produced by Hans Ulrich-Wehler in 1972: Ludwig August von Rochau, *Grundsätze der Realpolitik auf die staatlichen Zustände Deutschlands*, herausgegeben und eingeleitet von Hans-Ulrich Wehler (Frankfurt und Berlin: Ullstein Buch, 1972).
3. For the second volume, Ludwig von Rochau, *Grundsätze der Realpolitik, Angewendet auf die staatlichen Zustände Deutschlands*, vol. 2 (Heidelberg: J. C. B. Mohr, 1868), hereafter referred to as Rochau, *Realpolitik*, vol. 2.
4. Rochau, *Realpolitik*, vol. 1, p. 27.
5. Rochau, *Realpolitik*, vol. 1, pp. 1–9.
6. Rochau, *Realpolitik*, vol. 1, p. 23.
7. Rochau, *Realpolitik*, vol. 1, pp. 1–9.
8. Rochau, *Realpolitik*, vol. 1, pp. 1–9.
9. Lees, *Revolution and Reflection*, p. 35.
10. Rochau, *Realpolitik*, vol. 1, pp. 1–9.
11. Hohendahl, *Building a National Literature*, p. 62.
12. See *Realpolitik*, vol. 1, p. 18.
13. Rochau, *Realpolitik*, vol. 1, pp. 1–9.
14. Niccolò Machiavelli, *The Prince*, edited by Quentin Skinner and Russell Price (Cambridge: Cambridge University Press, 1988).
15. Rochau, *Realpolitik*, vol. 1, pp. 1–9.
16. Rochau, *Realpolitik*, vol. 1, pp. 1–9.
17. Rochau, *Realpolitik*, vol. 1, pp. 1–9.
18. Perry Anderson, *The New Old World* (London: Verso, 2009), pp. 490–491.
19. Rochau, *Realpolitik*, vol. 1, chapter 3, pp. 18–30.
20. Rochau, *Realpolitik*, vol. 1, chapter 2, pp. 9–12.

21. Rochau, *Realpolitik*, vol. 1, chapter 2, pp. 9–12.
22. Rochau, *Realpolitik*, vol. 1, chapter 2, pp. 12-15.
23. Rochau, *Realpolitik*, vol. 1, chapter 2, pp. 12–17.
24. Rochau, *Realpolitik*, vol. 1, chapter 2, pp. 12–17.
25. Rochau, *Realpolitik*, vol. 1, chapter 2, pp. 12–17.
26. Rochau, *Realpolitik*, vol 1, chapter 2, pp. 12–17.
27. Hohendahl, *Building a National Literature*, pp. 60–61.
28. Rochau, *Realpolitik*, vol. 1, chapter 2, p. 15
29. Ronald Beiner, "Machiavelli, Hobbes, and Rousseau on Civil Religion," *Review of Politics* 55.4 (Autumn 1993): 617–638.
30. Rochau, *Realpolitik*, vol. 1, chapter 2, p. 15
31. Rochau, *Realpolitik*, vol. 1, chapter 2, pp. 15-17.
32. Rochau, *Realpolitik*, vol. 1, chapter 2, pp. 15-17.
33. Rochau, *Realpolitik*, vol. 1, chapter 6, pp. 54–68.
34. Rochau, *Realpolitik*, vol. 1, pp. 218–224.
35. Rochau, *Realpolitik*, vol. 1, Introduction to second edition, pp. i–xvi.
36. Rochau, *Realpolitik*, vol. 1, Introduction to second edition, pp. i–xvi.
37. Rochau, *Realpolitik*, vol. 1, Introduction to second edition, pp. i–xvi.
38. Langewiesche, *Liberalism in Germany*, p. 59.
39. Rochau, *Realpolitik*, vol. 1, pp. i–xvi.

CHAPTER 3. LIBERALISM AND BISMARCK: A FATAL COMPROMISE?

1. Quoted by Friedrich Meinecke, *Machiavellianism: The Doctrine of Raison d'État and Its Place in Modern History*, edited by Werner Stark and translated by Douglas Scott (New Haven, CT: Yale University Press, 1957), pp. 395–396.
2. Edward Tannenbaum, *European Civilization since the Middle Ages* (New York: John Wiley, 1965), pp. 440–445.
3. Otto Pflanze, *Bismarck and the Development of Germany: The Period of Unification, 1815–1871* (Princeton, NJ: Princeton University Press, 1963), pp. 48, 215. It does not feature in the best recent biography by Jonathan Steinberg, *Bismarck: A Life* (Oxford: Oxford University Press, 2011).
4. Leonard Krieger, *The German Idea of Freedom: History of a Political Tradition* (Boston: Beacon Hill Press, 1957), pp. 349–389.
5. Doll, *Recht, Politik und "Realpolitik,"* p. 8.
6. James J. Sheehan, *German Liberalism in the Nineteenth Century* (Chicago: University of Chicago Press, 1978), pp. 123–124.
7. Langewiesche, *Liberalism in Germany*, pp. 74–95.
8. Gordon R. Monk, "Bismarck and the 'Capitulation' of German Liberalism," *Journal of Modern History* 43.1 (March, 1971): 59–75.
9. Krieger, *The German Idea of Freedom*, p. 387.
10. Krieger, *The German Idea of Freedom*, p. 397.
11. Jakob Venedey, *Ireland and the Irish during the Repeal Year, 1843* (Dublin, 1844).

12. Krieger, *The German Idea of Freedom*, pp. 420–421.

13. Constantin Frantz, "The Religion of National Liberalism," reviewed in *The Illustrated Review: A Fortnightly Journal of Literature, Science and Art* 4.5 (December 1872): 346.

14. Frantz, "The Religion of National Liberalism," p. 346.

15. "Spreading Propaganda in Germany," *Sun* (New York), 14 April 1918.

16. James J. Sheehan, *German History, 1770–1866* (Oxford: Oxford University Press, 1989), pp. 849–850.

17. Tannenbaum, *European Civilization*, pp. 440–445.

18. Rochau, *Foundations of Realpolitik*, vol. 2, Preface, pp. i–x.

19. Rochau, *Foundations of Realpolitik*, vol. 2, Preface, pp. i–x.

20. Rochau, *Foundations of Realpolitik*, vol. 2, Preface, pp. i–x.

21. Rochau, *Foundations of Realpolitik*, vol. 2, Preface, pp. i–x.

22. Michael Joseph Smith, *Realist Thought from Weber to Kissinger* (Baton Rouge: Louisiana State University Press, 1986).

23. James Alfred Aho, *German Realpolitik and American Sociology: An Inquiry into the Sources and Political Significance of the Sociology of Conflict* (Lewisburg: Bucknell University Press, 1975), p. 53.

24. Rochau, *Foundations of Realpolitik*, vol. 2, Preface, pp. viii.

25. Rochau, *Foundations of Realpolitik*, vol. 2, Preface, pp. iv–x.

26. Rochau, *Foundations of Realpolitik*, vol. 2, Preface, pp. iv–x.

27. Rochau, *Foundations of Realpolitik*, vol. 2, Preface, pp. iv–x.

28. Rochau, *Foundations of Realpolitik*, vol. 2, chapter 5, pp. 55–74.

29. Pflanze, *Bismarck*, p. 215.

30. Quoted in Sheehan, *German Liberalism*, p. 109.

31. The most considered discussion of Rochau's ideas is by Doll, *Recht, Politik und "Realpolitik,"* pp. 70–80.

32. Rochau, *Foundations of Realpolitik*, vol. 2, chapter 5, pp. 55–74.

33. Edmund Burke, *Reflections on the Revolution in France* (London: J. Dodsley, 1790), p. 318.

34. Rochau, *Foundations of Realpolitik*, vol. 2, chapter 5, pp. 55–74.

35. Rochau, *Foundations of Realpolitik*, vol. 2, chapter 5, pp. 55–74.

36. Burke, *Reflections*, p. 127.

37. Rochau, *Foundations of Realpolitik*, vol, 2, chapter 5, pp. 55–74.

38. Burke, *Reflections*, p. 8.

39. Rochau, *Foundations of Realpolitik*, vol. 2, chapter 5, pp. 55–74.

40. Menzel, "Rochau," pp. 75–79.

41. Rochau, *Foundations of Realpolitik*, vol. 2, pp. 172–220.

42. Rochau, *Foundations of Realpolitik*, vol. 2, pp. 172–220.

43. R. B. Elrod, "Realpolitik or Concert Diplomacy: The Debate over Austrian Foreign Policy in the 1860's," *Austrian History Yearbook* 17 (January 1981): 84–97.

44. Rochau, *Foundations of Realpolitik*, vol. 2, pp. 172–220.

45. Rochau, *Foundations of Realpolitik*, vol. 2, pp. 172–220.
46. Rochau, *Foundations of Realpolitik*, vol. 2, pp. 172–220.
47. Brendan Simms, *The Struggle for Mastery of Germany, 1779-1850* (New York: St. Martin's Press, 1998), pp. 190-194.
48. Eva Schmidt-Hartmann, *Thomas G. Masaryk's Realism Origins of a Czech Political Concept* (Munich: R. Oldenbourg Verlag, 1984), pp. 64–65.
49. A. J. P. Taylor, *The Course of German History: A Study of the Development of German History since 1815* (London: Routledge, 2001; first published 1946).
50. Rochau, *Foundations of Realpolitik*, vol., 2, chapter 10, p. 336. See also the discussion by Doll in *Recht, Politik und "Realpolitik,"* p. 29.

CHAPTER 4. *REALPOLITIK* AFTER ROCHAU

1. Menzel, "Rochau," pp. 75–80.
2. Gordon R. Monk, "Bismarck and the 'Capitulation' of German Liberalism," *Journal of Modern History* 43.1 (March, 1971): 59–75.
3. Robert C. Binkley, *Realism and Nationalism, 1852–1871* (New York: Harper and Brothers, 1935), pp. 28, 302.
4. Franco Moretti, *The Bourgeois: Between History and Literature* (London: Verso, 2013), p. 93.
5. Paul Hamilton, *Realpoetik: European Romanticism and Literary Politics* (Oxford: Oxford University Press, 2013).
6. Sheehan, *German Liberalism*. See a critical review by Geoff Eley, *Central European History* 14.3 (September 1981): 273–288.
7. Tannenbaum, *European Civilization*, pp. 440–445.
8. For the classic account of this, see Hans-Ulrich Wehler, *The German Empire, 1817–1918*, translated by Kim Traynor (Leamington Spa/Dover, NH: Berg, 1985). For another foundational text in the Sonderweg thesis, see Fritz Fischer, *Grift nach der Weltmacht: Die Kriegszielpolitik des kaiserlichen Deutschland, 1914–1918* (Düsseldorf: Droste Verlag, 1961).
9. Ludwig August von Rochau, *Grundsätze der Realpolitik auf die staatlichen Zustände Deutschlands*, herausgegeben und eingeleitet von Hans-Ulrich Wehler (Frankfurt und Berlin: Ullstein Buch, 1972).
10. Roger Fletcher, "Recent Developments in West German Historiography: The Bielefeld School and Its Critics," *German Studies Review* 7.3 (October 1984):451–480.
11. David Blackbourn and Geoff Eley, *The Peculiarities of German History: Bourgeois Society and Politics in Nineteenth-Century Germany* (Oxford: Oxford University Press, 1984). See chapter titled "The *Realpolitik* of the Bourgeoisie and the Redundancy of Liberalism," pp. 118–126. See also, Roger Fletcher, "Recent Developments in West German Historiography: The Bielefeld School and Its Critics," *German Studies Review* 7.3 (October 1984): 451–480.

12. Peter Viereck, *Conservatism Revisited: The Revolt against Ideology* (New Brunswick: Transaction, 2005), pp. 85–95.

13. Peter Viereck, *Conservatism Revisited,* pp. 85–95.

14. Peter Viereck, *Metapolitics: From Wagner and the German Romantics to Hitler* (New York: Alfred A. Knopf, 1965), pp. 189–208.

15. Hajo Holborn, "Bismarck's Realpolitik," *Journal of the History of Ideas* 21.1 (January–March 1960): 84–98.

16. Frederico Trocini, *L'invenzione della "Realpolitik" e la scoperta della "legge del potere"* (Bologna: Mulino, 2009).

17. Raymond J. Sontag, "The Germany of Treitschke," *Foreign Affairs* 18.1 (October 1939): 127–139.

18. Hohendahl, *Building a National Literature,* pp. 60–61.

19. Meinecke, *Machiavellianism,* pp. 396–397.

20. H. W. C. Davis, *The Political Thought of Heinrich von Treitschke* (London: Constable, 1914), pp. 1–33.

21. Hans Kohn, "Treitschke: National Prophet," *The Power of Politics* 7.4 (October 1945): 418–440.

22. Davis, *The Political Thought of Heinrich von Treitschke,* pp. 19–33.

23. Menzel, "Rochau," p. 11.

24. Menzel, "Rochau," pp. 75–78.

25. Haslam, *No Virtue like Necessity,* pp. 184–185.

26. Davis, *The Political Thought of Heinrich von Treitschke,* pp. 1–33.

27. Krieger, *The German Idea of Freedom,* pp. 366–368.

28. Sontag, "The Germany of Treitschke," pp. 127–139.

29. Davis, *The Political Thought of Heinrich von Treitschke,* pp. 1–33.

30. Hans Kohn, "Treitschke: National Prophet," *The Power of Politics* 7.4 (October 1945): 418–440.

31. Meinecke, *Machiavellianism,* pp. 396–397.

32. Heinrich von Treitschke, *His Life and Works* (London: Allen and Unwin, 1914), pp. 191–192. See also Heinrich von Treitschke, *Germany, France, Russia and Islam* (London: Allen and Unwin, 1914).

33. Davis, *The Political Thought of Heinrich von Treitschke,* pp. 19–33.

34. Treitschke, *His Life and Works,* pp. 28–29.

35. Davis, *The Political Thought of Heinrich von Treitschke,* pp. 1–33.

36. Treitschke, *His Life and Works,* pp. 28–29.

37. Hans Kohn, "Treitschke: National Prophet," pp. 418–440.

38. Quoted by Sheehan, *German Liberalism,* pp. 123–124.

39. Hans Kohn, "Treitschke: National Prophet," pp. 418–440.

40. Heinrich von Treitschke, *Politics,* with an introduction by Hans Kohn (New York: Harcourt, Brace and World), pp. ix–xviii.

41. Treitschke, *His Life and Works,* p. 105.

42. Ramsay Muir, *Britain's Case against Germany: An Examination of the Historical Background of the German Action in 1914* (Manchester: Manchester University Press, 1914), p. 67.

43. Theodore H. Von Laue, *Leopold Ranke: The Formative Years* (Princeton, NJ: Princeton University Press, 1950), pp. 87–88, 102–103, 204, 217.

44. He said this in his 1908 work *Weltbürgertum und Nationalstaat.* Quoted in Werner Stark, "Editor's Introduction," to Meinecke, *Machiavellianism,* pp. xi–xlvi.

45. Treitschke, *His Life and Works,* pp. 158–192.

46. Treitschke, *His Life and Works,* pp. 158–192.

47. Treitschke, *His Life and Works,* pp. 158–192.

48. Treitschke, *His Life and Works,* pp. 158–192.

49. Treitschke, *His Life and Works,* pp. 158–192.

50. Davis, *The Political Thought of Heinrich von Treitschke,* pp. 1–9, 35–38, 227–289.

51. Treitschke, *His Life and Works,* pp. 158–192.

52. Menzel, "Rochau," p. 80.

53. Treitschke, *Politics,* pp. 132–135.

54. Treitschke, *His Life and Works,* pp. 115–117.

55. Raymond J. Sontag, "The Germany of Treitschke."

56. Haslam, *No Virtue like Necessity,* pp. 184–185.

57. E. H. Carr, *What Is History?* (New York: Alfred A. Knopf, 1962), pp. 48–49.

58. Werner Stark, "Editor's Introduction," to Meinecke, *Machiavellianism,* pp. xi–xlvi.

59. Meinecke, *Machiavellianism,* pp. 396–397.

60. "The year 1848, shattering as it did the hopes of power and unity, directed people's thoughts all the more toward the aim. In 1853, A. L. von Rochau published his *Foundations of Realistic Policy, as Applied to the Conditions of the German State,* which brought the new slogan of *Realpolitik* into currency." Meinecke, *Machiavellianism,* pp. 396–397.

61. See Friedrich Meinecke, *Cosmopolitanism and the National State,* translated by Robert B. Kimber, introduction by Felix Gilbert (Princeton, NJ: Princeton University Press, 1970), pp. 100–103, 226, 343.

62. The most serious study of Rochau to date suggests that Meinecke came closest to the original meaning of "realpolitik." See Menzel, "Rochau," p. 83.

63. Friedrich Meinecke, *The Warfare of a Nation: Lectures and Essays,* translated by John A. Spaulding (Worcester, MA: Davis Press, 1915), pp. 10–11.

64. Meinecke, *Cosmopolitanism and the National State,* pp. 100–103, 226, 343.

65. Meinecke, *Cosmopolitanism and the National State,* pp. 226, 343.

66. Werner Stark, "Editor's Introduction," Meinecke, *Machiavellianism,* pp. xi–xlvi.

67. Hartmut Lehmann, ed., with the assistance of Kenneth F. Ledford, *An Interrupted Past: German-Speaking Refugee Historians in the United States after 1933* (Cambridge and Washington, DC: German Historical Institute, Washington DC, and Cambridge University, 1991).

68. Haslam, *No Virtue like Necessity,* pp. 184–185.

69. Woodruff Smith, *The Ideological Origins of Nazi Imperialism* (New York: Oxford University Press, 1996), pp. 18–19, 52–63.

70. Smith, *The Ideological Origins of Nazi Imperialism,* pp. 18–19, 52–63.

PART II: ANTI-REALPOLITIK AND
THE ANGLO-AMERICAN WORLDVIEW

1. Walter E. Weyl, "American Policy and European Opinion," *Annals of the American Academy of Political and Social Science* 666, *Preparedness and America's International Program* (July 1916): 140–146.

CHAPTER 5. THE ENGLISH DISCOVERY OF *REALPOLITIK*

1. For a brilliant rebuttal of this false and ahistorical dichotomy, see Lucian M. Ashworth, *A History of International Thought: From the Origins of the Modern State to Academic International Relations* (London: Routledge, 2014), pp. 134–180.
2. Constantin Frantz, "The Religion of National Liberalism," reviewed in *Illustrated Review: A Fortnightly Journal of Literature, Science and Art* 4.5 (December 1872): 346.
3. John A. Moses, "The British and German Churches and the Perception of War, 1908–1914," *War and Society* 5.1 (May 1987):23–44.
4. See David Runciman, *Political Hypocrisy: The Mask of Power, from Hobbes to Orwell and Beyond* (Princeton, NJ: Princeton University Press, 2008), pp. 142–168.
5. John Morley, "Machiavelli" (from a lecture delivered in Oxford, 2 June 1897), in John Morley, *Miscellanies*, fourth series (London: Macmillan, 1908), pp. 1–53.
6. Niall Ferguson, *The Pity of War, 1914–1918*, (Harmondsworth: Penguin, 1998), chapters 1–4.
7. *Bismarck: The Memoirs*, translated by A. J. Butler, 2 vols. (New York: Howard Fertig, 1966), vol. 1, p. 125.
8. A. J. P. Taylor, *Bismarck: The Man and the Statesman* (London: New English Library, 1965), pp. 186–187.
9. Paul Kennedy, *The Rise of the Anglo-German Antagonism, 1860–1914* (Boston: George Allen and Unwin, 1980), pp. 26–27, 392–393, 466–467.
10. *Times*, 3 December 1895.
11. Raymond J. Sontag, "The Cowes Interview and the Kruger Telegram," *Political Science Quarterly* 40.2 (June 1925): 217–247. See also Zara S. Steiner and Keith Nelson, *Britain and the Origins of the First World War* (Houndsmill: Palgrave Macmilllan, 2003), pp. 19–22.
12. Lieutenant-Colonel J. M. Grierson to Sir F. Lascelles, Berlin, 19 January 1898, in G. P. Gooch and Harold Temperley, eds., *British Documents on the Origins of the War, 1898–1914*, 3 vols. (London, 1927), vol. 1, pp. 42–43.
13. Lieutenant-Colonel J. M. Grierson to Sir F. Lascelles, Berlin, 1 February 1898, in Gooch and Temperley, *British Documents on the Origins of the War*, vol. 1, pp. 43–44.
14. Memorandum by Mr. Bertie, 9 November 1901, in Gooch and Temperley, *British Documents on the Origins of the War*, vol. 2, pp. 73–76.

15. Gooch and Temperley, *British Documents on the Origins of the War,* vol. 1, p. 334.

16. *Times,* 23 November 1901.

17. *Die Zeit,* 14 November 1902.

18. J. A. Hobson, *Imperialism: A Study* (London: James Nisbet, 1902), pp. 12–13.

19. Hobson, *Imperialism,* pp. 12–13.

20. Sidney Low, "Towards an Imperial Foreign Policy," *Fortnightly Review* 92.551 (November 1912): 789–802.

21. Duncan Bell, "The Victorian Idea of a Global State," in Duncan Bell, ed., *Victorian Visions of Global Order: Empire and International Relations in Nineteenth-Century Political Thought* (Cambridge: Cambridge University Press, 2007), pp. 159–185.

22. H. A. Sargeaunt and Geoffrey West, *Grand Strategy: The Search for Victory* (London: Jonathan Cape, 1942), pp. 60–76.

23. P. M. Kennedy, "Idealists and Realists: British Views of Germany, 1864–1939," *Transactions of the Royal Historical Society* 25 (December, 1975): 137–156. See J. A. Hobson, *The German Panic* (London, 1913).

24. Calchas, "The New German Intrigue," *Fortnightly Review* 76.453 (September 1904): 385–402.

25. Calchas, "The New German Intrigue," 385–402.

26. Zara Steiner, *The Foreign Office and Foreign Policy, 1898–1914* (Cambridge: Cambridge University Press, 1969).

27. "Memorandum on the Present State of British Relations with France and Germany," Foreign Office, 1 January 1907, in Gooch and Temperley, *British Documents on the Origins of the War,* vol. 3, pp. 397–420.

28. Zara S. Steiner and Keith Nelson, *Britain and the Origins of the First World War* (Houndsmill: Palgrave Macmillan, 2003), pp. 46–47.

29. Quoted in *New York Times,* 21 March 1909.

30. Count Osten-Sacken, Russian ambassador at Berlin to Iswolsky, 6–19 February 1909, in Benno Aleksandrovich fon-Zibert, *Entente Diplomacy and the World: Matrix of the History of Europe, 1909–14,* edited by George Abel Schreiner (London : Harper, 1921), pp. 491–492.

31. Quoted in M. L. Dockrill, "British Policy during the Agadir Crisis of 1911," in Francis Harry Hinsley, ed., *British Foreign Policy under Sir Edward Grey* (Cambridge: Cambridge University Press, 1977), pp. 271–287.

32. Friedrich von General Bernhardi, *Germany and the Next War,* translated by Allen H. Powles (London: Edward Arnold, 1914).

33. *Times,* 5 April 1912.

34. *Sun,* 14 May 1912.

35. *Times,* 5 April 1912.

36. Cited in P. M. Kennedy, "Idealists and Realists."

37. Quoted in Raymond J. Sontag, "The Germany of Treitschke," *Foreign Affairs* 18.1 (October 1939): 127–139.

38. Davis, *The Political Thought of Heinrich von Treitschke,* pp. 1–9, 35–38, 227–289.

39. *Spectator*, 28 September 1912.

40. *Spectator*, 1 March 1913.

41. *Saturday Review of Politics* 118.3067 (8 August 1914): 167–168.

42. "Psychology and Motives," by the editor, *English Review* (September 1914): 233–247.

43. Tenney Frank, "Commercialism and Roman Territorial Expansion," *Classical Journal* 5.3 (January 1910): 99–110.

44. Ramsay Muir, *Britain's Case against Germany: An Examination of the Historical Background of the German Action in 1914* (Manchester: Manchester University Press, 1914), pp. 26, 50, 67–77.

45. Muir, *Britain's Case against Germany*, pp. vii–ix, 164–194.

46. Radhakrishnan, *The Philosophy of Rabindranath Tagore*, pp. 268–269.

47. "A War Number of the Hibbert Journal," *Manchester Guardian*, 8 October 1914.

48. George Bernard Shaw, "Common Sense about the War," *New York Times*, 15 November 1914.

49. Shaw, "Common Sense about the War." See also "George Bernard Shaw Scores Junker Diplomacy," *Boston Daily Globe*, 22 November 1914.

50. Shaw, "Common Sense about the War."

51. John A. Moses, "The Mobilisation of the Intellectuals 1914–1915 and the Continuity of German Historical Consciousness," *Australian Journal of Politics and History* 48.3 (2002): 336–352.

52. Friedrich Meinecke, *The Warfare of a Nation: Lectures and Essays*, translated by John A. Spaulding (Worcester, MA: Davis Press, 1915), pp. 28, 57–59.

53. Edmund Fawcett, *Liberalism: The Life of an Idea* (Princeton, NJ: Princeton University Press, 2014), p. 166.

54. Meinecke, *Machiavellianism*, pp. 397–398.

55. Meinecke, "National Policy and Civilization" (Freiburg, 4 August 1914), in *The Warfare of a Nation*, pp. 32–37.

56. Friedrich Meinecke, *The Warfare of a Nation*, pp. 28, 57–59.

57. Richard W. Sterling, *Ethics in a World of Power: The Political Ideas of Friedrich Meinecke* (Princeton, NJ: Princeton University Press, 1958), pp. 145–147.

CHAPTER 6. AMERICAN REALPOLITIK

1. Robert Endicott Osgood, *Ideals and Self-Interest in America's Foreign Relations* (Chicago: University of Chicago Press, 1953), pp. 33–37.

2. Noel Maurer, *The Empire Trap: The Rise and Fall of US Intervention to Protect American Property Overseas (1893–2013)* (Princeton, NJ: Princeton University Press, 2013).

3. Robert Kagan, *Dangerous Nation: America and the World, 1600–1898* (London: Atlantic Books, 2006).

4. Osgood, *Ideals and Self-Interest*, pp. 33–37.

5. Quoted in Azar Gat, *The Development of Military Thought: The Nineteenth Century* (Oxford: Oxford University Press, 1992), p. 187.

6. Alfred Thayer Mahan, *The Interest of America in International Conditions* (New York: Sampson Low, Marston & Company, 1910), p. 168.

7. Mahan, quoted in Osgood, *Ideals and Self-Interest*, pp. 33–41.

8. David M. Kennedy, *Over Here: The First World War and American Society* (twenty-fifth anniversary edition) (Oxford; Oxford University Press, 2004), pp. 380–381.

9. Henry Kissinger, *World Order* (London: Allen Lane, 2014), pp. 247–256.

10. *Spectator*, 7 May 1910.

11. Sydney Brooks, "American Foreign Policy," *English Review*, November 1911, pp. 682–695.

12. Robert Holland, *Blue-Water Empire: The British in the Mediterranean since 1800* (London: Allen Lane, 2012).

13. Sydney Brooks, "American Foreign Policy."

14. Amos S. Hershey, *The Independent . . . Devoted to the Consideration of Politics, Social and Economic Tendencies, History, Literature, and the Arts (1848–1921)* 66.3155 (20 May 1909): 1071.

15. Osgood, *Ideals and Self-Interest*, pp. 130–134.

16. *New York Tribune*, 31 October 1914.

17. *Chicago Daily Tribune*, 9 April 1916.

18. *New York Tribune*, 21 November 1915.

19. *New York Times*, 10 June 1916.

20. *Spectator*, 14 October 1916.

21. David Lloyd George, *Memoirs of the Peace Conference* (New Haven, CT: Yale University Press, 1939), vol. 1, p. 21.

22. Osgood, *Ideals and Self-Interest*, pp. 130–134.

23. Walter E. Weyl, "American Policy and European Opinion," *Annals of the American Academy of Political and Social Science*, vol. 666: Preparedness and America's International Program (July 1916), pp. 140–146.

24. Walter Lippman, *U.S. Foreign Policy: Shield of the Republic* (Boston: Little, Brown, 1943), pp. vii–x.

25. Joel H. Rosenthal, *Righteous Realists: Political Realism, Responsible Power and American Culture in the Nuclear Age* (Baton Rouge: Louisiana State University Press, 1991), p. 21.

26. Walter Lippman, *The Stakes of Diplomacy* (New Brunswick: Transaction, 2008; first published 1917), pp. 111–126, 194–195.

27. Lippman, *The Stakes of Diplomacy*, pp. 226–229.

28. T. J. Jackson Lears, "Pragmatic Realism versus the American Century," in Andrew J. Bacevich, ed., *The Short American Century: A Postmortem* (Cambridge. MA: Harvard University Press, 2012), pp. 82–120.

29. Henry Raymond Mussey, "Neglected Realities in the Far East" [31 May 1917], *Proceedings of the Academy of Political Science* 7.3 (July 1917): 538–547.

30. *Nation* 99.2565 (27 August 1914): 251–252. For Bülow, see L. B. Namier, *In the Margin of History* (New York: Freeport, 1939), pp. 213–226.

31. "The Relations of Public Opinion and Foreign Affairs before and during the First World War," in A. O. Sarkisissian, ed., *Studies in Diplomatic History and Historiography in Honor of G. P. Gooch, C.H.* (London: Longmans, Green, 1961), pp. 199–216.

32. Robert C. Binkley, *Realism and Nationalism, 1852–1871* (New York: Harper and Brothers, 1935), pp. 300–302.

33. George Sylvester Viereck, *Confessions of a Barbarian* (New York: Moffat, Yard, 1910).

34. Quoted in Adam Tooze, *The Deluge: The Great War and the Remaking of Global Order* (London: Allen Lane, 2014), p. 66.

35. *Washington Herald*, 2 April 1917.

36. Harold Kellock, "Books Common and Preferred," *New York Tribune*, 8 April 1917.

37. Westel W. Willoughby, *Prussian Political Philosophy* (New York: D. Appleton, 1918), pp. 181–182.

38. "The Real 'Realpolitik,'" *Nation* 108.2805 (1918). The books reviewed were Willoughby, *Prussian Political Philosophy*; Gustavus Myers, *The German Myth*; and Karl Ludwig Krause, *What Is the German Nation Dying For?*

39. *El Paso Herald*, 29 May 1918.

40. *Washington Herald*, 16 March 1918.

CHAPTER 7. THE COMING PEACE AND THE ERADICATION
OF *REALPOLITIK*

1. Gilbert Murray, "Ethical Problems of the War," in Viscount James Bryce, David Lloyd George, et al., *The War of Democracy: The Allies' Statement* (London, 1917), pp. 123–124.

2. Sir Charles Waldstein, *What Is Germany Fighting For?* (London, 1917), p. 116.

3. Charles Sarolea, *German Problems and Personalities* (London, 1917), pp. 111–112, 178.

4. 27 February 1918, *Hansard*, fifth series, vol. 103, 1345–1522.

5. *Spectator*, 23 August 1918.

6. "'Realpolitik'—The First and Most Approved Specimen," *Spectator*, 19 October 1918.

7. Thucydides, *The History of the Peloponnesian War*, translated by Richard Crawley, updated by R. C. Feetham, 2 vols. (Avon, CT: Cardavon Press: 1974), Book Five, vol. 2, pp. 293–299.

8. "'Realpolitik'—The First and Most Approved Specimen," *Spectator*, 19 October 1918.

9. John T. Seaman Jr., *A Citizen of the World: The Life of James Bryce* (London: Taurus Academic Studies, 2006).

10. William Dunning, *The British Empire and the United States: A Review of Their Relations following the Treaty of Ghent* (New York: Charles Scribner's Sons, 1914).

11. Sidney Low, "England and America," *Times Literary Supplement*, 14 January 1915.

12. Casper Sylvester, "Continuity and Change in British Liberal Internationalism, c. 1900–1930," *Review of International Studies* 31.2 (April 2005): 263–283. See also Lucien M. Ashworth, *A History of International Thought: From the Origins of the Modern State to Academic International Relations* (New York: Routledge, 2014), pp.134–180.

13. Kennedy, "Idealists and Realists," pp. 137–156. See also, P. M. Kennedy, "The Decline of Nationalist History in the West," *Journal of Contemporary History* 8 (1973): 91–92.

14. Mark Mazower, *Governing the World: The History of an Idea* (London: Allen Lane, 2012).

15. Ashworth, *A History of International Thought*, pp. 116–121.

16. Niall Ferguson, *The Pity of War, 1914–1918* (Harmondsworth: Penguin, 1998), pp. 21–22.

17. Norman Angell, "The Break and Some English Guesses," *North British Review* 205.738 (May 1917): 698–705.

18. Sir Norman Angell, *The Political Conditions of Allied Success: A Plea for the Protective Union of Democracies* (New York: G.P. Putnam and Sons, 1918), pp. 271–274.

19. Quoted in Ronald Steel, *Walter Lippman and the American Century* (New Brunswick, NJ: Transaction, 1999), pp. 110–112.

20. "Internationalism versus Nationalism," *Athenaeum* 4632 (August 1918): 335–336.

21. David M. Kennedy, *Over Here: The First World War and American Society* (twenty-fifth anniversary edition) (Oxford: Oxford University Press, 2004), pp. 384–390.

22. Thorstein Veblen, *Imperial Germany and the Industrial Revolution, 1857–1929* (New York: Macmillan, 1915).

23. Thorstein Veblen, "The Modern Point of View and the New Order: VI. THE DIVINE RIGHT OF NATIONS," *Dial: A Semi-monthly Journal of Literary Criticism, Discussion and Information* 65 (28 December 1918): 605.

24. *Spectator*, 26 October 1918.

25. Kennedy, *Over Here: The First World War and American Society*, p. 359.

26. Sir Halford J. Mackinder, *Democratic Ideals and Reality: A Study in the Politics of Reconstruction* (London: Constable, 1919), pp. 5, 16.

PART III: INTERWAR REALPOLITIK

1. Article quoted by Labour Party leader, Clement Attlee, in House of Commons, 2 May 1938, *Hansard*, vol. 335, cc. 769–822.

CHAPTER 8. THE INGESTION OF REALPOLITIK

1. A. Chamberlain to Hilda, 26 December 1925, in Robert C. Self, ed., *The Austen Chamberlain Diary Letters: The Correspondence of Sir Austen Chamberlain* (Cambridge: Cambridge University Press, 1995), p. 271.
2. For Neville Chamberlain's reading of Castlereagh and George Canning during the 1930s, see John Bew, *Castlereagh: a Life* (Oxford: Oxford University Press, 2012), pp. xi–xii, 5, 178, 181, 409, 488,
3. Gordon Martel, "The Pre-history of Appeasement: Headlam-Morley, the Peace Settlement and Revisionism," *Diplomacy and Statecraft* 9.3 (November, 1998): 242–265.
4. Cabinet Memorandum: Weekly Report on Germany, 13 December 1917, UK National Register of Archives, London, CAB 24/35/72.
5. The Coming German Peace Offensive, by Political Intelligence Department at the Foreign Office, 28 August 2014, UK National Register of Archives, London, CAB 24/62/39.
6. Cabinet Memorandum: Report on the Pan-Turanian Movement, 1 October 1917, UK National Register of Archives, London, CAB 24/33/82.
7. Cabinet Memorandum: Weekly Report on Russia. XXXV. The Bolsheviks and the Peace Negotiations, 9 January 1918, UK National Register of Archives, London, CAB 24/38/85.
8. E. H. Carr, *The October Revolution* (New York: Alfred A. Knopf, 1969), pp. 174–175.
9. Martin Jay, *Marxism and Totality: The Adventures of a Concept from Lukács to Habermas* (Berkeley: University of California Press, 1984), p. 121.
10. *New York Tribune*, 18 March 1921.
11. Joseph Heller, "Britain and the Armenian Question, 1912–1914: A Study in Realpolitik," *Middle Eastern Studies* 16.1 (January 1980): 3–26.
12. Jeremy Wilson, *Lawrence of Arabia: The Authorized Biography* (New York: Atheneum, 1990), p. 220.
13. Minute by Vansittart, 19 June 1919. Cited in Erik Goldstein, *Winning the Peace: British Diplomatic Strategy, Peace Planning, and the Paris Peace Conference 1916–1920* (Oxford: Oxford University Press, 1991), p. 275.
14. Marvin Swartz, *The Union of Democratic Control in British Politics during the First World War* (Oxford: Clarendon, 1971), p. 132.
15. Hamilton Fish Armstrong, *Peace and Counterpeace: From Wilson to Hitler. Memoirs of Hamilton Fish Armstrong* (New York: Harper and Row, 1971), p. 238.
16. W. Alison Phillips, "The Peace Settlement: 1815 and 1919," *Edinburgh Review* 230.469 (July 1919): 1–21.

17. W. A. Phillips, *The Confederation of Europe: A Study of the European Alliance, 1813–1823* (London: Longmans, Green, 1914), p. 147.

18. Gordon Martel, "The Pre-History of Appeasement: Headlam-Morley, the Peace Settlement and Revisionism," *Diplomacy and Statecraft* 9.3 (November 1998): 242–265. In 1928, Headlam-Morley wrote an introduction to an edited collection of documents on German relations with Britain from 1871 to 1914 in which he recounted—with some sympathy—the missteps made by both. See James Headlam-Morley, "Introduction," in E. T. S. Dugdale, ed., *German Diplomatic Documents, 1871–1914,* vol 1: *Bismarck's Relations with England, 1871–1890* (London: Meuthen, 1928), pp. xi–xxviii.

19. "Realpolitik," *Times Literary Supplement,* 3 August 1922. See also Ferguson, *Pity of War,* p. xxxv.

20. Martel, "The Pre-History of Appeasement."

21. *New York Tribune,* 14 September 1920.

22. *New York Tribune,* 9 January 1921.

23. Bulletin of the Pan American Union 52, January–June 1921, US Congressional Serial Set, vol. 7891, Session vol. no. 97, 66th Congress, 3rd session, p.130.

24. [1928] Memorandum on the Monroe Doctrine, prepared by J. Reuben Clark, Undersecretary of State, presented by Mr. Dill, 6 January 1930, US Congressional Serial Set, vol. 9202, Session vol. no. 5, 71st Congress, 2nd session S. Doc. 114, p. 60. See also Phillips, *The Confederation of Europe,* p. 67.

25. James G. McDonald, "A New Code of International Morality," *Annals of the American Academy of Political and Social Science* 132 (July 1927): 193–196.

26. Adam Tooze, *The Deluge: The Great War and the Remaking of Global Order* (London: Allen Lane, 2014), pp. 511–518.

27. Sir Esme Howard, "The Way toward Peace," *Annals of the American Academy of Political and Social Science* 114 (July 1924): 132–134.

28. Cabinet Memorandum: Anglo-American Relations, Dispatch from Sir E. Howard to Sir A. Chamberlain, 31 January 1929, UK National Register of Archives, London, CAB 24/201/43.

CHAPTER 9. POSTWAR GERMAN AND THE *REALPOLITIK* REVIVAL

1. Quoted in Paul M. Kennedy, *The Realities behind Diplomacy: Background Influences on British External Policy, 1865–1980* (London: Fontana Press, 1985), p. 223.

2. Max Weber, "Politics as a Vocation," in H. H. Gerth and C. Wright Mills, eds., *From Max Weber: Essays in Sociology* (New York: Oxford University Press, 1946).

3. Michael Joseph Smith, *Realist Thought from Weber to Kissinger* (Baton Rouge: Louisiana State University Press, 1986).

4. Heikki Patomäki, *After International Relations: Critical Realism and the (Re) Construction of World Politics* (London: Routledge, 2002), pp. 34–37.

5. James Alfred Aho, *German Realpolitik and American Sociology: An Inquiry into the Sources and Political Significance of the Sociology of Conflict* (Lewisburg: Bucknell University Press, 1975), p. 53.

6. Wolfgang J. Mommsen, *Max Weber and German Politics, 1890–1920* (Chicago: Chicago University Press, 1984), pp. 8–9

7. Mommsen, *Max Weber*, pp. 43–44.

8. Stefan Eich and Adam Tooze, "Max Weber, Politics and the Crisis of Historicism" (Yale University, Departments of Political Science and History), unpublished paper, cited with permission of the authors.

9. Quoted in *New York Tribune*, 16 February 1920.

10. Dr. F. W. Foerster, "The League of Nations as League of Culture," *Living Age* 8.310 (2 July 1921).

11. E. A. Sonnenschein, "The German Professors," *Twentieth Century* 86 (August 1919): 321–332.

12. Cited in Eich and Tooze, "Max Weber, Politics and the Crisis of Historicism."

13. Quoted in Raymond James Sontag, *Germany and England: Background of Conflict, 1848–1898* (New York: D. Appleton Century, 1938), pp. 334–335.

14. Frederick Baumann, "Sir Thomas More," *Journal of Modern History* 4.4 (December 1932): 604–615.

15. Hajo Holborn, *A History of Modern Germany, 1840–1945* (New York: Alfred A. Knopf, 1969), pp. 656–661.

16. Hans Lühman, *Die Unfange August Ludwig von Rochaus, 1810–1850* (Heidelberg, 1921). Discussed in Menzel, "August Ludwig von Rochau," pp. 3–4.

17. Hermann Oncken, *Napoleon III and the Rhine: The Origin of the War of 1870–1871*, translated by Edwin H. Zeydel (New York: Russell and Russell, 1928).

18. Felix R. Hirsch, "Hermann Oncken and the End of an Era," *Journal of Modern History* 18.2 (June 1946):148–159.

19. Menzel, "August Ludwig von Rochau," pp. 3–5.

20. *New York Tribune*, 5 February 1920.

21. Harry Elmer Barnes, "Towards Historical Sanity," *Journal of Social Forces* 3.2 (January 1925): 365–369. The book was Mildred S. Wertheimer, *The Pan-German League, 1890–1914* (New York: Longmans, 1924).

22. Robert A. Pois, *Friedrich Meinecke and German Politics in the Twentieth Century* (Berkeley: University of California Press, 1972), pp. 35–37.

23. Eich and Tooze, "Max Weber, Politics and the Crisis of Historicism."

24. Meinecke, *Machiavellism*, pp. 424–425.

25. Meinecke, *Machiavellism*, pp. 424–433.

26. Meinecke, *Machiavellism*, pp. 392–408.

27. Meinecke, *Machiavellism*, pp. 397–398.

28. Meinecke, *Machiavellism*, pp. 424–433.

29. Quoted in Richard W. Sterling, *Ethics in a World of Power: The Political Ideas of Friedrich Meinecke* (Princeton, NJ: Princeton University Press, 1958), pp. 202–204.

30. Quoted in Sterling, *Ethics in a World of Power*, pp. 199–200, 248–250.

31. Meinecke, *Machiavellism,* pp. 424–33.

32. Cited in Tooze, *The Deluge,* p. 26.

33. Christian Gauss, "New Factors in Franco-German Relations," *Annals of the American Academy of Political and Social Science* 126 (July 1926): 19–21.

34. Pois, *Friedrich Meinecke and German Politics,* pp. 68–69.

35. "America: Slave or Free? Europe's 'Revolution' Is Counterrevolution," *Christian Science Monitor,* 4 April 1941.

36. Paul Mendes-Flour, *Divided Passions: Jewish Intellectuals and the Experience of Modernity* (Detroit: Wayne State University Press, 1991), pp. 318–320.

37. Mendes-Flour, *Divided Passions,* pp. 168–178, 234, 392, 396.

38. Hans Khon, *Prophets and Peoples: Studies in Nineteenth Century Nationalism* (New York: Macmillan, 1946).

39. Thomas G. Masaryk, "Reflections on the Question of War Guilt," in Hamilton Fish Armstrong, ed., *The Foreign Affairs Reader* (London and New York: Council on Foreign Relations/Harper and Brothers, 1947), pp. 1–23.

40. Eva Schmidt-Hartmann, *Thomas G. Masaryk's Realism: Origins of a Czech Political Concept* (Munich: R. Oldenbourg Verlag, 1984), pp. 64–65.

41. Wickham Steed, "Thomas Garrigue Masaryk: The Man and the Teacher," *Slavonic and East European Review* 8.24 (March 1930): 465–477.

42. A. J. P. Taylor, "Thomas Garrigue Masaryk: Humane Nationalism's Last Exponent," *Manchester Guardian,* 7 March 1950.

CHAPTER 10. REALPOLITIK, FASCISM, AND APPEASEMENT

1. William Kilborne Stewart, "The Mentors of Mussolini," *American Political Science Review* 22 (November 1928): 843–869.

2. Luigi Sturzo, "Politics versus Morality: From the Hibbert Journal London Quarterly of Philosophy and Theology," *Living Age* 353.4456 (January 1938): 312–319.

3. Rev. J. C. Hardwick, "Tyranny or Democracy?" *Saturday Review,* 13 September 1930, pp. 306–307.

4. Horace L. Friess, "The Progress of German Philosophy in the Last Hundred Years," *Journal of Philosophy* 27.15 (27 July 1930): 396–415.

5. Hans Kohn, "Treitschke: National Prophet," *The Power of Politics* 7.4 (October 1945): 418–440.

6. Hans Kohn, *Revolutions and Dictatorships* (Cambridge, MA: Harvard University Press, 1939), pp. 4–7, 76–80, 183–184.

7. Kohn, *Revolutions and Dictatorships,* pp. 4–7, 76–80, 128–143, 423.

8. Hans Speier, "Germany in Danger: Concerning Oswald Spengler's Latest Book," *Social Research* 1.2 (May 1934): 231–243.

9. Quoted in Fritz Stern, *The Politics of Cultural Despair: A Study in the Rise of Germanic Ideology* (Berkeley: University of California Press, 1961), p. 298.

10. John W. Wheeler-Bennett, "European Possibilities," *Virginia Quarterly Review,* Autumn 1937.

11. Peter Viereck, *Metapolitics: From Wagner and the German Romantics to Hitler* (New York: Alfred A. Knopf, 1965), pp. 189–208.

12. Quoted in Zara Steiner, *The Triumph of the Dark: European International History, 1933–1939* (Oxford: Oxford University Press, 2011), p. 33.

13. Robert Vansittart, Cabinet Memorandum: Disarmament. Proposed Anglo-Italian Conversations, 21 August 1933, UK National Register of Archives, London, CAB 24/243/4.

14. Francis Gower, "Mussolini: Realist or Romanticist," *Spectator*, 1 September 1935.

15. House of Lords, 7 May 1935, *Hansard*, vol. 96, cc. 769–822.

16. Quoted in House of Commons debate, 2 May 1938, *Hansard*, vol. 335, cc. 769–822.

17. John D. Fair, *Harold Temperley: A Scholar and Romantic in the Public Realm* (Newark: University of Delaware Press, 1992), pp. 50–51, 165, 278–279, 288.

18. J. A. de C. Hamilton, Cairo, 28 March 1937, Eastern Affairs, Further Correspondence, UK National Register Archives, London, Parts XL-XLI, FCO 406/75.

19. Karl Loewenstein, "Militant Democracy and Fundamental Rights," *American Political Science Review* 31.3 (June 1937): 417–432.

20. House of Commons, 2 May 1938, *Hansard*, vol. 335, cc. 769–822.

21. Arno Dosch-Fleurot, "European 'Realpolitik,'" *Sun*, 26 December 1938.

22. Joel Quirk and Darshan Vigneswaran, "The Construction of an Edifice: The Story of a First Great Debate," *Review of International Studies* 31 (2005): 89–107. See also Lucian M. Ashworth, "Did the Realist-Idealist Great Debate Really Happen? A Revisionist History of International Relations," *International Relations* 16.33 (2002): 33–51.

23. E. H. Carr, *The Twenty Years' Crisis, 1919–1939* (London: Macmillan, 1946), pp. 12, 25–26, 38–43.

24. Carr, *The Twenty Years' Crisis*, pp. 89–94.

25. Carr, *The Twenty Years' Crisis*, pp. 72, 76–83.

26. Carr, *The Twenty Years' Crisis*, pp. 72, 76–83, 234–235.

27. Jonathan Haslam, *The Vices of Integrity: E. H. Carr 1892–1928* (London: Verso, 2000).

28. See Michael Cox's introduction to E. H. Carr, *The Twenty Years' Crisis: An Introduction to the Study of International Relations*, ed. Michael Cox (Basingstoke: Palgrave, 2001). See also Michael Cox, ed., *E. H. Carr: A Critical Appraisal* (Basingstoke: Palgrave, 2000) and Michael Cox, "E. H. Carr and the Crisis of Twentieth Century Liberalism," *Millennium: Journal of International Studies* 38.3 (1999): 1–11.

29. Carr, *The Twenty Years' Crisis*, pp. 25–26, 32–38, 51.

30. Meinecke, *Machiavellism*, pp. 424–433.

31. Stefan Collini, *Common Reading: Critics, Historians, Publics* (Oxford: Oxford University Press, 2008), p. 166.

32. Quirk and Vigneswaran, "The Construction of an Edifice," pp. 89–107.

33. Ashworth, "Did the Realist-Idealist Great Debate Really Happen?" 33–51.

34. P. M. Kennedy, "Idealists and Realists: British Views of Germany, 1864–1939," *Transactions of the Royal Historical Society* 25 (December 1975): 137–156.

35. Lucian M. Ashworth, "Where Are the Idealists in Interwar International Relations?" *Review of International Studies* 32.2 (April 2006): 291–308; Lucian M. Ashworth, *Creating International Studies: Angell, Mitrany and the Liberal Tradition* (Aldershot: Ashgate, 1999).

36. Ashworth, "Did the Realist-Idealist Great Debate Really Happen?" See also Peter Wilson, "The Myth of the "First Great Debate," *Review of International Studies* 24.5 (December 1998): 1–15.

37. Quoted in Zara Steiner, *The Triumph of the Dark: European International History, 1933–1939* (Oxford University Press: Oxford, 2011), pp. 1048–1050. See also Zara Steiner, "British Decisions for Peace and War, 1938–1939: The Rise and Fall of Realism," in Ernest R. May, Richard Rosecrance, and Zara Steiner, eds., *History and Neo-realism* (Cambridge: Cambridge University Press, 2010), pp. 129–154

38. These quotations are from Ian Hall, "Power Politics and Appeasement: Political Realism in British International Thought, c. 1935-1955," *British Journal of Politics and International Relations*, vol. 8 (2006), pp. 174–192. For A. G. Arnold's article, see "Realpolitik," *Cambridge Journal* (1946) vol. 2, no. 7, pp. 410–419.

39. Quoted in David Runciman, *Political Hypocrisy: The Mask of Power, from Hobbes to Orwell and Beyond* (Princeton, NJ: Princeton University Press, 2008), pp. 180–181.

40. Attlee statement on death of Franklin Roosevelt, *Clement Attlee Papers*, Bodleian Library Oxford, Attlee MS dep. 17.

41. H. A. Sargeaunt and Geoffrey West, *Grand Strategy: The Search for Victory* (London: Jonathan Cape, 1942), pp. 13–24, 46–59.

42. F. A. Hayek, *The Road to Serfdom* (Abingdon: Routledge, 1944), pp. 222–223.

43. House of Commons, 23 January 1948, *Hansard*, vol. 446, cc. 529–622.

44. Carr, *The Twenty Years' Crisis*, pp. 151–152.

45. House of Commons, 23 January 1948, *Hansard*, vol. 446 cc. 529–622.

PART IV: REALPOLITIK AND THE TANGLED ROOTS
OF AMERICAN REALISM

1. Frank Tannenbaum, "Against Realpolitik," [Baltimore] *Sun*, 2 October 1953.

CHAPTER 11. GEOPOLITICS AND THE ETHICS
OF AMERICAN STATECRAFT

1. E. H. Carr, *The Twenty Years' Crisis*, p. 234.

2. Francis W. Coker, *Recent Political Thought* (New York: Appleton-Century-Crofts, 1934), pp. 433–459.

3. Harold G. Carlson, "American Loan Words from German," *American Speech* 15.2 (April 1940): 205–208.

4. *Forum and Century* 103.4 (April 1940): 209.

5. Walter Weyl to Reinhold Niebuhr, 24 October 1918, *The Reinhold Niebuhr Papers*, Library of Congress, Washington DC, Correspondence, Box 3.

6. Paul Merkley, *Reinhold Niebuhr: A Political Account* (Montreal: McGill-Queen's University Press, 1975), pp. 18–19.

7. Josef Joffe, "Bismarck or "Britain? Toward an American Grand Strategy after Bipolarity," *International Security* 19.4 (Spring 1995): 94–117.

8. Frederick Schuman, *International Politics: An Introduction to the Western State System* (New York: McGraw-Hill, 1937), pp. vii–xv.

9. Quoted in William R. Kinter and Robert L. Pfaltzgraff Jr., eds., *Strategy and Values: Selected Writings of Robert Strausz-Hupé* (Toronto: Lexington Books, 1973), pp. 81–83.

10. Sir Halford J. Mackinder, *Democratic Ideals and Reality: A Study in the Politics of Reconstruction* (London: Holt, 1942), pp. 5, 16.

11. For an excellent discussion of American geopolitics, see Robert Kaplan, *The Revenge of Geography: What the Map Tells Us about Coming Conflicts and the Battle against Fate* (New York: Random House, 2012), pp. 79–102.

12. Quoted in Hans Kohn, *Revolutions and Dictatorships* (Cambridge, MA: Harvard University Press, 1939), p. 410.

13. Walter Lippmann, *U.S. Foreign Policy: Shield of the Republic* (Boston: Little, Brown, 1943), pp. 175–177.

14. Ronald Steel, *Walter Lippmann and the American Century* (New Brunswick: Transaction, 1999), pp. 404–417.

15. Lippmann, *U.S. Foreign Policy*, pp. 175–177.

16. Quincy Wright, *A Study of War* (Chicago: University of Chicago Press, 1964), p. 365.

17. Robert Kaplan, *The Wizards of Armageddon* (Stanford, CA: Stanford University Press, 1991), pp. 10–15.

18. Matthew Farish, *The Contours of America's Cold War* (Minneapolis: University of Minnesota Press, 2010), p. 25.

19. Arnold Wolfers, *Britain and France between the Two Wars: Conflicting Strategies of Peace since Versailles* (New York: Harcourt, Brace, 1940).

20. Kaplan, *The Wizards of Armageddon*, pp. 20, 186–187.

21. Raymond L. Garthoff, *A Journey through the Cold War: A Memoir of Containment and Coexistence* (Washington, DC: Brookings Institution, 2001), p. 6.

22. Nicholas John Spykman, *America's Strategy in World Politics: The United States and the Balance of Power* (New York: Harcourt, Brace, 1942).

23. Spykman, *America's Strategy in World Politics*, p. 7.

24. Inderjeet Parmar, *Foundations of the American Century: The Ford, Carnegie, and Rockefeller Foundations in the Rise of American Power* (New York: Columbia University Press, 2012), p. 71.

25. Glenn Segel, *Nuclear Strategy: The Jim King Manuscripts* (London: Glenn Segel, 2006), pp. 47–49.

26. Parmar, *Foundations of the American Century*, pp. 68–73.

27. Kaplan, *The Wizards of Armageddon*, pp. 20, 186–187.

28. Parmar, *Foundations of the American Century*, pp. 68–73.

29. Edward Meade Earle, "National Security and Foreign Policy," *Yale Review* 29 (March 1940): 444–460.

30. Parmar, *Foundations of the American Century*, pp. 68–73, 96.

31. Edward Meade Earle, Gordon Alexander Craig, and Felix Gilbert, *Makers of Modern Military Strategy from Machiavelli to Hitler* (Princeton, NJ: Princeton University Press, 1943).

32. Farish, *The Contours of America's Cold War*, pp. 1–49.

33. This argument is made by Michael Lind, "The Case for American Nationalism," *National Interest*, 22 April 2014.

34. Quoted in John A. Thompson, "The Geopolitical Vision: The Myth of an Outdated USA," in Joel Isaac and Duncan Bell, ed., *Uncertain Empire: American History and the End of the Cold War* (Oxford: Oxford University Press, 2012), pp. 91–114.

35. Robert Endicott Osgood, *Ideals and Self-Interest in America's Foreign Relations* (Chicago: University of Chicago Press, 1953), pp. 381–402.

36. Osgood, *Ideals and Self-Interest*, p. 381–402.

37. Reinhold Niebuhr, "Augustine's Political Realism," in Robert McAfee Brown, ed., *The Essential Reinhold Niebuhr: Selected Essays and Addresses* (New Haven, CT: Yale University Press, 1986), pp. 123–142.

38. William Inboden, "The Prophetic Conflict: Reinhold Niebuhr, Christian Realism, and World War II," *Diplomatic History* 38.1 (2014): 49–82.

39. This is the argument of Robert Kaufman, "E. H. Carr, Winston Churchill, Reinhold Niebuhr, and Us: The Case for Principled, Prudential Leadership," in Benjamin Frankel, ed., *Roots of Realism* (London: Frank Cass, 1996), pp. 314–315.

40. Inboden, "The Prophetic Conflict," pp. 49–82.

41. Lucian M. Ashworth, "Did the Realist-Idealist Great Debate Really Happen? A Revisionist History of International Relations," *International Relations* 16.33 (2002): 33–51.

42. William E. Scheuerman, *The Realist Case for Global Reform* (Cambridge: Polity Press, 2001).

43. Osgood, *Ideals and Self-Interest*, p. 381–402.

44. Max Lerner, *Ideas for the Ice Age: Studies in a Revolutionary Era* (New Brunswick: Transaction, 1993), pp. 83–99.

45. Kenneth W. Thompson, "Niebuhr and the Foreign Policy Realists," in Daniel F. Rice, ed., *Reinhold Niebuhr Revisited: Engagements with an American Original* (Grand Rapids: William B. Eerdmans), pp. 139–160.

46. Reinhold Niebuhr, *The Irony of American History* (Chicago: University of Chicago Press, 1952), p. 69.

47. John Lewis Gaddis, *Strategies of Containment* (New York: Oxford University Press, 1982), pp. 32–33.

48. For anything concerning Kennan, the first source must be John Lewis Gaddis, *George F. Kennan: An American Life* (New York: Penguin, 2011).

49. X [George Kennan], "The Sources of Soviet Conduct," *Foreign Affairs*, 1947.

50. See Daniel F. Rice, *Reinhold Niebuhr and His Circle of Influence* (Cambridge: Cambridge University Press, 2013), pp. 174–204.

51. William Inboden, *Religion and American Foreign Policy: The Soul of Containment* (Cambridge: Cambridge University Press, 2008), pp. 18, 105–166.

52. George F. Kennan, *American Diplomacy, 1900–1950* (Chicago: Chicago University Press, 1951), pp. 66–69.

53. Raymond Aron, "The Case for Realpolitik: A French View of Mr. Kennan," *Manchester Guardian*, 21 February 1952.

54. "The Kennan Doctrine," *Washington Post*, 4 May 1952.

55. Inboden, *Religion and American Foreign Policy*, pp. 105–156.

CHAPTER 12. GERMAN ÉMIGRÉS AND AMERICAN REALISM

1. James Alfred Aho, *German Realpolitik and American Sociology: An Inquiry into the Sources and Political Significance of the Sociology of Conflict* (Lewisburg: Bucknell University Press, 1975), pp. 13–60.

2. Hartmut Lehmann, ed., with the assistance of Kenneth F. Ledford, *An Interrupted Past: German-Speaking Refugee Historians in the United States after 1933* (Cambridge and Washington, DC: Cambridge University Press and German Historical Institute, 1991).

3. Hajo Holborn, *A History of Modern Germany 1840–1945* (New York: Alfred A. Knopf, 1969), pp. 117–118, 151.

4. Felix Gilbert, "The Historical Seminar of the University of Berlin in the Twenties," in Lehmann, ed., *An Interrupted Past*, pp. 67–70.

5. Friedrich Meinecke, *Cosmopolitanism and the National State*, translated by Robert B. Kimber, introduction by Felix Gilbert (Princeton, NJ: Princeton University Press, 1970).

6. Holborn, *A History of Modern Germany*, pp. 656–661.

7. Otto P. Pflanze, "The Americanization of Hajo Holborn," in Lehmann, ed., *An Interrupted Past*, pp. 170–179.

8. Holborn, *A History of Modern Germany*, pp. 117–118, 151.

9. Pflanze, "The Americanization of Hajo Holborn," in Lehmann, ed., *An Interrupted Past*, pp. 170–179.

10. Felix Gilbert, *To the Farewell Address: Ideas of American Foreign Policy* (Princeton, NJ: Princeton University Press, 1961).

11. Franz Neumann, Herbert Marcuse, and Otto Kirchheimer, *Secret Reports on Nazi Germany: The Frankfurt School Contribution to the War Effort*, edited by Raffaele Laudani (Princeton, NJ: Princeton University Press, 2014).

12. Heikki Patomäki, *After International Relations: Critical Realism and the (Re) Construction of World Politics* (London: Routledge, 2002), pp. 34–37.

13. Hans J. Morgenthau, *Scientific Man versus Power Politics* (Chicago: Chicago University Press, 1946). See also, Michael C. Williams, *Realism Reconsidered: The Legacy of Hans J. Morgenthau* (Oxford: Oxford University Press, 2007).

14. Hans J. Morgenthau, "Fragments of an Intellectual Autobiography, 1904–1932," in K. Thompson and Robert J. Myers, eds., *A Tribute to Hans Morgenthau* (New Brunswick: Transaction, 1977), pp. 1–9.

15. Jan Willem Honig, "Totalitarianism and Realism: Hans Morgenthau's German Years," *Security Studies* 2.2 (1995): 283–313.

16. Hans Morgenthau to Kenneth Thompson, 24 December 1953, in *Hans J. Morgenthau Papers*, Library of Congress, Washington, DC, Box 56, Folder 7.

17. Greg Russell, *Hans J. Morgenthau and the Ethics of American Statecraft* (Baton Rouge: Louisiana State University, 1991), pp. 1–9.

18. Hans Morgenthau, *Politics among Nations: The Struggle for Power and Peace* (Chicago: University of Chicago Press, 1948), pp. 128–130.

19. George Kennan to Hans Morgenthau, 23 February 1950, *Hans J. Morgenthau Papers*, Box 33, Folder 7.

20. Hans Morgenthau to George Kennan, 10 June 1949, *Hans J. Morgenthau Papers*, Box 33, Folder 7.

21. Joel Quirk and Darshan Vigneswaran, "The Construction of an Edifice: The Story of a First Great Debate," *Review of International Studies* 31 (2005): 89–107.

22. Hans J. Morgenthau, *In Defense of the National Interest: A Critical Examination of American Foreign Policy* (New York: Alfred A. Knopf, 1951), pp. 3–39, 82–86.

23. *The Economist,* 7 June 1951.

24. Frank Tannenbaum, "Against Realpolitik," *Sun*, 2 October 1953. See also Frank Tannenbaum, *The American Tradition in Foreign Policy* (Norman: University of Oklahoma Press, 1955) and Brian C. Schmidt, "The American National Interest Debate," in B. C. Schmidt, ed., *International Relations and the First Great Debate* (Oxford: Routledge, 2012), pp. 94–117.

25. Carl J. Friedrich, "How Enlightened Should Self-Interest Be?" *Yale Review* (1952), in *Hans J. Morgenthau Papers*, Box 115, Folder 4.

26. J. M. Roberts, *Bradford Era*, 11 June 1951.

27. *Nation*, 8 September 1951.

28. Review by A. J. P. Taylor in *Nation*, 8 September 1951, and reply by Morgenthau on 10 November 1951, in *Hans J. Morgenthau Papers*, Box 115, Folder 5.

29. Peter Viereck, *The Shame and Glory of the Intellectuals* (New York: Capricorn Books, 1965), pp. 4, 100–101, 314.

30. Dean Acheson to Hans Morgenthau, 13 April 1958, *Hans J. Morgenthau Papers*, Box 2, Folder 8.

31. Hans Morgenthau to Walter Lippmann, 25 August 1950, *Hans J. Morgenthau Papers*, Box 26, Folder 16.

32. Hans Morgenthau to Walter Lippmann, 3 November 1952, *Hans J. Morgenthau Papers*, Box 26, Folder 16.

33. Hans Morgenthau to Walter Lippmann, 16 December 1955, *Hans J. Morgenthau Papers*, Box 26, Folder 16. Eric Fischer, *The Passing of the European Age* (Cambridge, MA: Harvard University Press, 1948).

34. Hans Morgenthau to George Kennan, 15 March 1954, *Hans J. Morgenthau Papers*, Box 33, Folder 7.

35. Hans Morgenthau to George Kennan, 7 March 1952, *Hans J. Morgenthau Papers*, Box 33, Folder 7.

36. George Kennan to Hans Morgenthau, 7 March 1952, *Hans J. Morgenthau Papers*, Box 33, Folder 7.

37. Hans Morgenthau, "Another 'Great Debate': The National Interest of the United States," *American Political Science Review* 46.4 (1952): 961–962.

38. Ernest W. Lefever, *Ethics and United States Foreign Policy* (New York: Living Age Books, 1957).

39. Hans Morgenthau to Dr. Gottfried-Karl Kindermann, 5 April 1961, *Hans J. Morgenthau Papers*, Box 33, Folder 12.

40. Nicholas Guilhot, ed., *The Invention of International Relations Theory: Realism, the Rockefeller Foundation, and the 1954 Conference on Theory* (New York: Columbia University Press, 2011).

41. Kenneth N. Waltz, *Man, the State and War: A Theoretical Analysis* (New York: Columbia University Press, 1959), pp. 216, 224–238.

42. Paul Schroeder, "Historical Reality vs. Neo-Realist Theory," *International Security* 19.1 (Summer 1994): 108–148 and Karl-Georg Faber, "Realpolitik als Ideologie," *Historiche Zeitschrift* 203.1 (August 1966): 1–45. See also Paul Schroeder, "The Nineteenth Century System: Balance of Power or Political Equilibrium?" *Review of International Studies* 15. 2 (1989): 135–153. For a more recent defense of classic realism against neo-realism, see Sean Molloy, *The Hidden History of Realism: A Genealogy of Power Politics* (Houndsmill: Palgrave, 2006).

43. Waltz, *Man, the State and War*, pp. 216, 224–238.

44. Dr. Gottfried-Karl Kindermann to Hans Morgenthau, 20 March 1961, *Hans J. Morgenthau Papers*, Box 33, Folder 12.

45. Hans Morgenthau to Dr. Gottfried-Karl Kindermann, 5 April 1961, *Hans J. Morgenthau Papers*, Box 33, Folder 12.

46. Hans Morgenthau to Dean Acheson, 30 March 1963, *Hans J. Morgenthau Papers*, Box 2, Folder 8.

47. Joel H. Rosenthal, *Righteous Realists: Political Realism, Responsible Power and American Culture in the Nuclear Age* (Baton Rouge: Louisiana State University Press, 1991), pp. 151–177.

48. Fritz Stern, *The Politics of Cultural Despair: A Study in the Rise of Germanic Ideology* (Berkeley: University of California Press, 1961), pp. xi–xxii. See also

Fritz Stern's *Gold and Iron: Bismarck, Bleichröder, and the Building of the German Empire* (New York: Alfred A. Knopf, 1977).

49. Robert E. Osgood, "Hans Morgenthau's Foreign Policy Impact," *Chicago Tribune*, 27 July 1980.

CHAPTER 13. THE BISMARCK DEBATE

1. Robert Kagan later praised Osgood as one of the most thoughtful of realist thinkers of the past century. See "Superpowers Don't Get to Retire," *New Republic*, 26 May 2014.
2. Osgood, *Ideals and Self-Interest*, pp. ix, 22–23.
3. Osgood, *Ideals and Self-Interest*, pp. 429–433.
4. Walter Lippman to Hans Morgenthau, 28 September 1953, *Hans J. Morgenthau Papers*, Box 26, Folder 16.
5. William Lee Miller, "The American Ethos and the Alliance System," in Arnold Wolfers, ed., *Alliance Policy and the Cold War* (Baltimore: Johns Hopkins University Press, 1959), pp. 31–48.
6. A. J. P. Taylor, *Bismarck: The Man and the Statesman* (London: New English Library, 1965), pp. 209–213.
7. William L. Langer's masterpiece was *An Encyclopedia of World History* (Boston: Houghton Mifflin, 1940). For his reinterpretation of Bismarck, see William L. Langer, "Bismarck as a Dramatist," in A. O. Sarkisissian, ed., *Studies in Diplomatic History and Historiography in Honor of G. P. Gooch, C.H.* (London: Longmans, Green, 1961), pp. 199–216.
8. George F. Kennan, *The Decline of Bismarck's European Order: Franco-Russian Relations 1875–1890* (Princeton, NJ: Princeton University Press, 1981).
9. William Langer review of Otto Hammann, *The World Policy of Germany 1890–1912*, in *Foreign Affairs* (October 1924).
10. Hans Rothfels, "1848—One Hundred Years After," *Journal of Modern History* 20.4 (December 1948): 291–319.
11. Holborn, *A History of Modern Germany*, pp. 656–661.
12. Holborn, *A History of Modern Germany*, pp. 117–118, 151. This built on his earlier work, "Bismarck's Realpolitik," *Journal of the History of Ideas* 21.1 (January–March 1960): 84–98.
13. Otto Pflanze, *Bismarck and the Development of Germany: The Period of Unification, 1815–1871* (Princeton, NJ: Princeton University Press, 1963), pp. 48, 215.
14. Otto Pflanze, "Bismarck's 'Realpolitik,'" *Review of Politics* 20.4 (October 1958): 492–514.
15. John L. Snell, *Illusion and Necessity: The Diplomacy of Global War, 1939–1945* (Boston: Houghton Mifflin, 1963), pp. 8–9, 91, 210, 214–215.
16. Richard Rosecrance, *Action and Reaction in World Politics: International Systems in Perspective* (Boston: Little, Brown, 1963), pp. 103–126.

17. Ludwig August von Rochau, *Grundsätze der Realpolitik auf die staatlichen Zustände Deutschlands*, herausgegeben und eingeleitet von Hans-Ulrich Wehler (Frankfurt and Berlin: Ullstein Buch, 1972).

18. Hans-Ulrich Wehler, "Bismarck's Imperialism, 1862–1890," in James Sheehan, ed., *Imperial Germany* (New York: Viewpoints, 1976), pp. 180–222.

19. Hans-Ulrich Wehler, *The German Empire, 1817–1918*, translated by Kim Traynor (Leamington Spa: Berg Publishers, 1985). Roger Fletcher, "Recent Developments in West German Historiography: The Bielefeld School and Its Critics," *German Studies Review* 7.3 (October 1984): 451–480.

20. Werner Stark, "Editor's Introduction" to Friedrich Meinecke, *Machiavellism: The Doctrine of Raison d'État and Its Place in Modern History*, translated by Douglas Scott (New Haven, CT: Yale University Press, 1957), pp. xi–xlvi. See also Werner Stark, *The Sociology of Knowledge: An Essay in Aid of a Deeper Understanding of Human Ideas* (Glencoe, IL: Free Press, 1958).

21. Arnold Wolfers and Laurence W. Martin, *The Anglo-American Tradition in Foreign Affairs: Readings from Thomas More to Woodrow Wilson* (New Haven, CT: Yale University Press, 1956), pp. ix–xxvii.

PART V: PRACTICAL REALPOLITIK

1. Frank W. Wayman and Paul F. Diehl, eds., *Reconstructing Realpolitik* (Ann Arbor: University of Michigan Press, 1994), pp. 205–225.

CHAPTER 14. REALPOLITIK BEFORE DÉTENTE

1. Alistair Horne, *Kissinger: 1973, the Crucial Year* (New York: Simon and Schuster, 1973), pp. 401–403.

2. Parmar, *Foundations of the American Century*, pp. 68–73.

3. Interview with John W. Holmes, 18 March 1996, Association for Diplomatic Studies and Training Foreign Affairs Oral History Project, Frontline Diplomacy Archive, Library of Congress.

4. David Maraniss, "Bill Clinton and Realpolitik," *Washington Post*, 25 October 1992.

5. Schuman, *International Politics*, pp. vii–xv.

6. Henry Kissinger, "Memorial Remarks for Hans Morgenthau," 23 July 1980, http://www.henryakissinger.com/eulogies/072380.html.

7. Interview with John J. Harter, 22 July 1997, Frontline Diplomacy Archive, Library of Congress.

8. Interview with David Michael Adamson, 5 June 2002, Frontline Diplomacy Archive, Library of Congress.

9. Interview with Frederick A. Becker, 16 November 2004, Frontline Diplomacy Archive, Library of Congress.

10. Hans Morgenthau to Dean Acheson, 30 March 1963, *Hans Morgenthau Papers*, Box 2, Folder 8.

11. Dean Acheson to Hans Morgenthau, 25 March 1963, *Hans Morgenthau Papers*, Box 2 Folder 8.

12. David Halberstam, *The Best and the Brightest* (New York: Modern Library, 2001), p. 706.

13. Herbert Marcuse to Hans J. Morgenthau, [undated] May 1965, *Hans J. Morgenthau Papers*, Box 37, Folder 9.

14. Herbert Marcuse, *Reason and Revolution: Hegel and the Rise of Social Theory* (Atlantic Highlands, NJ: Humanities Press, 1954).

15. Herbert Marcuse, *The New Left and the 1960s: Collected Papers of Herbert Marcuse*, vol. 3 (London: Routledge, 2005).

16. Jeremy Suri, *Power and Protest: Global Revolution and the Rise of Détente* (Cambridge, MA: Harvard University Press, 2003).

17. Noam Chomsky, *American Power and the New Mandarins* (New York: Random House, 2002), p. 416.

18. Chomsky, *American Power and the New Mandarins*, pp. 12, 32, 45, 480.

19. Chomsky, *American Power and the New Mandarins*, p. 416.

20. Chomsky, *American Power and the New Mandarins*, p. 416.

21. Irving Kristol, "Machiavelli and the Profanation of Politics," in Polanyi Festschrift Committee, ed., *The Logic of Personal Knowledge: Essays by Various Contributors Presented to Michael Polanyi on His Seventieth Birthday* (London: Routledge and Kegan Paul, 1961), pp. 151–164.

22. Irving Kristol, "American Intellectuals and Foreign Policy," *Foreign Affairs* (July 1967).

23. Kristol, "American Intellectuals and Foreign Policy."

24. Norman Podhoretz, "Following Irving," in Christopher C. DeMuth and William Kristol, eds., *The Neoconservative Imagination: Essays in Honor of Irving Kristol* (Washington, DC: American Enterprise Institute, 1995), pp. 57–62.

25. Cited in Richard A. Falk, "What's Wrong with Henry Kissinger's Foreign Policy," *Alternatives* 1 (1975): 79–100.

26. Dean Acheson, *Present at the Creation: My Years in the State Department* (New York: W.W. Norton, 1969), p. 164.

27. Ambassador to China (Stuart) to the Secretary of State, Nanking, 20 August 1946, *Foreign Relations of the United States*, vol. 8: *The Far East* (Washington, DC, 1971), pp. 301–302.

28. Lord Kennett, House of Lords debate, 31 July 1963, *Hansard*, vol. 252, cc. 1214–1248.

29. House of Commons, 16 July 1958, *Hansard*, vol. 591, cc. 1240–1371.

30. Cabinet Memorandum: Gaullism by Richard A. Butler [sharing a paper by Dr. David Thomson of Cambridge University], 12 May 1964, UK National Register of Archives, CAB 129/118/2.

31. Instruction from the Department of State to the Legation in Hungary, Washington, October 21, 1960, *Foreign Relations of the United States, 1958–1960,* Vol. 10, Part 1, Eastern Europe Region, Soviet Union, Cyprus, Document 33, Department of State, Central Files, 033.6411/10–2160. Secret; Limited Distribution. Drafted by Steven D. Zagorski (INR/IRC), accessed on 18 August 2014, http://history.state.gov/historicaldocuments/frus1958-60v10p1/d33#fn-source.

32. Interview with Robert Gerald Livingston, 6 February 1998, Frontline Diplomacy Archive, Library of Congress.

33. "World Objectives of International Communism," address to the Inter-American Defense Board, 9 December 1958, available in the CIA files, *CREST,* US National Archives.

34. "Recent Soviet Tactics in the Sino-Soviet Dispute," *Central Intelligence Agency: Intelligence Memorandum,* 18 November 1963, *CREST,* US National Archives, CIA/RS 63-18, 18 November 1963.

35. Telegram from the Embassy in India to the Department of State, New Delhi, March 5, 1963, 9 PM, *Foreign Relations of the United States, 1961–1963,* Volume 19, South Asia, Document 262, Source: Department of State, Central Files, DEF 1-4 INDIA. Top Secret; Operational Immediate, accessed on 18 August 2014, http://history.state.gov/historicaldocuments/frus1961-63v19/d262#fn-source.

36. Special National Intelligence Estimate 31'72, Washington, August 3, 1972, *Foreign Relations of the United States, 1969–1976,* Volume E–7, Documents on South Asia, 1969–1972, Document 298, Central Intelligence Agency, Job 79'R01012A, NIC Files. Secret; Sensitive; Controlled Dissem., http://history.state.gov/historicaldocuments/frus1969-76ve07/d298#fn1.

37. Paper by Robert W. Komer of the National Security Council Staff, Washington, 20 October 1962, *Foreign Relations of the United States, 1961–1963,* Volume 18, Near East, 1962–1963, Document 85, Source: Kennedy Library, President's Office Files, Countries, Iran 11/1/62–11/30/62. Secret. Accessed on 18 August 2014, http://history.state.gov/historicaldocuments/frus1961-63v18/d85#fn1.

38. Letter from the Deputy Assistant Secretary of Defense for International Security Affairs (Bundy) to the Under Secretary of State (Ball), Washington, 30 December 1963, *Foreign Relations of the United States, 1961–1963,* Volume 9, Foreign Economic Policy, Document 177, Source: Department of State, S/S Briefing Books, 1962–1966: Lot 66 D 219, Executive Branch Committee on Foreign Aid. Personal and Confidential, accessed on 18 August 2014, http://history.state.gov/historicaldocuments/frus1961-63v09/d177#fn-source.

39. John Stothoff Badeau, *The American Approach to the Arab World* (New York and London: Council on Foreign Relations and Harper and Row, 1968), pp. 180–197.

CHAPTER 15. THE KISSINGER EFFECT

1. Walter Laqueur, "Kissinger and the Politics of Détente," *Commentary* (December, 1973).
2. Interview with Henry Kissinger, *Der Spiegel*, 7 June 2009.
3. Kissinger, "The Limits of Universalism," *New Criterion* (June, 2012).
4. Walter Isaacson, *Kissinger: A Biography* (New York: Simon and Schuster, 1992), p. 75.
5. Klitzing, *The Nemesis of Stability: Henry A. Kissinger's Ambivalent Relationship with Germany* (Trier: Wissenschaftlicher Verlag Trier, 2007), pp. 54–62.
6. Fritz Kraemer obituary, *Daily Telegraph*, 10 November 2003.
7. Isaacson, *Kissinger*, pp. 72–79.
8. Henry Kissinger, "Memorial Remarks for Hans Morgenthau," 23 July 1980, http://www.henryakissinger.com/eulogies/072380.html.
9. Henry A. Kissinger, "The Meaning of History: Reflections on Spengler, Toynbee and Kant" (undergraduate honors thesis, Harvard University, 1950).
10. Klitzing, *The Nemesis of Stability*, pp. 63–75.
11. Carl J. Friedrich, "How Enlightened Should Self-Interest Be?" *Yale Review* (1952), in *Hans J. Morgenthau Papers*, Library of Congress, Box 115, Folder 4.
12. Author interview with Henry Kissinger, New York, 7 July 2014.
13. T. G. Otte, "Kissinger," in G. R. Berridge, Maurice Keens-Soper, and T.G. Otte, eds., *Diplomatic Theory from Machiavelli to Kissinger* (Houndsmill: Palgrave, 2001), pp. 181–211.
14. Henry Kissinger, *A World Restored: Metternich, Castlereagh and the Problems of Peace, 1812–1822* (London: Weidenfeld and Nicholson, 1999), pp. 312–322.
15. Thomas J. Noer, "Henry Kissinger's Philosophy of History," *Modern Age* 19 (Spring, 1975): 180–189.
16. Michael Joseph Smith, "Henry Kissinger and the Values of American Realism," in Kenneth W. Thompson, ed., *Traditions and Values: American Diplomacy, 1945 to the Present* (Lanham: United Press of America, 1984), pp. 59–79.
17. Isaacson, *Kissinger*, p. 77.
18. Brendan Simms, *Europe: The Struggle for Supremacy, 1453 to the Present* (London: Penguin, 2014), p. 449.
19. Henry A. Kissinger, "The White Revolutionary: Reflections on Bismarck," *Daedalus* 97.3 (Summer 1968): 888–924.
20. George F. Kennan, *The Decline of Bismarck's European Order: Franco-Russian Relations 1875–1890* (Princeton, NJ: Princeton University Press, 1981).
21. John Lewis Gaddis, *George F. Kennan: An American Life* (New York: Penguin, 2011), pp. 641–642.
22. Henry Kissinger, *Diplomacy* (New York: Simon and Schuster, 1994), Chapter 6, "Realpolitik Turns on Itself."
23. Henry Kissinger, "The Age of Kennan," *New York Times*, 10 November 2011.

24. Henry Kissinger, "Memorial Remarks for Hans Morgenthau," 23 July 1980, http://www.henryakissinger.com/eulogies/072380.html.

25. Hans Morgenthau to Henry Kissinger, 22 October 1968, in *Hans J. Morgenthau Papers*, Box 22, Folder 14.

26. Hans Morgenthau to Reinhold Niebuhr, 12 May 1970, in *Hans J. Morgenthau Papers*, Box 44, Folder 1.

27. Hans J. Morgenthau, "The Pathology of American Power," *International Security* 1.3 (Winter 1977): 3–20.

28. Henry Kissinger, *Years of Renewal* (New York: Touchstone, 2000), p. 476.

29. Michael Hunt, *Ideology and U.S. Foreign Policy* (New Haven, CT: Yale University Press, 1987), pp. 132, 174, 182–187. A salient criticism of Hunt's book is that it was essentially a study of public discourse.

30. See Henry Kissinger, *World Order* (London: Allen Lane, 2014). See review by John Bew, "Altered States," *New Statesman*, 30 October 2015.

31. Interview with the Honorable David L. Mack, 2011, Frontline Diplomacy Archive, Library of Congress.

32. For the best study of the relationship between the two, see Robert Dallek, *Nixon and Kissinger: Partners in Power* (London: Penguin, 2007). See also Alistair Horne, *Kissinger: 1973, The Crucial Year* (New York: Simon and Schuster, 1973), pp. 1–34.

33. Richard Reeves, *President Nixon: Alone in the White House* (New York: Simon and Schuster, 2001), pp. 432–433.

34. Richard Nixon, *RN: The Memoirs of Richard Nixon* (New York: Simon and Schuster, 1978), p. 343.

35. Andrew Johns, *Vietnam's Second Front: Domestic Politics, the Republican Party, and the War* (Lexington: University of Kentucky Press, 2010), p. 196.

36. From the Nixon tapes, quoted in Douglas Brinkley and Luke A. Nichter, "Nixon Unbound," *Vanity Fair*, August 2014.

37. Kissinger, *A World Restored*.

38. Josef Joffe, "'Bismarck' or 'Britain'? Toward an American Grand Strategy after Bipolarity," *International Security* 19.4 (Spring 1995): 94–117.

39. John Bew, "Rethinking Nixon," *New Statesman*, 19 September 2014.

40. Henry A. Kissinger, "Reflections on a Partnership: British and American Attitudes to Postwar Foreign Policy," *Royal Institute of International Affairs*, 10 May 1982, available in the CIA Files, National Archives, College Park, Maryland.

41. Interview with Samuel R. Gammon III, 2 February 1989, Frontline Diplomacy Archive, Library of Congress.

42. Interview with Maurice Williams, 15 May 1996, Frontline Diplomacy Archive, Library of Congress.

43. Interview with Winston Lord, 28 April 1998, Frontline Diplomacy Archive, Library of Congress.

44. Interview with LaRue R. Lutkins, 18 February 1990, Frontline Diplomacy Archive, Library of Congress.

45. Trends in Communist Propaganda, 20 June 1973, CIA files, *CREST*, US National Archives.

46. Secretary of State Kissinger, "Moral Purposes and Policy Choices," 8 October 1973, *Foreign Relations of the United States, 1969–1976*, vol. 38, part 1, Foundations of Foreign Policy, 1973–1976, Document 19.

47. Interview with Robert J. Martens, 13 September 1991, Frontline Diplomacy Archive, Library of Congress.

48. Interview with the Honorable Ints Silins, 25 February 1998, Frontline Diplomacy Archive, Library of Congress.

49. Arthur Schlesinger Jr., *Cycles of American History* (Boston: Mariner Books, 1999), p. 96.

50. Thomas Probert, "The Innovation of the Jackson-Vanik Amendment," in B. Simms and D. Trim, eds., *Humanitarian Intervention; A History* (Cambridge: Cambridge University Press, 2011), pp. 323–342.

51. Interview with Montcrieff J. Spear, 6 April 1993, Frontline Diplomacy Archive, Library of Congress.

52. Horne, *Kissinger*, p. 387.

53. Interview with Walter J. Silva, 23 January 1995, Frontline Diplomacy Archive, Library of Congress. See also Christos P. Ioannides, *Realpolitik in the Eastern Mediterranean: From Kissinger and the Cyprus Crisis to Carter and the Lifting of the Turkish Arms Embargo* (Ann Arbor: University of Michigan, 2001).

54. Interview with Ambassador Thomas D. Boyatt, 8 March 1990, Frontline Diplomacy Archive, Library of Congress.

55. Summary of Paper on Policies on Human Rights and Authoritarian Regimes, Washington, October 1974, *Foreign Relations of the United States, 1969–1976*, Volume E–3, Documents on Global Issues, 1973–1976, Document 243, Source: National Archives, RG 59, L/HR Files: Lot 80 D 275, Human Rights S/P Study—Policy Planning Vol. II. Confidential, accessed on 19 August 2014, http://history.state.gov/historicaldocuments/frus1969-76ve03/d243.

56. Quoted in Ben J. Wattenberg and Richard James Whalen, *The Wealth Weapon: U.S. Foreign Policy and Multinational Corporations* (New Brunswick, NJ: Transaction, 1980), p. 122.

57. Interview with Donald F. McHenry, 23 March 1993, Frontline Diplomacy Archive, Library of Congress.

58. Interview with Dell Pendergrast, 24 June 1999, Frontline Diplomacy Archive, Library of Congress.

59. See Joshua Muravchik, *The Uncertain Crusade: Jimmy Carter and the Dilemmas of Human Rights Policy* (Washington, DC: American Enterprise Institute for Policy Research, 1988).

60. Irving Kristol, "The 'Human Rights' Muddle," *Wall Street Journal*, 20 March 1978.

61. Walter Laqueur, "The Issue of Human Rights," *Commentary*, May 1977.

62. Anthony Lake and Roger Morris, "The Human Reality of Realpolitik," *Foreign Policy* (Fall 1971): 157–162.

63. Memorandum from the Director of the Policy Planning Staff (Lake) to the Deputy Secretary of State (Christopher), Washington, March 25, 1977, *Foreign Relations of the United States, 1977–1980*, vol. II, Human Rights and Humanitarian Affairs, Document 29. Source: National Archives, RG 59, Office of the Deputy Secretary: Records of Warren Christopher, 1977–1980, Lot 81D113, Withdrawn Material, RC #1126, Box 12 of 13. Secret, accessed on 19 August 2014, at http://history.state.gov/historicaldocuments/frus 1977-80v02/d29#fn1.

64. Interview with Ronald J. Neitzke, 1 December 2006, Frontline Diplomacy Archive, Library of Congress.

65. Interview with the Honorable Chester A. Croker, 5 June 2006, Frontline Diplomacy Archive, Library of Congress.

66. Interview with William C. Harrop, 24 August 1993, Frontline Diplomacy Archive, Library of Congress.

67. Interview with Theodore S. Wilkinson, 10 December 1996, Frontline Diplomacy Archive, Library of Congress.

68. Interview with Ambassador Richard W. Teare, 31 July 1998, Frontline Diplomacy Archive, Library of Congress.

69. Charles Gati, *Zbig: The Strategy and Statecraft of Zbigniew Brzezinski* (Baltimore: Johns Hopkins University Press, 2013).

70. For a fascinating discussion of Brzezinski's thinking, see Perry Anderson, *American Foreign Policy and its Thinkers* (London and New York: Verson, 2015), pp. 197-209.

71. Interview with Warren Zimmerman, 10 December 1996, Frontline Diplomacy Archive, Library of Congress.

72. Labour prime minister, Harold Wilson, quoted in John Bew, "Rethinking Nixon," *New Statesman*, 19 September 2014.

CHAPTER 16. FROM COLD WAR TO NEW WORLD ORDER

1. Address by the Honorable Dr. Henry A. Kissinger to the Annual Convention of the American Society of Newspaper Editors, Washington, DC, 10 April 1980, in *Hans J. Morgenthau Papers*, Box 33, Folder 14.

2. Douglas Little, *American Orientalism: The United States and the Middle East since 1945* (Chapel Hill: University of North Carolina Press, 2008), p. 149.

3. Author interview with Jimmy Carter, *New Statesman*, 17 April 2014.

4. Zbigniew Brezinski, "The Twin Strands of American Foreign Policy," *Sun*, 9 May 1980.

5. Jennifer Seymour Whitaker, "Rights and Realpolitik," *New York Times*, 24 February 1981.

6. Hans J. Morgenthau, "The Pathology of American Power," *International Security* 1.3 (Winter 1977): 3–20.

7. Robert E. Osgood, "Hans Morgenthau's Foreign Policy Impact," *Chicago Tribune*, 27 July 1980.

8. Kenneth Waltz, *Theory of International Politics* (New York: McGraw Hill, 1979), p. 117.

9. Paul Schroeder, "Historical Reality vs. Neo-Realist Theory," *International Security* 19.1 (Summer 1994): 108–148 and Karl-Georg Faber, "Realpolitik als Ideologie," *Historiche Zeitschrift* 203.1 (August 1966): 1–45. See also Paul Schroeder, "The Nineteenth Century System: Balance of Power or Political Equilibrium?" *Review of International Studies* 15.2 (1989): 135–153. For a more recent defense of classic realism against neo-realism, see Sean Molloy, *The Hidden History of Realism: A Genealogy of Power Politics* (Houndsmill: Palgrave, 2006).

10. Kenneth W. Thompson, *Traditions and Values in Politics and Diplomacy: Theory and Practice* (Baton Rouge: Louisiana State University, 1992), pp. 135, 189–194. See also Kenneth W. Thompson, *Morality and Foreign Policy* (Baton Rouge: Louisiana State University, 1980).

11. Nicholas Thompson, *The Hawk and the Dove: Paul Nitze, George Kennan, and the History of the Cold War* (New York: Picador, 2010).

12. Richard A. Melanson, "Paul H. Nitze to Norman Podhoretz: The Tradition of Anti-Communist Containment," in Kenneth W. Thompson, ed., *Traditions and Values: American Diplomacy, 1945 to the Present* (Lanham, MD: United Press of America, 1984), pp. 147–179.

13. Murray Friedman, *The Neoconservative Revolution: Jewish Intellectuals and the Shaping of Public Policy* (Cambridge: Cambridge University Press, 2005), pp. 146–175.

14. Jeane Kirkpatrick, "Dictatorships and Double Standards," *Commentary Magazine* 68.5 (November 1979): 34–45.

15. Benjamin Balint, *Running Commentary: The Contentious Magazine That Transformed the Jewish Left into the Neoconservative Right* (New York: Public Affairs, 2010), pp. 155–156.

16. Jacob Heilbrunn, *They Knew They Were Right* (New York: Anchor Books, 2009), p. 169.

17. David J. Hoeveler, *Watch on the Right: Conservative Intellectuals in the Reagan Era* (Milwaukee: University of Wisconsin Press, 1991), pp. 151–153, 171–172.

18. Melanson, "Paul H. Nitze to Norman Podhoretz."

19. Norman Podhoretz, "Kissinger Reconsidered," *Commentary*, June 1982.

20. Stuart Kinross, *Clausewitz and America: Strategic Thought and Practice from Vietnam to Iraq* (New York: Routledge, 2008), pp. 105–106.

21. William E. Pemberton, *Exit with Honor: The Life and Presidency of Ronald Reagan* (New York: M. E. Sharpe, 1998), p. 149.

22. Statement by Secretary of State-Designate (Haig) before the Senate Foreign Relations Committee, 9 January 1981, *Nomination of Alexander M. Haig, Jr: Hearings before the Committee on Foreign Relations, United States Senate, Ninety-Seventh Congress, First Session, Part I* (Washington, DC, 1981), pp. 12–18.

23. Interview with Ambassador Samuel F. Hart, 12 January 1992, Frontline Diplomacy Archive.

24. Michael Krepon, "Neo-Conservative War of the Worlds," *Bulletin of Atomic Scientists* (March 1986): 6–7.

25. Charles Krauthammer, "The Poverty of Realism: The Newest Challenge to the Reagan Doctrine," *New Republic*, 17 February 1986.

26. Charles Krauthammer, *Democratic Realism: An American Foreign Policy for a Unipolar World* [2004 Irving Kristol Memorial Lecture] (Washington, DC: American Enterprise Institute for Public Policy Research, 2004), pp. 10–13. Democratic realism had a longer heritage, of course. See A. C. Hill, *Democratic Realism* (London: Jonathan Cape, 1945).

27. Charles Krauthammer, "Double Standard," *Washington Post*, 5 April 1985.

28. Charles Krauthammer, "Now, Tilt toward Iran," *Washington Post*, 16 September 1988.

29. George Kennan, "Morality and Foreign Policy," *Foreign Affairs* 64.2 (Winter 1985–6): 205–218.

30. Mr. Bruce George, House of Commons debate, 23 June 1981, *Hansard*, vol. 7, cc. 140–222.

31. John Vincour, "Régis Debray: At Home in the Realm of Realpolitik," *New York Times*, 3 May 1984.

32. Written evidence from Lord Howe of Aberavon, *Foreign Affairs Committee—Written Evidence*, the Role of the FCO in UK Government, 28 January 1997.

33. An account of the meeting of 22 December 1984 is available in the archives of the Margaret Thatcher Foundation, http://www.margaretthatcher.org/archive/displaydocument.asp?docid=109185.

34. Harry C. Cochran, Special Assistant for Warning, "The International Arena in the Year 2000," 17 April 1985, CIA files, CREST, US National Archives.

35. *New York Times*, 17 July 1990.

36. "Building a Newly Democratic International Society," address by Secretary of State James Baker Before the World Affairs Council, Dallas, 30 March 1990, *American Foreign Policy* (Washington DC: Department of State, 1990), pp. 12–13.

37. Joel Kotkin, "Bush and China: Un-Realpolitik," *Washington Post*, 17 December 1989.

38. Robert Kagan, "Superpowers Don't Get to Retire," *New Republic*, 26 May 2014.

39. Elliot Abrahams, "Bush's Unrealpolitik," *New York Times*, 30 April 1990.

40. Zamir Meir, "Unrealistic Realpolitik toward Syria," *Wall Street Journal*, 21 November 1990.

41. *Wall Street Journal*, 19 April 1991.

42. Christopher Hitchens, "Realpolitik in the Gulf," *Harper's* 282.1688 (January 1991).

43. "The Omics," *New York Times*, 1 November 1992.

44. Interview with Herman J. Cohen, 15 August 1996, Frontline Diplomacy Archive, Library of Congress.

45. Interview with Ambassador James Dobbins, Frontline Diplomacy Archive, Library of Congress.

46. Jonathan Clarke, "Getting *Realpolitik* about Bosnia," *Washington Post*, 11 October 1992.

47. Andrew Marr, "Do We Want a Europe Ruled by Blood?" *Independent*, 13 July 1995.

48. Brendan Simms, *Unfinest Hour: Britain and the Destruction of Bosnia* (London: Penguin, 2002).

49. *Guardian*, 12 May 1997.

50. Robin Cook, House of Commons debate, 12 May 1998, *Hansard*, vol. 312, cc. 153–166.

51. John Kampfner, *Blair's Wars* (London: Free Press, 2004).

52. Tony Blair, Speech to the Economic Club of Chicago, 22 April 1999, http://www.pbs.org/newshour/bb/international-jan-june99-blair_doctrine4-23/.

53. Jonathan Powell, "No Higher Honor," *New Statesman*, 14 November 2011.

54. *Washington Post*, 2 August 2000.

55. Marcus Mabry, *Twice as Good: Condoleezza Rice and Her Path to Power* (New York: Modern Times, 2008), pp. 80–85.

56. James Mann, *Rise of the Vulcans: The History of Bush's War Cabinet* (New York: Penguin Press, 2004).

57. John Mearsheimer, "Morgenthau and the Iraq war: Realism versus Neo-Conservatism," 18 May 2005. See also John Mearsheimer, *The Tragedy of Great Power Politics* (New York: W.W. Norton, 2001).

58. Richard Lowry, "Reaganism versus Neo-Reaganism," *National Interest* (Spring 2005).

59. Condoleezza Rice, Remarks at the American University Cairo, June 2005. http://2001-2009.state.gov/secretary/rm/2005/48328.htm.

60. Tony Blair, *A Global Alliance for Global Values* (London: Foreign Policy Center, 2006). See also Tony Blair, "The Roots of Extremism," *Foreign Affairs*, January–February, 2007.

61. Barry Gerwin, "Why Are We in Iraq: A Realpolitik Perspective," *World Policy Journal* 24.3 (Fall 2007).

62. James Mann, "For Bush, Realpolitik Is no Longer a Dirty Word," *New York Times*, 11 April 2004.

63. Gerhard Spörl, "Realpolitik Returns to the Middle East," *Der Spiegel*, 6 December 2006.

64. Thomas Ricks, *The Gamble: General Petraeus and the American Military Adventure in Iraq* (London: Penguin Books, 2010).

65. Hubert Védrine, *History Strikes Back: How States, Nations, and Conflicts Are Shaping the Twenty-First Century* (Washington, DC: Brookings Institution, 2008), pp. xi, 3–5, 109–123.

66. Robert J. Art, *America's Grand Strategy and World Politics* (New York: Routledge, 2009).

67. Arthur Schlesinger Jr., "Forgetting Reinhold Niebuhr," *New York Times*, 18 September 2005.

68. David Brooks, "Obama, Gospel, and Verse," *New York Times*, 26 April 2007.

69. "Remarks by the President at the Acceptance of the Nobel Peace Prize," 10 December 2009, http://www.whitehouse.gov/the-press-office/remarks-president-acceptance-nobel-peace-prize.

70. See R. Ward Holder and Peter B. Josephson, *The Irony of Barack Obama: Barack Obama, Reinhold Niebuhr and the Problem of Statecraft* (Farnham: Ashgate, 2012).

71. Interview with *Vox* magazine, 9 February 2015, http://www.vox.com/a/barack-obama-interview-vox-conversation/obama-foreign-policy-transcript.

72. Reinhold Niebuhr, "Augustine's Political Realism," in Robert McAfee Brown, ed., *The Essential Reinhold Niebuhr: Selected Essays and Addresses* (New Haven, CT: Yale University Press, 1986), pp. 123–142.

CONCLUSION: A RETURN TO FOUNDATIONS

1. Ludwig von Rochau, *Grundsätze der Realpolitik, Angewendet auf die staatlichen Zustände Deutschlands* [vol. 1] (Stuttgart: Karl Göpel, 1859).

2. Gerhard Spörl, "Realpolitik Returns to the Middle East," *Der Spiegel*, 6 December 2006.

3. Lawrence Freedman, *Strategy: A History* (Oxford: Oxford University Press, 2013), pp. 247–260.

4. For a brilliant critique of such failures of analysis, see M. G. Frampton and E. Rosen, "Reading the Runes? The United States and the Muslim Brotherhood as seen through the Wikileaks Cables," *Historical Journal* 56.3 (2013): 827–856.

5. Paul Schroeder, "Historical Reality vs. Neo-Realist Theory," *International Security* 19.1 (Summer 1994): 108–148. See also Paul Schroeder, "The Nineteenth Century System: Balance of Power or Political Equilibrium?" *Review of International Studies* 15.2 (1989): 135–153.

6. David Runciman, *Political Hypocrisy: The Mask of Power, from Hobbes to Orwell and Beyond* (Princeton, NJ: Princeton University Press, 2008), p. 15.

7. Manuel Castells, *The Information Age: Economy, Society and Culture*, 3 vols. (Oxford: Blackwell, 1996–7). For a discussion of Castells's work, see

Felix Stadler, "The Network Paradigm: Social Formations in the Age of Information," *Information Society* 14.4 (1998).

8. Michael Bess, *Realism, Utopia and the Mushroom Cloud: Four Activist Intellectuals and Their Strategies for Peace, 1945–1989* (Chicago: University of Chicago Press, 1993), p. 222.

9. Walter Russell Mead, "Literary Saturday: Revolutionary Reads," *American Interest*, http://www.the-american-interest.com/2010/05/16/literary-saturday-revolutionary-reads/.

10. Franz Neumann, Herbert Marcuse, and Otto Kirchheimer, *Secret Reports on Nazi Germany: The Frankfurt School Contribution to the War Effort*, edited by Raffaele Laudani (Princeton, NJ: Princeton University Press, 2014).

11. Wolfgang J. Mommsen, *Max Weber and German Politics, 1890–1920* (Chicago: University of Chicago Press, 1984), pp. 43–44.

12. Walter E. Weyl, "American Policy and European Opinion," *Annals of the American Academy of Political and Social Science*, vol. 666: *Preparedness and America's International Program* (July 1916), pp. 140–146.

13. John Bew, "Pax Anglo-Saxonica," *American Interest* (May–June 2015), pp. 3–11.

Bibliography

MANUSCRIPT SOURCES

US National Archives, College Park, Maryland
CREST (CIA archives)
State Department Central Files

UK National Register of Archives, Kew, London
CAB (Cabinet) papers
FCO (Foreign and Commonwealth Office) papers
PEM (Prime Ministerial) papers

Library of Congress, Washington DC
Frontline Diplomacy Archive (The Association for Diplomatic Studies and Training Foreign Affairs Oral History Project)
Hans J. Morgenthau Papers
Daniel P. Moynihan Papers
Reinhold Niebuhr Papers

Bodleian Library, Oxford University, Oxford
Clement Attlee Papers

Edited Manuscript Collections
Dugdale, E. T. S. ed., *German Diplomatic Documents, 1871–1914,* vol 1: *Bismarck's Relations with England, 1871–1890,* London: Methuen, 1928.
Gooch, G. P. and Harold Temperley, eds., *British Documents on the Origins of the War, 1898–1914,* 3 vols., London: His Majesty's Stationery Office, 1927.

Databases, Digital Archives, and Online Sources
Commentary Magazine archive, https://www.commentarymagazine.com/archive/.
Margaret Thatcher Foundation online archive—www.margeretthatcher.org.
JSTOR—www.jstor.org.
New York Times online archive, http://www.nytimes.com/content/help/search/archives/archives.html.
ProQuest Historical Newspapers Archive, Library of Congress. Washington, DC.
ProQuest Dissertation and Theses Archive, Library of Congress, Washington, DC.
The Times digital database, British Library, London

The Spectator archive, http://archive.spectator.co.uk/.
Times Literary Supplement digital database, British Library, London.
US State Department Archives—www.history.state.gov/historicaldocuments.
Whitehouse archive—www.whitehouse.gov.

Official Publications

American Foreign Policy (US Department of State)
Congressional Serial Set (US Congress)
Foreign Relations of the United States (US Department of State)
Foreign Affairs Committee written evidence (UK Parliament)
Hansard's Parliamentary Debates (UK Parliament)
Hearings before the Committee on Foreign Relations (US Senate)

Newspapers and Periodicals

American Interest
American Speech
Annals of the American Academy of Political and Social Science
Atlantic
Athenaeum
Boston Daily Globe
Bradford Era
British Quarterly Review
Bulletin of the Pan American Union
Chicago Daily Tribune
Christian Science Monitor
Classical Journal
Commentary
Daedalus
Der Spiegel
Dial
Die Zeit
Daily Telegraph
Edinburgh Review
El Paso Herald
English Review
Foreign Affairs
Foreign Policy
Fortnightly Review
Forum and Century
Guardian
Hibbert's Journal
Illustrated Review
Independent
International Security

Journal of Philosophy
Journal of Social Forces
Living Age
Manchester Guardian
Modern Age
Nation
National Interest
New Criterion
New Statesman
New Republic
New York Times
New York Tribune
North British Review
Observer
Political Science Quarterly
Power of Politics
Proceedings of the Academy of Political Science
Saturday Review
Saturday Review of Politics
Slate
Slavonic and East European Review
Spectator
Sun (New York)
Sun (Baltimore)
Times
Times Literary Supplement
Twentieth Century
Virginia Quarterly Review
Wall Street Journal
Washington Herald
Washington Post
Washington Times
Yale Review

Books, Journal Articles, and Unpublished Papers

Acheson, Dean, *Present at the Creation: My Years in the State Department*, New York: W.W. Norton, 1969.

Aho, James Alfred, *German Realpolitik and American Sociology: An Inquiry into the Sources and Political Significance of the Sociology of Conflict*, Lewisburg: Bucknell University Press, 1975.

Aleksandrovich fon-Zibert, Benno, *Entente Diplomacy and the World: Matrix of the History of Europe, 1909–14*, London: Harper, 1921.

Anderson, Perry, *American Foreign Policy and its Thinkers*, London and New York: Verso, 2015.

Angell, Norman, "The Break and Some English Guesses," *North British Review* 205.738, May 1917, 698–705.

Angell, Norman, *The Political Conditions of Allied Success: A Plea for the Protective Union of Democracies*, New York: G.P. Putnam and Sons, 1918, pp. 271–274.

Applebaum, Anne, "Every Revolution Is Different," *Slate*, 21 February 2011.

Armstrong, Hamilton Fish, *Peace and Counterpeace: From Wilson to Hitler: Memoirs of Hamilton Fish Armstrong*, New York: Harper and Row, 1971.

Arnold. A. G., "Realpolitik," *Cambridge Journal* 2.7, 1949, 410–419.

Art, Robert J., *America's Grand Strategy and World Politics*, London: Routledge, 2009.

Ashworth, Lucian M., *Creating International Studies: Angell, Mitranyi and the Liberal Tradition*, Aldershot: Ashgate, 1999.

Ashworth, Lucian M., "Did the Realist-Idealist Great Debate Really Happen? A Revisionist History of International Relations," *International Relations* 16.33, 2002, 33–51.

Ashworth, Lucian M., "Where Are the Idealists in Interwar International Relations?" *Review of International Studies* 32.2, April 2006, 291–308.

Ashworth, Lucian M., *A History of International Thought: From the Origins of the Modern State to Academic International Relations*, London: Routledge, 2014.

Bacevich, Andrew J., ed., *The Short American Century: A Postmortem*, Cambridge, MA: Harvard University Press, 2012.

Badeau, John Stothoff, *The American Approach to the Arab World*, New York and London: Council on Foreign Relations and Harper and Row, 1968.

Balibar, Etienne, *Cinq Etudes du Materialisme Historique*, Paris: Maspero, 1974.

Balint, Benjamin, *Running Commentary: The Contentious Magazine That Transformed the Jewish Left into the Neoconservative Right*, New York: Public Affairs, 2010.

Barnes, Harry Elmer, "Towards Historical Sanity," *Journal of Social Forces* 3.2, January 1925, 365–369.

Baumann, Frederick, "Sir Thomas More," *Journal of Modern History* 4.4, December 1932, 604–615.

Beiner, Ronald, "Machiavelli, Hobbes, and Rousseau on Civil Religion," *Review of Politics* 55.4, Autumn 1993, 617–638.

Bell, Duncan, "Political Theory and the Function of Intellectual History: A Response to Emmanuel Navon," *Review of International Studies* 29.1, January 2003, 151–160.

Bell, Duncan, ed., *Victorian Visions of Global Order: Empire and International Relations in Nineteenth-Century Political Thought*, Cambridge: Cambridge University Press, 2007.

Bell, Duncan, ed., *Political Thought and International Relations: Variations on a Realist Theme,* Oxford: Oxford University Press, 2009.

Bennett Woods, Randall, *A Changing of the Guard: Anglo-American Relations, 1941–1946,* Chapel Hill: University of North Carolina Press, 1990.

Bernhardi, Friedrich von, *Germany and the Next War*, London: Edward Arnold, 1914.

Berridge, Geoff R., Harold Maurice Alvar Keens-Soper, and Thomas G. Otte, eds., *Diplomatic Theory from Machiavelli to Kissinger*, Houndsmill: Palgrave, 2001.

Bess, Michael, *Realism, Utopia and the Mushroom Cloud: Four Activist Intellectuals and Their Strategies for Peace, 1945–1989*, Chicago: University of Chicago Press, 1993.

Bew, John, *Castlereagh: A Life*, Oxford: Oxford University Press, 2012.

Bew, John, "The Real Origins of Realpolitik," *National Interest* 130, March–April 2014, 40–52.

Bew, John, "Pax Anglo-Saxonica," *American Interest*, May–June 2015.

Binkley, Robert C., *Realism and Nationalism, 1852–1871*, New York: Harper and Brothers, 1935.

Blackbourn, David and Geoff Eley, *The Peculiarities of German History: Bourgeois Society and Politics in Nineteenth-Century Germany*, Oxford: Oxford University Press, 1984.

Blair, Tony, "A Global Alliance for Global Values," London: Foreign Policy Center, 2006.

Blair, Tony, "The Roots of Extremism," *Foreign Affairs*, January–February 2007.

Bobbitt, Philip, *The Garments of Court and Palace: Machiavelli and the World That He Made*, New York: Atlantic, 2013.

Boucoyannis, Deborah, "The International Wanderings of a Liberal Idea, or Why Liberals Can Stop Worrying and Love the Balance of Power," *Perspectives on Politics* 5.4, December 2007, 703–727.

Brooks, Sydney, "American Foreign Policy," *English Review*, November 1911, 682–695.

Burk, Kathleen, *The Troublemaker: The Life and History of A. J. P. Taylor*, New Haven, CT: Yale University Press, 2000.

Burke, Edmund, *Reflections on the Revolution in France*, London: J. Dodsley, 1790.

Burleigh, Michael, *Blood and Rage: A Cultural History of Terrorism*, London: Harper Collins, 2008.

Butler, A. J., *Bismarck: The Memoirs*, New York: Howard Fertig, 1966.

Carlson, Harold G., "American Loan Words from German," *American Speech* 15.2, April 1940, 205–258.

Carr, E. H., *The Twenty Years' Crisis, 1919–1939*, London: Macmillan, 1946.

Carr, E. H., *What Is History?* New York: Alfred A. Knopf, 1962.

Carr, E. H., *The October Revolution*, New York: Alfred A. Knopf, 1969.

Castells, Manuel, *The Information Age: Economy, Society and Culture*, 3 vols., Oxford: Blackwell, 1996–7.

Cesa, Marco, ed., *Machiavelli on International Relations*, Oxford: Oxford University Press, 2014.

Chesterton, G. K., *The Collected Works of G. K. Chesterton*, San Francisco: Ignatius Press, 1987.

Chomsky, Noam, *American Power and the New Mandarins*, New York: Random House, 2002.

Clarke, Christopher, *Iron Kingdom: The Rise and Downfall of Prussia, 1600–1947*, London: Allen Lane, 2006.

Coker, Francis W., *Recent Political Thought*, New York: Appleton-Century-Crofts, 1934.

Collini, Stefan, *Common Reading: Critics, Historians, Publics*, Oxford: Oxford University Press, 2008.

Comte, Auguste, *Système de politique positive, ou Traité de Sociologie instituant la Religion de l'Humanité* (1851–1854), vol. 1, Paris, Carilian-Goeury, 1880.

Cox, Michael, "E. H. Carr and the Crisis of Twentieth Century Liberalism," *Millennium: Journal of International Studies* 38.3, 1999, 1–11.

Cox, Michael, ed., *E. H. Carr: A Critical Appraisal*, Basingstoke: Palgrave, 2000.

Dallek, Robert, *Nixon and Kissinger: Partners in Power*, London: Penguin, 2007.

Davis, H. W. C., *The Political Thought of Heinrich von Treitschke*, London: Constable, 1914.

Del Pero, Mario, *The Eccentric Realist: Henry Kissinger and the Shaping of American Foreign Policy*, Ithaca, NY: Cornell University Press, 2010.

DeMuth, Christopher C., and William Kristol, eds., *The Neoconservative Imagination: Essays in Honor of Irving Kristol*, Washington, DC: American Enterprise Institute, 1995.

Doll, Natasha, *Recht, Politik und "Realpolitik" bei August Ludwig von Rochau (1810–1873): Ein wissenschaftsgeschichtlicher Beitrag zum Verhältnis von Politik und Recht im 19. Jahrhundert*, Frankfurt am Main: Vittorio Klostermann, 2005.

Dunning, William, *The British Empire and the United States: A Review of Their Relations Following the Treaty of Ghent*, New York: Charles Scribner's Sons, 1914.

Earle, Edward Meade, "National Security and Foreign Policy," *Yale Review* 29, March 1940.

Earle, Edward Meade, Gordon Alexander Craig, and Felix Gilbert, *Makers of Modern Military Strategy from Machiavelli to Hitler*, Princeton, NJ: Princeton University Press, 1943.

Eich, Stefan and Adam Tooze, "Max Weber, Politics and the Crisis of Historicism" (Yale University, Departments of Political Science and History), unpublished paper, cited with permission of the authors.

Eley, Geoff, "James Sheehan and the German Liberals: A Critical Appreciation," *Central European History* 14.3, September 1981, 273–288.

Elrod, R. B., "Realpolitik or Concert Diplomacy: The Debate over Austrian Foreign Policy in the 1860's," *Austrian History Yearbook* 17, January 1981, 84–97.

Faber, Karl-Georg, "Realpolitik als Ideologie," *Historiche Zeitschrift* 203.1, August 1966, 1–45.

Fair, John D., *Harold Temperley: A Scholar and Romantic in the Public Realm*, Newark, NJ: University of Delaware Press, 1992.

Farge, Arlette, *The Allure of the Archives*, translated by Thomas Scott-Railton, New Haven, CT: Yale University Press, 2013

Farish, Matthew, *The Contours of America's Cold War*, Minneapolis: University of Minnesota Press, 2010.

Fawcett, Edmund, *Liberalism: The Life of an Idea*, Princeton, NJ: Princeton University Press, 2014.

Ferguson, Niall, *The Pity of War, 1914–1918*, Harmondsworth: Penguin, 1998.

Fischer, Fritz, *Grift nach der Weltmacht: Die Kriegszielpolitik des kaiserlichen Deutschland, 1914–1918*, Düsseldorf: Droste Verlag, 1961.

Fletcher, Roger, "Recent Developments in West German Historiography: The Bielefeld School and Its Critics," *German Studies Review* 7.3, October 1984, 451–480.

Frampton, M. G., and Rosen, U., "Reading the Runes? The United States and the Muslim Brotherhood as Seen through the Wikileaks Cables," *Historical Journal* 56.3, 2013, 827–856.

Frank, Tenney, "Commercialism and Roman Territorial Expansion," *Classical Journal* 5.3, January 1910, 99–110.

Frankel, Benjamin, ed., *Roots of Realism*, London: Frank Cass, 1996.

Frantz, Constantin, "The Religion of National Liberalism," reviewed in *Illustrated Review: A Fortnightly Journal of Literature, Science and Art* 4.5, December 1872.

Freedman, Lawrence, *Strategy: A History*, Oxford: Oxford University Press, 2013.

Friedman, Murray, *The Neoconservative Revolution: Jewish Intellectuals and the Shaping of Public Policy*, Cambridge: Cambridge University Press, 2005.

Friedrich, Carl J., "How Enlightened Should Self-Interest Be?" *Yale Review* 1952.

Friess, Horace L., "The Progress of German Philosophy in the Last Hundred Years," *Journal of Philosophy* 27.15, 27 July 1930, 396–415.

Gaddis, John Lewis, *Strategies of Containment*, New York: Oxford University Press, 1982.

Gaddis, John Lewis, *George F. Kennan: An American Life*, New York: Penguin, 2011.

Garthoff, Raymond L., *A Journey through the Cold War: A Memoir of Containment and Coexistence*, Washington, DC: Brookings Institution, 2001.

Garvin, J. [Calchas], "The New German Intrigue," *Fortnightly Review*, September 1904, 385–402.

Gati, Charles, *Zbig: The Strategy and Statecraft of Zbigniew Brzezinski*, Baltimore: Johns Hopkins University Press, 2013.

Gauss, Christian, "New Factors in Franco-German Relations," *Annals of the American Academy of Political and Social Science* 126, July 1926, 19–21.

Gerth, H. H. and C. Wright Mills, eds., *From Max Weber: Essays in Sociology*, New York: Oxford University Press, 1946.

Gewen, Barry, "Why Are We in Iraq: A Realpolitik Perspective," *World Policy Journal* 24.3, Fall 2007.

Gilbert, Felix, *To the Farewell Address: Ideas of American Foreign Policy*, Princeton, NJ: Princeton University Press, 1961.

Goldstein, Erik, *Winning the Peace: British Diplomatic Strategy, Peace Planning, and the Paris Peace Conference 1916–1920*, Oxford: Oxford University Press, 1991.

Gooch, G. P. and Harold Temperley, eds., *British Documents on the Origins of the War, 1898–1914*, 3 vols., London: His Majesty's Stationery Office, 1927.

Guilhot, Nicholas, ed., *The Invention of International Relations Theory: Realism, the Rockefeller Foundation, and the 1954 Conference on Theory*, New York: Columbia University Press, 2011.

Halberstam, David, *The Best and the Brightest*, New York: Modern Library, 2001.

Hall, Ian, "Power Politics and Appeasement: Political Realism in British International Thought, c. 1935–1955," *British Journal of Politics and International Relations* 8, 2006, 174–192.

Hamilton, Paul, *Realpoetik: European Romanticism and Literary Politics*, Oxford: Oxford University Press, 2013.

Haslam, Jonathan, *The Vices of Integrity: E. H. Carr 1892–1928*, London: Verso, 2000.

Haslam, Jonathan, *No Virtue like Necessity: Realist Thought in International Relations since Machiavelli*, New Haven, CT: Yale University Press, 2002.

Hayek, F. A., *The Road to Serfdom*, Abingdon: Routledge, 1944.

Heilbrunn, Jacob, *They Knew They Were Right: The Rise of the Neocons*, New York: Anchor Books, 2009.

Heller, Joseph, "Britain and the Armenian Question, 1912–1914: A Study in Realpolitik," *Middle Eastern Studies* 16.1, January 1980, 3–26.

Hill, A. C., *Democratic Realism*, London: Jonathan Cape, 1945.

Hinsley, Francis Harry, ed., *British Foreign Policy under Sir Edward Grey*, Cambridge: Cambridge University Press, 1977.

Hirsch, Felix R., "Herman Oncken and the End of an Era," *Journal of Modern History* 18.2, June 1946, 148–159.

Hirst, Paul, "The Eighty Years' Crisis, 1919–1999: Power," *Review of International Studies* 24.5, 1998, 133–148.

Hobson, J. A., *Imperialism: A Study*, London: James Nisbet, 1902.

Hobson, J. A., *The German Panic*, London: Cobden Club, 1913.

Hoeveler, David J., *Watch on the Right: Conservative Intellectuals in the Reagan Era*, Milwaukee: University of Wisconsin Press, 1991.

Hohendahl, Peter Uwe, *Building a National Literature: The Case of Germany, 1830–1870*, Ithaca, NY: Cornell University Press, 1989.

Holborn, Hajo, "Bismarck's Realpolitik," *Journal of the History of Ideas* 21.1, January–March 1960, 84–98.

Holborn, Hajo, *A History of Modern Germany, 1840–1945*, New York: Alfred A. Knopf, 1969.

Holland, Robert, *Blue-Water Empire: The British in the Mediterranean since 1800*, London: Allen Lane, 2012.

Honig, Jan Willem, "Totalitarianism and Realism: Hans Morgenthau's German Years," *Security Studies* 2.2, 1995, 283–313.

Horne, Alistair, *Kissinger: 1973, the Crucial Year*, New York: Simon and Schuster, 1973.

Howard, Esme, "The Way toward Peace," *Annals of the American Academy of Political and Social Science* 114, July 1924, 132–134.

Hunt, Michael, *Ideology and U.S. Foreign Policy*, New Haven, CT: Yale University Press, 1987.

Inboden, William, *Religion and American Foreign Policy: The Soul of Containment*, Cambridge: Cambridge University Press, 2008.

Inboden, William, "The Prophetic Conflict: Reinhold Niebuhr, Christian Realism, and World War II," *Diplomatic History* 38.1, 2014, 49–82.

Isaac, Joel and Duncan Bell, eds., *Uncertain Empire: American History and the End of the Cold War*, Oxford: Oxford University Press, 2012.

Jones, Greta, *Social Darwinism and English Thought*, Brighton: Harvester Press, 1980.

Kaplan, Robert, *The Wizards of Armageddon*, Stanford, CA: Stanford University Press, 1991.

Kagan, Robert, *Dangerous Nation: America and the World, 1600–1898*, London: Atlantic Books, 2006.

Kagan, Robert, *The Return of History and the End of Dreams*, New York: Vintage Books, 2009

Kaplan, Robert, *The Revenge of Geography: What the Map Tells Us about Coming Conflicts and the Battle against Fate*, New York: Random House, 2012.

Kennan, George F., "The Sources of Soviet Conduct," *Foreign Affairs* 25, 1946.

Kennan, George F., *American Diplomacy, 1900–1950*, Chicago: University of Chicago Press, 1951.

Kennan, George F., *The Decline of Bismarck's European Order: Franco-Russian Relations 1875–1890*, Princeton, NJ: Princeton University Press, 1981.

Kennan, George F., "Morality and Foreign Policy," *Foreign Affairs* 64.2, Winter 1985–6, 205–218.

Kennedy, P. M., "The Decline of Nationalist History in the West, 1900–1970," *Journal of Contemporary History* 8, 1973, 77–100.

Kennedy, P. M., "Idealists and Realists: British Views of Germany, 1864–1939," *Transactions of the Royal Historical Society* 25, December 1975, 137–156.

Kennedy, P. M., *The Rise of the Anglo-German Antagonism, 1860–1914*, Boston: George Allen and Unwin, 1980.

Kennedy, P. M., *The Realities behind Diplomacy: Background Influences on British External Policy, 1865–1980*, London: Fontana Press, 1985.

Kennedy, P. M., *Over Here: The First World War and American Society* (twenty-fifth anniversary edition), Oxford; Oxford University Press, 2004.

Kinross, Stuart, *Clausewitz and American Strategic Thought and Practice from Vietnam to Iraq,* New York: Routledge, 2008.

Kinter, William R. and Robert L. Pfaltzgraff Jr., eds., *Strategy and Values: Selected Writings of Robert Strausz-Hupé,* Toronto: Lexington Books, 1973.

Kissinger, Henry, "The Meaning of History: Reflections on Spengler, Toynbee and Kant" (Undergraduate honors thesis, Harvard University, 1950).

Kissinger, Henry, "The White Revolutionary: Reflections on Bismarck," *Daedalus* 97.3, Summer 1968, 888–924.

Kissinger, Henry, *A World Restored: Metternich, Castlereagh and the Problems of Peace, 1812–1822*, London: Weidenfeld and Nicholson, 1999.

Kissinger, Henry, *Years of Renewal*, New York: Touchstone, 2000.

Kissinger, Henry, "The Limits of Universalism," *New Criterion* 30.10, June 2012.

Kissinger, Henry, *World Order*, London: Allen Lane, 2014.

Klitzing, Holger, *The Nemesis of Stability: Henry A. Kissinger's Ambivalent Relationship with Germany,* Trier: Wissenschaftlicher Verlag Trier, 2007.

Kohn, Hans, *Revolutions and Dictatorships*, Cambridge, MA: Harvard University Press, 1939.

Kohn, Hans, "Treitschke: National Prophet," *Power of Politics* 7.4, October 1945, 418–440.

Khon, Hans, *Prophets and Peoples: Studies in Nineteenth Century Nationalism*, New York: Macmillan, 1946.

Krauthammer, Charles, "Democratic Realism: An American Foreign Policy for a Unipolar World" [2004 Irving Kristol Memorial Lecture], Washington, DC: American Enterprise Institute for Public Policy Research, 2004.

Krieger, Leonard, *The German Idea of Freedom: History of a Political Tradition*, Boston: Beacon Hill Press, 1957.

Kristol, Irving, "American Intellectuals and Foreign Policy," *Foreign Affairs,* July 1967.

Lane, Christopher, *The Peace of Illusions: American Grand Strategy from 1940 to the Present*, Ithaca, NY: Cornell University Press, 2006.

Langer, William L., *An Encyclopedia of World History*, Boston: Houghton Mifflin, 1940.

Langewiesche, Dieter, *Liberalism in Germany*, Princeton, NJ: Princeton University Press, 2000.

Laue, Theodore H. von, *Leopold Ranke: The Formative Years*, Princeton, NJ: Princeton University Press, 1950.

Lees, Andrew, *Revolution and Reflection: Intellectual Change in Germany during the 1850s*, The Hague: Martinus Nijhoff, 1974.

Lefever, Ernest W., *Ethics and United States Foreign Policy*, New York: Living Age Books, 1957.

Lehmann, Hartmut, ed., *An Interrupted Past: German-Speaking Refugee Historians in the United States after 1933*, Cambridge: German Historical Institute, 1991.

Lerner, Max, *Ideas for the Ice Age: Studies in a Revolutionary Era*, New Brunswick, NJ: Transaction, 1993.

Lieven, Anatol, *Ethical Realism: A Vision for America's Role in the World*, London: Pantheon Books, 2006.

Lippmann, Walter, *The Stakes of Diplomacy*, New Brunswick, NJ: Transaction, 2008; first published 1917.

Lippmann, Walter, *U.S. Foreign Policy: Shield of the Republic*, Boston: Little Brown, 1943.

Little, Douglas, *American Orientalism: The United States and the Middle East since 1945*, Chapel Hill: University of North Carolina Press, 2008.

Lloyd George, David, *Memoirs of the Peace Conference*, New Haven, CT: Yale University Press, 1939, vol. 1.

Lloyd George, David and Viscount James Bryce, *The War of Democracy: The Allies' Statement,* New York: Doubleday, 1917.

Loewenstein, Karl, "Militant Democracy and Fundamental Rights," *American Political Science Review* 31.3, June 1937, 417–432.

Low, Sidney, "Towards an Imperial Foreign Policy," *Fortnightly Review*, November 1912, 789–802.

Lühman, Hans, *Die Unfange August Ludwig von Rochau, 1810–1850*, Heidelberg, 1921.

Mabry, Marcus, *Twice as Good: Condoleezza Rice and Her Path to Power*, New York: Modern Times, 2008.

Mackinder, Halford J., *Democratic Ideals and Reality: A Study in the Politics of Reconstruction*, London: Constable, 1919; reissued London: Holt, 1942.

Mann, James, *Rise of the Vulcans: The History of Bush's War Cabinet,* New York: Penguin Press, 2004.

Marcuse, Herbert, *Reason and Revolution: Hegel and Rise of Social Theory*, Atlantic Highlands, NJ: Humanities Press, 1954.

Marcuse, Herbert, *The New Left and the 1960s: Collected Papers of Herbert Marcuse*, vol. 3, London: Routledge, 2005.

Martel, Gordon, "The Pre-History of Appeasement: Headlam-Morley, the Peace Settlement and Revisionism," *Diplomacy and Statecraft* 9.3, November 1998, 242–265.

Marx, Karl, *The First International and After*, Harmondsworth: Penguin, 1974.

Marx, Karl, *Collected Works*, vol. 11, New York: International, 1976.

Marx, Karl, *The Eighteenth Brumaire of Louis Bonaparte,* Moscow: Progress, 1977

Masaryk, Thomas G., "Reflections on the Question of War Guilt," in Hamilton Fish Armstrong, ed., *The Foreign Affairs Reader*, London and New York: Council on Foreign Relations/Harper and Brothers, 1947.

Maurer, Noel, *The Empire Trap: The Rise and Fall of US Intervention to Protect American Property Overseas (1893–2013)*, Princeton, NJ: Princeton University Press, 2013.

May, Ernest R., R. Rosecrance, and Zara Steiner, eds., *History and Neo-Realism*, Cambridge: Cambridge University Press, 2010.

Mazower, Mark, *Governing the World: The History of an Idea*, London: Allen Lane, 2012.

McAfee, Robert, ed., *The Essential Reinhold Niebuhr: Selected Essays and Addresses*, New Haven, CT: Yale University Press, 1986.

McDonald, James G., "A New Code of International Morality," *Annals of the American Academy of Political and Social Science* 132, July 1927, 193–196.

Mead, Walter Russell, *God and Gold: Britain, America and the Making of the Modern World*, London: Atlantic Books, 2007.

Mearsheimer, John, *The Tragedy of Great Power Politics*, New York: W. W. Norton, 2001.

Meinecke, Friedrich, *The Warfare of a Nation: Lectures and Essays,* translated by John A. Spaulding, Worcester, MA: Davis Press, 1915.

Meinecke, Friedrich, *Machiavellism: The Doctrine of Raison d'État and Its Place in Modern History,* translated by Douglas Scott, New York: Frederick A. Praeger, 1965.

Meinecke, Friedrich, *Cosmopolitanism and the National State*, translated by Robert B. Kimber, Princeton, NJ: Princeton University Press, 1970.

Mendes-Flour, Paul, *Divided Passions: Jewish Intellectuals and the Experience of Modernity*, Detroit: Wayne State University Press, 1991.

Menzel, Johanna Margarette, "August Ludwig von Rochau: A Study on the Concept of Realpolitik" (MA dissertation, University of Chicago, August 1953).

Merkley, Paul, *Reinhold Niebuhr: A Political Account*, Montreal: McGill-Queen's University Press, 1975.

Meyer, Christopher, *Getting Our Own Way: 500 Years of British Diplomacy*, London: Weidenfeld and Nicolson, 2009.

Molloy, Sean, *The Hidden History of Realism*, Houndsmill: Palgrave Macmillan, 2006.

Mommsen, Wolfgang J., *Max Weber and German Politics, 1890–1920*, Chicago: Chicago University Press, 1984.

Mommsen, Wolfgang J., "German Liberalism in the Nineteenth Century by James J. Sheehan," *Journal of Modern History* 66. 2, June 1994, 431–433.

Monk, Gordon R., "Bismarck and the 'Capitulation' of German Liberalism," *Journal of Modern History* 43.1, March 1971.

Moretti, Franco, *The Bourgeois: Between History and Literature,* London: Verso, 2013.

Morgenthau, Hans J., *Scientific Man versus Power Politics*, Chicago: University of Chicago Press, 1946.

Morgenthau, Hans J., *Politics among Nations: The Struggle for Power and Peace*, Chicago: University of Chicago Press, 1948.

Morgenthau, Hans J., *In Defense of the National Interest: A Critical Examination of American Foreign Policy*, New York: Alfred A. Knopf, 1951.

Morgenthau, Hans J., "Another 'Great Debate': The National Interest of the United States," *American Political Science Review* 46.4, 1952, 961–962.

Morgenthau, Hans J., "Fragments of an Intellectual Autobiography, 1904–1932," in K. Thompson and Robert J. Myers, ed., *A Tribute to Hans Morgenthau*, New Brunswick, NJ: Transaction, 1977, pp. 1–9.

Morgenthau, Hans J., "The Pathology of American Power," *International Security* 1.3, Winter 1977, 3–20.

Morley, John, *Miscellanies*, fourth series, London: Macmillan, 1908.

Moses, John A., "The British and German Churches and the Perception of War, 1908–1914," *War and Society* 5.1, May 1987, 23–44.

Moses, John A., "The Mobilisation of the Intellectuals 1914–1915 and the Continuity of German Historical Consciousness," *Australian Journal of Politics and History* 48.3, 2002, 336–352.

Muir, Ramsay, *Britain's Case against Germany: An Examination of the Historical Background of the German Action in 1914*, Manchester: Manchester University Press, 1914.

Muravchik, Joshua, *The Uncertain Crusade: Jimmy Carter and the Dilemmas of Human Rights Policy,* Washington, DC: American Enterprise Institute for Policy Research, 1988.

Mussey, Henry Raymond, "Neglected Realities in the Far East" [31 May 1917], *Proceedings of the Academy of Political Science* 7.3, July 1917, 538–547.

Namier, L. B., *In the Margin of History*, New York: Freeport, 1939.

Namier, L. B., *1848: The Revolution of the Intellectuals* (The Raleigh Lecture on History), *Proceedings of the British Academy*, Oxford: Oxford University Press, 1993.

Nardin, Terry, "Middle-Ground Ethics: Can One Be Politically Realistic without Being a Political Realist," *Ethics and International Affairs* 25.1, Spring 2011.

Neumann, Franz, Herbert Marcuse, and Otto Kirchheimer, *Secret Reports on Nazi Germany: The Frankfurt School Contribution to the War Effort*, edited by Raffaele Laudani, Princeton, NJ: Princeton University Press, 2014.

Niebuhr, Reinhold, *The Irony of American History*, Chicago: University of Chicago Press, 1952.

Nixon, Richard, *RN: The Memoirs of Richard Nixon*, New York: Simon and Schuster, 1978.

Oncken, Herman, *Napoleon III and the Rhine: The Origin of the War of 1870–1871*, translated by Edwin H. Zeydel, New York: Russell and Russell, 1928.

Osgood, Robert Endicott, *Ideals and Self-Interest in America's Foreign Relations*, Chicago: University of Chicago Press, 1953.

Parmar, Inderjeet, *Foundations of the American Century: The Ford, Carnegie, and Rockefeller Foundations in the Rise of American Power*, New York: Columbia University Press, 2012.

Patomäki, Heikki, *After International Relations: Critical Realism and the (Re) Construction*, London: Routledge, 2002.

Pemberton, William E., *Exit with Honor: The Life and Presidency of Ronald Reagan*, New York: M. E. Sharpe, 1998.

Pflanze, Otto, "Bismarck's 'Realpolitik,'" *Review of Politics* 20. 4, October 1958, 492–514.

Pflanze, Otto, *Bismarck and the Development of Germany: The Period of Unification, 1815–1871*, Princeton, NJ: Princeton University Press, 1963.

Phillips, Walter Alison, *The Confederation of Europe: A Study of the European Alliance, 1813–1823,* London: Longmans, Green, 1914.

Phillips, Walter Alison, "The Peace Settlement: 1815 and 1919," *Edinburgh Review* 230.469, July 1919, 1–21.

Pocock, J. G. A. *The Machiavellian Moment: Florentine Political Thought and the Atlantic Republican Tradition*, Princeton, NJ: Princeton University Press, 2003.

Pois, Robert A., *Friedrich Meinecke and German Politics in the Twentieth Century*, Berkeley: University of California Press, 1972.

Polanyi Festschrift Committee, ed., *The Logic of Personal Knowledge: Essays by Various Contributors Presented to Michael Polanyi on His Seventieth Birthday*, London: Routledge and Kegan Paul, 1961.

Powell, Jonathan, *The New Machiavelli: How to Wield Power in the Modern World*, Random House: London, 2010.

Quirk, Joel and Darshan Vigneswaran, "The Construction of an Edifice: The Story of a First Great Debate," *Review of International Studies* 31, 2005, 89–107.

Radhakrishnan, Sarvepalli, *The Philosophy of Rabindranath Tagore*, London: Macmillan, 1918.

Reeves, Richard, *President Nixon: Alone in the White House*, New York: Simon and Schuster, 2001.

Rice, Daniel F., ed., *Reinhold Niebuhr Revisited: Engagements with an American Original*, Grand Rapids, MI: William B. Eerdmans, 2009.

Rice, Daniel F., *Reinhold Niebuhr and His Circle of Influence*, Cambridge: Cambridge University Press, 2013.

Ricks, Thomas, *The Gamble: General Petraeus and the American Military Adventure in Iraq*, London: Penguin Books, 2010.

Rochau, August Ludwig von, *Geschite Frankreichs von 1814 bis 1852*, Leipzig: Nizel; London: Williams and Morgate, 1859.

Rochau, August Ludwig von, *Grundsätze der Realpolitik, Angewendet auf die staatlichen Zustände Deutschlands* [*Foundations of Realpolitik, applied to the current state of Germany*], vol. 1, Stuttgart: Karl Göpel, 1859.

Rochau, August Ludwig von, *Grundsätze der Realpolitik, Angewendet auf die staatlichen Zustände Deutschlands* [*Foundations of Realpolitik, applied to the current state of Germany*], vol. 2, Heidelberg: J. C. B. Mohr, 1868.

Rochau, August Ludwig von, *Wanderings in the Cities of Italy in 1850 and 1851*, translated by Percy Sinnett, London: R. Bentley, 1853.

Rosecrance, Richard, *Action and Reaction in World Politics: International Systems in Perspective*, Boston: Little, Brown, 1963.

Rosenthal, Joel H., *Righteous Realists: Political Realism, Responsible Power and American Culture in the Nuclear Age*, Baton Rouge: Louisiana State University Press, 1991.

Rothfels, Hans, "1848-One Hundred Years After," *Journal of Modern History* 20.4, December 1948, 291–319.

Runciman, David, *Political Hypocrisy: The Mask of Power, from Hobbes to Orwell and Beyond*, Princeton, NJ: Princeton University Press, 2008.

Russell, Greg, *Hans J. Morgenthau and the Ethics of American Statecraft*, Baton Rouge: Louisiana State University Press, 1991.

Sargeaunt, H. A. and Geoffrey West, *Grand Strategy: The Search for Victory*, London: Jonathan Cape, 1942.

Sarkisissian, A. O., ed., *Studies in Diplomatic History and Historiography in Honor of G. P. Gooch, C.H.*, London: Longmans, Green, 1961.

Sarolea, Charles, *German Problems and Personalities*, London: Chatto and Windus, 1917.

Scheuerman, William E., *The Realist Case for Global Reform*, Cambridge: Polity Press, 2001.

Schlesinger, Arthur, *Cycles of American History*, Boston: Mariner Books, 1999.

Schmidt, B. C., ed., *International Relations and the First Great Debate*, London: Routledge, 2012.

Schmidt-Hartmann, Eva, *Thomas G. Masaryk's Realism: Origins of a Czech Political Concept*, Munich: R. Oldenbourg Verlag, 1984.

Schreiner, George Abel, *The Craft Sinister: A Diplomatico-Political History of the Great War and Its Causes—Diplomacy and International Politics and Diplomatists as Seen at Close Range by an American Newspaperman Who Served in Central Europe as War and Political Correspondent*, New York: G. Albert Geyer, 1920.

Schroeder, Paul, "The Nineteenth Century System: Balance of Power or Political Equilibrium?" *Review of International Studies* 15.2, 1989, 135–153.

Schroeder, Paul, "Historical Reality vs. Neo-Realist Theory," *International Security* 19.1, Summer 1994, 108–148.

Schuman, Frederick, *International Politics: An Introduction to the Western State System*, New York: McGraw-Hill, 1937.

Seaman, John T. Jr., *A Citizen of the World: The Life of James Bryce*, London: Taurus Academic Studies, 2006.

Segel, Glenn, *Nuclear Strategy: The Jim King Manuscripts*, London: Glenn Segel, 2006.

Sheehan, James J., ed., *Imperial Germany*, New York: New Viewpoints, 1976.

Sheehan, James J., *German Liberalism in the Nineteenth Century*, Chicago: University of Chicago Press, 1978.

Sheehan, James J., *German History, 1770–1866*, Oxford: Oxford University Press, 1989.

Sidgwick, Rose, "The League of Nations," *Rice Institute Pamphlet* 6.2, April 1919, 33–62.

Simms, Brendan, *The Struggle for Mastery in Germany, 1779–1850*, New York: St. Martin's Press, 1998.

Simms, Brendan, *Unfinest Hour: Britain and the Destruction of Bosnia*, London: Penguin, 2002.

Simms, Brendan, *Europe: The Struggle for Supremacy, 1453 to the Present*, London: Penguin, 2014.

Simms, Brendan, *The Longest Afternoon: The 400 Men Who Decided the Battle of Waterloo*, Harmondsworth: Penguin, 2014.

Simms, Brendan and David J. B. Trim, eds., *Humanitarian Intervention: A History*, Cambridge: Cambridge University Press, 2011.

Skinner, Quentin, *Liberty before Liberalism*, Cambridge: Cambridge University Press, 1998.

Smith, Michael Joseph, *Realist Thought from Weber to Kissinger*, Baton Rouge: Louisiana State University Press, 1986.

Smith, Woodruff, *The Ideological Origins of Nazi Imperialism*, New York: Oxford University Press, 1996.

Snell, John L., *Illusion and Necessity: The Diplomacy of Global War, 1939–1945*, Boston: Houghton Mifflin, 1963.

Sonnenschein, E. A., "The German Professors," *Twentieth Century* 86, August 1919, 321–332.

Sontag, Raymond James, "The Cowes Interview and the Kruger Telegram," *Political Science Quarterly* 40.2, June 1925, 217–247.

Sontag, Raymond James, *Germany and England: Background of Conflict, 1848–1898*, New York: D. Appleton Century, 1938.

Sontag, Raymond James, "The Germany of Treitschke," *Foreign Affairs* 18.1, October 1939, 127–139.

Speier, Hans, "Germany in Danger: Concerning Oswald Spengler's Latest Book," *Social Research* 1.2, May 1934, 231–243.

Spykman, Nicholas John, *America's Strategy in World Politics: The United States and the Balance of Power*, New York: Harcourt, Brace, 1942.

Stadler, Felix, "The Network Paradigm: Social Formations in the Age of Information," *Information Society* 14.4, 1998.

Stark, Werner, *The Sociology of Knowledge: An Essay in Aid of a Deeper Understanding of Human Ideas*, Glencoe, IL: Free Press, 1958.

Steed, Wickham, "Thomas Garrigue Masaryk: The Man and the Teacher," *Slavonic and East European Review* 8.24, March 1930, 465–477.

Steel, Ronald, *Walter Lippman and the American Century*, New Brunswick: Transaction, 1999.

Steinberg, Jonathan, *Bismarck: A Life*, Oxford: Oxford University Press, 2011.

Steiner, Zara S., *The Foreign Office and Foreign Policy, 1898–1914*, Cambridge: Cambridge University Press, 1969.

Steiner, Zara S., *The Triumph of the Dark: European International History, 1933–1939*, Oxford: Oxford University Press, 2011.

Steiner, Zara S. and Keith Nelson, *Britain and the Origins of the First World War*, Houndsmill: Palgrave Macmilllan, 2003.

Sterling, Richard W., *Ethics in a World of Power: The Political Ideas of Friedrich Meinecke*, Princeton, NJ: Princeton University Press, 1958.

Stern, Fritz, *The Politics of Cultural Despair: A Study in the Rise of Germanic Ideology*, Berkeley: University of California Press, 1961.

Stern, Fritz, *Gold and Iron: Bismarck, Bleichröder, and the Building of the German Empire*, New York: Alfred A. Knopf, 1977.

Stewart, William Kilborne, "The Mentors of Mussolini," *American Political Science Review* 22, November 1928, 843–869.

Stolleis, Michael, *Public Law in Germany, 1800–1914*, Oxford: Bergahn Books, 2001.

Sturzo, Luigi, "Politics versus Morality: From the Hibbert Journal London Quarterly of Philosophy and Theology," *Living Age* 353.4456, January 1938, 312–319.

Suri, Jeremy, *Power and Protest: Global Revolution and the Rise of Détente*, Cambridge, MA: Harvard University Press, 2003.

Swartz, Marvin, *The Union of Democratic Control in British Politics during the First World War*, Oxford: Clarendon, 1971.

Sylvester, Casper, "Continuity and Change in British Liberal Internationalism, c. 1900–1930," *Review of International Studies* 31.2, April 2005, 263–283.

Tannenbaum, Edward, *European Civilization since the Middle Ages*, New York: John Wiley, 1965.

Taylor, A. J. P., *The Course of German History: A Survey of the Development of German History since 1815*, London: Methuen, 1961.

Taylor, A. J. P., *Bismarck: The Man and the Statesman*, London: New English Library, 1965.

Thompson, Kenneth W., *Morality and Foreign Policy*, Baton Rouge: Louisiana State University, 1980.

Thompson, Kenneth W., ed., *Traditions and Values: American Diplomacy, 1945 to the Present*, Lanham, MD: United Press of America, 1984.

Thompson, Kenneth W., *Traditions and Values in Politics and Diplomacy: Theory and Practice*, Baton Rouge: Louisiana State University, 1992.

Thompson, Nicholas, *The Hawk and the Dove: Paul Nitze, George Kennan, and the History of the Cold War*, New York: Picador, 2010.

Thucydides, *The History of the Peloponnesian War*, translated by Richard Crawley, 2 vols., Avon, CT: Cardavon Press, 1974.

Tooze, Adam, *The Deluge: The Great War and the Remaking of Global Order*, London: Allen Lane, 2014.

Treitschke, Heinrich von, *Germany, France, Russia and Islam*, London: Allen and Unwin, 1914.

Treitschke, Heinrich von, *His Life and Works*, London: Allen and Unwin, 1914.

Treitschke, Heinrich von and Hans Kohn, eds., *Politics*, New York: Harcourt, Brace and World, 1963.

Trocini, Frederico, *L'invenzione della "Realpolitik" e la scoperta della "legge del potere." August Ludwig von Rochau tra radicalismo e nazional-liberalismo*, Bologna: Il Mulino, 2009.

Trubowitz, Peter, *Defining the National Interest: Conflict and Change in American Foreign Policy*, Chicago: University of Chicago Press, 1998.

Ulrich-Wehler, Hans, *Ludwig August von Rochau, Grundsätze der Realpolitik auf die staatlichen Zustände Deutschlands, herausgegeben und eingeleitet von Hans-Ulrich Wehler,* Frankfurt: Ullstein Buch, 1972.

Veblen, Thorstein, *Imperial Germany and the Industrial Revolution, 1857–1929,* New York: Macmillan, 1915.

Veblen, Thorstein, "The Modern Point of View and the New Order: VI. THE DIVINE RIGHT OF NATIONS," *The Dial: A Semi-Monthly Journal of Literary Criticism, Discussion and Information,* December 28, 1918.

Védrine, Hubert, *History Strikes Back: How States, Nations, and Conflicts Are Shaping the Twenty-First Century,* Washington, DC: Brookings Inistitution, 2008.

Venedey, Jacob, *Ireland and the Irish during the Repeal Year, 1843,* Dublin: James Duffy, 1844.

Viereck, George Sylvester, *Confessions of a Barbarian,* New York: Moffat, Yard and Company, 1910.

Viereck, Peter, *Metapolitics: From Wagner and the German Romantics to Hitler,* New York: Alfred A. Knopf, 1965.

Viereck, Peter, *The Shame and Glory of the Intellectuals,* New York: Capricorn Books, 1965.

Viereck, Peter, *Conservatism Revisited: The Revolt against Ideology,* New Brunswick, NJ: Transaction, 2005.

Waldstein, Charles, *What Is Germany Fighting For?* London: Longmans, Green, 1917.

Waltz, Kenneth N., *Man, the State and War: A Theoretical Analysis,* New York: Columbia University Press, 1959.

Waltz, Kenneth N., *Theory of International Politics,* New York: McGraw-Hill, 1979.

Wattenberg, Ben J. and Richard James Whalen, *The Wealth Weapon: U.S. Foreign Policy and Multinational Corporations,* New Brunswick, NJ: Transaction, 1980.

Wayman, Frank W. and Paul F. Diehl, eds., *Reconstructing Realpolitik,* Ann Arbor: University of Michigan Press, 1994.

Wehler, Hans-Ulrich, "Bismarck's Imperialism, 1862–1890," in James Sheehan, ed., *Imperial Germany,* New York: Viewpoints, 1976.

Wehler, Hans-Ulrich, *The German Empire, 1817–1918,* translated by Kim Traynor, Leamington Spa: Berg, 1985.

Weyl, Walter E., "American Policy and European Opinion," *Annals of the American Academy of Political and Social Science* 66, July 1916, 140–146.

Weyland, Kurt, "The Arab Spring: Why the Surprising Similarities with the Revolutionary Wave of 1848?" *Perspectives on Politics* 10.4, December 2010, 917–934.

Wheeler-Bennett, John W., "European Possibilities," *Virginia Quarterly Review* Autumn 1937.

Whitehead, Andrew, "Eric Hobsbawm on 2011: 'It Reminds Me of 1848,'" *BBC News Magazine,* 23 December 2011.

Williams, Michael C., *Realism Reconsidered: The Legacy of Hans J. Morgenthau*, Oxford: Oxford University Press, 2007.

Williams, Raymond, *Keywords: A Vocabulary of Culture and Society*, Guilford: Fontana/Croom Helm, 1976.

Willoughby, Westel W., *Prussian Political Philosophy*, New York: D. Appleton, 1918.

Wilson, Jeremy, *Lawrence of Arabia: The Authorized Biography*, New York: Atheneum, 1990.

Wilson, Peter, "The Myth of the 'First Great Debate,'" *Review of International Studies* 24.5, 1998, 1–16.

Wolfers, Arnold, ed., *Alliance Policy and the Cold War*, Baltimore: Johns Hopkins University Press, 1959.

Wolfers, Arnold, *Britain and France between the Two Wars: Conflicting Strategies of Peace since Versailles*, New York: Harcourt, Brace, 1940.

Wolfers, Arnold and Laurence W. Martin, *The Anglo-American Tradition in Foreign Affairs: Readings from Thomas More to Woodrow Wilson*, New Haven, CT: Yale University Press, 1956.

Wright, Quincy, *A Study of War*, Chicago: University of Chicago Press, 1964.

Zamoyski, Adam, *Phantom Terror: The Threat of Revolution and the Repression of Liberty 1789–1848*, William Collins: London, 2014.

Index

Note: Material in figures or tables is indicated by italic page numbers. Endnotes are indicated by n after the page number.